PCED™ – CERTIFIED ENTRY-LEVEL DATA ANALYST WITH PYTHON

EXAM CODE: PCED-30-01

- ✓ FAST TRACK PREPARATION,
- ✓ 10 PRACTICE TESTS,
- ✓ 450 FOUNDATIONAL QUESTIONS,
- ✓ 400+ EXAM FOCUSED TIPS,
- ✓ 400+ CAUTION ALERTS AND CONCISE EXPLANATIONS

D1709722

ANAND M
AMEENA PUBLICATIONS

DEDICATION

To the Visionaries in My Professional Odyssey

This book is dedicated to the mentors and leaders who guided me through triumph and adversity in my professional universe. Your guidance has illuminated the path to success and taught me to seize opportunities and surmount obstacles. Thank you for imparting the advice to those who taught me the value of strategic thinking and the significance of innovation to transform obstacles into stepping stones. Your visionary leadership has inspired my creativity and motivated me to forge new paths.

Thank you for sharing the best and worst of your experiences with me, kind and severe employers. As I present this book to the world, I am aware that you have been my inspiration. All of your roles as mentors, advisors, and even occasional adversaries have helped me become a better professional and storyteller.

This dedication is a tribute to your impact on my journey, a narrative woven with threads of gratitude, introspection, and profound gratitude for the lessons you've inscribed into my story.

With deep gratitude and enduring respect,
Anand M

FROM TECH TO LIFE SKILLS – MY EBOOKS COLLECTION

Dive into my rich collection of eBooks, curated meticulously across diverse and essential domains.

Pro Tips and Tricks Series*: Empower yourself with life-enhancing skills and professional essentials with our well-crafted guides.*

Hot IT Certifications and Tech Series*: Stay ahead in the tech game. Whether you're eyeing certifications in AWS, PMP, or prompt engineering, harnessing the power of ChatGPT with tools like Excel, PowerPoint, Word, and more!, we've got you covered!*

Essential Life Skills*: Embark on a journey within. From yoga to holistic well-being, Master the art of culinary, baking, and more delve deep and rediscover yourself.*

Stay Updated & Engaged
For an entire world of my knowledge, tips, and treasures, follow me on Amazon
https://www.amazon.com/author/anandm

Your Feedback Matters!
Your support, feedback, and ratings are the wind beneath my wings. It drives me to curate content that brings immense value to every aspect of life. Please take a moment to share your thoughts and rate the books. Together, let's keep the flame of knowledge burning bright!

★ ★ ★ ★ ★

Best Regards,

ANAND M

INTRODUCTION

Embark on an in-depth journey to excel in the **PCED™ – Certified Entry-Level Data Analyst with Python** exam with this essential guide: *"PCED™ – CERTIFIED ENTRY-LEVEL DATA ANALYST WITH PYTHON: PRACTICE TESTS: FAST TRACK PREPARATION, 10 PRACTICE TESTS, 450 FOUNDATIONAL QUESTIONS, 400+ EXAM FOCUSED TIPS, 400+ CAUTION ALERTS AND CONCISE EXPLANATIONS."* This question bank is meticulously crafted to help you navigate the complexities of data analysis using Python and achieve success in the PCED™ certification exam.

As the demand for data-driven insights continues to grow in every industry, Python has emerged as a leading tool for data analysis. The PCED™ – Certified Entry-Level Data Analyst with Python certification is a pivotal milestone for individuals looking to establish their credentials in this rapidly evolving field. Attaining this certification not only validates your analytical skills but also deepens your understanding of essential data analysis techniques and Python programming practices that will enhance your career prospects.

This question bank is carefully designed to challenge your knowledge across key topics in data analysis with Python, aligned with the latest syllabus. It covers Python basics, data manipulation, data visualization, exploratory data analysis, and foundational statistics. Each of the 450 questions is thoughtfully formulated to assess your comprehension, with detailed explanations that reinforce your understanding of the concepts behind the correct answers.

In an era where data is critical to decision-making, earning the PCED™ certification can set you apart as a skilled and knowledgeable data analyst. This certification is indispensable for those looking to advance in fields such as business intelligence, data science, and data-driven decision-making.

Here's an overview of the PCED™ exam:

Exam Name: PCED™ – Certified Entry-Level Data Analyst with Python
Exam Code & Current Exam Version: PCED-30-0x (Status: Active)
Prerequisites: None
Validity: Lifetime
Exam Duration: 60 minutes (including NDA/tutorial time)
Number of Questions: 45 to 50
Format: Single- and multiple-select questions, data-related problem-solving, and Python coding challenges | Python 3.x
Passing Score: 65%
Languages: English

This book is your go-to resource for mastering the foundational PCED™ exam, offering strategic insights, in-depth knowledge, and the confidence to succeed.

Start your path to becoming a proficient data analyst with Python, and let this eBook guide you through every step of your preparation journey.

ADVANTAGES OF CERTIFICATION

As you set out to achieve the **PCED™ – Certified Entry-Level Data Analyst with Python** Certification, it's crucial to recognize the significant advantages this credential brings to your professional journey. Here are the key benefits of earning this certification:

Recognition in a Data-Driven Industry: With the growing importance of data in decision-making processes across various industries, the demand for skilled data analysts continues to rise. The PCED™ certification serves as a robust endorsement of your expertise in Python-based data analysis. It is more than just a certificate—it is a symbol of your specialized knowledge in one of the most critical and rapidly expanding sectors.

Career Advancement and Expanded Opportunities: Earning the PCED™ certification can be a transformative step in your career. It opens doors to new and exciting opportunities in data analysis, business intelligence, and data science. Many professionals find that this certification was pivotal in advancing their careers, leading to more fulfilling and diverse roles in organizations that rely on data-driven strategies.

Increased Earning Potential: Certifications often have a positive impact on salary prospects. Attaining the PCED™ certification demonstrates your expertise in Python for data analysis, which is highly valued by employers. This proven skillset can position you for roles with better compensation, as certified professionals are often seen as more capable and proficient in handling data-related tasks.

Enhanced Professional Visibility: Standing out in a competitive job market is essential, and the PCED™ certification helps you do just that. It elevates your professional profile, making you a more attractive candidate to employers. Whether you're looking for a new job or seeking advancement within your current role, this certification showcases your commitment to professional growth and mastery in data analysis.

Practical and Theoretical Mastery: The PCED™ certification ensures that you gain both a deep theoretical understanding and practical application skills in data analysis using Python. It equips you with the ability to apply data analysis techniques in real-world scenarios, giving you a practical edge over non-certified individuals and helping you solve complex business problems with data-driven insights.

Versatility in Multiple Fields: Python is not just limited to programming—it is widely used in various fields, including finance, healthcare, marketing, and technology. The PCED™ certification equips you with versatile skills that can be applied in multiple sectors, broadening your career possibilities and enhancing your adaptability in a rapidly evolving job market.

In conclusion, the **PCED™ certification** acts as a powerful asset in your data analysis career. It solidifies your standing in the industry, paving the way for continued professional growth, greater opportunities, and long-term success in data analysis and related fields.

EXAM OBJECTIVE

Welcome to your comprehensive question bank for the **PCED™ – Certified Entry-Level Data Analyst with Python Exam**! This book is designed to thoroughly prepare you by evaluating your ability to understand and apply Python-based data analysis concepts. Below is a detailed breakdown of the syllabus sections and their weightings.

Exam Section	*Weightage*
Data Acquisition and Pre-Processing	33%
Programming Skills	29%
Statistical Analysis	9%
Data Analysis and Modeling	16%
Data Communication and Visualization	13%

DATA ACQUISITION AND PRE-PROCESSING (33%): This section covers the critical steps required to acquire, clean, and prepare data for analysis. You will learn about different data sources, including databases, APIs, and flat files, and explore methods to handle missing, inconsistent, or erroneous data. By mastering this section, you will gain a solid foundation in extracting useful data and transforming it into formats suitable for analysis, ensuring that you work with high-quality, reliable datasets.

PROGRAMMING SKILLS (29%): Python is a versatile programming language widely used in data analysis. This section tests your understanding of Python programming fundamentals, such as variables, data types, loops, conditionals, and functions. You will also be assessed on your ability to write efficient code for data manipulation, including working with libraries such as pandas and NumPy. Strengthening your programming skills will equip you to handle diverse tasks related to data processing and analysis.

STATISTICAL ANALYSIS (9%): Understanding basic statistics is crucial for interpreting data and drawing meaningful conclusions. This section evaluates your knowledge of statistical concepts such as measures of central tendency, variability, probability, and statistical significance. You will also learn how to apply statistical methods to real-world datasets, laying the groundwork for deeper data analysis and decision-making.

DATA ANALYSIS AND MODELING (16%): Data analysis and modeling are at the heart of any data analyst's role. In this section, you will explore techniques for exploratory data analysis (EDA) and predictive modeling. You will also learn how to apply machine learning algorithms, such as linear regression, decision trees, and clustering, using Python libraries like scikit-learn. Mastery of this section will enable you to analyze data effectively and build models that predict trends and behaviors.

DATA COMMUNICATION AND VISUALIZATION (13%): The ability to communicate data-driven insights is a vital skill for data analysts. This section focuses on data visualization techniques using Python libraries such as Matplotlib and Seaborn. You will learn how to create clear, informative charts, graphs, and dashboards that convey complex data insights to stakeholders. This section ensures that you can effectively present your findings and support decision-making processes within an organization.

By mastering these objectives, you will be well-prepared to excel in the **PCED™ certification exam**, demonstrating your expertise in data analysis using Python and advancing your career as a data analyst.

OBJECTIVE MAP

This question bank has been meticulously designed to align with the PCED™ – Certified Entry-Level Data Analyst with Python exam syllabus, ensuring comprehensive coverage of key Python-based data analysis concepts. Each question is carefully crafted to simulate real-world challenges that data analysts might face, with a strong focus on practical and advanced Python scenarios.

Many questions in this collection are rooted in detailed data analysis situations, highlighting specific constraints and complexities commonly encountered in the field. These questions often require selecting multiple correct answers, encouraging a deeper understanding and quick application of Python techniques for data manipulation and analysis. This structured approach aims to thoroughly equip you, helping you quickly grasp concepts, identify knowledge gaps, and confidently apply your expertise in real-world scenarios.

Additionally, each question includes targeted exam tips and strategic caution alerts in the answer section. These insights are tailored to enhance your exam performance by emphasizing critical concepts and highlighting common mistakes in Python-based data analysis.

The table below methodically aligns each question with practical use cases drawn from the exam syllabus. This ensures that your preparation is not only thorough but also strategically focused on maximizing your effectiveness in the exam.

DOMAIN 1 - DATA ACQUISITION AND PRE-PROCESSING (33%)
Note: P indicates Practice Test and Q indicates Question

S.No	KNOWLEDGE AREA	MAPPED QUESTIONS
1	Understanding of data collection techniques	P1Q1,P2Q1,P3Q1,P4Q1,P5Q1
2	Techniques for combining data from multiple sources	P6Q1,P7Q1,P8Q1,P9Q1,P10Q1
3	Handling missing values and standardization	P1Q2,P2Q2,P3Q2,P4Q2,P5Q2
4	Understanding of different storage solutions	P6Q2,P7Q2,P8Q2,P9Q2,P10Q2
5	Characteristics of structured and unstructured data	P1Q3,P2Q3,P3Q3,P4Q3,P5Q3
6	Understanding normalization and scaling methods	P6Q3,P7Q3,P8Q3,P9Q3,P10Q3
7	Detecting and managing outliers	P1Q4,P2Q4,P3Q4,P4Q4,P5Q4
8	Preparing data for analysis	P6Q4,P7Q4,P8Q4,P9Q4,P10Q4
9	Ensuring data accuracy	P1Q5,P2Q5,P3Q5,P4Q5,P5Q5
10	Understanding of basic Python programming syntax	P6Q5,P7Q5,P8Q5,P9Q5,P10Q5
11	SQL basics for data retrieval	P1Q6,P2Q6,P3Q6,P4Q6,P5Q6
12	Understanding database connections using Python	P6Q6,P7Q6,P8Q6,P9Q6,P10Q6
13	Understanding basic descriptive statistics	P1Q7,P2Q7,P3Q7,P4Q7,P5Q7
14	Grasp of basic inferential statistics concepts	P6Q7,P7Q7,P8Q7,P9Q7,P10Q7
15	Using Pandas for effective data manipulation	P1Q8,P2Q8,P3Q8,P4Q8,P5Q8
16	Using NumPy for efficient numerical computations	P6Q8,P7Q8,P8Q8,P9Q8,P10Q8
17	Introduction to basic machine learning concepts	P1Q9,P2Q9,P3Q9,P4Q9,P5Q9
18	Creating visual representations using Matplotlib	P6Q9,P7Q9,P8Q9,P9Q9,P10Q9

S.No	KNOWLEDGE AREA	MAPPED QUESTIONS
19	Advanced visualization using Seaborn	P1Q10,P2Q10,P3Q10,P4Q10,P5Q10
20	Presenting data insights clearly	P6Q10,P7Q10,P8Q10,P9Q10,P10Q10
21	Understanding the data gathering process	P1Q11,P2Q11,P3Q11,P4Q11,P5Q11
22	Awareness of ethical implications in data collection	P6Q11,P7Q11,P8Q11,P9Q11,P10Q11
23	Understanding legal constraints in data collection	P1Q12,P2Q12,P3Q12,P4Q12,P5Q12
24	Role of data collection in business strategy	P6Q12,P7Q12,P8Q12,P9Q12,P10Q12
25	Understanding Python data structures	P1Q13,P2Q13,P3Q13,P4Q13,P5Q13
26	Proficiency in Python control structures	P6Q13,P7Q13,P8Q13,P9Q13,P10Q13
27	Using Pandas for advanced data aggregation	P1Q14,P2Q14,P3Q14,P4Q14,P5Q14
28	Applying data transformation techniques in Pandas	P6Q14,P7Q14,P8Q14,P9Q14,P10Q14
29	Preparing data for effective presentation	P1Q15,P2Q15,P3Q15,P4Q15,P5Q15
30	Ensuring consistency in datasets	P6Q15,P7Q15,P8Q15,P9Q15,P10Q15

DOMAIN 2 - PROGRAMMING SKILLS (29%)
Note: P indicates Practice Test and Q indicates Question

S.No	KNOWLEDGE AREA	MAPPED QUESTIONS
31	Understanding Python syntax and control flow	P1Q16,P2Q16,P3Q16,P4Q16,P5Q16
32	Designing and using Python functions effectively	P6Q16,P7Q16,P8Q16,P9Q16,P10Q16
33	Navigating the Python ecosystem for data science	P1Q17,P2Q17,P3Q17,P4Q17,P5Q17
34	Organizing data using Python's core data structures	P6Q17,P7Q17,P8Q17,P9Q17,P10Q17
35	Writing clean and maintainable Python scripts	P1Q18,P2Q18,P3Q18,P4Q18,P5Q18
36	Managing modules and packages in Python	P6Q18,P7Q18,P8Q18,P9Q18,P10Q18
37	Handling errors and exceptions in Python scripts	P1Q19,P2Q19,P3Q19,P4Q19,P5Q19
38	Composing and executing SQL queries	P6Q19,P7Q19,P8Q19,P9Q19,P10Q19
39	Performing CRUD operations in SQL	P1Q20,P2Q20,P3Q20,P4Q20,P5Q20
40	Establishing database connections using Python	P6Q20,P7Q20,P8Q20,P9Q20,P10Q20
41	Executing parameterized SQL queries in Python	P1Q21,P2Q21,P3Q21,P4Q21,P5Q21
42	Managing and converting SQL data types in Python	P6Q21,P7Q21,P8Q21,P9Q21,P10Q21
43	Understanding essential database security concepts	P1Q22,P2Q22,P3Q22,P4Q22,P5Q22
44	Understanding advanced function concepts	P6Q22,P7Q22,P8Q22,P9Q22,P10Q22
45	Understanding the basics of OOP in Python	P1Q23,P2Q23,P3Q23,P4Q23,P5Q23
46	Managing Python code with modules and packages	P6Q23,P7Q23,P8Q23,P9Q23,P10Q23
47	Working with file input and output	P1Q24,P2Q24,P3Q24,P4Q24,P5Q24
48	Handling structured data formats in Python	P6Q24,P7Q24,P8Q24,P9Q24,P10Q24
49	Creating and using custom exception classes	P1Q25,P2Q25,P3Q25,P4Q25,P5Q25
50	Writing and managing complex SQL queries	P6Q25,P7Q25,P8Q25,P9Q25,P10Q25
51	Understanding different types of joins and subqueries	P1Q26,P2Q26,P3Q26,P4Q26,P5Q26
52	Optimizing SQL queries for performance	P6Q26,P7Q26,P8Q26,P9Q26,P10Q26

53	Enforcing data integrity in SQL databases	P1Q27,P2Q27,P3Q27,P4Q27,P5Q27
54	Using views for data abstraction in SQL	P6Q27,P7Q27,P8Q27,P9Q27,P10Q27
55	Implementing and managing indexes in SQL databases	P1Q28,P2Q28,P3Q28,P4Q28,P5Q28
56	Managing SQL transactions for data consistency	P6Q28,P7Q28,P8Q28,P9Q28,P10Q28

DOMAIN 3 - STATISTICAL ANALYSIS (9%)
Note: P indicates Practice Test and Q indicates Question

S.No	KNOWLEDGE AREA	MAPPED QUESTIONS
57	Understanding central tendency measures	P1Q29,P2Q29,P3Q29,P4Q29,P5Q29
58	Understanding variability in data	P6Q29,P7Q29,P8Q29,P9Q29,P10Q29
59	Identifying and interpreting distributions	P1Q30,P2Q30,P3Q30,P4Q30,P5Q30
60	Understanding and interpreting correlations	P6Q30,P7Q30,P8Q30,P9Q30,P10Q30
61	Applying bootstrapping in data analysis	P1Q31,P2Q31,P3Q31,P4Q31,P5Q31
62	Applying linear regression in data analysis	P6Q31,P7Q31,P8Q31,P9Q31,P10Q31
63	Understanding and applying logistic regression	P1Q32,P2Q32,P3Q32,P4Q32,P5Q32
64	Identifying and managing outliers in data	P6Q32,P7Q32,P8Q32,P9Q32,P10Q32

DOMAIN 4 - DATA ANALYSIS AND MODELING (16%)
Note: P indicates Practice Test and Q indicates Question

S.No	KNOWLEDGE AREA	MAPPED QUESTIONS
65	Organizing and manipulating data using Pandas	P1Q33,P2Q33,P3Q33,P4Q33,P5Q33
66	Conceptual understanding of Pandas DataFrame and Series	P6Q33,P7Q33,P8Q33,P9Q33,P10Q33
67	Performing efficient array operations using NumPy	P1Q34,P2Q34,P3Q34,P4Q34,P5Q34
68	Reshaping and organizing data for analysis	P6Q34,P7Q34,P8Q34,P9Q34,P10Q34
69	Applying descriptive statistics for data analysis	P1Q35,P2Q35,P3Q35,P4Q35,P5Q35
70	Importance of test datasets in model evaluation	P6Q35,P7Q35,P8Q35,P9Q35,P10Q35
71	Analyzing and applying supervised learning models	P1Q36,P2Q36,P3Q36,P4Q36,P5Q36
72	Applying linear regression in Python for data modeling	P6Q36,P7Q36,P8Q36,P9Q36,P10Q36
73	Applying logistic regression in Python for binary outcomes	P1Q37,P2Q37,P3Q37,P4Q37,P5Q37
74	Using Pandas groupby for advanced data analysis	P6Q37,P7Q37,P8Q37,P9Q37,P10Q37
75	Applying broadcasting and vectorization in NumPy	P1Q38,P2Q38,P3Q38,P4Q38,P5Q38
76	Creating pivot tables and cross tables for data analysis	P6Q38,P7Q38,P8Q38,P9Q38,P10Q38
77	Understanding and preventing overfitting/underfitting in models	P1Q39,P2Q39,P3Q39,P4Q39,P5Q39
78	Evaluating machine learning model accuracy	P6Q39,P7Q39,P8Q39,P9Q39,P10Q39

DOMAIN 5 - DATA COMMUNICATION AND VISUALIZATION (13%)

Note: P indicates Practice Test and Q indicates Question

S.No	KNOWLEDGE AREA	MAPPED QUESTIONS
79	Creating visualizations using Matplotlib	P1Q40,P2Q40,P3Q40,P4Q40,P5Q40
80	Visualizing complex datasets with Seaborn	P6Q40,P7Q40,P8Q40,P9Q40,P10Q40
81	Evaluating different chart types for data representation	P1Q41,P2Q41,P3Q41,P4Q41,P5Q41
82	Labeling and annotating plots for clarity	P6Q41,P7Q41,P8Q41,P9Q41,P10Q41
83	Improving the readability of plots by customizing display	P1Q42,P2Q42,P3Q42,P4Q42,P5Q42
84	Customizing data presentations for diverse audiences	P6Q42,P7Q42,P8Q42,P9Q42,P10Q42
85	Communicating key insights clearly through data visualizations	P1Q43,P2Q43,P3Q43,P4Q43,P5Q43
86	Using a mix of text and visuals for compelling presentations	P6Q43,P7Q43,P8Q43,P9Q43,P10Q43
87	Using data visualizations to tell a compelling story	P1Q44,P2Q44,P3Q44,P4Q44,P5Q44
88	Using colors effectively for data clarity	P6Q44,P7Q44,P8Q44,P9Q44,P10Q44
89	Summarizing complex data into concise insights	P1Q45,P2Q45,P3Q45,P4Q45,P5Q45
90	Supporting data claims with solid evidence and reasoning	P6Q45,P7Q45,P8Q45,P9Q45,P10Q45

CONTENTS

PRACTICE TEST 1 - QUESTIONS ONLY 1

PRACTICE TEST 1 - ANSWERS ONLY 11

PRACTICE TEST 2 - QUESTIONS ONLY 25

PRACTICE TEST 2 - ANSWERS ONLY 34

PRACTICE TEST 3 - QUESTIONS ONLY 49

PRACTICE TEST 3 - ANSWERS ONLY 57

PRACTICE TEST 4 - QUESTIONS ONLY 71

PRACTICE TEST 4 - ANSWERS ONLY 81

PRACTICE TEST 5 - QUESTIONS ONLY 95

PRACTICE TEST 5 - ANSWERS ONLY 103

PRACTICE TEST 6 - QUESTIONS ONLY 118

PRACTICE TEST 6 - ANSWERS ONLY 127

PRACTICE TEST 7 - QUESTIONS ONLY 141

PRACTICE TEST 7 - ANSWERS ONLY 150

PRACTICE TEST 8 - QUESTIONS ONLY 165

PRACTICE TEST 8 - ANSWERS ONLY 177

PRACTICE TEST 9 - QUESTIONS ONLY 191

PRACTICE TEST 9 - ANSWERS ONLY 200

PRACTICE TEST 10 - QUESTIONS ONLY 215

PRACTICE TEST 10 - ANSWERS ONLY 228

ABOUT THE AUTHOR 243

PRACTICE TEST 1 - QUESTIONS ONLY

QUESTION 1

A company wants to collect data through web scraping and analyze customer reviews from an e-commerce website. They need to ensure that the collected data respects ethical considerations. Write a Python script to scrape data from a website and filter reviews containing the word "great." Which option best ensures ethical web scraping practices in Python?

A) Use requests and BeautifulSoup for scraping without checking robots.txt
B) Use requests with a sleep interval and check robots.txt for allowed URLs
C) Bypass website's robots.txt
D) Use selenium to scrape pages rapidly
E) Scrape data but ignore terms of service

QUESTION 2

You have a dataset with missing values in several columns. You are asked to handle these missing values using appropriate methods. Which Python code snippets correctly fill missing values in numerical columns using the median? (Select 2 answers)

```
A) df.fillna(df.mean(), inplace=True)
B) df.fillna(df.median(), inplace=True)
C) df.replace(np.nan, df.median(),
inplace=True)
D) df.interpolate(method='linear')
E) df.dropna()
```

QUESTION 3

You are tasked with processing both structured and unstructured data for a machine learning project. The structured data is stored in a relational database, while the unstructured data includes customer reviews in text format. How would you load and combine these data types into a Pandas DataFrame? (Select 2 answers)

A) Use pd.read_sql() for structured data
B) Use pd.read_json() for structured data
C) Use pd.read_csv() for unstructured text data

D) Use Python's re module to process unstructured text data
E) Use pd.concat() to combine both data sources

QUESTION 4

You are analyzing a dataset of customer purchases and want to identify outliers in the purchase_amount column. Which Python techniques can be used to detect numerical outliers in the dataset? (Select 2 answers)

A) Use the Z-score method to detect outliers
B) Use Min-Max scaling to normalize outliers
C) Use the Interquartile Range (IQR) method
D) Use Label Encoding for categorical outlier detection
E) Use pd.read_csv() to load the dataset

QUESTION 5

You are validating a dataset of employee records and need to ensure that the age column only contains values between 18 and 65. What Python code would you use to apply this validation rule? (Select 2 answers)

```
A) df[(df['age'] >= 18) & (df['age'] <=
65)]
B) df['age'].between(18, 65)
C) df[df['age'] == [18, 65]]
D) df.filter('age', lambda x: 18 <= x <=
65)
E) df.query('age >= 18 and age <= 65')
```

QUESTION 6

You are retrieving data from a database table called employees using Python. Which SQL query would correctly fetch all records where the salary is greater than 50000? (Select 2 answers)

```
A) SELECT * FROM employees WHERE salary >
50000
B) SELECT * employees WHERE salary = 50000
C) SELECT * FROM employees WHERE salary >=
50000
```

```
D) SELECT salary FROM employees
E) SELECT * FROM employees WHERE salary >
'50000'
```

QUESTION 7

You are tasked with calculating the mean, median, and mode of a dataset in Python using the statistics library. Which of the following correctly calculates these measures of central tendency? (Select 2 answers)

```
A) import statistics
mean_val = statistics.mean(data)
median_val = statistics.median(data)
mode_val = statistics.mode(data)

B) import statistics
mean_val = statistics.mean(datA) mode_val =
statistics.median(data)

C) import numpy as np
mean_val = np.mean(datA) median_val =
np.median(data)
mode_val = np.mode(data)

D) import statistics
mean_val = statistics.mean(data)
median_val = statistics.mean(data)

E) import pandas as pd
mean_val = pd.mean(data)
```

QUESTION 8

You are tasked with reading a CSV file and performing data cleaning using Pandas. Which of the following code snippets correctly reads a CSV and handles missing data by filling NaN values with the mean of each column? (Select 2 answers)

```
A) import pandas as pd
df = pd.read_csv('data.csv')
df.fillna(df.mean(), inplace=True)

B) import pandas as pd
df = pd.read_csv('data.csv')
df.fillna(mean(), inplace=True)

C) import pandas as pd
df = pd.read_csv('data.csv')
df.dropna(inplace=True)

D) import pandas as pd
df = pd.read_csv('data.csv')
df = df.fillna(df.median())

E) import pandas as pd
df = pd.read_csv('data.csv')
df['col1'].fillna(df['col1'].mean(),
inplace=True)
```

QUESTION 9

You are building a linear regression model in Python to predict house prices based on square footage and number of bedrooms. Which steps are correct for fitting the model? Select 2 correct options.

```
A) from sklearn.linear_model import
LinearRegression
model = LinearRegression()
model.fit(X_train[['sqft', 'bedrooms']],
y_train)

B) model.predict(X_test[['sqft',
'bedrooms']])

C) model.fit(X_train, y_train)

D) from sklearn.tree import
DecisionTreeClassifier
model = DecisionTreeClassifier()

E) model.score(X_test, y_test)
```

QUESTION 10

You are tasked with creating a correlation heatmap using Seaborn. Which steps are correct? Select 2 correct options.

```
A) import seaborn as sns
corr = df.corr()
sns.heatmap(corr)

B) sns.heatmap(df)
C) sns.heatmap(corr, annot=True)
D) sns.barplot(df)
E) sns.heatmap(df.pivot_table())
```

QUESTION 11

You are designing a survey for a market research project to gather data on customer preferences. After receiving the data, you notice missing values and inconsistencies. Which Python operations will you use to handle missing data and ensure consistency? (Select 2 correct answers)

```
A) df.fillna(method='ffill')
B) df.dropna(axis=0)
C) df.isnull().sum()
D) df.replace(np.nan, '0')
E) df['age'].astype(int)
```

QUESTION 12

You are tasked with collecting and storing healthcare patient data under GDPR. What actions should be taken to ensure compliance with the GDPR while processing Personally Identifiable Information (PII)? (Select 2 correct answers)

 A) Use Python's cryptography package to encrypt PII before storing it in a database
 B) Allow patients to update or request deletion of their data via a Python-based API
 C) Automatically share patient data with third-party partners for analytics purposes without explicit consent
 D) Store patient data on servers located outside the EU without considering GDPR transfer rules
 E) Generate anonymized versions of the data using Python libraries like pandas to protect privacy

QUESTION 13

You are given a dataset with missing values and duplicates. You need to clean the dataset by removing all rows with missing values and duplicates using Python's Pandas. Select the correct scripts. (Select 2 answers)

```
A)   df.dropna(inplace=TruE)
B)   df.drop_duplicates(inplace=TruE)
C)   df.dropna(axis=1)
D)   df.fillna(0)
E)   df.isna().drop_duplicates()
```

QUESTION 14

You are working with a dataset that contains sales transactions across multiple regions. You need to group the data by 'region' and calculate the total sales for each region using Pandas. Which of the following scripts accomplishes this task? Select 2 correct answers.

```
A) df.groupby('region').agg({'sales':
'sum'})
B) df.groupby(['region'])['sales'].sum()
C) df.groupby('region').apply(lambda x:
x.sum())
D) df.groupby('region')['sales'].count()
E) df.groupby('region').transform('sum')
```

QUESTION 15

You are tasked with formatting a sales report for your team. The report needs to be exported to Excel with properly formatted headers, including totals at the bottom and numbers rounded to two decimal places. What is the best way to achieve this using Python and Pandas? (Select 2 answers)

```
A) df.to_excel('sales_report.xlsx',
index=False, float_format='%.2f')

B) df.style.format({'Sales':
'{:.2f}'}).to_excel('sales_report.xlsx',
index=FalsE)

C) df.to_excel('sales_report.xlsx',
header=False, float_format='%.2f')

D)
df.round(2).to_excel('sales_report.xlsx',
index=FalsE)

E) df['Total'] = df.sum(axis=1);
df.to_excel('sales_report.xlsx',
index=FalsE)
```

QUESTION 16

You are processing a sales dataset and need to iterate through each row to check if the sales value is greater than 500. If it is, you must apply a 10% discount to that sale. Which code structure will correctly implement this logic using Python? (Select 2 answers)

```
A) for i in range(len(df)): if df.loc[i,
'Sales'] > 500: df.loc[i, 'Sales'] *= 0.9

B) df['Sales'] = df.apply(lambda row:
row['Sales'] * 0.9 if row['Sales'] > 500
else row['Sales'], axis=1)

C) for sale in df['Sales']: if sale > 500:
sale *= 0.9

D) df['Sales'] = df[df['Sales'] >
500]['Sales'] * 0.9

E) for index, row in df.iterrows(): if
row['Sales'] > 500: df.at[index, 'Sales']
*= 0.9
```

QUESTION 17

You are working on a dataset where you need to handle missing values in a column named 'Age'. You are required to fill the missing values with the mean of the column. Which Python data science library and function should you use? (Select 2 answers)

```
A) df['Age'].fillna(df['Age'].mean(),
inplace=TruE)

B) df['Age'] = df['Age'].replace(np.nan,
df['Age'].mean())

C) from sklearn.impute import
SimpleImputer; imputer =
```

```
SimpleImputer(strategy='mean'); df['Age'] =
imputer.fit_transform(df[['Age']])

D) df['Age'].interpolate(method='linear',
inplace=TruE)

E) df['Age'].fillna(np.mean(df['Age']),
inplace=TruE)
```

QUESTION 18

You are tasked with writing a Python script to preprocess customer data. As part of the script, you want to ensure that your code follows the PEP 8 style guide for readability and best practices. Which of the following code snippets adheres to PEP 8 standards? (Select 2 answers)

```
A) def process_data(): total=0 for i in
range(10): total+=i return total

B) def process_data(): total = 0 for i in
range(10): total += i return total

C) def processData(): total=0 for i in
range(10): total+=i return total

D) def process_data(): total = 0 for i in
range(10): total+=i return total

E) def process_data(): total = 0 for i in
range(10): total += i return total
```

QUESTION 19

You are developing a data acquisition script that fetches data from an API. You want to handle network errors and ensure that your script can display a custom error message. Which of the following snippets handles this scenario correctly? (Select 2 answers)

```
A) try:
data = fetch_data(api_url)
except TimeoutError:
print("API timed out.")

B) try:
data = fetch_data(api_url)
except ConnectionError:
print("Failed to connect to the API.")
raise

C) try:
data = fetch_data(api_url)
except Exception:
print("An error occurred.")
raise

D) try:
data = fetch_data(api_url)
```

```
except Exception:
raise("Custom message")

E) try:
data = fetch_data(api_url)
except (ConnectionError, TimeoutError):
print("A network error occurred.")
```

QUESTION 20

You are creating a new table to store customer information in a SQL database. The table should store customer_id as a primary key, customer_name as text, and total_purchase as a numeric field. Which SQL statement correctly creates this table? (Select 2 answers)

```
A) CREATE TABLE customers (
customer_id INT PRIMARY KEY,
customer_name VARCHAR(100),
total_purchase DECIMAL(10,2));

B) CREATE TABLE customers (
customer_id INTEGER PRIMARY KEY,
customer_name TEXT,
total_purchase NUMERIC(10,2));

C) CREATE TABLE customers (
customer_id INT,
customer_name VARCHAR(100),
total_purchase DECIMAL(10,2),
PRIMARY KEY (customer_id));

D) CREATE TABLE customers (
customer_id INTEGER AUTO_INCREMENT,
customer_name TEXT,
total_purchase DECIMAL(10,2),
PRIMARY KEY (customer_id));

E) CREATE TABLE customers (
customer_id INT UNIQUE,
customer_name VARCHAR(100),
total_purchase FLOAT);
```

QUESTION 21

You are tasked with writing a Python script that retrieves customer data from a SQLite database using a parameterized query. Which of the following code snippets correctly retrieves data where customer_id equals a user-supplied value, ensuring protection against SQL injection? (Select 2 answers)

```
A) import sqlite3
conn = sqlite3.connect('database.db')
cursor = conn.cursor()
cursor.execute("SELECT * FROM customers
WHERE customer_id = ?", (customer_id,))
rows = cursor.fetchall()
```

```
B) import sqlite3
conn = sqlite3.connect('database.db')
cursor = conn.cursor()
cursor.execute("SELECT * FROM customers
WHERE customer_id = '" + str(customer_id) +
"'")
rows = cursor.fetchall()

C) import sqlite3
conn = sqlite3.connect('database.db')
cursor = conn.cursor()
cursor.execute("SELECT * FROM customers
WHERE customer_id = :id", {'id':
customer_id})
rows = cursor.fetchall()

D) import sqlite3
conn = sqlite3.connect('database.db')
cursor = conn.cursor()
cursor.execute("SELECT * FROM customers
WHERE customer_id = %s", (customer_id,))
rows = cursor.fetchall()

E) import sqlite3
conn = sqlite3.connect('database.db')
cursor = conn.cursor()
cursor.execute("SELECT * FROM customers
WHERE customer_id = ?", [customer_id])
rows = cursor.fetchall()
```

QUESTION 22

You are tasked with retrieving sensitive customer data such as names and emails from a SQL database. What is the best way to avoid SQL injection attacks when querying this data? (Select 2 answers)

```
A) cur.execute("SELECT name, email FROM
customers WHERE id = " + customer_id)

B) cur.execute("SELECT name, email FROM
customers WHERE id = ?", (customer_id,))

C) cur.execute("SELECT * FROM customers
WHERE id=%s", (customer_id))

D) query = f"SELECT * FROM customers WHERE
id = {customer_id}"
    cur.execute(query)

E) cur.execute("SELECT * FROM customers
WHERE id=:id", {"id": customer_id})
```

QUESTION 23

You are implementing a class for managing employee records. Which constructor implementation allows setting the name and age of an employee? (Select 2 answers)

```
A) class Employee:
```

```
def __init__(self, name, age):
self.name = name
self.age = age

 B) class Employee:
def init(self, name, age):
self.name = name
self.age = age

 C) class Employee:
def __init__(self, name, age):
self.name(name)
self.age(agE)   D) class Employee:
def __init__(self):
self.name = "default"
self.age = 30

 E) class Employee:
def __init__(name, age):
self.name = name
self.age = age
```

QUESTION 24

You need to open a file, read its contents, and handle any exceptions that occur. Which of the following Python scripts is the best way to handle this?

```
 A) with open('data.txt', 'r') as f:
print(f.read())

 B) f = open('data.txt', 'r')
print(f.read())

 C) try: with open('data.txt', 'r') as f:
print(f.read()) except FileNotFoundError:
print("File not found")

D) with open('data.txt', 'r') as f:
print(f.readlines()) except
FileNotFoundError: print("File not found")

E) f = open('data.txt', 'r') try:
print(f.read()) except FileNotFoundError:
print("File not found")
```

QUESTION 25

You are tasked with creating a custom exception class for handling invalid file formats in a data processing application. Which of the following code snippets would correctly define and raise this custom exception? (Select 2 correct answers)

```
A) class InvalidFileFormatError(Exception):
pass
raise InvalidFileFormatError()

 B) class
InvalidFileFormatError(Exception):
```

```
def __init__(self, message):
self.message = message
raise InvalidFileFormatError('Invalid file
format')

 C) class
FileError(InvalidFileFormatError):
raise FileError()

 D) class
InvalidFileFormatError(ValueError):
def __init__(self):
super().__init__('File format is invalid')
raise InvalidFileFormatError()

 E) raise
Exception('InvalidFileFormatError')
```

QUESTION 26

You have two tables: employees and departments. You want to retrieve all employees along with their department names, even if some employees are not assigned to any department. Which SQL query will achieve this? (Select 2 correct answers)

```
A) SELECT e.employee_name,
d.department_name FROM employees e LEFT
JOIN departments d ON e.department_id =
d.department_id;

B) SELECT e.employee_name,
d.department_name FROM employees e INNER
JOIN departments d ON e.department_id =
d.department_id;

C) SELECT e.employee_name,
d.department_name FROM employees e RIGHT
JOIN departments d ON e.department_id =
d.department_id;

D) SELECT e.employee_name,
d.department_name FROM employees e FULL
JOIN departments d ON e.department_id =
d.department_id;

E) SELECT e.employee_name,
d.department_name FROM employees e CROSS
JOIN departments d;
```

QUESTION 27

A table employees has a department_id column that is a foreign key referencing the departments table. How can you ensure that if a department is deleted, the corresponding employees are also deleted to maintain referential integrity? (Select 2 correct answers)

```
A) ALTER TABLE employees ADD FOREIGN KEY
```

```
(department_id) REFERENCES
departments(department_id) ON DELETE
CASCADE;

B) ALTER TABLE employees ADD FOREIGN KEY
(department_id) REFERENCES
departments(department_id) ON UPDATE
CASCADE;

C) ALTER TABLE employees DROP FOREIGN KEY
department_id;

D) DELETE FROM departments WHERE
department_id = 1;

E) ALTER TABLE employees ADD CONSTRAINT
FK_dept_emp FOREIGN KEY (department_id)
REFERENCES departments(department_id) ON
DELETE CASCADE;
```

QUESTION 28

You have a large dataset in a table called sales_data. To optimize the performance of queries that frequently filter by customer_id, which indexing strategy should be used? (Select 2 correct answers)

```
A) CREATE INDEX idx_customer ON
sales_data(customer_id);

B) CREATE UNIQUE INDEX idx_sales ON
sales_data(sales_id);

C) CREATE CLUSTERED INDEX idx_date ON
sales_data(order_date);

D) CREATE INDEX idx_customer_order ON
sales_data(customer_id, order_id);

E) CREATE NONCLUSTERED INDEX idx_price ON
sales_data(price);
```

QUESTION 29

You have a dataset of monthly salaries. How would you calculate the mean, median, and mode using Python? (Select 2 correct answers)

```
A) import statistics;
statistics.mean(salaries)

B) import statistics;
statistics.median(salaries)

C) import numpy as np; np.mean(salaries)
D) salaries.median()
E) statistics.mode(salaries)
```

QUESTION 30

You are analyzing the distribution of a company's annual sales data. How would you calculate the variance and standard deviation of this data using Python? (Select 2 correct answers)

```
A) import statistics;
statistics.variance(sales)
```

```
B) import statistics;
statistics.stdev(sales)
```

```
C) import numpy as np; np.var(sales)
D) sales.variance()
```

```
E) import statistics;
statistics.mean(sales)
```

QUESTION 31

You are tasked with applying bootstrapping to a dataset containing the heights of individuals to estimate the mean height. How would you implement bootstrapping to resample the dataset and calculate the bootstrapped means in Python using the numpy library? (Select 2 correct answers)

```
A) import numpy as np; means =
[np.mean(np.random.choice(df['height'],
size=len(df['height']), replace=True)) for
_ in range(1000)]
```

```
B) np.median(np.random.choice(df['height'],
size=len(df['height']), replace=False))
```

```
C) import numpy as np; means =
np.mean(np.random.choice(df['height'],
size=len(df['height']), replace=True,
size=1000))
```

```
D) import pandas as pd; means =
df['height'].bootstrap(1000)
```

```
E) import numpy as np; bootstrapped_means =
[np.mean(np.random.choice(df['height'],
size=len(df['height']), replace=True)) for
_ in range(1000)]
```

QUESTION 32

You are tasked with implementing a logistic regression model to predict whether customers will purchase a product based on their age and income. Which Python code correctly implements logistic regression using scikit-learn? (Select 2 correct answers)

```
A) from sklearn.linear_model import
LogisticRegression; model =
LogisticRegression(); X = df[['age',
'income']]; y = df['purchased'];
model.fit(X, y)
```

```
B) from sklearn.linear_model import
LinearRegression; model =
LinearRegression(); X = df[['age',
'income']]; y = df['purchased'];
model.fit(X, y)
```

```
C) import statsmodels.api as sm; X =
df[['age', 'income']]; y = df['purchased'];
X = sm.add_constant(X); model = sm.Logit(y,
X).fit()
```

```
D) from sklearn.model_selection import
train_test_split; X_train, X_test, y_train,
y_test = train_test_split(df[['age',
'income']], df['purchased']); model =
LogisticRegression(); model.fit(X_train,
y_train)
```

```
E) import numpy as np; model =
np.log(df[['age', 'income']])
```

QUESTION 33

You are working with a dataset containing missing values and want to fill the missing values in the 'sales' column with the median value of the column. Which of the following is the correct way to fill the missing values using Pandas? (Select 2 correct answers)

```
A) df['sales'] =
df['sales'].fillna(df['sales'].median())
```

```
B) df['sales'].fillna(df['sales'].mean(),
inplace=True)
```

```
C) df['sales'] =
df['sales'].fillna(df['sales'].mean())
```

```
D) df.fillna({'sales':
df['sales'].median()}, inplace=True)
```

```
E) df['sales'] =
df['sales'].fillna(df['sales'].mode()[0])
```

QUESTION 34

You are working with NumPy arrays and Python lists. Which of the following correctly demonstrates a key difference between arrays and lists in Python? (Select 2 correct answers)

A) Arrays allow element-wise operations, while lists require loops for such operations.
B) Arrays can only contain numerical data, while lists can store any data type.
C) Lists support broadcasting, while arrays do not.
D) Arrays are more efficient in memory usage than lists for large datasets.
E) Arrays require the use of explicit loops for

element-wise operations.

QUESTION 35

You are analyzing a dataset with numerical values in Pandas and want to calculate the mean, median, and standard deviation of a column age. Which of the following scripts will give the correct result? (Select 2 correct answers)

```
A) df['age'].mean()
B) df['age'].median()
C) df['age'].std()
D) df.mean(df['age'], df['salary'])
E) np.mean(df['age'], df['salary'])
```

QUESTION 36

You are building a linear regression model to predict house prices based on the size of the house (in square feet). Which of the following Python scripts will correctly implement a linear regression using Scikit-learn? (Select 2 correct answers)

```
A) from sklearn.linear_model import
LinearRegression; model =
LinearRegression(); model.fit(X_train,
y_train)

B) from sklearn.linear_model import
LogisticRegression; model =
LogisticRegression(); model.fit(X_train,
y_train)

C) model = sm.OLS(y_train, X_train).fit()

D) from sklearn.model_selection import
LinearRegression; model =
LinearRegression().fit(X_test, y_test)

E) from sklearn.linear_model import Ridge;
model = Ridge().fit(X_train, y_train)
```

QUESTION 37

You are tasked with building a linear regression model to predict house prices based on square footage. Which Python script would correctly create and fit the model using scikit-learn?

```
A) from sklearn.linear_model import
LinearRegression
 model = LinearRegression()
 model.fit(X_train, y_train)

 B) from sklearn.linear_model import
LogisticRegression
 model = LogisticRegression()
```

```
model.fit(X_train, y_train)

 C) from sklearn.preprocessing import
StandardScaler
 model = StandardScaler()
 model.fit(X_train, y_train)

 D) from sklearn.neighbors import
KNeighborsRegressor
 model = KNeighborsRegressor()
 model.fit(X_train, y_train)

 E) from sklearn.ensemble import
RandomForestClassifier
 model = RandomForestClassifier()
 model.fit(X_train, y_train)
```

QUESTION 38

You are analyzing customer purchase data and need to group sales data by region and find the average sales per region. Which of the following is the correct way to achieve this using Pandas? Select TWO correct answers.

```
 A)
df.groupby('region').agg({'sales':'mean'})

 B) df.groupby('region')['sales'].mean()
 C) df.sales.groupby('region').agg('mean')
 D) df.sales.groupby('region').mean()
 E) df.groupby('sales').mean()
```

QUESTION 39

A machine learning model is trained on a dataset with a high training accuracy but performs poorly on unseen test data. This is an example of overfitting. To reduce overfitting, you can apply regularization techniques. Which of the following scripts would implement L2 regularization using the Ridge regression model in scikit-learn? Select two answers.

```
A) from sklearn.linear_model import Ridge;
ridge = Ridge(alpha=1.0);
ridge.fit(X_train, y_train)

B) from sklearn.linear_model import Lasso;
lasso = Lasso(alpha=1.0);
lasso.fit(X_train, y_train)

C) from sklearn.linear_model import
RidgeCV; ridge_cv = RidgeCV(alphas=[0.1,
1.0, 10.0]); ridge_cv.fit(X_train, y_train)

D) from sklearn.linear_model import
ElasticNet; enet = ElasticNet(alpha=1.0,
l1_ratio=0.5); enet.fit(X_train, y_train)

E) from sklearn.linear_model import
```

```
LinearRegression; lr = LinearRegression();
lr.fit(X_train, y_train)`
```

QUESTION 40

You are tasked with visualizing the sales
performance of different product categories over
time using Matplotlib. Which of the following scripts
will help you create a line plot to represent this
data? Select two correct answers.

```
A) plt.plot(df['Date'], df['Sales'])

B) plt.bar(df['Product Category'],
df['Sales'])

C) plt.plot(df['Product Category'],
df['Sales'])

D) plt.plot(df['Date'], df['Sales'],
label='Sales by Date')`

E) plt.scatter(df['Date'], df['Sales'])
```

QUESTION 41

You are analyzing sales data over time and want to
visualize it with a time-series line plot using
Matplotlib. Which of the following will produce an
accurate representation? Select two correct answers.

```
A) plt.plot(df['date'], df['sales'])
B) plt.bar(df['date'], df['sales'])
C) plt.scatter(df['date'], df['sales'])
D) plt.plot(df['sales'], df['date'])
E) plt.line(df['date'], df['sales'])
```

QUESTION 42

You are visualizing a bar plot showing sales data
across regions. You want to apply a consistent color
palette for readability. How would you implement a
"Blues" color palette in Matplotlib for this bar plot?

```
A) plt.bar(df['Region'], df['Sales'],
color='Blues')

B) plt.bar(df['Region'], df['Sales'],
cmap='Blues')

C) plt.bar(df['Region'], df['Sales'],
color=plt.cm.Blues(df['Sales']))

D) plt.bar(df['Region'], df['Sales'],
palette='Blues')

E) plt.bar(df['Region'], df['Sales'],
```
```
color='blue')
```

QUESTION 43

You are preparing a report on customer behavior
using Matplotlib to visualize the distribution of
purchases across regions. The plot needs to highlight
key regions where purchases are highest. How would
you effectively emphasize these regions with
annotations?

```
A) plt.bar(df['Region'], df['Purchases']);
plt.text(df['Purchases'], ha='left')

B) plt.bar(df['Region'], df['Purchases']);
for i, v in enumerate(df['Purchases']):
plt.text(i, v, str(v), ha='center')

C) plt.bar(df['Region'], df['Purchases']);
plt.annotate('Highest', xy=(0, 200))

D) plt.bar(df['Region'], df['Purchases'],
label='Purchases')
```

QUESTION 44

You are tasked with visualizing customer acquisition
trends over the last 3 years using Python and
Matplotlib. You need to create a narrative that
highlights key peaks and valleys. Which Python script
approach effectively crafts this narrative? Select two
correct answers.

```
A) plt.plot(dates, acquisitions)
 plt.title('Customer Acquisitions')
 plt.annotate('Peak', xy=(date[10],
acquisitions[10]), xytext=(date[5],
acquisitions[10]),
arrowprops=dict(facecolor='black',
shrink=0.05))

B) plt.bar(dates, acquisitions)
 plt.title('Acquisitions Over Time')

C) plt.scatter(dates, acquisitions)
 plt.text(date[10], acquisitions[10],
'Peak', fontsize=12)

D) plt.plot(dates, acquisitions)
 plt.annotate('Valley', xy=(date[15],
acquisitions[15]),
arrowprops=dict(arrowstyle='->'))

E) plt.plot(dates, acquisitions) with no
labels or annotations
```

QUESTION 45

You have analyzed sales data for different regions and need to summarize key findings for a management report. The sales trend shows a steady increase in Region A, but fluctuating sales in Region B. Which Python code would best summarize this trend in a bar plot?

```
A) plt.bar("Region A", sales_A); plt.bar("Region B", sales_B); plt.xlabel("Regions");
plt.ylabel("Sales"); plt.title("Sales Trends")

B) plt.barh(["Region A", "Region B"], [sales_A, sales_B]); plt.xlabel("Regions");
plt.ylabel("Sales")

C) sns.lineplot(x="time", y="sales_A", label="Region A"); sns.lineplot(x="time", y="sales_B",
label="Region B"); plt.title("Sales Trends Over Time")

D) plt.scatter(sales_A, sales_B, color="blue"); plt.title("Sales Trends")

E) sns.histplot(data=sales_df, x="Region", hue="Sales", multiple="stack"); plt.title("Sales
Distribution")
```

PRACTICE TEST 1 - ANSWERS ONLY

QUESTION 1

Answer - B

A) Incorrect – Not checking robots.txt is unethical as it bypasses restrictions set by websites. Scraping without permission can lead to legal consequences.
B) Correct – This method respects ethical scraping practices by following robots.txt and using a sleep interval to avoid overwhelming the server.
C) Incorrect – Deliberately bypassing robots.txt is a violation of ethical standards.
D) Incorrect – Scraping rapidly using selenium may cause server overload, leading to IP blocking or legal action.
E) Incorrect – Ignoring terms of service could result in violation of the website's policy.

EXAM FOCUS	Ethical web scraping requires adhering to a website's robots.txt file and terms of service. Always incorporate delays to avoid overwhelming servers.
CAUTION ALERT	Ignoring robots.txt or scraping too fast can result in your IP getting banned or legal actions. Ensure you follow all website guidelines.

QUESTION 2

Answer - B, D

A) Incorrect – This method uses the mean to fill missing values, not the median.
B) Correct – fillna(df.median(), inplace=True) correctly fills missing values with the median.
C) Incorrect – The replace() method is used for replacing specific values, not suitable for filling NaNs with median.
D) Correct – interpolate() is a valid method for filling missing values in a linear fashion.
E) Incorrect – dropna() removes rows with missing values, which may result in loss of important data.

EXAM FOCUS	Use fillna() for imputation to maintain data integrity. Remember to choose between median or mean based on data distribution.
CAUTION ALERT	Be cautious with replace() for filling missing values; it's meant for replacing specific values, not statistical imputation.

QUESTION 3

Answer - A, D

A) Correct – pd.read_sql() is the standard way to load structured data from SQL databases into a Pandas DataFrame.
B) Incorrect – pd.read_json() is primarily used for JSON, not relational databases.
C) Incorrect – CSV is typically structured, not unstructured data, and wouldn't apply to text reviews directly.
D) Correct – The re module is useful for processing unstructured text, extracting patterns, and converting it into a usable format.
E) Incorrect – While pd.concat() can combine DataFrames, it's better suited for structured data, and not for merging structured with unstructured data without first processing the unstructured data.

EXAM FOCUS	Use pd.read_sql() for structured data and re for processing unstructured text. Ensure proper handling of each data type before combining.
CAUTION ALERT	pd.concat() is better for combining similar datasets. Avoid directly concatenating structured and unstructured data without first processing the unstructured data.

QUESTION 4

Answer - A, C

A) Correct – The Z-score method identifies outliers by measuring how many standard deviations a data point is from the mean.
B) Incorrect – Min-Max scaling is used for normalization, not for detecting outliers.
C) Correct –IQR method detects outliers by identifying points that fall below Q1 or above Q3 by 1.5 times IQR.
D) Incorrect – Label Encoding is used for converting categorical variables, not for detecting outliers.
E) Incorrect – pd.read_csv() is used for loading datasets and does not detect outliers.

EXAM FOCUS	Use Z-score and IQR methods to reliably detect numerical outliers. Focus on these statistical techniques for outlier detection in datasets.
CAUTION ALERT	Don't confuse normalization methods like Min-Max scaling with outlier detection. Min-Max scaling won't detect outliers, only normalize the range of data.

QUESTION 5

Answer - A, E

A) Correct – This code uses Boolean indexing to filter rows where age is between 18 and 65.
B) Incorrect – The between() method is useful but doesn't ensure data validity since it won't filter out invalid rows in-place without further steps.
C) Incorrect – This syntax is incorrect for filtering the column for a range.
D) Incorrect – filter() does not support the provided lambda format for column validation.
E) Correct – The query() function allows querying based on conditions in Pandas, and this query ensures that age values meet the required range.

EXAM FOCUS	Use Boolean indexing and query() to filter datasets based on conditions like age validation. These methods are efficient for filtering large datasets.
CAUTION ALERT	Be cautious with methods like filter() and incorrect syntax in filtering. Ensure you're applying the correct method when working with numerical ranges.

QUESTION 6

Answer - A, C

A) Correct – This SQL query correctly retrieves all columns from the employees table where the salary > 50000.
B) Incorrect – This query lacks the FROM clause and uses the wrong condition (= instead of >).
C) Correct – This query also retrieves employees with a salary greater than or equal to 50000.
D) Incorrect – This query only retrieves the salary column and doesn't filter by salary condition.
E) Incorrect – The value '50000' is treated as a string, which will result in an error.

EXAM FOCUS	Use SELECT * FROM to retrieve all records in SQL, but always ensure correct comparison operators like >, >=.
CAUTION ALERT	Avoid comparing numeric values with strings like '50000'. This mismatch leads to errors in SQL queries.

QUESTION 7

Answer - A, C

A) Correct – This is the correct usage of the statistics library to calculate mean, median, and mode.

B) Incorrect – median() and mode() are swapped in this syntax.

C) Correct – NumPy's mean() and median() are correctly used, but NumPy does not have a direct mode() function.

D) Incorrect – This mistakenly calculates the mean twice, instead of calculating both mean and median.

E) Incorrect – The correct method for Pandas would be data.mean(), not pd.mean().

EXAM FOCUS	*Use statistics.mean(), median(), and mode() or NumPy for basic statistical measures. These libraries offer reliable built-in functions for central tendency.*
CAUTION ALERT	*NumPy lacks a direct mode() function. Use scipy.stats.mode() or statistics.mode() for calculating mode values in your dataset.*

QUESTION 8

Answer - A, E

A) Correct – This code reads a CSV and fills NaN values with the mean of the columns using df.mean().

B) Incorrect – The function mean() is not defined here; it must be applied to the DataFrame.

C) Incorrect – This drops missing values instead of filling them.

D) Incorrect – It fills NaN values with the median, which is not what the question asks.

E) Correct – This fills NaN values for a specific column using its mean.

EXAM FOCUS	*Use df.fillna(df.mean()) to fill missing data in Pandas with the column mean. It's useful for numerical data imputation.*
CAUTION ALERT	*Avoid using undefined functions like mean(). Always call statistical functions directly on DataFrame columns, e.g., df.mean().*

QUESTION 9

Answer - A, B

A) Correct: The linear regression is correctly initialized and fitted with the right feature set.

B) Correct: Predicting house prices using the trained model.

C) Incorrect: It misses feature specification ('sqft', 'bedrooms').

D) Incorrect: Decision tree classifier is not relevant.

E) Incorrect: Scoring is useful but not for fitting the model.

EXAM FOCUS	*Always specify feature columns in X_train[['feature1', 'feature2']] when using fit() in linear regression. Use .predict() for predictions on unseen data.*
CAUTION ALERT	*Avoid using classifiers like DecisionTreeClassifier when regression is required. Always choose the correct model for prediction tasks.*

QUESTION 10

Answer - A, C

A) Correct: This imports Seaborn and creates a heatmap for correlation matrix which is a valid use case for visualizing relationships.

B) Incorrect: df without corr() would cause an error as heatmap requires numeric data input, not raw data frames.

C) Correct: Adding annot=True allows for annotations on heatmap, improving clarity & understanding of the plot.

D) Incorrect: barplot is for bar charts, not heatmaps, so this would not visualize correlations properly.

E) Incorrect: pivot_table() generates tables for summary stats, but it's not required for basic heatmap plotting.

EXAM FOCUS	*Always use df.corr() before sns.heatmap() to compute the correlation matrix for numeric columns. Use annot=True to add values on the heatmap.*
CAUTION ALERT	*Avoid using a DataFrame directly without correlation when generating heatmaps. This can cause errors if non-numeric data is present.*

QUESTION 11

Answer - A, B

A) Forward fill (ffill) is used to propagate non-null values to fill missing data.
B) Dropping rows with missing data is a valid approach when large amounts of data are missing.
C) This only checks for missing data, it doesn't handle it.
D) Replacing missing values with '0' may distort data integrity.
E) Converting columns to integers may cause loss of important data.

EXAM FOCUS	*Forward filling (ffill) and dropping rows (dropna) are commonly used to handle missing data. Choose wisely based on the data importance.*
CAUTION ALERT	*Avoid replacing missing data with arbitrary values like 0 or string placeholders like 'Unknown', as they may distort analysis.*

QUESTION 12

Answer - A, B

A) Encryption ensures that data stored is not vulnerable to unauthorized access.
B) GDPR grants users the right to modify or delete their data, so a Python-based API allows for compliance.
C) Sharing data without consent breaches GDPR regulations as explicit consent is required.
D) Transferring data outside the EU without considering GDPR can lead to legal penalties.
E) While anonymizing is good practice, it does not replace the need for consent for sensitive data.

EXAM FOCUS	*Encryption (cryptography) is essential when storing PII. Ensure users have control over their data via API access, complying with GDPR requirements.*
CAUTION ALERT	*Avoid transferring patient data outside the EU without GDPR-compliant safeguards in place, as it can lead to significant legal penalties.*

QUESTION 13

Answer - A, B

A) Correct, dropna removes rows with missing values.
B) Correct, drop_duplicates removes duplicate rows.
C) Drops columns, not rows, so it's not needed here.
D) Fills missing values but doesn't remove them.
E) Invalid syntax, combining isna() and drop_duplicates.

EXAM FOCUS	*Use df.dropna() to clean missing values and df.drop_duplicates() to remove duplicates, ensuring your dataset is ready for analysis.*
CAUTION ALERT	*Don't use axis=1 in dropna() if you're dealing with row-based missing values. Dropping columns can lead to loss of essential data.*

QUESTION 14

Answer - A, B

A) Correct: This uses groupby and agg to sum sales by region.
B) Correct: This method groups by 'region' and sums 'sales'.
C) Incorrect: While apply is valid, it's unnecessary here.
D) Incorrect: This calculates count, not sum.
E) Incorrect: transform is for transformation, not aggregation.

EXAM FOCUS	Use groupby() with agg() or .sum() to calculate sales by region, which is essential for analyzing grouped data efficiently.
CAUTION ALERT	Avoid using transform() when aggregating; it's designed for element-wise operations, not for summarizing data.

QUESTION 15

Answer - B, D

Option A: Incorrect – No rounding mechanism applied.
Option B: Correct – It uses style.format to format specific columns and round values.
Option C: Incorrect – Missing headers, which is not specified in the requirement.
Option D: Correct – This applies round(2) to format the numbers and exports correctly.
Option E: Incorrect – Although adding totals, no rounding is applied to the output.

EXAM FOCUS	Use df.to_excel() with style.format() or round() to ensure precision and clarity in reports, especially when working with financial data.
CAUTION ALERT	Be cautious when using header=False; omitting headers can cause confusion and misinterpretation in exported reports.

QUESTION 16

Answer - A, B

Option A: Correct – Uses a loop with loc to access and modify rows based on condition.
Option B: Correct – Uses apply with a lambda function, applying the discount efficiently.
Option C: Incorrect – sale is a copy, so changes won't reflect back in the DataFrame.
Option D: Incorrect – This modifies only the filtered subset, not the entire DataFrame.
Option E: Incorrect – iterrows() is inefficient for large datasets compared to apply().

EXAM FOCUS	Use apply() with a lambda function to modify DataFrame values efficiently when applying discounts based on conditions like sales amounts.
CAUTION ALERT	Avoid using iterrows() for large datasets as it is slower compared to vectorized operations like apply().

QUESTION 17

Answer - A, C

Option A: Correct – fillna() is a Pandas function used to replace missing values with the column mean.
Option B: Incorrect – replace() is not the right function for replacing NaN values.
Option C: Correct – Uses Scikit-learn's SimpleImputer to impute missing values with the column mean.

Option D: Incorrect – interpolate() is used for linear interpolation, not mean replacement.

Option E: Incorrect – np.mean() should be applied directly, but this syntax is not supported in this context.

EXAM FOCUS	*Use fillna() or Scikit-learn's SimpleImputer to efficiently handle missing values, ensuring your dataset is ready for analysis.*
CAUTION ALERT	*Be cautious when using replace() to handle missing values; it's better suited for replacing specific values, not handling NaNs.*

QUESTION 18

Answer - B, E

Option A: Incorrect – Missing spaces around operators (total+=i).
Option B: Correct – Follows proper indentation and spacing per PEP 8.
Option C: Incorrect – The function name processData does not follow PEP 8 naming conventions (should use underscores).
Option D: Incorrect – Missing space after +=.
Option E: Correct – Proper spacing, indentation, and naming conventions as per PEP 8.

EXAM FOCUS	*PEP 8 matters: Use proper spacing around operators and ensure function names follow snake_case convention to improve code readability and maintainability.*
CAUTION ALERT	*Be mindful of operator spacing: Missing spaces around operators or inconsistent naming conventions are common PEP 8 violations that reduce readability.*

QUESTION 19

Answer - B, E

Option A: Incorrect – TimeoutError is valid, but there's no broader exception handling for other potential network issues.
Option B: Correct – Handles ConnectionError and uses raise to re-raise the original exception after printing a custom message.
Option C: Incorrect – Provides a generic error message but doesn't specify the nature of the error.
Option D: Incorrect – raise cannot take a custom message directly without an exception class.
Option E: Correct – Handles both ConnectionError and TimeoutError, which are common in network-related issues.

EXAM FOCUS	*Handle multiple errors: Use exception handling blocks that account for common issues like ConnectionError and TimeoutError when fetching data from APIs.*
CAUTION ALERT	*Don't re-raise blindly: Always raise exceptions with context, ensuring you retain original error details for better debugging and transparency.*

QUESTION 20

Answer - A, B

Option A: Correct – Defines the customer_id as an INT primary key, customer_name as VARCHAR, and total_purchase as DECIMAL, a correct and common format.
Option B: Correct – Uses INTEGER and TEXT for column types, which are valid data types in many SQL implementations.
Option C: Incorrect – This syntax is valid but redundant as the primary key can be defined within the column definition, making Option A more efficient.

Option D: Incorrect – AUTO_INCREMENT is specific to MySQL but not universally accepted, and it's not a requirement in the scenario.
Option E: Incorrect – Using FLOAT is not optimal for financial data, where DECIMAL or NUMERIC should be used.

EXAM FOCUS	*Primary keys and data types matter: Always use primary keys to uniquely identify records, and opt for DECIMAL for precise financial values in databases.*
CAUTION ALERT	*Avoid using FLOAT for money: Financial data requires precision; use DECIMAL or NUMERIC, not FLOAT, to avoid rounding errors in financial computations.*

QUESTION 21

Answer - A, C

Option A: Correct – This code uses a parameterized query with a ? placeholder, protecting against SQL injection.
Option B: Incorrect – Concatenating SQL query strings with user input opens the code to SQL injection.
Option C: Correct – Uses named placeholders (:id) with a dictionary, ensuring query safety.
Option D: Incorrect – %s is not the correct placeholder for SQLite (which uses ?).
Option E: Incorrect – Although the use of ? is correct, passing a list instead of a tuple is non-standard.

EXAM FOCUS	*Use parameterized queries: Always use ? or :param placeholders to avoid SQL injection when accepting user input in queries.*
CAUTION ALERT	*Never concatenate SQL: Avoid combining strings in SQL queries with user input as it makes your code vulnerable to SQL injection.*

QUESTION 22

Answer - B, E

Option A: Incorrect – This is vulnerable to SQL injection due to string concatenation in the query.
Option B: Correct – Using parameterized queries with placeholders prevents SQL injection by escaping input properly.
Option C: Incorrect – Using %s is not standard for SQLite or certain databases; also requires proper parameterization.
Option D: Incorrect – String interpolation is unsafe as it does not sanitize the input, leaving the code vulnerable to SQL injection.
Option E: Correct – Parameterized queries using named placeholders (e.g., :id) prevent SQL injection effectively.

EXAM FOCUS	*Use parameterized queries: Always use ? or named placeholders in SQL queries to prevent SQL injection attacks, especially when retrieving sensitive data like emails.*
CAUTION ALERT	*Avoid string concatenation: Never build SQL queries by concatenating strings with user input, as it opens up vulnerabilities to SQL injection.*

QUESTION 23

Answer - A, D

Option A: Correct – This defines a constructor with __init__ and correctly assigns name and age to the instance.
Option B: Incorrect – The function name is misspelled as init instead of __init__, making it an invalid constructor.
Option C: Incorrect – The syntax for setting attributes is wrong.
Option D: Correct – This constructor assigns default values for name and age, which is valid for the class.
Option E: Incorrect – The method lacks the self argument, which is required for constructors.

EXAM FOCUS	*Use double underscores for private attributes: To make attributes private, use __attribute in Python. It's a common practice for encapsulation.*
CAUTION ALERT	*Encapsulation matters: Avoid using single underscore _ for private attributes; it only marks the attribute as protected, not fully private.*

QUESTION 24

Answer - C

Option A: Incorrect – This does not handle exceptions, so it will raise an error if the file is missing.
Option B: Incorrect – Similar to option A, no exception handling is provided.
Option C: Correct – This script uses a try block with exception handling and a context manager, which is a best practice.
Option D: Incorrect – The except block is incorrectly placed outside the context of the try block.
Option E: Incorrect – While it handles the exception, it does not use a context manager, which is less efficient.

EXAM FOCUS	*Use context managers (with): Always use with open() for file operations. It ensures files are properly closed even in case of exceptions.*
CAUTION ALERT	*Avoid missing context managers: Manually closing files without with can lead to resource leaks, especially in scripts that process many files.*

QUESTION 25

Answer - A, B

A) Correct: This defines and raises a basic custom exception.
B) Correct: This custom exception class defines an __init__ method, which provides flexibility with a message.
C) Incorrect: The custom exception class does not follow the correct inheritance hierarchy, and the base exception InvalidFileFormatError is not defined properly.
D) Incorrect: Inheriting from ValueError is unnecessary in this context.
E) Incorrect: Raising a generic exception with a string doesn't define a custom exception.

EXAM FOCUS	*Custom exceptions enhance clarity: Use custom exceptions to provide detailed error messages relevant to your application context, helping with debugging and clarity.*
CAUTION ALERT	*Don't use generic exceptions: Avoid raising generic Exception classes without context, as it can make error handling and debugging more difficult.*

QUESTION 26

Answer - A, D

Option A: Correct, the LEFT JOIN retrieves all employees even if they are not assigned to a department.
Option B: Incorrect, INNER JOIN would exclude employees with no department.
Option C: Incorrect, RIGHT JOIN focuses on departments, not employees.
Option D: Correct, FULL JOIN retrieves all employees and departments, regardless of assignment.
Option E: Incorrect, CROSS JOIN results in a Cartesian product of both tables.

EXAM FOCUS	*Use LEFT JOIN to preserve unmatched records: LEFT JOIN ensures you retrieve all rows from the left table, even if there are no matches in the right table.*
CAUTION ALERT	*INNER JOIN excludes unmatched records: Remember, INNER JOIN only includes rows that have matches in both tables, which may exclude essential data in your query.*

QUESTION 27

Answer - A, E

Option A: Correct, ON DELETE CASCADE ensures related employees are deleted when a department is deleted.
Option B: Incorrect, ON UPDATE CASCADE applies to updates, not deletes.
Option C: Incorrect, dropping the foreign key constraint would break referential integrity.
Option D: Incorrect, manually deleting the department doesn't ensure employees are removed unless ON DELETE CASCADE is set.
Option E: Correct, adding the constraint with ON DELETE CASCADE ensures proper behavior.

EXAM FOCUS	Use ON DELETE CASCADE for referential integrity: Applying ON DELETE CASCADE ensures that related records, such as employees, are automatically deleted when the associated department is removed.
CAUTION ALERT	Be cautious of ON UPDATE CASCADE: This applies only to updates, not deletions. Ensure you're using the correct constraint for the task.

QUESTION 28

Answer - A, D

Option A: Correct, creating a non-clustered index on customer_id will improve query performance for filters on this column.
Option B: Incorrect, although unique indexes improve performance, it is unnecessary for customer_id in this case.
Option C: Incorrect, clustered indexes organize data physically, and order_date might not be optimal for queries on customer_id.
Option D: Correct, a composite index on customer_id and order_id can be effective for queries filtering both columns.
Option E: Incorrect, indexing price doesn't benefit queries filtering by customer_id.

EXAM FOCUS	Use non-clustered indexes for filtering: Indexing frequently queried columns like customer_id with non-clustered indexes significantly boosts query performance.
CAUTION ALERT	Avoid unnecessary indexes: Indexes add overhead during INSERT, UPDATE, and DELETE operations, so only create indexes on frequently filtered columns.

QUESTION 29

Answer - A, C

Option A: Correct, the statistics library is used to calculate the mean.
Option B: Incorrect, while this calculates the median, it's not a valid option if calculating the mean.
Option C: Correct, NumPy's mean function can calculate the mean.
Option D: Incorrect, DataFrame methods apply only to Pandas objects, and the syntax is incorrect here.
Option E: Incorrect, this calculates mode but does not calculate mean.

EXAM FOCUS	Use statistics or NumPy for central tendency: The statistics and NumPy libraries both offer methods to calculate mean, median, and mode efficiently.
CAUTION ALERT	Not all methods work with lists directly: Functions like .median() work only on specific objects like Pandas DataFrames, not Python lists.

QUESTION 30

Answer - A, C

Option A: Correct, statistics.variance() calculates the variance of the dataset.
Option B: Correct, statistics.stdev() is used to compute the standard deviation of the dataset.
Option C: Correct, np.var() computes the variance using NumPy.
Option D: Incorrect, sales.variance() is not a valid method.
Option E: Incorrect, mean is not a measure of spread.

EXAM FOCUS	Use statistics or NumPy for variance and standard deviation: Both libraries provide efficient methods to compute variance and standard deviation for analyzing data spread.
CAUTION ALERT	Avoid using .variance() on lists directly: The .variance() function is not valid on list objects directly. Use the correct library methods like statistics.variance() or np.var().

QUESTION 31

Answer - A, E

Option A: Correct, this is the correct method for implementing bootstrapping with 1000 samples.
Option B: Incorrect, replace=False would not allow resampling.
Option C: Incorrect, the function does not handle size=1000 correctly in this case.
Option D: Incorrect, there is no bootstrap method in pandas.
Option E: Correct, same as Option A but restated.

EXAM FOCUS	Understand bootstrapping: It involves resampling with replacement to generate multiple samples. Use numpy.random.choice with replace=True for effective resampling in Python.
CAUTION ALERT	Resampling requires replacement: Ensure you use replace=True in np.random.choice() to resample with replacement for bootstrapping.

QUESTION 32

Answer - A, C

Option A: Correct, this is the standard way to implement logistic regression in scikit-learn.
Option B: Incorrect, LinearRegression should not be used for binary outcomes.
Option C: Correct, Logit from statsmodels is another correct way to perform logistic regression.
Option D: Incorrect, although this splits data, it doesn't complete the prediction.
Option E: Incorrect, using np.log is unrelated to logistic regression.

EXAM FOCUS	Logistic regression for binary outcomes: Use logistic regression models in scikit-learn or statsmodels for binary classification tasks like predicting purchase likelihood.
CAUTION ALERT	Linear regression is unsuitable for binary outcomes: Don't use linear regression for classification problems, as it assumes continuous output. Logistic regression is designed for binary outcomes.

QUESTION 33

Answer - A, D

A) Correct: Fills missing values in 'sales' using the median value and assigns it back to the column
B) Incorrect: This fills missing values with the mean, not the median
C) Incorrect: Similar to B, this uses the mean instead of the median
D) Correct: This method fills missing values using a dictionary and works correctly with the median value
E) Incorrect: Uses the mode instead of the median.

EXAM FOCUS	Use median for skewed data: Replacing missing values with the median helps maintain robustness when the data is skewed or contains outliers.

QUESTION 34

Answer - A, D

A) Correct: Arrays support element-wise operations directly, which makes them efficient, whereas lists do not. Element-wise operations must be manually looped in lists.

B) Incorrect: NumPy arrays can handle various data types, not just numerical values, although they are most commonly used for numerical computations.

C) Incorrect: Broadcasting is a feature of NumPy arrays, not lists. Arrays can automatically align and operate on arrays of different shapes, which lists cannot.

D) Correct: Arrays are more memory-efficient than lists for handling large datasets, as they store data in contiguous blocks of memory.

E) Incorrect: Arrays do not require explicit loops for element-wise operations due to their built-in broadcasting and vectorized operations.

EXAM FOCUS	*Use arrays for element-wise operations: NumPy arrays provide better performance and efficiency for element-wise arithmetic operations compared to Python lists.*
CAUTION ALERT	*Avoid loops with NumPy: Unlike lists, you don't need explicit loops to perform element-wise operations on arrays, thanks to NumPy's vectorization.*

QUESTION 35

Answer - A, B, C

A) Correct: df['age'].mean() will correctly return the mean of the age column.

B) Correct: df['age'].median() will return the correct median for the age column.

C) Correct: df['age'].std() correctly calculates the standard deviation for the age column.

D) Incorrect: This uses an invalid syntax for the mean() method, which would raise an error.

E) Incorrect: np.mean() cannot handle multiple columns as arguments in this way and would result in an error.

EXAM FOCUS	*Use basic Pandas functions: For numerical statistics, rely on Pandas functions like .mean(), .median(), and .std() for quick descriptive analysis.*
CAUTION ALERT	*Avoid invalid Pandas syntax: Functions like df.mean(df['age'], df['salary']) and np.mean(df['age'], df['salary']) will result in syntax errors in Pandas and NumPy.*

QUESTION 36

Answer - A, C

A) Correct: This correctly uses LinearRegression from Scikit-learn and fits it to the training data.

B) Incorrect: LogisticRegression is used for classification, not regression.

C) Correct: This uses OLS (Ordinary Least Squares) from the statsmodels library for linear regression.

D) Incorrect: The training set, not the test set, should be used for fitting the model.

E) Incorrect: Ridge is a type of regularized linear regression, but the question specifically asks for standard linear regression.

EXAM FOCUS	*Linear regression setup: Use LinearRegression() from Scikit-learn or OLS() from Statsmodels to correctly implement linear regression in Python.*

| CAUTION ALERT | *Avoid classification models: Don't confuse LogisticRegression() with LinearRegression(). Logistic regression is for classification, not continuous target predictions.* |

QUESTION 37

Answer - A

A) Correct – Linear regression is the appropriate model for predicting continuous target values like house prices.
B) Incorrect – Logistic regression is used for classification, not regression.
C) Incorrect – StandardScaler is used for scaling features, not for modeling regression.
D) Incorrect – K-Neighbors is another model but not the best for basic linear regression tasks.
E) Incorrect – RandomForestClassifier is a classification model, not suitable for predicting continuous values.

| EXAM FOCUS | *Use LinearRegression for regression: Scikit-learn's LinearRegression() is designed for continuous target values like house prices. Avoid using classification models for regression tasks.* |
| CAUTION ALERT | *Wrong model type: Don't confuse logistic regression (LogisticRegression) for linear regression tasks. Use LinearRegression for continuous prediction like house prices.* |

QUESTION 38

Answer - A, B

A) Correct – This method groups by region and calculates the mean of the sales column.
B) Correct – This syntax is also valid for grouping by region and calculating the mean for sales.
C) Incorrect – Aggregation functions are applied to grouped objects, not directly to columns.
D) Incorrect – The correct approach is to apply groupby before aggregating.
E) Incorrect – Grouping by sales is illogical in this case, as the question requires grouping by region.

| EXAM FOCUS | *Pandas groupby() syntax: When grouping by columns and calculating statistics like the mean, use the correct groupby() structure followed by the appropriate aggregation function like mean() or agg().* |
| CAUTION ALERT | *Avoid incorrect column references: Ensure you're applying groupby on the correct column like 'region' or 'department'. Grouping on irrelevant columns will not provide meaningful insights.* |

QUESTION 39

Answer - A, C

A) Correct because Ridge(alpha=1.0) implements L2 regularization (Ridge regression) to reduce overfitting.
B) Incorrect because Lasso(alpha=1.0) applies L1 regularization (Lasso regression), not L2 regularization.
C) Correct as RidgeCV performs cross-validated Ridge regression, helping prevent overfitting by tuning the regularization parameter alpha.
D) Incorrect because ElasticNet combines L1 and L2 regularization, but it is not purely an L2 regularization technique.
E) Incorrect because LinearRegression() does not apply any regularization and would likely lead to overfitting.

| EXAM FOCUS | *L2 Regularization Tip: Ridge regression applies L2 regularization. Use it to prevent overfitting, especially when your model has high complexity and overlearns the training data.* |
| CAUTION ALERT | *L1 vs. L2: Don't confuse Lasso (L1 regularization) with Ridge (L2 regularization). Lasso performs feature selection by shrinking some coefficients to zero, unlike Ridge.* |

QUESTION 40

Answer - A, D

A) Correct because plt.plot(df['Date'], df['Sales']) creates a simple line plot of sales over time.
B) Incorrect because plt.bar() is for creating bar plots, which does not fit the question's requirement for a line plot.
C) Incorrect because product categories are not typically plotted using a line plot, as they represent categorical data.
D) Correct because adding a label helps to enhance the clarity of the plot, aligning with the requirement to visualize sales over time.
E) Incorrect because a scatter plot does not show trends over time as effectively as a line plot.

EXAM FOCUS	*Matplotlib Tip: Use plt.plot() for visualizing trends over time. It's most effective for time series data where dates or time intervals are involved.*
CAUTION ALERT	*Line vs. Scatter: For trends over time, always use a line plot. Scatter plots are better for relationships between numerical variables, not time series data.*

QUESTION 41

Answer - A, D

A) Correct because plt.plot() is the proper Matplotlib function to create a line plot, where x is the date, and y is the sales value over time.
B) Incorrect because plt.bar() generates a bar chart, which is not optimal for visualizing continuous time-series data.
C) Incorrect because plt.scatter() creates a scatter plot, not a line plot, which is better for time-series visualization.
D) Correct because although x and y are reversed, the plot still generates an accurate line graph, just with inverted axes.
E) Incorrect because plt.line() is not a valid function in Matplotlib.

EXAM FOCUS	*Time-Series Tip: Use plt.plot() for visualizing trends over time. Ensure dates are on the x-axis and values like sales are on the y-axis.*
CAUTION ALERT	*Incorrect Plot Choice: Avoid using bar or scatter plots for continuous time-series data. They don't show trends as effectively as a line plot.*

QUESTION 42

Answer - C

A) Incorrect because color='Blues' is not valid. Color palettes must be applied using a colormap like plt.cm.Blues().
B) Incorrect because cmap is used for scatter plots, not directly with bar plots.
C) Correct because plt.cm.Blues() applies a color palette to the bars using the values from the Sales column.
D) Incorrect because palette is not a valid argument for the plt.bar() function; it's used in Seaborn.
E) Incorrect because this assigns a single color 'blue' instead of using a color palette.

EXAM FOCUS	*Color Palette Tip: Use plt.cm.Blues() to apply consistent color palettes in bar plots. This helps maintain a professional look and improve readability.*
CAUTION ALERT	*Common Error: Avoid using color='Blues'. Instead, apply the colormap via plt.cm to set color gradients for your bar plot based on data values.*

QUESTION 43

Answer - C

A) Incorrect because plt.text() is not being correctly used to place the text at the correct value.
B) Incorrect because although it shows the values, it does not specifically highlight any key region as the highest.
C) Correct because plt.annotate('Highest', xy=(0, 200)) correctly highlights a specific region with a label at the maximum value, making it clear to the reader.
D) Incorrect because it adds a legend label but does not highlight the highest purchase value.

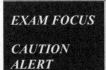	
EXAM FOCUS	*Annotation Tip: Use plt.annotate() to highlight key regions with high values on bar plots for clear emphasis, especially in reports or presentations.*
CAUTION ALERT	*Annotation Placement: Avoid placing annotations randomly—use xy coordinates that align with key data points to ensure clarity and accuracy in the plot.*

QUESTION 44

Answer - A, D

A) Correct because using a plot with annotations on key data points and adding an arrow helps visualize trends in a narrative-driven manner.
B) Incorrect because a bar plot doesn't effectively emphasize trends over time when compared to a line plot.
C) Incorrect because using a scatter plot here does not help in representing continuous time series data as well as line charts would.
D) Correct because using annotations to mark valleys in the data reinforces key points in the narrative while maintaining focus on dips and rises.
E) Incorrect because omitting labels and annotations makes it difficult for the audience to follow the narrative, reducing the clarity of the message.

EXAM FOCUS	*Annotations Help: Use plt.annotate() to highlight key peaks and valleys in time-series data, which is essential for emphasizing important trends in your narrative.*
CAUTION ALERT	*Avoid Scatter Plots: For time-series trends, use line plots over scatter plots, as scatter plots don't effectively show continuous data or trends over time.*

QUESTION 45

Answer - C

A) Incorrect because while it plots a bar chart, it doesn't show the trend over time that the scenario asks for.
B) Incorrect because a horizontal bar chart doesn't summarize trends effectively in this case.
C) Correct because the line plot effectively shows trends over time, which is the focus of the analysis.
D) Incorrect because a scatter plot is not suitable for showing sales trends over time for different regions.
E) Incorrect because a histogram stacked plot doesn't convey trends or fluctuations.

EXAM FOCUS	*Line Plot for Trends: When summarizing trends over time, always use line plots for better clarity. Bar charts are better for static comparisons between categories.*
CAUTION ALERT	*Scatter Plot Limitation: Avoid scatter plots for time series trends, as they do not effectively represent continuous data like sales fluctuations over time.*

PRACTICE TEST 2 - QUESTIONS ONLY

QUESTION 1

A marketing analyst is collecting survey responses to analyze customer satisfaction. The data collected is representative of the company's customer base. What Python function would be used to generate a random sample of 100 responses from a dataset to ensure this?

```
A) random.sample(df, 100)
B) df.sample(n=100)
C) numpy.random.choice(df, 100)
D) df.random_sample(100)
E) df[:100]
```

QUESTION 2

A dataset contains customer demographics data. Some entries in the age column are missing and need to be handled. What are the advantages of using imputation methods over exclusion methods for handling missing values? (Select 2 answers)

A) Imputation preserves the dataset's size
B) Imputation introduces bias into the dataset
C) Exclusion improves model accuracy
D) Imputation minimizes data loss
E) Exclusion maintains dataset variability

QUESTION 3

You have two datasets: one containing structured sales data from a SQL database and another containing unstructured product reviews in JSON format. Which steps are needed to analyze both datasets using Python? (Select 2 answers)

A) Use SQL queries to extract structured data
B) Use json.loads() to parse the JSON data
C) Load both datasets into a relational database before analysis
D) Use pd.read_sql() for both structured and unstructured data
E) Use Pandas to perform sentiment analysis on structured data

QUESTION 4

You have detected several outliers in a dataset and need to decide how to handle them. What are the correct methods for handling numerical outliers to improve data quality for machine learning models? (Select 2 answers)

A) Remove rows with outliers
B) Impute outliers with the median
C) Use one-hot encoding for numerical outliers
D) Use Z-score normalization on outliers
E) Leave the outliers unhandled in the data

QUESTION 5

You are tasked with checking if all values in the salary column are within a valid range (greater than zero). Which methods can you use to validate that the salary column contains only positive values? (Select 2 answers)

```
A) df['salary'].all() > 0
B) df[df['salary'] > 0]
C) df[df['salary'].gt(0)]
D) df['salary'].gt(0).all()
E) df.validate('salary', lambda x: x > 0)
```

QUESTION 6

You need to join two tables in a database: employees and departments. The common column between the two tables is department_id. Which SQL query correctly retrieves the name of employees along with their department_name? (Select 2 answers)

```
A) SELECT employees.name,
departments.department_name FROM employees
INNER JOIN departments ON
employees.department_id =
departments.department_id

B) SELECT employees.name,
departments.department_name FROM employees
JOIN departments WHERE
employees.department_id =
departments.department_id

C) SELECT name, department_name FROM
employees JOIN departments USING
(department_id)

D) SELECT employees.name, department_name
FROM employees, departments

E) SELECT employees.name,
departments.department_name FROM employees
```

```
WHERE employees.department_id =
departments.department_id
```

QUESTION 7

You are given a dataset and asked to compute the variance and standard deviation in Python using both the statistics and numpy libraries. Which of the following Python code snippets correctly calculates these measures of variability? (Select 2 answers)

```
A) import statistics
variance_val = statistics.variance(data)
stdev_val = statistics.stdev(data)

 B) import numpy as np
variance_val = np.var(data)
stdev_val = np.std(data)

 C) import statistics
variance_val = statistics.stdev(data)
stdev_val = statistics.variance(data)

 D) import numpy as np
variance_val = np.std(data)
stdev_val = np.var(data)

 E) import pandas as pd
variance_val = pd.DataFrame(data).var()
```

QUESTION 8

You need to group a DataFrame by a categorical column and calculate the mean for each group in Pandas. Which of the following code snippets accomplishes this task?

```
A) import pandas as pd
grouped_df =
df.groupby('Category')['Value'].mean()

 B) import pandas as pd
grouped_df = df.groupby(['Category']).sum()

 C) import pandas as pd
grouped_df = df.groupby('Category').mean()

 D) import pandas as pd
grouped_df = df.groupby('Value').mean()

 E) import pandas as pd
grouped_df =
df.groupby('Category')['Value'].sum()
```

QUESTION 9

You are tasked with clustering customer purchase data based on their purchase amounts and frequency using K-Means clustering. Which steps are correct for K-Means clustering? Select 2 correct

options.

```
A) from sklearn.cluster import KMeans
kmeans = KMeans(n_clusters=3,
random_state=42)
kmeans.fit(data[['purchase_amount',
'purchase_frequency']])

B) predictions =
kmeans.predict(data[['purchase_amount',
'purchase_frequency']])
C) kmeans.fit(data[['purchase_amount',
'purchase_frequency']], y)
D) model = KMeans(n_clusters=3)
E) cluster_centers =
kmeans.cluster_centers_
```

QUESTION 10

You want to create pairwise relationships in your dataset using Seaborn. Which steps are correct for using pairplot? Select 2 correct options.

```
A) import seaborn as sns
sns.pairplot(df)

B) sns.pairplot(df, hue="species")
C) sns.pairplot(df, diag_kind='kde')
D) sns.lineplot(df)
E) sns.catplot(df)
```

QUESTION 11

You are tasked with collecting data from different sources for a business strategy report. How would you merge two datasets in Python using the common key customer_id? (Select 2 correct answers)

```
 A) pd.merge(df1, df2, on='customer_id',
how='inner')
 B) df1.join(df2, lsuffix='_left',
rsuffix='_right')
 C) df1.append(df2)
 D) pd.concat([df1, df2], axis=1)
 E) df1.merge(df2,
left_on='customer_id_left',
right_on='customer_id_right')
```

QUESTION 12

Your organization collects user data for marketing under CCPA. What Python-based solutions should you implement to comply with CCPA regulations? (Select 2 correct answers)

 A) Develop a Python script that allows users to opt out of the sale of their personal information
 B) Automatically store and process users' data

indefinitely without providing an option for deletion

C) Allow users to request deletion of their personal data through a Python-based API

D) Automatically share collected data with third-party advertisers without users' consent

E) Implement Python encryption functions to secure personal data in transit and at rest

QUESTION 13

You need to calculate the correlation matrix and visualize it using a heatmap in Python. Select the scripts you would use. (Select 2 answers)

```
A)  df.corr()
B)  sns.heatmap(df)
C)  df.cov()
D)  sns.heatmap(df.corr())
E)  sns.lineplot(df)
```

QUESTION 14

You are analyzing a dataset and want to calculate both the mean and count of sales for each product category using Pandas. Which of the following options provide the correct output? Select 2 correct answers.

```
A) df.groupby('category').agg({'sales':
['mean', 'count']})
B) df.groupby('category').agg({'sales':
'mean', 'sales': 'count'})
C) df.groupby('category').agg(['mean',
'count'])
D)
df.groupby('category')['sales'].agg(['mean'
, 'count'])
E)
df.groupby('category')['sales'].apply(['mea
n', 'count'])
```

QUESTION 15

A marketing team needs a dashboard displaying quarterly revenue and product performance. They want bar charts with each product colored based on performance tiers. What is the best approach to visualize this using Python's Matplotlib? (Select 3 answers)

```
A) plt.bar(x, y, color='blue')
B) colors = ['green' if value > 100 else
'red' for value in y]; plt.bar(x, y,
color=colors)
C) df.plot(kind='bar',
```

```
color='performance')
D) plt.bar(x, y); plt.xlabel('Quarter');
plt.ylabel('Revenue')
E) plt.barh(x, y, color=['green',
'orange', 'red'])
```

QUESTION 16

You are given a dataset and tasked with finding all rows where the 'Age' is between 30 and 40, and 'Salary' is greater than 50000. Which control structure best implements this logic in Python? (Select 2 answers)

```
A) df[(df['Age'] > 30) & (df['Age'] < 40)
& (df['Salary'] > 50000)]
B) df.query('30 < Age < 40 and Salary >
50000')
C) df[df['Age'].between(30, 40) &
(df['Salary'] > 50000)]
D) for index, row in df.iterrows(): if 30
< row['Age'] < 40 and row['Salary'] >
50000: print(row)
E) df = df[(30 < df['Age']) & (df['Age'] <
40) & (df['Salary'] > 50000)]
```

QUESTION 17

You are tasked with converting a large dataset into a NumPy array for faster numerical operations. What is the best way to achieve this using Pandas? (Select 2 answers)

```
A)  arr = np.array(df)
B)  arr = df.to_numpy()
C)  arr = df.values
D)  arr = pd.DataFrame(df).as_matrix()
E)  arr = np.asarray(df)
```

QUESTION 18

You are documenting your Python functions with docstrings to improve code readability and maintainability. Which of the following examples follows the PEP 257 conventions for docstrings? (Select 2 answers)

```
A) def calculate_mean(data): """Calculate
the mean of a list of numbers.""" return
sum(data) / len(datA)

B) def calculate_mean(data): """Calculates
the mean of the numbers.""" return
sum(data) / len(datA)

C) def calculate_mean(data): """Calculate
the mean of a list of numbers. Args: data
```

```
(list): A list of numeric values. Returns:
float: The mean of the list.""" return
sum(data) / len(datA)

D) def calculate_mean(data): """Calculates
the mean of the numbers Args: data (list):
A list of numeric values. Returns: float:
The mean.""" return sum(data) / len(datA)

E) def calculate_mean(data): """Calculate
the mean. Args: list: Returns: float."""
return sum(data) / len(datA)
```

QUESTION 19

You are cleaning data and want to handle missing
values in a CSV file. Your script should raise an
exception if the file does not exist or is unreadable,
and it should handle errors related to missing values
in the file. Which of the following exception handling
blocks accomplishes this? (Select 2 answers)

```
A) try:
df = pd.read_csv('data.csv')
except FileNotFoundError:
print("File not found.")

B) try:
df = pd.read_csv('data.csv')
except (FileNotFoundError, IOError):
print("File error.")

C) try:
df = pd.read_csv('data.csv')
if df.isnull().values.any():
raise ValueError("Missing values
detected.")
except FileNotFoundError:
print("File not found.")

D) try:
df = pd.read_csv('data.csv')
if df.isnull().values.any():
raise Exception("Missing data.")
except FileNotFoundError:
print("File not found.")
except IOError:
print("File error.")

E) try:
df = pd.read_csv('data.csv')
if df.isnull().values.any():
raise MissingDataError("Data missing.")
```

QUESTION 20

You are inserting a new record into the customers
table. The new customer has an ID of 101, a name of
"John Doe," and a total purchase of $150.50. Which
SQL statement correctly inserts this data? (Select 2

answers)

```
A) INSERT INTO customers (customer_id,
customer_name, total_purchase)
VALUES (101, 'John Doe', 150.50);

B) INSERT INTO customers VALUES (101,
'John Doe', 150.50);

C) INSERT INTO customers (customer_id,
total_purchase)
VALUES (101, 150.50);

D) INSERT INTO customers (customer_id,
customer_name, total_purchase)
VALUES (101, 'John Doe', 150.50)
ON DUPLICATE KEY UPDATE
total_purchase=150.50;

E) INSERT INTO customers (customer_id,
customer_name, total_purchase)
VALUES ('101', 'John Doe', '150.50');
```

QUESTION 21

You need to write a Python script that inserts new
customer data into the customers table in a MySQL
database. The customer's name and total purchases
are provided by the user. How would you safely
insert the data to prevent SQL injection? (Select 2
answers)

```
A) import pymysql
conn = pymysql.connect(host='localhost',
user='root',
password='password',
database='sales')
cursor = conn.cursor()
cursor.execute("INSERT INTO customers
(customer_name, total_purchase) VALUES (%s,
%s)", (customer_name, total_purchase))
conn.commit()

B) import pymysql
conn = pymysql.connect(host='localhost',
user='root',
password='password',
database='sales')
cursor = conn.cursor()
cursor.execute("INSERT INTO customers
(customer_name, total_purchase) VALUES ('"
+ customer_name + "', " +
str(total_purchase) + ")")
conn.commit()

C) import pymysql
conn = pymysql.connect(host='localhost',
user='root',
password='password',
database='sales')
```

```
cursor = conn.cursor()
cursor.execute("INSERT INTO customers
(customer_name, total_purchase) VALUES
(%(name)s, %(purchase)s)", {'name':
customer_name, 'purchase': total_purchase})
conn.commit()

 D) import pymysql
conn = pymysql.connect(host='localhost',
user='root',
password='password',
database='sales')
cursor = conn.cursor()
cursor.execute("INSERT INTO customers
(customer_name, total_purchase) VALUES (?,
?)", (customer_name, total_purchase))
conn.commit()

 E) import pymysql
conn = pymysql.connect(host='localhost',
user='root',
password='password',
database='sales')
cursor = conn.cursor()
query = f"INSERT INTO customers
(customer_name, total_purchase) VALUES
('{customer_name}', {total_purchase})"
cursor.execute(query)
conn.commit()
```

QUESTION 22

A database containing salary information is being accessed via Python. What practices should you follow to protect sensitive data during query execution? (Select 2 answers)

```
 A) cur.execute("SELECT salary FROM
employees WHERE emp_id=?", (emp_id,))

 B) cur.execute("SELECT salary FROM
employees WHERE emp_id=" + emp_iD)

 C) conn.set_secure_option('encrypt')
cur.execute("SELECT salary FROM employees
WHERE emp_id=:id", {"id": emp_id})

 D) cur.execute("SELECT salary FROM
employees WHERE emp_id = %s", emp_iD)

 E) query = "SELECT salary FROM employees
WHERE emp_id=%s"
cur.execute(query)
```

QUESTION 23

You want to implement inheritance in a class Manager, which inherits from the class Employee. Which implementations are correct? (Select 2 answers)

```
A) class Manager(Employee):
def __init__(self, name, age):
Employee.__init__(self, name, agE)

B) class Manager(Employee):
def __init__(self, name, age):
super().__init__(name, agE)

C) class Manager(Employee):
def __init__(self):
super(Manager).__init__(self)

D) class Manager(Employee):
def __init__(self, name):
Employee.__init__(namE)  E) class
Manager(Employee):
pass
```

QUESTION 24

You are working on a project where you need to append data to an existing file without overwriting it. Which of the following methods correctly achieves this?

```
 A) with open('output.txt', 'w') as f:
f.write('New data')
 B) f = open('output.txt', 'a')
f.write('More data')
 C) with open('output.txt', 'a') as f:
f.write('More data')
 D) f = open('output.txt', 'w')
f.write('Appending data')
 E) with open('output.txt', 'r+') as f:
f.write('Data')
```

QUESTION 25

In a financial data processing script, you need to handle errors related to invalid transaction types using custom exceptions. What is the correct way to define and catch these exceptions in Python? (Select 3 correct answers)

```
 A) class
InvalidTransactionError(Exception):
pass
try:
raise InvalidTransactionError()
except InvalidTransactionError:
print('Invalid transaction')

 B) class
InvalidTransactionError(ValueError):
pass
raise InvalidTransactionError()

 C) try:
raise InvalidTransactionError('Invalid
```

```
type')
except InvalidTransactionError as e:
print(E)

D) class
InvalidTransactionError(Exception):
def __init__(self, message):
self.message = message
raise InvalidTransactionError('Invalid
type')

 E) raise ValueError('Invalid
transaction').
```

QUESTION 26

You are tasked with retrieving the total number of orders per customer from the orders table. However, you want to filter out customers who have placed fewer than 5 orders. Which query will achieve this? (Select 1 correct answer)

```
A) SELECT customer_id, COUNT(order_id) FROM
orders GROUP BY customer_id HAVING
COUNT(order_id) >= 5;
B) SELECT customer_id, COUNT(order_id) FROM
orders WHERE COUNT(order_id) >= 5 GROUP BY
customer_id;
C) SELECT customer_id, COUNT(order_id) FROM
orders GROUP BY customer_id WHERE
COUNT(order_id) >= 5;
D) SELECT * FROM orders WHERE customer_id
IN (SELECT customer_id FROM orders GROUP BY
customer_id HAVING COUNT(order_id) >= 5);
E) SELECT customer_id FROM orders GROUP BY
customer_id HAVING COUNT(order_id) > 5;
```

QUESTION 27

You need to enforce a rule where the salary column in the employees table must be greater than 3000. Which SQL constraint would you use? (Select 1 correct answer)

```
A) ALTER TABLE employees ADD CONSTRAINT
salary_check CHECK (salary > 3000);
B) ALTER TABLE employees ADD PRIMARY KEY
(salary);
C) ALTER TABLE employees ADD UNIQUE
(salary);
D) ALTER TABLE employees ADD CONSTRAINT
salary_check CHECK (salary < 3000);
E) ALTER TABLE employees ADD DEFAULT salary
= 3000;
```

QUESTION 28

You have noticed slow query performance when inserting data into a table with multiple indexes. How should you address this performance issue? (Select 1 correct answer)

```
A) DROP INDEX idx_customer ON sales_data;
B) CREATE CLUSTERED INDEX idx_sales_date ON
sales_data(sales_date);
C) CREATE NONCLUSTERED INDEX idx_sales_id
ON sales_data(sales_id);
D) Disable all indexes before performing
batch inserts and then rebuild them
afterward;
E) REBUILD INDEX idx_customer;
```

QUESTION 29

You are analyzing house prices and find that the data is heavily skewed. Which measure of central tendency is least affected by the skewness? (Select 1 correct answer)

```
A) statistics.mean(prices)
B) statistics.median(prices)
C) statistics.mode(prices)
D) np.mean(prices)
E) statistics.stdev(prices)
```

QUESTION 30

You have a dataset with exam scores for two different classes. How would you compare the variability of scores between the two classes? (Select 2 correct answers)

```
A) np.std(class1) > np.std(class2)
B) statistics.stdev(class1) >
statistics.stdev(class2)
C) max(class1) - min(class1) > max(class2)
- min(class2)
D) np.mean(class1) > np.mean(class2)
E) import pandas as pd;
pd.DataFrame.std([class1, class2])
```

QUESTION 31

When applying bootstrapping to estimate the 95% confidence interval of the mean salary of employees, which Python function or method will you use to calculate the confidence interval based on bootstrapped samples? (Select 1 correct answer)

```
A) np.percentile(bootstrapped_means, [2.5,
97.5])
B) np.mean(bootstrapped_means)
C) np.var(bootstrapped_means)
D) np.std(bootstrapped_means)
```

```
E) np.random.choice(bootstrapped_means)
```

QUESTION 32

After building a logistic regression model, you want to evaluate the performance of the model. Which metric should you primarily consider when assessing a classification model like logistic regression? (Select 1 correct answer)

A) Mean Squared Error (MSE)
B) R-squared
C) Precision
D) Mean Absolute Error (MAE)
E) Adjusted R-squared

QUESTION 33

You have two DataFrames, df1 and df2, and you want to merge them based on the 'id' column while retaining all rows from df1 and any matching rows from df2. What is the correct way to merge these DataFrames in Pandas? (Select 2 correct answers)

```
A) pd.merge(df1, df2, on='id', how='outer')
B) pd.merge(df1, df2, on='id', how='inner')
C) pd.merge(df1, df2, on='id', how='left')
D) pd.merge(df1, df2, on='id', how='right')
E) df1.merge(df2, on='id', how='left')
```

QUESTION 34

You want to perform basic arithmetic operations on two NumPy arrays, a and b. Which of the following demonstrates proper broadcasting in NumPy? (Select 2 correct answers)

A) c = a + b, where a and b have compatible shapes.
B) c = np.dot(a, b), where a and b are 1D arrays of the same length.
C) c = a + b, where a is a (2x1) array and b is a (1x2) array.
D) c = np.add(a, b), where a and b have compatible shapes.
E) c = a + b, where a and b have different dimensions.

QUESTION 35

You have a Pandas DataFrame with missing values in the salary column and you want to fill those missing values with the median. Which script would accomplish this? (Select 2 correct answers)

```
A)
df['salary'].fillna(df['salary'].median(),
inplace=True)
B) df.fillna(method='median', inplace=True)
C) df['salary'] = df['salary'].apply(lambda
x: x.fillna(df['salary'].median()))
D) df.replace(np.nan,
df['salary'].median())
E) df.fillna(df.median(), inplace=True)
```

QUESTION 36

You are evaluating a logistic regression model and want to check its accuracy using Scikit-learn. Which Python script correctly calculates the model's accuracy? (Select 2 correct answers)

```
A) from sklearn.metrics import
accuracy_score; acc =
accuracy_score(y_test, y_pred)
B) from sklearn.metrics import
precision_score; acc =
precision_score(y_test, y_pred)
C) acc = model.score(X_test, y_test)
D) acc = accuracy_score(y_test, model)
E) acc = model.evaluate(X_test, y_test)
```

QUESTION 37

You want to evaluate the fit of your linear regression model using R-squared. Which of the following steps should you take? (Select 2 correct answers)

```
A) from sklearn.metrics import r2_score
r2_score(y_test, y_preD)

B) model.predict(X_test)
C) model.coef_

D) from sklearn.metrics import
accuracy_score
accuracy_score(y_test, y_preD)   E)
model.intercept_
```

QUESTION 38

In a dataset of employee information, you want to find the count of employees in each department and their average salary. Which Pandas functions would you use? (Select two correct options) Select TWO correct answers.

```
A)
df.groupby('department').agg({'salary':'mea
n', 'name':'count'})
B) df.groupby('department').count()
C)
df.groupby('department')['salary'].mean()
```

```
D) df.groupby('name').count()
E)
df.salary.groupby('department').agg('count'
)
```

QUESTION 39

You are trying to evaluate the performance of a linear regression model. To ensure that the model is not overfitting, you decide to implement K-Fold cross-validation. Which script correctly implements 5-fold cross-validation to evaluate the model's performance? Select two correct answers.

```
A) from sklearn.model_selection import
cross_val_score; cross_val_score(model, X,
y, cv=5)
B) from sklearn.model_selection import
train_test_split; X_train, X_test, y_train,
y_test = train_test_split(X, y,
test_size=0.2)
C) from sklearn.model_selection import
KFold; kf = KFold(n_splits=5); for
train_index, test_index in kf.split(X):
X_train, X_test = X[train_index],
X[test_index] y_train, y_test =
y[train_index], y[test_index]
D) from sklearn.linear_model import
LinearRegression; model =
LinearRegression(); model.fit(X_train,
y_train)
E) cross_val_score(LinearRegression(), X,
y, cv=10)`
```

QUESTION 40

You need to visualize the relationship between two variables, "Height" and "Weight," in a dataset using a scatter plot in Matplotlib. Which of the following options will correctly generate this scatter plot? Select one answer.

```
A) plt.plot(df['Height'], df['Weight'])
B) plt.bar(df['Height'], df['Weight'])
C) plt.scatter(df['Height'], df['Weight'])
D) plt.plot(df['Height'], df['Weight'],
marker='o')
E) plt.boxplot(df[['Height', 'Weight']])
```

QUESTION 41

You have been asked to create a histogram to visualize the distribution of product prices. Which of the following scripts will generate the correct

visualization in Matplotlib? (Select 2 answers)

```
A) plt.hist(df['Price'])
B) plt.plot(df['Price'])
C) plt.scatter(df['Price'], df['Sales'])
D) plt.hist(df['Price'], bins=20)
E) plt.bar(df['Price'], df['Sales'])
```

QUESTION 42

You want to adjust the font size of the legend in your line plot to improve clarity. Which of the following methods will help you adjust the font size of the legend? (Select two correct answers)

```
A) plt.legend(fontsize=14)
B) plt.legend(title_fontsize=14)
C) plt.legend(prop={'size':14})
D) plt.legend(font='Arial', size=14)
E) plt.legend(size='14pt')
```

QUESTION 43

You are presenting monthly sales data to a non-technical audience and want to make the x-axis labels clearer by reducing clutter. What techniques could help with this? Select two correct answers.

```
A) plt.xticks(rotation=45)
B) plt.locator_params(axis='x', nbins=6)
C)
plt.xaxis.set_major_locator(mdates.MonthLoc
ator())
D) plt.xticks(fontsize=10)
E) plt.set_xticks(['Jan', 'Feb', 'Mar',
'Apr', 'May'])
```

QUESTION 44

You want to visualize product sales across various categories for a quarterly review. You plan to structure the narrative around the top three performing products. Which Python script best supports this goal?

```
A) plt.pie(sales, labels=categories,
autopct='%1.1f%%')
B) plt.barh(categories, sales)
 plt.text(0.9, sales[0], 'Highest',
ha='center')
C) plt.bar(categories, sales)
D) sns.boxplot(x=categories, y=sales)
E) plt.scatter(sales, categories) with no
annotations
```

QUESTION 45

After calculating monthly profit margins, you need to highlight key takeaways for stakeholders using a simple visualization. You want to emphasize the months with the highest profit margins. Which Python visualization technique would best summarize these key findings?

```
A) plt.pie(profit_margin, labels=months, explode=explodE)

B) plt.bar(months, profit_margin); plt.title("Monthly Profit Margins"); plt.xlabel("Months");
plt.ylabel("Profit Margin")

C) sns.heatmap(data=profit_margin)
D) plt.scatter(profit_margin, months, color="red")
E) sns.kdeplot(data=profit_margin)
```

PRACTICE TEST 2 - ANSWERS ONLY

QUESTION 1

Answer - B

A) Incorrect – random.sample works on lists but not DataFrames, making it unsuitable for sampling from a Pandas DataFrame.
B) Correct – df.sample(n=100) is the standard way to randomly sample 100 rows from a Pandas DataFrame, making it ideal for this task.
C) Incorrect – While numpy.random.choice works with NumPy arrays, it is not applicable directly to Pandas DataFrames.
D) Incorrect – random_sample is not a valid method in Pandas, so it won't work for this operation.
E) Incorrect – Slicing df[:100] selects the first 100 rows rather than providing a random sample, leading to potential bias.

EXAM FOCUS	Use Pandas' sample() method for efficient random sampling of rows in a DataFrame. Ideal for large datasets needing representative subsets for analysis.
CAUTION ALERT	Don't confuse random.sample() with Pandas sample(); the former works only for lists, not DataFrames. Ensure proper method usage.

QUESTION 2

Answer - A, D

A) Correct – Imputation allows you to retain all rows, preserving the dataset's size.
B) Incorrect – While imputation may introduce some bias, it is often a better alternative to exclusion for retaining the dataset size.
C) Incorrect – Excluding rows with missing data can lead to reduced sample size and may affect model accuracy.
D) Correct – Imputation minimizes data loss by filling in missing values, preserving the structure of the dataset.
E) Incorrect – Exclusion often reduces variability as it removes rows, which can skew the dataset.

EXAM FOCUS	Imputation retains dataset size, which is critical for maintaining sample representativeness in analysis. Avoid exclusion unless justified.
CAUTION ALERT	Exclusion reduces the dataset size, potentially causing loss of valuable insights and leading to biased results. Imputation minimizes this risk.

QUESTION 3

Answer - A, B

A) Correct – SQL queries are necessary for extracting and loading structured data from relational databases.
B) Correct – json.loads() is a common Python function for converting JSON (unstructured data) into a Python dictionary that can then be analyzed.
C) Incorrect – Loading unstructured data into a relational database adds unnecessary complexity, and JSON data can be handled directly.
D) Incorrect – pd.read_sql() only works with structured data and would not parse JSON properly.
E) Incorrect – Pandas is typically used for structured data analysis, but specialized libraries like nltk or TextBlob would be used for sentiment analysis of unstructured text data.

EXAM FOCUS	Use json.loads() to easily convert JSON data into a Python dictionary for analysis, while SQL queries

	work best for structured data extraction.
CAUTION ALERT	*Don't mix structured SQL and unstructured data like JSON in the same query method. Each data type requires separate handling in Python.*

QUESTION 4

Answer - A, B

A) Correct – Removing outliers can help improve the accuracy of machine learning models by eliminating extreme values that may skew the results.

B) Correct – Imputing outliers with the median can reduce the impact of extreme values while preserving the data.

C) Incorrect – One-hot encoding is used for categorical variables, not for handling numerical outliers.

D) Incorrect – Z-score normalization is used to standardize data, but it doesn't directly handle outliers.

E) Incorrect – Leaving outliers unhandled can negatively affect the accuracy and performance of machine learning models.

EXAM FOCUS	*Imputing outliers with the median reduces their impact without losing data. Consider removing extreme outliers that severely skew the analysis.*
CAUTION ALERT	*One-hot encoding is only used for categorical variables, not for numerical outliers. Z-score normalization helps standardize but doesn't fix outliers.*

QUESTION 5

Answer - B, D

A) Incorrect – all() checks if all values are True, but the code should be checking if salary > 0 for all rows.

B) Correct – This code filters the rows to include only those with positive salary values.

C) Incorrect – While gt() works for comparison, this code doesn't ensure that all salary values are positive without additional steps.

D) Correct – This checks that all values in the salary column are greater than 0 using gt() and all(), which returns True only if all values meet the condition.

E) Incorrect – The syntax for validate() does not exist in Pandas.

EXAM FOCUS	*Use .gt(0).all() to validate positive values in the salary column. Combining comparison methods with all() ensures all values meet the condition.*
CAUTION ALERT	*Avoid using .all() directly without first checking conditions. It's necessary to ensure all values meet the criteria with the right comparison.*

QUESTION 6

Answer - A, C

A) Correct – This is the proper use of an INNER JOIN to retrieve employee names and their department names based on the matching department_id.

B) Incorrect – The use of JOIN without ON or USING is incorrect and will result in an error.

C) Correct – The USING clause is a shorthand method for joining tables when the columns have the same name in both tables.

D) Incorrect – This query doesn't specify how the tables are joined, which results in a Cartesian product.

E) Incorrect – The WHERE clause is improperly used here for joining the two tables.

QUESTION 7

Answer - A, B

A) Correct – This code correctly calculates variance and standard deviation using the statistics library.
B) Correct – This is the correct usage of NumPy to compute variance and standard deviation.
C) Incorrect – Variance and standard deviation are swapped in this example.
D) Incorrect – This incorrectly calculates standard deviation using var() and variance using std().
E) Incorrect – While Pandas can calculate variance, the syntax shown is incomplete and will not execute properly.

EXAM FOCUS	Variance and standard deviation are easily calculated with statistics or numpy. Remember, variance measures spread, while standard deviation indicates data dispersion.
CAUTION ALERT	Don't confuse variance() with std()—the former measures variability, while the latter measures the spread of data in the same units as the data.

QUESTION 8

Answer - A

A) Correct – This groups by the 'Category' column and calculates the mean of the 'Value' column for each group.
B) Incorrect – This calculates the sum, not the mean.
C) Incorrect – While it calculates the mean, it applies to all columns, which may not be intended.
D) Incorrect – It groups by 'Value', not 'Category'.
E) Incorrect – This calculates the sum for 'Value', not the mean as required.

EXAM FOCUS	Use groupby() to group data in Pandas and apply aggregation functions like mean(), sum(), etc. Grouping helps summarize categorical data efficiently.
CAUTION ALERT	Be cautious with groupby().mean()—it applies the function to all columns by default. Use specific column indexing if needed.

QUESTION 9

Answer - A, B

A) Correct: Initializing KMeans and specifying features is essential for clustering.
B) Correct: Predicting cluster labels based on the features.
C) Incorrect: y is not required for unsupervised learning.
D) Incorrect: This only defines the model but lacks fitting.
E) Incorrect: Cluster centers are retrieved post-fitting, not a step in fitting.

EXAM FOCUS	For unsupervised learning like K-Means, fit() requires only feature data, no target (y). Always run the algorithm multiple times to avoid empty clusters.
CAUTION ALERT	Ensure that K-Means initializes well by setting n_init to avoid random clusters and prevent empty ones from appearing during clustering.

QUESTION 10

Answer - A, C

A) Correct: The basic syntax for creating pairwise relationships using Seaborn's pairplot, which is effective for visualizing feature relationships in a dataset.
B) Incorrect: hue can be used in pairplot but needs to be mapped to valid categorical values in the dataset, otherwise it would generate an error.
C) Correct: diag_kind='kde' modifies the diagonal plots to use Kernel Density Estimate (KDE), offering better insights into data distributions.
D) Incorrect: lineplot is not relevant for visualizing pairwise relationships, it's used for time-series or line-based visualizations.
E) Incorrect: catplot is used for categorical data plots, not for pairwise relationships, so it's unsuitable here.

EXAM FOCUS	*Seaborn's pairplot() helps visualize pairwise relationships in the dataset. Use diag_kind='kde' for a better understanding of data distribution on the diagonal.*
CAUTION ALERT	*Ensure you use categorical columns for the hue parameter; otherwise, it might generate unintended results or errors.*

QUESTION 11

Answer - A, E

A) Merging on a common key using pd.merge() is a common method for joining datasets.
B) join() is index-based and won't work with a column-based key like customer_id.
C) Appending datasets adds rows but does not merge based on keys.
D) Concatenation stacks datasets either horizontally or vertically.
E) merge() with different column names works when columns in both datasets differ.

EXAM FOCUS	*Use pd.merge() for merging datasets on a common key like customer_id, and ensure column names match or use left_on and right_on.*
CAUTION ALERT	*Avoid using join() if you need to merge on a specific column rather than indexes, as it may lead to unintended results.*

QUESTION 12

Answer - A, C

A) CCPA gives users the right to opt-out from data sales, and implementing this option via Python is necessary for compliance.
B) CCPA mandates data deletion upon request, so indefinite storage would violate the law.
C) Allowing users to delete their data complies with the CCPA's data handling regulations.
D) Sharing data without user consent violates CCPA's user privacy rights.
E) While encryption is critical, it doesn't directly address user opt-out and deletion rights under CCPA.

EXAM FOCUS	*Implementing user opt-out of data sales via a Python script ensures compliance with CCPA. Data deletion options are essential for user rights.*
CAUTION ALERT	*Storing user data indefinitely without offering deletion violates CCPA. Always inform users of their rights to deletion and data control.*

QUESTION 13

Answer - A, D

A) Correct, df.corr() calculates the correlation matrix.
B) Incorrect, using heatmap directly without a correlation matrix.
C) Covariance doesn't calculate correlation.
D) Correct, heatmap visualizes the correlation matrix.
E) Incorrect as lineplot is used for trend lines, not correlation.

EXAM FOCUS	*To visualize correlations, always compute df.corr() first, then use sns.heatmap() to visualize the matrix effectively.*
CAUTION ALERT	*Don't confuse covariance (df.cov()) with correlation. Covariance measures variability, while correlation quantifies the relationship between variables.*

QUESTION 14

Answer - A, D

A) Correct: This groups by category and aggregates both mean and count.
B) Incorrect: This script is incorrect due to duplicate keys in agg.
C) Incorrect: Without specifying the column, the output is ambiguous.
D) Correct: This directly aggregates 'sales' by category.
E) Incorrect: apply is not appropriate for this type of aggregation.

EXAM FOCUS	*agg() can handle multiple functions like mean and count for each group, making it versatile for summary statistics.*
CAUTION ALERT	*Don't use apply() for simple aggregation. It's slower and less readable compared to agg() or groupby().sum().*

QUESTION 15

Answer - B, D, E

Option A: Incorrect – Uses a single color instead of conditional formatting.
Option B: Correct – This approach conditionally colors the bars based on performance.
Option C: Incorrect – The performance column is not used properly.
Option D: Correct – Properly adds labels, which are essential for communicating data.
Option E: Correct – Horizontal bar chart using multiple colors.

EXAM FOCUS	*Conditional formatting in Matplotlib can be easily done by setting colors based on conditions, making visualizations more insightful.*
CAUTION ALERT	*Avoid using a single color in bar charts when multiple categories need to be differentiated visually.*

QUESTION 16

Answer - A, B

Option A: Correct – Uses logical operators and the & operator for filtering.
Option B: Correct – query() allows for a clear and readable query string.
Option C: Incorrect – .between() includes the boundaries, so it won't exclude 30 and 40.

Option D: Incorrect – iterrows() is inefficient compared to vectorized operations.
Option E: Incorrect – Syntax is wrong; the assignment to df overwrites previous data.

EXAM FOCUS	Use query() or logical operators for efficient row filtering when dealing with conditions across multiple columns in Pandas.
CAUTION ALERT	.between() includes boundaries, so it may not exclude exact values when filtering ranges in a DataFrame.

QUESTION 17

Answer - B, C

Option A: Incorrect – While this works, it's not the optimal or recommended way to convert a DataFrame to a NumPy array.
Option B: Correct – to_numpy() is the most efficient and recommended method in Pandas to convert a DataFrame to a NumPy array.
Option C: Correct – df.values returns a NumPy array of the DataFrame's values, but it is deprecated in favor of to_numpy().
Option D: Incorrect – as_matrix() is deprecated and not recommended.
Option E: Incorrect – np.asarray() works but is not optimal for Pandas DataFrames.

EXAM FOCUS	Use to_numpy() to convert a DataFrame into a NumPy array for optimal performance in numerical operations.
CAUTION ALERT	Avoid deprecated methods like as_matrix() or unnecessary conversions with np.array() when working with Pandas.

QUESTION 18

Answer - A, C

Option A: Correct – Single-line docstring that is simple and concise, following PEP 257.
Option B: Incorrect – The verb "Calculates" should be in the imperative ("Calculate").
Option C: Correct – Follows proper multi-line docstring format with clear description, arguments, and return type.
Option D: Incorrect – Improper punctuation and format for the docstring.
Option E: Incorrect – Incorrect argument and return type formatting.

EXAM FOCUS	Use imperative mood in docstrings: When writing function docstrings, always start with a verb in the imperative mood (e.g., "Calculate", not "Calculates").
CAUTION ALERT	Docstring structure matters: Incorrect formatting of arguments and return types in multi-line docstrings can confuse readers and lead to poor maintainability.

QUESTION 19

Answer - C, D

Option A: Incorrect – This handles the file not being found but does not handle missing data in the file.
Option B: Incorrect – Broadly catches file-related errors but doesn't handle missing values.
Option C: Correct – Handles both file reading and missing data errors appropriately.
Option D: Correct – Properly checks for missing values and includes multiple exception types for file handling.
Option E: Incorrect – MissingDataError is not a built-in Python exception.

QUESTION 20

Answer - A, B

Option A: Correct – Standard syntax for inserting a record with specified columns and their values.
Option B: Correct – This version works as long as values for all columns are provided in the correct order.
Option C: Incorrect – Omits the customer_name, which is required based on the schema.
Option D: Incorrect – The ON DUPLICATE KEY UPDATE clause is specific to MySQL and adds unnecessary complexity to a simple insert operation.
Option E: Incorrect – The customer_id and total_purchase should not be enclosed in single quotes as they are numeric types.

QUESTION 21

Answer - A, C

Option A: Correct – Uses parameterized queries (%s placeholders) for MySQL, preventing SQL injection.
Option B: Incorrect – Concatenating user input into the SQL query opens the code to SQL injection.
Option C: Correct – Uses named placeholders with a dictionary in MySQL, providing protection against SQL injection.
Option D: Incorrect – ? placeholders are for SQLite, not MySQL; MySQL uses %s or named placeholders.
Option E: Incorrect – String interpolation (f-strings) with user input directly in the query is vulnerable to SQL injection.

QUESTION 22

Answer - A, C

Option A: Correct – Parameterized queries secure sensitive data and avoid SQL injection.
Option B: Incorrect – This concatenation exposes the query to SQL injection.
Option C: Correct – Enforcing encryption on the database connection ensures data is encrypted during transmission.
Option D: Incorrect – %s parameterization may not work with some Python database connectors, and it lacks explicit security features.
Option E: Incorrect – This query is vulnerable to SQL injection attacks due to unsafe string formatting.

EXAM FOCUS	*Encrypt sensitive data in transit: Use SSL/TLS for encrypting sensitive data like salaries during transmission between Python scripts and databases.*
CAUTION ALERT	*Avoid concatenation for SQL queries: Combining strings to build SQL queries can lead to SQL injection vulnerabilities and is unsafe, especially with sensitive data.*

QUESTION 23

Answer - A, B

Option A: Correct – This uses the parent class's constructor with Employee.__init__.
Option B: Correct – It uses super() to inherit from the Employee class.
Option C: Incorrect – The super() call is wrongly structured with the class name and self.
Option D: Incorrect – Employee.__init__(name) is missing self, which is required.
Option E: Incorrect – While technically valid for inheritance, it doesn't implement constructor behavior.

EXAM FOCUS	*Inheritance needs super(): Use super().__init__() to ensure the child class correctly inherits and initializes attributes from the parent class.*
CAUTION ALERT	*Don't forget self: Forgetting to pass self when calling parent class methods like Employee.__init__ will cause errors in Python.*

QUESTION 24

Answer - C

Option A: Incorrect – This will overwrite the existing file because it opens the file in write mode.
Option B: Incorrect – While it uses append mode, it does not use a context manager, which is not the best practice.
Option C: Correct – This opens the file in append mode and uses a context manager for safe handling.
Option D: Incorrect – This opens the file in write mode, which will overwrite the file contents.
Option E: Incorrect – The r+ mode allows both reading and writing but does not ensure appending to the file.

EXAM FOCUS	*Use append mode for non-overwriting: When writing to a file without overwriting, use 'a' mode to append data while preserving existing content.*
CAUTION ALERT	*Beware of write mode ('w'): Using 'w' overwrites existing file content. Always double-check your file mode before writing to avoid accidental data loss.*

QUESTION 25

Answer - A, C, D

A) Correct: This is the correct way to define and catch a custom exception.
B) Incorrect: Inheriting from ValueError is not necessary for transaction-specific errors.
C) Correct: The custom exception is raised and caught using a message, demonstrating proper exception handling.
D) Correct: This defines a custom exception with a message and raises it.
E) Incorrect: Raising ValueError instead of a custom exception loses the specificity of the custom error class, which is important in this case.

EXAM FOCUS	*Message in exceptions matters: Always include meaningful messages in custom exceptions to help understand the cause of the error when caught.*
CAUTION ALERT	*Inheriting wrong exception types: Be mindful of which base class you inherit from; improper choices can confuse the intended meaning of your custom error.*

QUESTION 26

Answer - A

Option A: Correct, the HAVING clause filters customers with 5 or more orders.
Option B: Incorrect, COUNT cannot be used directly in the WHERE clause.
Option C: Incorrect, WHERE clause is misplaced in this query structure.
Option D: Incorrect, this query unnecessarily uses a subquery.
Option E: Incorrect, this excludes customers with exactly 5 orders.

EXAM FOCUS	*HAVING is used after GROUP BY: When filtering aggregated data, use the HAVING clause to apply conditions on groups created by GROUP BY.*
CAUTION ALERT	*WHERE vs. HAVING: Don't confuse WHERE and HAVING—WHERE is for filtering rows before grouping, and HAVING filters groups after aggregation.*

QUESTION 27

Answer - A

Option A: Correct, CHECK (salary > 3000) enforces the rule that salary must be greater than 3000.
Option B: Incorrect, PRIMARY KEY is for uniquely identifying records, not enforcing salary rules.
Option C: Incorrect, UNIQUE ensures all salary values are different, which is unrelated to the salary threshold.
Option D: Incorrect, this constraint checks if salary is less than 3000, which is the opposite of the requirement.
Option E: Incorrect, DEFAULT only sets the initial value but doesn't enforce the salary being greater than 3000.

EXAM FOCUS	*CHECK constraints ensure data integrity: Use CHECK (salary > 3000) to enforce business rules like ensuring salaries meet minimum thresholds in SQL databases.*
CAUTION ALERT	*PRIMARY KEY doesn't enforce rules on column values: While it ensures uniqueness and non-null values, it does not enforce conditions like the value being greater than 3000.*

QUESTION 28

Answer - D

Option A: Incorrect, dropping the index improves performance temporarily but loses the index benefits afterward.
Option B: Incorrect, adding a clustered index may not resolve the performance issue with inserts.
Option C: Incorrect, adding another index increases the overhead on insert performance.
Option D: Correct, disabling indexes during batch inserts reduces overhead and improves performance. Rebuilding afterward restores index performance.
Option E: Incorrect, rebuilding the index alone doesn't directly address slow insert performance.

EXAM FOCUS	*Disable indexes for batch inserts: Temporarily disabling indexes during bulk data inserts and rebuilding them afterward can improve performance significantly.*
CAUTION ALERT	*Don't drop indexes permanently: Dropping important indexes may lead to faster inserts but will degrade query performance over time.*

QUESTION 29

Answer - B

Option A: Incorrect, mean is sensitive to skewed data because outliers can greatly impact the result.
Option B: Correct, the median is least affected by skewed data and outliers.

Option C: Incorrect, mode is not the most reliable measure of central tendency in continuous, skewed distributions.
Option D: Incorrect, like statistics.mean(), np.mean() is impacted by skewed data.
Option E: Incorrect, this calculates standard deviation, not central tendency.

EXAM FOCUS	*Median handles skewed data well: For skewed distributions, the median is a better representation of central tendency as it is less influenced by extreme values.*
CAUTION ALERT	*Mean is sensitive to outliers: Always consider how skewness and outliers can distort the mean, particularly in distributions with significant skew.*

QUESTION 30

Answer - A, B

Option A: Correct, comparing standard deviations gives insight into variability.
Option B: Correct, using statistics.stdev() is also valid for comparing variability.
Option C: Incorrect, range does not give as much insight into variability as standard deviation.
Option D: Incorrect, comparing means does not address variability.
Option E: Incorrect, the syntax for calculating standard deviation is wrong here.

EXAM FOCUS	*Compare variability using standard deviation: Standard deviation provides a clear insight into the variability between datasets. Use either statistics.stdev() or np.std().*
CAUTION ALERT	*Range is not the best measure of variability: Comparing the range gives limited insight into data spread. Use standard deviation for better accuracy.*

QUESTION 31

Answer - A

Option A: Correct, np.percentile() calculates the confidence interval based on percentiles.
Option B: Incorrect, mean gives a point estimate, not a confidence interval.
Option C: Incorrect, variance is a measure of spread, not confidence interval.
Option D: Incorrect, standard deviation measures spread, not the confidence interval.
Option E: Incorrect, random choice does not compute confidence intervals.

EXAM FOCUS	*Use percentiles for confidence intervals: To estimate confidence intervals, calculate percentiles (2.5, 97.5) from bootstrapped means using np.percentile().*
CAUTION ALERT	*Mean and variance do not give confidence intervals: Avoid using mean or variance to calculate confidence intervals, as they only provide central tendency and spread.*

QUESTION 32

Answer - C

Option A: Incorrect, MSE is used for regression, not classification.
Option B: Incorrect, R-squared is not relevant to logistic regression.
Option C: Correct, Precision is a key metric for evaluating logistic regression models.
Option D: Incorrect, MAE is a metric for regression problems.
Option E: Incorrect, Adjusted R-squared applies to linear regression.

EXAM FOCUS	*Focus on classification metrics: Precision, recall, and F1-score are the most relevant metrics for evaluating logistic regression, especially when data is imbalanced.*

QUESTION 33

Answer - C, E

A) Incorrect: 'outer' merge keeps all rows from both DataFrames, not just df1
B) Incorrect: 'inner' merge retains only rows that match between both DataFrames
C) Correct: 'left' merge retains all rows from df1 and matches from df2
D) Incorrect: 'right' merge keeps all rows from df2, not df1
E) Correct: Same as C, but using a method attached to df1 instead of pd.merge().

EXAM FOCUS	*Left join retains unmatched rows: A left join keeps all rows from the left DataFrame (df1) and only matches rows from the right (df2) based on the key column.*
CAUTION ALERT	*Avoid inner join if you want unmatched rows: An inner join only keeps rows with matches in both DataFrames. Use left join if you need to retain all rows from one DataFrame.*

QUESTION 34

Answer - A, D

A) Correct: Broadcasting allows element-wise addition of arrays when their shapes are compatible, such as arrays with shapes (n, 1) and (1, n).
B) Incorrect: While np.dot() performs matrix multiplication, it is not considered broadcasting because it doesn't perform element-wise operations.
C) Incorrect: The shapes of a (2x1) and b (1x2) are not compatible for broadcasting addition, as the dimensions do not align properly.
D) Correct: The np.add() function allows broadcasting when the shapes of the arrays are compatible, such as arrays with aligned or extendable dimensions.
E) Incorrect: Broadcasting only works if the dimensions of the arrays are compatible, i.e., they can be aligned or "stretched" along their dimensions.

EXAM FOCUS	*Broadcasting simplifies array operations: NumPy broadcasting allows efficient element-wise operations on arrays of different shapes without writing loops. Understand how shapes align for broadcasting.*
CAUTION ALERT	*Ensure compatible shapes: Arrays must have compatible shapes for broadcasting. Mismatched shapes will result in errors or unexpected results in arithmetic operations.*

QUESTION 35

Answer - A, E

A) Correct: This fills missing values in the salary column with its median using fillna().
B) Incorrect: There is no method='median' option in fillna(); this would raise an error.
C) Incorrect: While apply() can work with lambda, the syntax here is unnecessarily complex for this task.
D) Incorrect: Using replace() here is inefficient and unconventional for filling missing values.
E) Correct: This fills missing values in the entire DataFrame with the respective column medians.

EXAM FOCUS	*Filling missing data: Use fillna() with appropriate statistical measures like median for effective handling of missing values.*
CAUTION	*Watch out for incorrect methods: fillna(method='median') is invalid in Pandas. Ensure the method*

QUESTION 36

Answer - A, C

A) Correct: accuracy_score() is the correct function for calculating accuracy.
B) Incorrect: precision_score calculates precision, not accuracy.
C) Correct: model.score() is used to calculate accuracy directly for classification models in Scikit-learn.
D) Incorrect: accuracy_score() requires predicted labels, not the model object.
E) Incorrect: Scikit-learn does not use evaluate() for accuracy; that is more typical of Keras models.

| EXAM FOCUS | Model accuracy: Use accuracy_score() and model.score() to evaluate model performance for classification problems. These functions simplify accuracy calculation. |
| CAUTION ALERT | Wrong function usage: model.evaluate() is typical in Keras, not in Scikit-learn. Stick with model.score() and accuracy_score() in Scikit-learn for classification tasks. |

QUESTION 37

Answer - A, B

A) Correct – R-squared is a common metric for evaluating the goodness of fit of a linear regression model.
B) Correct – Predictions need to be made using model.predict() to compare with actual values.
C) Incorrect – Coefficients represent feature weights but are not used directly for evaluating the fit of the model.
D) Incorrect – Accuracy is used for classification tasks, not regression.
E) Incorrect – The intercept is part of the model but not used for model evaluation.

| EXAM FOCUS | Evaluate with R-squared: Use R-squared to assess linear regression model fit. Combine it with other metrics to get a holistic understanding of model performance. |
| CAUTION ALERT | Accuracy is for classification, not regression: Avoid using accuracy_score() for regression evaluation. Stick to R-squared or mean squared error for regression tasks. |

QUESTION 38

Answer - A, C

A) Correct – The agg function allows for multiple operations such as counting and calculating the mean.
B) Incorrect – The count() function applied alone will count all non-null values, not calculate the average.
C) Correct – This is a valid option to calculate the average salary per department.
D) Incorrect – Grouping by name is not relevant to the question as we are grouping by department.
E) Incorrect – Grouping by salary will not give meaningful insights in this context.

| EXAM FOCUS | Combining aggregation in agg(): You can apply multiple aggregation functions simultaneously by passing a dictionary or list to agg()—useful for calculating multiple statistics at once. |
| CAUTION ALERT | Avoid groupby on irrelevant columns: Grouping by columns like name or salary when asked to group by department is a common error that results in incorrect aggregation. |

QUESTION 39

Answer - A, C

A) Correct because cross_val_score(model, X, y, cv=5) correctly applies 5-fold cross-validation to the model.
B) Incorrect because train_test_split is not a cross-validation technique. It splits data once, not multiple times as cross-validation does.
C) Correct because KFold(n_splits=5) correctly implements a manual 5-fold cross-validation split for the model.
D) Incorrect as this only fits a model without any cross-validation, leading to potential overfitting without validation.
E) Incorrect because although cross_val_score is valid, this uses cv=10, which does not match the 5-fold cross-validation asked in the question.

EXAM FOCUS	K-Fold Cross-Validation: Cross-validation divides the data into multiple folds to ensure better generalization. Use cross_val_score() to evaluate models with folds like 5 or 10.
CAUTION ALERT	Cross-validation vs. Train-test Split: Remember that train_test_split() does not perform cross-validation. It's only used for creating one training and test set.

QUESTION 40

Answer - C

A) Incorrect because plt.plot() generates a line plot, not a scatter plot, which is needed here.
B) Incorrect because a bar plot is unsuitable for visualizing the relationship between two continuous variables.
C) Correct because plt.scatter() generates a scatter plot, which is the best choice to visualize the relationship between Height and Weight.
D) Incorrect because this option generates a line plot, not a scatter plot.
E) Incorrect because plt.boxplot() generates a boxplot, which is not appropriate for this task.

EXAM FOCUS	Scatter Plot Tip: Use plt.scatter() for visualizing relationships between two continuous variables, like "Height" and "Weight". This helps identify potential correlations.
CAUTION ALERT	Line Plot Caution: Don't confuse plt.plot() for scatter plots. It is used for continuous trends and not for scatter plots where data points are distinct.

QUESTION 41

Answer - A, D

A) Correct because plt.hist() generates a histogram in Matplotlib to visualize the distribution of a numerical variable like price.
B) Incorrect because plt.plot() creates a line plot, not a histogram.
C) Incorrect because plt.scatter() creates a scatter plot, which is not suitable for visualizing distributions.
D) Correct because adding bins=20 in plt.hist() customizes the histogram with 20 bins, which can provide a more granular view of price distribution.
E) Incorrect because plt.bar() generates a bar chart and is not used for distribution analysis.

EXAM FOCUS	Histogram Tip: Use plt.hist() to visualize the distribution of numerical data like prices. Customize the number of bins to get more granularity in the distribution.
CAUTION ALERT	Avoiding Mistakes: Don't use plt.plot() or plt.scatter() for distributions. These are designed for relationships between variables, not for frequency visualization.

QUESTION 42

Answer - A, C

A) Correct because plt.legend(fontsize=14) correctly adjusts the legend font size.
B) Incorrect because title_fontsize only adjusts the size of the title in the legend, not the font size of the legend labels.
C) Correct because using prop={'size':14} also adjusts the font size of the legend labels.
D) Incorrect because font and size are not valid arguments for plt.legend().
E) Incorrect because size='14pt' is not a valid syntax in Matplotlib for legends.

EXAM FOCUS	*Legend Font Tip: Use plt.legend(fontsize=14) or prop={'size':14} to adjust the legend's font size for clarity when presenting multiple lines or categories in a plot.*
CAUTION ALERT	*Legend Mistake: Avoid using font='Arial', size=14 in plt.legend()—these parameters don't exist for legends. Use fontsize or prop instead.*

QUESTION 43

Answer - A, B

A) Correct because rotating the x-axis labels helps reduce overlap and clutter.
B) Correct because reducing the number of ticks with locator_params() simplifies the presentation for non-technical audiences.
C) Incorrect because mdates.MonthLocator() is more suitable for time-series data, not categorical x-axis values like months.
D) Incorrect because reducing font size alone might not address clutter caused by long labels or too many ticks.
E) Incorrect because manually setting ticks without considering the full data might misrepresent information.

EXAM FOCUS	*Reducing Clutter: Rotate labels with plt.xticks(rotation=45) or use locator_params() to reduce ticks. This prevents x-axis clutter when presenting categorical or time-based data.*
CAUTION ALERT	*Tick Overload: Adding too many ticks or long labels without reducing their frequency can overwhelm the viewer and cause clutter in your visualizations.*

QUESTION 44

Answer - B

A) Incorrect because a pie chart is less effective in showing the magnitude differences between categories in a quarterly review where the top three performers need emphasis.
B) Correct because using a horizontal bar chart with text annotation highlighting the top performer draws attention to the best-performing categories, supporting the narrative effectively.
C) Incorrect because a simple bar chart without further annotations won't sufficiently emphasize the top performers.
D) Incorrect because a boxplot visualizes distribution rather than emphasizing the top performers as needed here.
E) Incorrect because a scatter plot doesn't fit the context of category sales and lacks necessary emphasis without annotations.

EXAM FOCUS	*Highlight Top Performers: When reviewing performance, use annotations like plt.text() to emphasize key performers in bar charts. This draws focus to critical data points.*
CAUTION ALERT	*Beware Pie Charts: Pie charts are less effective for comparing product sales or rankings. Use bar charts for clearer differentiation and easier interpretation.*

QUESTION 45

Answer - A

A) Correct because a pie chart with the explode feature effectively emphasizes the highest profit margins, making it easier for stakeholders to identify key months.

B) Incorrect because while a bar chart visualizes the data, it doesn't emphasize the key takeaways, which is the focus of this task.

C) Incorrect because a heatmap is not suitable for summarizing one-dimensional data like monthly profit margins.

D) Incorrect because a scatter plot doesn't summarize or emphasize specific months effectively.

E) Incorrect because a kernel density plot is more suited for distributions than summarizing key monthly profit margins.

EXAM FOCUS	*Emphasize Key Insights: Use plt.pie() with the explode option to emphasize specific data points, such as months with the highest profit margins.*
CAUTION ALERT	*Limitations of Pie Charts: Be cautious when using pie charts for complex data. They work best for simple comparisons with a limited number of categories.*

PRACTICE TEST 3 - QUESTIONS ONLY

QUESTION 1

You've collected a dataset containing missing values for various attributes. You need to handle these missing values before conducting an analysis. Which Python code snippet best replaces missing values in numerical columns with the mean of that column?

```
A) df.fillna(df.mean(), inplace=True)
B) df.replace(np.nan, df.mean(),
inplace=True)
C) df.fillna(method='ffill')
D) df.dropna()
E) df.interpolate()
```

QUESTION 2

A dataset includes variables that are suspected to have missing data that is "Missing Not At Random" (MNAR). How would the presence of MNAR data impact your analysis?

A) It can lead to biased analysis results
B) MNAR data is easier to handle compared to MCAR data
C) Standard imputation techniques can solve MNAR issues
D) Excluding MNAR data can improve model accuracy

QUESTION 3

You are working with unstructured text data from customer reviews and want to convert it into a structured format for analysis. Which of the following Python methods can be used to process unstructured text data into structured form? (Select 2 answers).

```
A) Use json.dumps() to convert the text to
structured data
B) Use Python's re module to extract
structured information
C) Use pd.read_csv() to load text data
D) Use pd.DataFrame() to create a
structured format from the extracted
information
```

QUESTION 4

You are working with a dataset of housing prices and have identified an outlier in the price column. The outlier has a Z-score of 4.5. How should you handle this outlier before running a regression analysis? (Select 2 answers).

A) Remove the outlier to prevent it from skewing the regression results
B) Use Min-Max scaling to handle the outlier
C) Impute the outlier with the median value
D) Ignore the outlier, as it has little impact on the analysis

QUESTION 5

A dataset contains inconsistent data formats in the date column. You want to validate that all entries in the column follow the YYYY-MM-DD format. Which of the following methods would help you achieve this validation? (Select 2 answers).

```
A) Use pd.to_datetime() to ensure
consistent date formatting
B) Use df['date'].apply(lambda x:
datetime.strptime(x, '%Y-%m-%d'))
C) Use df['date'] =
df['date'].strftime('%Y-%m-%d')
D) Use pd.date_range() to validate date
consistency
```

QUESTION 6

You are running a SQL query in Python to retrieve data from a database. Which Python function allows you to execute SQL queries and fetch results using the sqlite3 library? (Select 2 answers).

```
A) cursor.execute('SELECT * FROM
employees')
B) cursor.fetchall()
C) cursor.fetchall('SELECT * FROM
employees')
D) cursor.fetchone()
```

QUESTION 7

You are analyzing a dataset and want to visualize its distribution using Seaborn. Which of the following Python code snippets correctly creates a histogram with a KDE (Kernel Density Estimate) plot? (Select 2 answers).

```
A) import seaborn as sns
sns.histplot(data, kde=True)

 B) import seaborn as sns
sns.hist(data, kde=True)

 C) import seaborn as sns
sns.distplot(data, kde=False)

 D) import matplotlib.pyplot as plt
plt.hist(data)
```

QUESTION 8

You are required to merge two DataFrames on a common column using an inner join. Which of the following code snippets correctly merges the DataFrames in Pandas?

```
A) import pandas as pd
merged_df = pd.merge(df1, df2, on='ID',
how='inner')

 B) import pandas as pd
merged_df = pd.merge(df1, df2,
left_on='ID', right_on='ID', how='outer')

 C) import pandas as pd
merged_df = df1.merge(df2, on='ID',
how='left')

 D) import pandas as pd
merged_df = df1.join(df2, how='inner',
on='ID')

 E) import pandas as pd
merged_df = df1.append(df2)
```

QUESTION 9

You are tasked with evaluating the accuracy of a classification model using accuracy and confusion matrix. Which are the correct steps to compute them? Select 2 correct options.

```
A) from sklearn.metrics import
accuracy_score, confusion_matrix
accuracy = accuracy_score(y_test, y_pred)
matrix = confusion_matrix(y_test, y_pred)

B) from sklearn.metrics import
precision_score
```

```
C) accuracy = model.predict(X_train)
D) confusion = confusion_matrix(X_test,
y_pred)
E) precision = precision_score(y_test,
y_pred, average='weighted')
```

QUESTION 10

You want to visualize the distribution of your numerical data using Seaborn's distplot function. Which options are correct? Select 2 correct options.

```
A) import seaborn as sns
sns.distplot(df['column'])

B) sns.distplot(df['column'], kde=False)
C) sns.distplot(df['column'], hist=False)
D) sns.catplot(df)
E) sns.kdeplot(df)
```

QUESTION 11

While preparing data for an audience survey, you need to anonymize customer identifiers in compliance with GDPR. Which Python techniques will help you anonymize the data? (Select 2 correct answers)

```
 A) df['customer_id'] =
df['customer_id'].apply(lambda x: hash(x))
 B) df.drop(columns=['customer_id'])
 C) df['customer_id'].apply(lambda x:
'XXXX' + str(x)[-4:])
 D) df.replace(df['customer_id'],
'Unknown')
 E) df['customer_id'].replace(r'\d+',
'####', regex=True)
```

QUESTION 12

You are building a Python-based system to collect customer feedback for a company that operates in both the EU and the US. What features should you include to ensure compliance with both GDPR and CCPA? (Select 2 correct answers)

A) Use Python scripts to generate encrypted backups of the feedback data
 B) Automatically share collected feedback data with third-party vendors without user consent
 C) Provide a Python-based API for users to access, delete, or update their feedback
 D) Store all collected feedback indefinitely without providing any deletion option
 E) Anonymize feedback data using Python to prevent re-identification of users

QUESTION 13

You are tasked with efficiently storing unique customer IDs. Which data structures would you use for fast membership testing? (Select 2 answers)

A) Set
B) List
C) Dictionary
D) Tuple
E) Array

QUESTION 14

A dataset contains sales data that needs to be combined with product details stored in another DataFrame. You are tasked with merging the sales data with product details on the 'product_id' column. Which of the following scripts would achieve this? Select 2 correct answers.

```
A) merged_df = pd.merge(sales_df,
product_df, on='product_id')
 B) merged_df = pd.merge(sales_df,
product_df, how='outer', on='product_id')
 C) merged_df = pd.merge(sales_df,
product_df, left_on='product_id')
 D) merged_df = sales_df.join(product_df,
on='product_id')
 E) merged_df = pd.concat([sales_df,
product_df], axis=1)
```

QUESTION 15

Your task is to clean a dataset and remove all rows with missing values in the "Price" column, then export the cleaned data to a CSV file for your team. Which methods should you use in Python? (Select 2 answers)

```
A)
df.dropna(subset=['Price']).to_csv('cleaned
_data.csv', index=FalsE)
B) df.fillna(0).to_csv('cleaned_data.csv',
index=FalsE)
C)
df[df['Price'].notnull()].to_csv('cleaned_d
ata.csv', index=FalsE)
D) df.dropna().to_csv('cleaned_data.csv')
E)
df.drop(columns='Price').to_csv('cleaned_da
ta.csv', index=FalsE)
```

QUESTION 16

You need to define a function that checks if a

number is even or odd, and prints "Even" or "Odd" accordingly. However, the function should also count the number of even and odd numbers it processes, and return these counts at the end. Which code structures are correct? (Select 3 answers)

```
A) def even_odd_counter(numbers):
even_count, odd_count = 0, 0 for num in
numbers: if num % 2 == 0: print('Even')
even_count += 1 else: print('Odd')
odd_count += 1 return even_count, odd_count

 B) def even_odd_counter(numbers):
even_count = len([n for n in numbers if n %
2 == 0]) odd_count = len(numbers) -
even_count return even_count, odd_count

 C) def even_odd_counter(numbers):
even_count, odd_count = 0, 0 for num in
numbers: if num % 2 == 0: print('Even')
even_count += 1 else: print('Odd')
odd_count += 1 return {'Even': even_count,
'Odd': odd_count}

 D) def even_odd_counter(numbers): counts =
{'Even': 0, 'Odd': 0} for num in numbers:
if num % 2 == 0: counts['Even'] += 1 else:
counts['Odd'] += 1 return counts

 E) def even_odd_counter(numbers): evens =
[num for num in numbers if num % 2 == 0]
odds = [num for num in numbers if num % 2
!= 0] return len(evens), len(odds)
```

QUESTION 17

You are analyzing a dataset and need to scale the numerical features using standardization (mean=0, std=1) to prepare it for a machine learning model. Which library and methods will allow you to standardize the data? (Select 2 answers)

```
A) from sklearn.preprocessing import
StandardScaler; scaler = StandardScaler();
df_scaled = scaler.fit_transform(df)

 B) from sklearn.preprocessing import
MinMaxScaler; scaler = MinMaxScaler();
df_scaled = scaler.fit_transform(df)
 C) df_scaled = (df - df.mean()) / df.std()
 D) df['scaled'] = df.apply(lambda x: (x -
x.mean()) / x.std())
 E) df_scaled = df / df.std()
```

QUESTION 18

You are writing a Python script to analyze sales data. Your manager has asked you to organize your code into modules to improve maintainability. Which of the following approaches represents best practices for organizing the code into modules? (Select 2 answers)

A) Create a single script sales_analysis.py for all processing tasks

B) Create separate modules: data_processing.py, data_visualization.py, and model_building.py

C) Create a module sales_data.py that handles everything including data processing, visualization, and modeling

D) Create a main script sales_main.py that calls functions from data_processing.py, data_visualization.py, and model_building.py

E) Create a single script sales.py and import all libraries at the top of the file

QUESTION 19

You are writing a Python script that connects to a database and executes SQL queries. If a query fails, you want to raise a custom exception with a relevant error message. Which code snippet implements this correctly? (Select 2 answers)

```
A) try:
execute_query(sql)
except DatabaseError:
raise

 B) try:
execute_query(sql)
except Exception as e:
raise Exception(f"Query failed: {e}")

 C) try:
execute_query(sql)
except Exception as e:
raise DatabaseError(f"Database error
occurred: {e}")

 D) try:
execute_query(sql)
except DatabaseError:
print("Error running the query.")
raise

 E) try:
execute_query(sql)
except Exception as e:
raise ValueError(f"SQL failed with error:
{e}")
```

QUESTION 20

You need to update the total_purchase for customer 101 in the customers table. The new total should be

$200. Which SQL query correctly updates this record? (Select 2 answers)

```
A) UPDATE customers
SET total_purchase = 200.00
WHERE customer_id = 101;

 B) UPDATE customers
SET total_purchase = 200.00;

 C) UPDATE customers
SET total_purchase = 200.00
WHERE customer_id = '101';

 D) UPDATE customers
SET total_purchase = '200.00'
WHERE customer_id = 101;

 E) UPDATE customers
total_purchase = 200
WHERE customer_id = 101;
```

QUESTION 21

You are tasked with updating the total purchases for a customer in the customers table using a parameterized query in Python. Which of the following options ensures the query is both secure and efficient? (Select 2 answers)

```
A) import sqlite3
conn = sqlite3.connect('database.db')
cursor = conn.cursor()
cursor.execute("UPDATE customers SET
total_purchase = ? WHERE customer_id = ?",
(total_purchase, customer_id))
conn.commit()

 B) import sqlite3
conn = sqlite3.connect('database.db')
cursor = conn.cursor()
query = "UPDATE customers SET
total_purchase = " + str(total_purchase) +
" WHERE customer_id = " + str(customer_id)
cursor.execute(query)
conn.commit()

 C) import sqlite3
conn = sqlite3.connect('database.db')
cursor = conn.cursor()
cursor.execute("UPDATE customers SET
total_purchase = :total WHERE customer_id =
:id", {'total': total_purchase, 'id':
customer_id})
conn.commit()

 D) import sqlite3
conn = sqlite3.connect('database.db')
cursor = conn.cursor()
cursor.execute("UPDATE customers SET
```

```
total_purchase = ? AND customer_id = ?",
(total_purchase, customer_id))
conn.commit()

 E) import sqlite3
conn = sqlite3.connect('database.db')
cursor = conn.cursor()
cursor.execute("UPDATE customers SET
total_purchase = '1000' WHERE customer_id =
?", (customer_id,))
conn.commit()
```

QUESTION 22

You are implementing access controls for a database. How would you ensure the principle of least privilege for SQL users in your Python application? (Select 2 answers)

 A) Grant SELECT and INSERT permissions only to the necessary tables.
 B) Grant all privileges (SELECT, INSERT, UPDATE, DELETE) on all tables to the application user.
 C) Use a specific role with limited permissions for each database user in the app.
 D) Use a superuser role with global access to the entire database for the application.
 E) Create different users for different operations, like one for SELECT and another for INSERT.

QUESTION 23

You want to enforce encapsulation in a class by making the salary attribute private. Which approaches work correctly? (Select 2 answers)

```
A) class Employee:
def __init__(self, salary):
self._salary = salary

 B) class Employee:
def __init__(self, salary):
self.__salary = salary

 C) class Employee:
def __init__(self, salary):
self.salary = salary
def get_salary(self):
return self.salary

 D) class Employee:
def __init__(self, salary):
self.__salary = salary
def get_salary(self):
return self.__salary

 E) class Employee:
def __init__(self, salary):
```

```
self.salary = salary
def _get_salary(self):
return self.salary
```

QUESTION 24

You are processing a large file and want to read it line by line instead of loading the entire file into memory. Which Python code snippet achieves this efficiently?

```
 A) with open('largefile.txt', 'r') as f:
data = f.read()
 B) with open('largefile.txt', 'r') as f:
for line in f: process(linE)  C) f =
open('largefile.txt', 'r') for line in
f.readlines(): process(linE)

 D) with open('largefile.txt', 'r') as f:
data = f.readlines()
 E) with open('largefile.txt', 'r+') as f:
process(f)
```

QUESTION 25

You are building a data validation system for incoming data streams. You need to implement a custom exception that handles invalid data types and provides a clear error message. How would you structure the custom exception class and handle it? (Select 2 correct answers)

```
A) class InvalidDataTypeError(Exception):
def __init__(self, message):
super().__init__(message)
try:
raise InvalidDataTypeError('Invalid data
type')
except InvalidDataTypeError as e:
print(E)

B) class InvalidDataTypeError(TypeError):
def __init__(self, message):
self.message = message
raise InvalidDataTypeError('Invalid data
type')

 C) try:
raise InvalidDataTypeError('Data type not
allowed')
except InvalidDataTypeError:
print('Handled invalid data')

 D) class InvalidDataTypeError(ValueError):
def __init__(self, msg):
super().__init__(msg)
raise InvalidDataTypeError()

 E) raise
```

```
TypeError('InvalidDataTypeError').
```

QUESTION 26

You want to select all products from a products table, along with their category names from a categories table. Some products might not have a category. Which of the following SQL queries will achieve this? (Select 1 correct answer)

```
A) SELECT p.product_name, c.category_name
FROM products p LEFT JOIN categories c ON
p.category_id = c.category_id;

B) SELECT p.product_name, c.category_name
FROM products p INNER JOIN categories c ON
p.category_id = c.category_id;

C) SELECT p.product_name, c.category_name
FROM products p RIGHT JOIN categories c ON
p.category_id = c.category_id;

D) SELECT p.product_name, c.category_name
FROM products p CROSS JOIN categories c;

E) SELECT p.product_name, c.category_name
FROM products p FULL JOIN categories c ON
p.category_id = c.category_id;
```

QUESTION 27

You are tasked with ensuring that employee_id in the employees table is unique and not null. Which SQL statement would best accomplish this? (Select 1 correct answer)

```
A) ALTER TABLE employees ADD PRIMARY KEY
(employee_id);
B) ALTER TABLE employees ADD FOREIGN KEY
(employee_id) REFERENCES
departments(employee_id);
C) ALTER TABLE employees ADD CONSTRAINT
employee_unique UNIQUE (employee_id);
D) ALTER TABLE employees ADD CONSTRAINT
employee_id_not_null CHECK (employee_id IS
NOT NULL);
E) ALTER TABLE employees ADD INDEX
(employee_id);
```

QUESTION 28

What is the main difference between clustered and non-clustered indexes in SQL? (Select 1 correct answer)

A) Clustered indexes store data physically in sorted order, while non-clustered indexes store pointers to the data.
B) Non-clustered indexes store data physically, while clustered indexes store pointers to the data.
C) Clustered indexes can be created multiple times on a table.
D) Non-clustered indexes always require more storage than clustered indexes.
E) Non-clustered indexes improve the performance of INSERT operations.

QUESTION 29

In a dataset with some extreme outlier values, which measure of central tendency would best represent the typical data point? (Select 1 correct answer)

```
A) statistics.mean(data)
B) statistics.median(data)
C) statistics.mode(data)
D) np.mean(data)
E) sum(data) / len(data)
```

QUESTION 30

You have two datasets: one with salaries and one with house prices. Both datasets are skewed. What measure of spread would you use to compare their variability? (Select 1 correct answer)

```
A) statistics.mean(salaries)
B) statistics.stdev(salaries)
C) statistics.variance(house_prices)
D) max(house_prices) - min(house_prices)
E) np.mean(salaries)
```

QUESTION 31

You want to validate the robustness of your machine learning model using bootstrapping techniques. How can you implement bootstrapping for model validation in Python? (Select 2 correct answers)

```
A) from sklearn.utils import resample;
X_resampled, y_resampled = resample(X, y,
replace=True, n_samples=1000)

B) from sklearn.bootstrap import
bootstrap(X, y)
C) from sklearn.utils import resample;
bootstrapped_data = resample(X,
replace=False)
D) import numpy as np; bootstrapped_data =
np.random.choice(X, size=1000,
replace=True)

E) from sklearn.model_selection import
cross_val_score; bootstrapped_scores =
cross_val_score(model, X_resampled,
```

```
y_resampled, cv=5)
```

QUESTION 32

You want to interpret the coefficients of a logistic regression model predicting whether a customer will churn based on their account balance. What does a positive coefficient for the balance feature imply? (Select 1 correct answer)

A) A higher balance increases the likelihood of churn
B) A higher balance decreases the likelihood of churn
C) A higher balance has no impact on churn
D) A higher balance implies a non-linear relationship with churn
E) The balance feature should be one-hot encoded before interpretation

QUESTION 33

You are tasked with identifying outliers in a dataset using the Interquartile Range (IQR) method. Which options are valid for identifying outliers in the 'age' column of a DataFrame named df? (Select 3 correct answers)

```
A) df_outliers = df[df['age'] > Q3 + 1.5 *
IQR]

B) IQR = np.percentile(df['age'], 75) -
np.percentile(df['age'], 25); df_outliers =
df[df['age'] > np.percentile(df['age'], 75)
+ 1.5 * IQR]

C) df_outliers = df[df['age'] >
df['age'].mean() + 3 * df['age'].std()]

D) IQR = np.median(df['age']); df_outliers
= df[df['age'] < IQR]

E) outliers = df[df['age'] >
df['age'].median() * 1.5]
```

QUESTION 34

You are performing aggregation operations on a NumPy array arr. Which of the following demonstrates valid use of aggregation functions in NumPy? (Select 2 correct answers)

```
A) total_sum = arr.sum()
B) mean_value = arr.mean(axis=0)
C) variance = arr.var()
D) median_value = arr.median()
E) maximum_value = arr.max(axis=1)
```

QUESTION 35

You want to create a boxplot for the salary column in your dataset to identify outliers. Which of the following Python commands correctly plots the boxplot? (Select 2 correct answers)

```
A) plt.boxplot(df['salary'])
B) sns.boxplot(x='salary', data=df)
C) plt.plot(df['salary'].boxplot())
D) df['salary'].plot(kind='box')
E) plt.boxplot(x=df['salary'])
```

QUESTION 36

You are concerned about overfitting while training a machine learning model. Which strategies can help you avoid overfitting? (Select 2 correct answers)

A) Applying L2 regularization (Ridge)
B) Reducing the size of the training dataset
C) Using early stopping in training
D) Removing the validation set
E) Increasing the depth of the decision tree

QUESTION 37

A higher R-squared value always means a better model in linear regression.

A) True
B) False

QUESTION 38

When using the Pandas groupby function, the resulting grouped object can be directly visualized using Matplotlib without converting it to a DataFrame first.

A) True
B) False

QUESTION 39

A machine learning model is trained with a high complexity model that captures almost every detail in the training data, but it fails to generalize well on new unseen data. This is an example of underfitting.

A) True
B) False

QUESTION 40

You are tasked with visualizing the distribution of a numerical variable using Matplotlib. A histogram is an effective way to visualize the distribution of a numerical variable in a dataset.

A) True
B) False

QUESTION 41

You are asked to compare the relationship between two numerical variables (height and weight) in a scatter plot. In Matplotlib, plt.scatter() is the correct function to generate this plot.

A) True
B) False

QUESTION 42

You have created a scatter plot comparing profit and sales. You need to move the legend to the upper left corner of the plot and adjust the background color to light gray. Which of the following commands will correctly adjust the legend?

```
A) plt.legend(loc='upper left',
frameon=True, facecolor='lightgray')
B) plt.legend(loc='upper left',
backgroundcolor='lightgray')
C) plt.legend(position='upper left',
frameon=True, facecolor='gray')
D) plt.legend(loc='upper left',
shadow=True, bg='gray')
E) plt.legend(loc='top', bg='lightgray')
```

QUESTION 43

You have created a line plot that includes multiple product categories and want to adapt it for an executive presentation. How can you simplify the chart without losing key information? Select two correct answers.

```
A) plt.plot(df['Month'], df['Category1'],
label='Category 1')
```

```
B) plt.plot(df['Month'], df['Category2'],
label='Category 2')
C) plt.legend(loc='upper left', fontsize=8)
```

```
D) plt.plot(df['Month'], df['Category1'],
color='blue'); plt.plot(df['Month'],
df['Category2'], linestyle='--',
color='green')
```

```
E) plt.ylabel('Sales')
```

QUESTION 44

In your quarterly data presentation, you're asked to create a clear Python-based visualization for revenue trends, highlighting seasonal spikes and dips. How would you effectively present this data using Matplotlib and annotations? Select two correct answers.

```
A) plt.plot(months, revenuE)
plt.annotate('Winter Spike', xy=(months[2],
revenue[2]), xytext=(months[3],
revenue[2]+50),
arrowprops=dict(facecolor='red',
shrink=0.05))
```

```
B) plt.plot(months, revenue) without any
labels or annotations
C) plt.scatter(months, revenuE)
plt.title('Seasonal Revenue Trends')
D) plt.bar(months, revenue) with
plt.text(months[2], revenue[2], 'Spike')
E) plt.pie(revenue, labels=months)
```

QUESTION 45

A client is interested in understanding the growth of their customer base over the last year. How would you summarize this growth visually to highlight the months with the highest and lowest customer sign-ups?

```
A) plt.plot(months, signups, color="blue")
B) sns.boxplot(data=signups, x="months")
C) plt.bar(months, signups);
plt.title("Customer Sign-ups Growth");
plt.xlabel("Months"); plt.ylabel("Sign-
ups")
D) plt.hist(signups)
E) sns.violinplot(data=signups)
```

PRACTICE TEST 3 - ANSWERS ONLY

QUESTION 1

Answer - A

A) Correct – df.fillna(df.mean(), inplace=True) fills missing values in numerical columns with the mean, which is the correct approach for numerical imputation.
B) Incorrect – replace does not handle missing values effectively in this context; fillna is the proper method.
C) Incorrect – Forward filling (ffill) uses previous values and is better suited for time series, not for imputing numerical data.
D) Incorrect – dropna() removes rows with missing values, which could lead to loss of important data.
E) Incorrect – interpolate() fills missing values by estimating intermediate values, which may not match the required mean-based imputation for numerical data.

EXAM FOCUS	*Use fillna() with the mean for numerical imputation. It's a common approach when missing values need to be replaced with a statistical measure.*
CAUTION ALERT	*Replacing missing values using methods like replace() or forward filling may not suit numerical data. Understand the difference in approach.*

QUESTION 2

Answer - A

A) Correct – MNAR data is missing in a systematic way, and failing to address it can lead to biased results.
B) Incorrect – MNAR is harder to handle compared to MCAR, as its missingness depends on unobserved factors.
C) Incorrect – Standard imputation techniques like mean or median imputation may not effectively handle MNAR data.
D) Incorrect – Excluding MNAR data can introduce bias into the analysis, as it may not be missing at random.

EXAM FOCUS	*Identifying MNAR data early is crucial. It often requires specialized methods beyond simple imputation, like modeling missingness itself.*
CAUTION ALERT	*Avoid using standard imputation techniques like mean or median for MNAR data. It can lead to skewed results due to the non-random nature of the missingness.*

QUESTION 3

Answer - B, D

A) Incorrect – json.dumps() is used to convert a Python object to a JSON string, not for converting unstructured text to structured data.
B) Correct – Python's re module can extract patterns and structured information from unstructured text data.
C) Incorrect – pd.read_csv() is used for structured CSV files, not unstructured text.
D) Correct – pd.DataFrame() can create a structured format from the extracted text information, allowing further analysis.

EXAM FOCUS	*The re module in Python is highly effective for pattern extraction in unstructured text, while pd.DataFrame() structures extracted data for analysis.*
CAUTION ALERT	*Don't confuse JSON conversion functions like json.dumps() with tools for extracting structured information from raw text. They're not interchangeable.*

QUESTION 4

Answer - A, C

A) Correct – Removing outliers with high Z-scores can prevent them from skewing the results of a regression analysis.
 B) Incorrect – Min-Max scaling does not handle outliers; it scales data but does not address extreme values.
 C) Correct – Imputing the outlier with the median is a valid technique to minimize its impact without losing the data.
 D) Incorrect – Ignoring an outlier with a high Z-score (like 4.5) can significantly impact the regression results.

EXAM FOCUS	*Remove or impute outliers to avoid skewing regression models. Outliers with Z-scores greater than 3 often distort results and should be handled carefully.*
CAUTION ALERT	*Ignoring outliers with high Z-scores (e.g., 4.5) will likely distort regression models. Always address such extreme values before analysis.*

QUESTION 5

Answer - A, B

A) Correct – pd.to_datetime() converts the column to a datetime object, ensuring that all dates follow the same format.
 B) Correct – This lambda function applies strptime to convert string entries into a consistent format.
 C) Incorrect – strftime() is used for formatting a datetime object to a string, but it does not validate or enforce the format of string entries.
 D) Incorrect – pd.date_range() generates a range of dates but does not validate whether the column entries are consistent.

EXAM FOCUS	*Use pd.to_datetime() to standardize date formats. Apply strptime for more control over formatting strings into datetime objects.*
CAUTION ALERT	*Avoid using strftime() for date validation. It formats dates but doesn't enforce or check the consistency of string entries in the dataset.*

QUESTION 6

Answer - A, B

A) Correct – The execute() function allows executing SQL queries in Python using sqlite3.
 B) Correct – fetchall() retrieves all results after the query is executed.
 C) Incorrect – fetchall() doesn't accept a SQL query string as an argument; the query must first be executed with execute().
 D) Incorrect – fetchone() retrieves only a single result, but this isn't a function for executing SQL queries.

EXAM FOCUS	*Use execute() to run SQL queries and fetchall() to retrieve all results when working with the sqlite3 Python library.*
CAUTION ALERT	*fetchall() only retrieves results after executing a query. It cannot execute a SQL query directly. Always pair it with execute().*

QUESTION 7

Answer - A, D

A) Correct – histplot() with kde=True is the correct way to create a histogram with a KDE plot in Seaborn.

B) Incorrect – hist() is not a valid Seaborn function; histplot() is correct.

C) Incorrect – This uses distplot(), which has been deprecated in recent versions of Seaborn.

D) Correct – This code creates a simple histogram using Matplotlib, though it doesn't include KDE.

EXAM FOCUS	*Use sns.histplot(data, kde=True) to create histograms with KDE in Seaborn. For simple histograms, plt.hist() works well.*
CAUTION ALERT	*Seaborn's distplot() is deprecated. Always opt for histplot() or kdeplot() for newer versions of Seaborn.*

QUESTION 8

Answer - A

A) Correct – This performs an inner join on the 'ID' column of both DataFrames.

B) Incorrect – This performs an outer join, not an inner join.

C) Incorrect – This performs a left join instead of an inner join.

D) Incorrect – The join() method requires indexes to be aligned for joining, and it doesn't use 'ID'.

E) Incorrect – append() concatenates DataFrames, not merge them on a column.

EXAM FOCUS	*Use pd.merge() with the on parameter to join DataFrames based on common columns. how='inner' performs an inner join, excluding unmatched records.*
CAUTION ALERT	*Don't confuse merge() with join(). join() works based on DataFrame indexes, while merge() joins on specific columns.*

QUESTION 9

Answer - A, E

A) Correct: Both accuracy_score and confusion_matrix are used for classification metrics.

B) Incorrect: Precision is relevant but not part of the question.

C) Incorrect: Accuracy requires true labels and predictions.

D) Incorrect: Confusion matrix requires y_test, not X_test.

E) Correct: Precision can complement the accuracy metric for further analysis.

EXAM FOCUS	*When evaluating a classification model, compute accuracy_score and confusion_matrix to understand overall performance and the distribution of errors.*
CAUTION ALERT	*Don't mix up X and y when calculating confusion matrix. It always compares true labels (y_test) with predictions (y_pred).*

QUESTION 10

Answer - A, B

A) Correct: This is the basic syntax for using distplot, which includes both a histogram and a KDE by default, making it useful for visualizing distributions.

B) Correct: kde=False disables the KDE, leaving only the histogram for those who prefer pure histograms without density estimates.

C) Incorrect: Disabling histograms and only showing KDE might hide important data trends if not used correctly in certain data sets.

D) Incorrect: catplot is meant for categorical variables, and not for continuous data distributions like distplot visualizes.

E) Incorrect: kdeplot only plots density estimations, but it's not equivalent to distplot, which also includes a histogram.

EXAM FOCUS	*Seaborn's distplot() is deprecated. Use histplot() for histograms and kdeplot() for density plots. Disable KDE or hist when not required.*
CAUTION ALERT	*Avoid relying on deprecated functions like distplot() as it can cause compatibility issues with newer versions of Seaborn.*

QUESTION 11

Answer - A, C

A) Hashing customer identifiers ensures anonymization while preserving uniqueness.
B) Dropping the customer ID will result in data loss, not anonymization.
C) Masking part of the customer ID can retain some usefulness in tracking.
D) Replacing values with 'Unknown' may result in data ambiguity.
E) This replaces numerical data but does not fully anonymize.

EXAM FOCUS	*Anonymizing data with hash() or partially masking sensitive data helps comply with GDPR while preserving data integrity for analysis.*
CAUTION ALERT	*Be cautious when replacing sensitive data with ambiguous values like 'Unknown' or deleting it, as this may lead to loss of valuable information.*

QUESTION 12

Answer - A, C

A) Encrypted backups ensure data security and protect user data under both GDPR and CCPA.
B) Sharing feedback data without user consent breaches GDPR and CCPA.
C) Providing a user-facing API that supports data access, deletion, and modification ensures compliance with user rights.
D) Storing data indefinitely without deletion options violates GDPR and CCPA's right to erasure.
E) Anonymizing data is helpful but should be accompanied by explicit consent and deletion options.

EXAM FOCUS	*An encrypted backup system (cryptography or ssl) and an API to manage user data are vital for GDPR/CCPA compliance in customer feedback collection.*
CAUTION ALERT	*Do not share feedback data with third parties without explicit user consent, as it violates both GDPR and CCPA requirements.*

QUESTION 13

Answer - A, C

A) Correct, sets allow O(1) membership testing.
B) Lists have O(n) complexity for membership testing.
C) Correct, dictionaries also offer O(1) membership testing.
D) Tuples are immutable and inefficient for testing.
E) Arrays don't optimize for membership testing.

EXAM FOCUS	*Use sets and dictionaries for fast membership testing. Both have O(1) lookup time, making them ideal for efficiently handling unique values.*

QUESTION 14

Answer - A, B

A) Correct: This performs an inner join on 'product_id'.
B) Correct: This performs an outer join, ensuring all entries are merged.
C) Incorrect: left_on is not enough without specifying right_on.
D) Incorrect: join requires an index-based merge.
E) Incorrect: concat combines dataframes side by side, not by keys.

EXAM FOCUS	*When merging datasets, pd.merge() is flexible for key-based joins, while join() is index-based and not ideal for column-based merges.*
CAUTION ALERT	*Don't use concat() for merging by key; it stacks datasets but doesn't align based on columns.*

QUESTION 15

Answer - A, C

Option A: Correct – Drops rows where 'Price' is missing and exports to CSV.
Option B: Incorrect – Fills missing values instead of dropping them.
Option C: Correct – Filters out rows where 'Price' is null and exports correctly.
Option D: Incorrect – Drops rows with any missing values, which is not the requirement.
Option E: Incorrect – Drops the entire 'Price' column, which is incorrect.

EXAM FOCUS	*Use df.dropna() to remove rows with missing values and to_csv() for exporting cleaned data. This ensures data quality in exported reports.*
CAUTION ALERT	*Avoid using fillna(0) when dealing with missing price data, as filling with zeros can distort analysis.*

QUESTION 16

Answer - A, C, D

Option A: Correct – Counts even and odd numbers, prints values, and returns the counts.
Option B: Incorrect – Returns the correct counts but does not print anything.
Option C: Correct – Returns the counts as a dictionary, which is acceptable.
Option D: Correct – Efficiently uses a dictionary to store and return the counts.
Option E: Incorrect – Does not print whether the number is even or odd.

EXAM FOCUS	*Use dictionaries or counters to store results of even and odd counts for efficient processing and returning results in Python functions.*
CAUTION ALERT	*Ensure that the function prints even and odd values as required, while maintaining count logic inside the loop.*

QUESTION 17

Answer - A, C

Option A: Correct – StandardScaler() is the correct tool from Scikit-learn for standardization.
Option B: Incorrect – MinMaxScaler() is used for normalization, not standardization.
Option C: Correct – This manually standardizes the dataset by subtracting the mean and dividing by the standard deviation.
Option D: Incorrect – This applies the function row-wise and may not achieve the desired standardization for all columns.
Option E: Incorrect – Dividing by the standard deviation alone is not full standardization.

EXAM FOCUS	Scikit-learn's StandardScaler() is a key tool for machine learning preprocessing to standardize features, ensuring consistency in feature scaling.
CAUTION ALERT	Avoid using MinMaxScaler when standardization is required; MinMaxScaler is for normalization, which has different scaling requirements.

QUESTION 18

Answer - B, D

Option A: Incorrect – A single script may lead to poor maintainability as the project grows.
Option B: Correct – Organizing code into specific modules based on functionality is a best practice for maintainability and clarity.
Option C: Incorrect – Combining all tasks in one module defeats the purpose of modularity.
Option D: Correct – Having a main script that calls functions from well-separated modules follows best practices for Python projects.
Option E: Incorrect – A single script approach can become unmanageable as the project scales.

EXAM FOCUS	Modularization helps: Organizing code into separate, task-specific modules makes it scalable, easier to maintain, and easier to debug in the future.
CAUTION ALERT	Avoid combining everything: Combining data processing, visualization, and modeling into a single module makes the code harder to maintain and understand as it grows.

QUESTION 19

Answer - B, C

Option A: Incorrect – Simply raising the error without a custom message does not provide enough context.
Option B: Correct – Raises a custom exception message while retaining the original exception for context.
Option C: Correct – Raises a DatabaseError with a custom error message.
Option D: Incorrect – Prints the error but doesn't modify or customize the exception message.
Option E: Incorrect – A ValueError is not appropriate for database-related issues.

EXAM FOCUS	Custom exception messages matter: When raising exceptions, always provide context-specific error messages to make debugging easier and more meaningful.
CAUTION ALERT	Use appropriate exceptions: Don't raise unrelated exceptions like ValueError for database issues; stick to relevant exceptions like DatabaseError.

QUESTION 20

Answer - A, C

Option A: Correct – Correctly updates the total_purchase for the customer with customer_id = 101.
Option B: Incorrect – Missing a WHERE clause, which would update all records, not just for customer 101.

Option C: Correct – This query works, but the customer_id is unnecessarily enclosed in quotes, which is redundant for an integer.
Option D: Incorrect – The total_purchase is quoted as a string, which is incorrect for a numeric value.
Option E: Incorrect – Missing the SET keyword in the UPDATE statement.

EXAM FOCUS	*Always use a WHERE clause: When updating records, ensure the query contains a WHERE clause to avoid updating all rows in the table unintentionally.*
CAUTION ALERT	*Quote carefully: Quoting numbers as strings ('101') works but is unnecessary. Use proper data types to maintain clean, efficient queries.*

QUESTION 21

Answer - A, C

Option A: Correct – Uses ? placeholders for a parameterized query and ensures secure handling.
Option B: Incorrect – Concatenating strings for SQL statements allows for SQL injection attacks.
Option C: Correct – Uses named parameters (:total and :id), which is secure and efficient.
Option D: Incorrect – The query structure is incorrect (AND should not be used when updating a single record).
Option E: Incorrect – Hardcoding the total_purchase value makes the query inflexible, and the placeholders should apply to both parameters.

EXAM FOCUS	*Update with parameters: Always use parameterized queries for UPDATE statements to ensure that user inputs are handled securely and efficiently.*
CAUTION ALERT	*No concatenation: Concatenating strings into queries can expose your application to SQL injection and should always be avoided.*

QUESTION 22

Answer - A, C

Option A: Correct – Granting only the necessary permissions ensures the principle of least privilege.
Option B: Incorrect – Granting all permissions, especially DELETE, is against the least privilege principle.
Option C: Correct – Using role-based access limits privileges to only what the application needs.
Option D: Incorrect – Using a superuser role violates the least privilege principle and creates security risks.
Option E: Incorrect – While better than using a superuser, it's inefficient and may cause management challenges.

EXAM FOCUS	*Least privilege principle: Assign only the necessary permissions for users accessing the database to minimize security risks and prevent unauthorized changes.*
CAUTION ALERT	*Avoid granting global permissions: Giving superuser or global permissions violates the least privilege principle and increases the risk of security breaches.*

QUESTION 23

Answer - B, D

Option A: Incorrect – The single underscore _salary indicates a protected attribute, not fully private.
Option B: Correct – Double underscores make __salary private and not accessible directly outside the class.
Option C: Incorrect – This does not enforce encapsulation; salary is publicly accessible.
Option D: Correct – This makes the __salary attribute private and uses a getter method for access.
Option E: Incorrect – The single underscore in _get_salary() does not imply full encapsulation.

EXAM FOCUS	Use double underscores (__) for private attributes: To enforce encapsulation, use double underscores to restrict access to class variables.
CAUTION ALERT	Avoid public variables: Public variables (those without an underscore) can be accessed and modified freely, violating encapsulation principles.

QUESTION 24

Answer - B

Option A: Incorrect – f.read() loads the entire file into memory, which is inefficient for large files.
Option B: Correct – This reads the file line by line without loading it all into memory, which is efficient.
Option C: Incorrect – f.readlines() reads all lines at once into memory, which is not memory-efficient for large files.
Option D: Incorrect – Similar to option C, it reads the entire file at once.
Option E: Incorrect – Using r+ mode is unnecessary here and does not efficiently handle line-by-line reading.

EXAM FOCUS	Read large files line by line: For large files, read them line by line using for line in f to save memory instead of reading the entire file at once.
CAUTION ALERT	Avoid readlines() for large files: Using readlines() or read() loads the entire file into memory, which is inefficient for large files and may cause memory issues.

QUESTION 25

Answer - A, C

A) Correct: This defines and raises the custom exception with an error message and handles it properly.
B) Incorrect: While this defines a custom error, inheriting from TypeError is unnecessary when a specific custom error is preferred.
C) Correct: This raises and handles the custom exception correctly.
D) Incorrect: The ValueError inheritance is unnecessary and doesn't align with custom exception handling best practices.
E) Incorrect: Raising a generic TypeError with a string doesn't define a custom exception, which defeats the purpose of creating a custom error.

EXAM FOCUS	Use super() for flexibility: In custom exception handling, using super() allows for better inheritance and ensures the correct behavior of built-in exception methods.
CAUTION ALERT	Avoid manual message assignment: Manually assigning the message attribute may lead to mistakes—use super().__init__(message) for better consistency.

QUESTION 26

Answer - A

Option A: Correct, LEFT JOIN retrieves all products even without categories.
Option B: Incorrect, INNER JOIN excludes products without categories.
Option C: Incorrect, RIGHT JOIN prioritizes categories, not products.
Option D: Incorrect, CROSS JOIN gives a Cartesian product of both tables.
Option E: Incorrect, FULL JOIN includes all categories, which is unnecessary here.

EXAM FOCUS	Use LEFT JOIN for missing categories: When some products might not have a category, LEFT JOIN ensures that all products are listed, even if their category is missing.

QUESTION 27

Answer - A

Option A: Correct, a PRIMARY KEY ensures that employee_id is both unique and not null.
Option B: Incorrect, FOREIGN KEY does not ensure uniqueness or null checks.
Option C: Incorrect, UNIQUE enforces uniqueness but doesn't guarantee the column is not null.
Option D: Incorrect, CHECK (employee_id IS NOT NULL) enforces not null but doesn't ensure uniqueness.
Option E: Incorrect, adding an index doesn't enforce uniqueness or not null constraints.

EXAM FOCUS	*PRIMARY KEY ensures uniqueness and non-null: A PRIMARY KEY constraint automatically ensures that values are unique and not null, which is ideal for identifiers like employee_id.*
CAUTION ALERT	*UNIQUE and CHECK constraints aren't equivalent to PRIMARY KEY: UNIQUE ensures distinct values but allows nulls, and CHECK only enforces a condition without ensuring uniqueness.*

QUESTION 28

Answer - A

Option A: Correct, clustered indexes store data in sorted order, and non-clustered indexes store pointers to the data.
Option B: Incorrect, it is the opposite—clustered indexes store data physically, and non-clustered store pointers.
Option C: Incorrect, only one clustered index can be created per table.
Option D: Incorrect, storage requirements depend on the index type and data, not simply non-clustered vs. clustered.
Option E: Incorrect, non-clustered indexes generally slow down INSERT operations due to additional overhead.

EXAM FOCUS	*Clustered vs. non-clustered indexes: A clustered index organizes physical data in order, while a non-clustered index stores pointers to the data without altering its physical order.*
CAUTION ALERT	*Only one clustered index per table: Keep in mind that a table can only have one clustered index due to its physical data arrangement.*

QUESTION 29

Answer - B

Option A: Incorrect, mean is influenced by outliers and may not represent the typical data point.
Option B: Correct, the median is resistant to outliers and provides a better central measure when outliers are present.
Option C: Incorrect, mode is useful for categorical data but not for continuous data with outliers.
Option D: Incorrect, np.mean() is also affected by outliers.
Option E: Incorrect, this is a manual way to compute the mean, which still gets affected by outliers.

EXAM FOCUS	*Median for data with outliers: The median is often the best measure of central tendency when extreme values (outliers) are present in the dataset.*
CAUTION ALERT	*Mode works better for categorical data: Use mode for categorical or discrete data, not for continuous data when there are outliers.*

QUESTION 30

Answer - C

Option A: Incorrect, the mean is not a measure of spread.
Option B: Incorrect, standard deviation alone may not provide enough insight in skewed data.
Option C: Correct, variance is a good measure of spread to compare skewed distributions.
Option D: Incorrect, range does not consider the shape of the data.
Option E: Incorrect, mean does not represent spread.

EXAM FOCUS	*Variance captures spread in skewed distributions: Variance is useful when comparing spread in skewed datasets, providing better insight into variability than standard deviation alone.*
CAUTION ALERT	*Standard deviation alone may not be enough for skewed data: In skewed datasets, variance offers a broader perspective on data variability compared to just standard deviation.*

QUESTION 31

Answer - A, E

Option A: Correct, resample() from sklearn.utils allows bootstrapping by resampling with replacement.
Option B: Incorrect, no bootstrap method in sklearn.
Option C: Incorrect, replace=False does not allow bootstrapping.
Option D: Incorrect, NumPy choice is not efficient for model validation.
Option E: Correct, cross_val_score() with resampled data validates the model.

EXAM FOCUS	*Use bootstrapping for model validation: sklearn.utils.resample helps resample the dataset with replacement. Combine with cross_val_score() for model validation with bootstrapped data.*
CAUTION ALERT	*Avoid replace=False when bootstrapping: Always use replace=True to ensure proper bootstrapping. Otherwise, the sample won't reflect the original dataset.*

QUESTION 32

Answer - A

Option A: Correct, a positive coefficient implies that as the balance increases, the likelihood of the event (churn) increases.
Option B: Incorrect, a positive coefficient increases likelihood, not decreases it.
Option C: Incorrect, coefficients in logistic regression indicate the impact of the feature.
Option D: Incorrect, the relationship is assumed to be linear in logistic regression.
Option E: Incorrect, one-hot encoding is for categorical variables, not numerical.

EXAM FOCUS	*Positive coefficient interpretation: In logistic regression, a positive coefficient means that as the feature increases, the likelihood of the target class (event) also increases.*
CAUTION ALERT	*Don't confuse coefficient signs: A negative coefficient means the probability of the event decreases, while a positive one increases the probability.*

QUESTION 33

Answer - A, B, C

A) Correct: This applies the IQR method with the correct formula for identifying outliers
B) Correct: This calculates the IQR manually and applies it to detect outliers

C) Correct: This uses the standard deviation to identify extreme outliers
D) Incorrect: Using the median for outlier detection is incorrect
E) Incorrect: Median multiplied by 1.5 is not a valid method for detecting outliers.

EXAM FOCUS	IQR is robust for outlier detection: The Interquartile Range (IQR) is a robust way to detect outliers in a dataset, especially when the data is skewed.
CAUTION ALERT	Standard deviation vs. IQR: Don't rely solely on standard deviation for outlier detection when data is skewed; the IQR method is more reliable for identifying extreme values.

QUESTION 34

Answer - A, C

A) Correct: .sum() is a valid aggregation function in NumPy that returns the sum of all the elements in the array.
B) Incorrect: While .mean() is a valid aggregation function, specifying axis=0 may not always be applicable depending on the shape of the array. For a 1D array, axis does not apply.
C) Correct: .var() is the correct function for calculating the variance of the array, which is a valid aggregation function in NumPy.
D) Incorrect: arr.median() is not a valid function in NumPy. The correct function for calculating the median is np.median(arr).
E) Incorrect: .max() is a valid function, but the use of axis=1 will throw an error if the array is 1D or its shape is not aligned with this axis.

EXAM FOCUS	Aggregation functions in NumPy: Use functions like .sum(), .mean(), and .var() to efficiently perform aggregation operations on arrays.
CAUTION ALERT	Correct function for median: Unlike other operations, use np.median(arr) to calculate the median. arr.median() will raise an error.

QUESTION 35

Answer - A, B, D

A) Correct: plt.boxplot() can be used to create a simple boxplot of the salary column.
B) Correct: Using Seaborn's sns.boxplot() provides a more flexible way to plot a boxplot.
C) Incorrect: plt.plot() is for line plots, not for boxplots, and this will result in an error.
D) Correct: Pandas' built-in plotting functionality allows for boxplots using plot(kind='box').
E) Incorrect: plt.boxplot() does not take x=df['salary'] as a valid input; this will raise an error.

EXAM FOCUS	Use Seaborn or Matplotlib for visualizations: Both libraries provide simple commands like sns.boxplot() and plt.boxplot() for creating boxplots.
CAUTION ALERT	Avoid mixing functions: plt.plot() is for line plots, not boxplots. Always use the correct plotting function depending on the chart type.

QUESTION 36

Answer - A, C

A) Correct: L2 regularization reduces overfitting by penalizing large coefficients.
B) Incorrect: Reducing the training size may lead to underfitting, not overfitting.
C) Correct: Early stopping halts training when the performance on the validation set stops improving, preventing overfitting.

D) Incorrect: Removing the validation set eliminates a key check for overfitting.

E) Incorrect: Increasing the depth of a decision tree makes it more prone to overfitting.

EXAM FOCUS	Prevent overfitting: Apply L2 regularization (Ridge) and early stopping to prevent your model from overfitting the training data.
CAUTION ALERT	Avoid harmful actions: Reducing the training data size or removing validation sets can worsen model performance, leading to underfitting or poor generalization.

QUESTION 37

Answer - B

A) Incorrect – A higher R-squared can indicate better fit, but it can also mean the model is overfitting. Other factors such as residuals should also be considered.

B) Correct – R-squared is a measure of fit but does not guarantee that the model generalizes well, particularly if it leads to overfitting.

EXAM FOCUS	High R-squared can indicate overfitting: A high R-squared value is not always a good sign. Check residuals and cross-validate to ensure the model generalizes well.
CAUTION ALERT	Beware of overfitting: Don't assume that high R-squared always equals a better model. Overfitting can occur, especially with too many features or insufficient data.

QUESTION 38

Answer - B

A) Incorrect – Grouped objects need to be converted to DataFrame or series before they can be visualized.

B) Correct – Grouped objects cannot be directly visualized using Matplotlib without further conversion to a DataFrame or Series.

EXAM FOCUS	Convert grouped objects before plotting: When visualizing grouped data, first convert the groupby object into a DataFrame or Series before passing it to Matplotlib or other visualization libraries.
CAUTION ALERT	Grouped objects can't be plotted directly: Groupby objects need conversion into DataFrames or Series for plotting. Direct plotting of grouped objects without conversion will raise errors.

QUESTION 39

Answer - B

A) Incorrect as the scenario described is an example of overfitting, where the model captures noise and complexities of the training data but performs poorly on new data.

B) Correct because the description provided fits the definition of overfitting, not underfitting. Underfitting occurs when a model is too simple and fails to capture the patterns in the data.

EXAM FOCUS	Overfitting Clarification: Overfitting happens when the model fits noise and details in the training data but struggles with unseen data. Combat it with techniques like regularization.
CAUTION ALERT	Overfitting ≠ Underfitting: Don't confuse overfitting with underfitting. Overfitting occurs when the model is too complex, while underfitting happens when the model is too simple.

QUESTION 40

Answer - A

A) Correct because histograms are designed to show the distribution of numerical data by splitting the data into bins and plotting the frequency of values in each bin, making them effective for understanding data distribution.
B) Incorrect because histograms are, in fact, the most common and appropriate method for visualizing distributions of numerical data, so the statement is not false.

EXAM FOCUS	*Histograms for Distribution: Histograms are perfect for visualizing the distribution of numerical data by grouping values into bins and showing frequency.*
CAUTION ALERT	*Histogram Misuse: Avoid using histograms for categorical data. They are designed for continuous numerical variables, not categorical or discrete data.*

QUESTION 41

Answer - A

A) Correct because plt.scatter() is indeed the correct function in Matplotlib to generate a scatter plot for visualizing the relationship between two numerical variables such as height and weight.
B) Incorrect because plt.scatter() is the proper function for creating scatter plots, so this statement is not false.

EXAM FOCUS	*Scatter Plot Insight: Always use plt.scatter() to plot the relationship between two numerical variables like height and weight. This helps reveal correlations.*
CAUTION ALERT	*Function Confusion: Don't mistake plt.plot() for plt.scatter(). plt.plot() is used for continuous data trends, while plt.scatter() focuses on discrete points.*

QUESTION 42

Answer - A

A) Correct because plt.legend(loc='upper left', frameon=True, facecolor='lightgray') correctly positions the legend in the upper left and changes the background to light gray.
B) Incorrect because backgroundcolor is not a valid argument; it should be facecolor for legend background color.
C) Incorrect because position is not a valid argument for plt.legend(); the correct argument is loc.
D) Incorrect because bg is not a valid argument for background color in Matplotlib.
E) Incorrect because loc='top' is invalid; valid values include upper left, upper right, etc.

EXAM FOCUS	*Legend Positioning Tip: plt.legend(loc='upper left', frameon=True, facecolor='lightgray') properly adjusts the legend's position and background color for better visualization.*
CAUTION ALERT	*Positioning Error: Don't use backgroundcolor or position in plt.legend(). Always use loc and facecolor for setting legend placement and color.*

QUESTION 43

Answer - D, E

A) Incorrect because plotting individual categories without visual distinctions might confuse the audience.
B) Incorrect because adding one more category does not help simplify or make the chart clearer.
C) Incorrect because although adjusting the legend font helps readability, it does not directly simplify the chart for executives.
D) Correct because using distinct colors and line styles makes it easier for the audience to differentiate between

categories.

E) Correct because adding a y-axis label ensures that the audience understands the metric being visualized.

EXAM FOCUS	*Chart Simplification: Use distinct line styles or colors like linestyle='--', color='green' for better differentiation in line plots. Add axis labels for clarity.*
CAUTION ALERT	*Line Plot Confusion: Avoid plotting multiple categories without visual distinction (colors/line styles). This may confuse the audience, especially in executive presentations.*

QUESTION 44

Answer - A, D

A) Correct because plotting the revenue with annotation on key points ensures that spikes and dips are highlighted, aligning with the need to emphasize seasonal trends.

B) Incorrect because presenting the plot without annotations or labels diminishes the clarity of the seasonal narrative.

C) Incorrect because scatter plots are not as effective as line charts in showing continuous data, especially in revenue over time.

D) Correct because using a bar chart with added text can also effectively highlight the spikes and dips in the narrative.

E) Incorrect because pie charts don't represent time-based trends well.

EXAM FOCUS	*Revenue Trends: Use plt.annotate() to label seasonal spikes and dips in revenue, reinforcing trends and making it easier for non-technical audiences to understand fluctuations.*
CAUTION ALERT	*Scatter Plots for Trends: Scatter plots are not ideal for visualizing trends over time. Stick with line or bar plots to represent changes and highlight key points.*

QUESTION 45

Answer - C

A) Incorrect because while a line plot shows the growth, it doesn't clearly highlight the highest and lowest sign-ups.

B) Incorrect because a box plot is more useful for showing the distribution of data, but not for summarizing the overall growth pattern month by month.

C) Correct because a bar plot provides a clear summary of the monthly growth and effectively highlights the months with the highest and lowest sign-ups.

D) Incorrect because a histogram doesn't provide a clear summary of monthly changes.

E) Incorrect because a violin plot is too complex and doesn't summarize growth over time effectively.

EXAM FOCUS	*Use Bar Charts for Growth: When presenting monthly changes like customer sign-ups, bar charts provide a clear visual of the highest and lowest values, offering an easy-to-read summary.*
CAUTION ALERT	*Box Plot Misuse: Avoid box plots for showing monthly changes or growth trends. Box plots are better for showing data distributions rather than specific changes over time.*

PRACTICE TEST 4 - QUESTIONS ONLY

QUESTION 1

You have been tasked with analyzing a dataset on customer orders. You need to calculate the average order amount grouped by customer type. Which Python code using Pandas would allow you to group the data by customer_type and calculate the average order_amount?

```
 A)
df.groupby('customer_type')['order_amount']
.mean()
 B) df.groupby('customer_type').sum()
 C) df.pivot_table(index='customer_type',
values='order_amount', aggfunc='mean')
 D)
df.groupby('customer_type').agg({'order_amo
unt': 'mean'})
 E) df.mean('order_amount')
```

QUESTION 2

You are working on standardizing data formats across different datasets. One dataset stores dates in the format MM/DD/YYYY and another in DD-MM-YYYY. Which Python code snippets will correctly standardize these date formats to YYYY-MM-DD for consistency? (Select 2 answers)

```
 A) df['date'] = pd.to_datetime(df['date'],
format='%m/%d/%Y')
 B) df['date'] = pd.to_datetime(df['date'],
format='%d-%m-%Y')
 C) df['date'] =
pd.to_datetime(df['date']).dt.strftime('%Y-
%m-%d')
 D) df['date'] = df['date'].str.replace('-
', '/')
 E) df['date'] =
df['date'].astype('datetime64')
```

QUESTION 3

You are storing both structured sales data and unstructured product review data in a cloud storage solution. Which storage method is NOT ideal for handling both data types?

A) A cloud-based data lake
B) A traditional relational database

C) Cloud object storage like Amazon S3
D) A data warehouse optimized for SQL queries
E) A hybrid storage solution combining relational and NoSQL databases

QUESTION 4

Which of the following methods is NOT a recommended approach for detecting or handling outliers in a dataset?

A) Use Z-score to detect outliers
B) Use IQR to identify outliers
C) Remove rows with outliers
D) Normalize outliers using Min-Max scaling
E) Impute outliers with the mean value

QUESTION 5

You are validating a dataset by cross-referencing two tables: employees and departments. The department_id column in the employees table must match valid department_id values in the departments table. Which approach would NOT be appropriate for validating the department_id column?

A) Use pd.merge() to cross-reference the tables based on department_id
B) Use SQL JOIN queries to cross-reference the two tables
C) Use df['department_id'].isin(df_departments['department_id'])
D) Use df['department_id'].fillna('Unknown') to fill missing values
E) Use validate() function to ensure data integrity between the tables

QUESTION 6

You are trying to retrieve only distinct values from a column called job_title in the employees table. Which SQL query would NOT be appropriate for this task?

```
 A) SELECT DISTINCT job_title FROM
```

```
employees
 B) SELECT * FROM employees WHERE job_title
IS NOT NULL
 C) SELECT job_title FROM employees GROUP
BY job_title
 D) SELECT DISTINCT job_title FROM
employees WHERE job_title = 'Manager'
 E) SELECT job_title, COUNT(*) FROM
employees GROUP BY job_title
```

QUESTION 7

You are tasked with visualizing the relationship between two variables in a dataset using a scatter plot with a regression line. Which of the following Seaborn methods can be used to accomplish this task?

```
A) import seaborn as sns
sns.regplot(x='var1', y='var2', data=df)

 B) import seaborn as sns
sns.lineplot(x='var1', y='var2', data=df)

 C) import seaborn as sns
sns.lmplot(x='var1', y='var2', data=df)

 D) import matplotlib.pyplot as plt
plt.scatter(x='var1', y='var2')

 E) import seaborn as sns
sns.boxplot(x='var1', y='var2', data=df)
```

QUESTION 8

Which of the following Pandas code snippets correctly identifies and drops duplicate rows from a DataFrame based on a specific column?

```
A) import pandas as pd
df = df.drop_duplicates(subset=['Column1'],
keep='first')

 B) import pandas as pd
df.drop(subset=['Column1'], inplace=True)

 C) import pandas as pd
df.drop_duplicates(keep='last')

 D) import pandas as pd
df = df.drop_duplicates(subset=['Column1'])

 E) import pandas as pd
df = df.drop(subset='Column1')
```

QUESTION 9

While using K-Means clustering, you find that some clusters are empty. How can this issue be addressed? Select 2 correct options.

```
A) max_iter=1000
B) random_state=42
C) init='random'
D) n_init=10
E) increase n_clusters=5
```

QUESTION 10

You are asked to create a box plot to visualize the distribution of multiple categories. Which steps are correct? Select 2 correct options.

```
A) sns.boxplot(x="category", y="value",
data=df)
B) sns.boxplot(x="value", y="category",
data=df)
C) sns.catplot(x="category", y="value",
kind="box", data=df)
D) sns.boxplot(x="value", data=df)
E) sns.boxplot(y="value", data=df)
```

QUESTION 11

You need to ensure that the collected survey data is aligned with business strategy goals, and you need to clean the dataset using Python. How would you handle missing data and ensure data quality? (Select 2 correct answers)

```
 A) df.interpolate()
 B) df.drop_duplicates()
 C) df.dropna(subset=['important_column'])
 D) df.fillna(method='bfill')
 E) df.apply(pd.to_numeric)
```

QUESTION 12

In a Python-based web application collecting user data, how can you ensure compliance with GDPR and avoid legal penalties? (Select 2 correct answers)

 A) Implement a Python-based form to explicitly ask users for consent before collecting any personal data
 B) Allow users to view, edit, or request the deletion of their data using a Python-based user portal
 C) Collect and store user data without informing them of its intended use
 D) Transfer data to third-party partners without notifying users
 E) Encrypt all stored data using Python libraries such as pycryptodome

QUESTION 13

You have a dataset with missing values in multiple columns. You want to fill missing values using the mean of each column. Which of the following scripts would you use? (Select 2 answers)

```
A)  df.fillna(df.mean())
B)  df.interpolate()
C)  df.fillna(df.median())
D)  df.fillna(method='ffill')
E)  df.dropna()
```

QUESTION 14

You are working with sales data and need to group the data by 'region' and apply a custom function that calculates the percentage of total sales for each region. Which of the following approaches would work best? Select 2 correct answers.

```
A) df.groupby('region').apply(lambda x:
x['sales'].sum()/df['sales'].sum())
B)
df.groupby('region')['sales'].apply(lambda
x: x.sum()/df['sales'].sum())
C)
df.groupby('region')['sales'].transform(lam
bda x: x / df['sales'].sum())
D)
df.groupby('region')['sales'].sum().apply(l
ambda x: x / df['sales'].sum())
E) df.groupby('region').agg({'sales':
lambda x: x.sum() / df['sales'].sum()})
```

QUESTION 15

You need to create a summary table showing the mean, median, and standard deviation of sales data for a report. Which methods in Python using Pandas should you use to calculate and display these statistics? (Select 2 answers)

```
A) df.describe()
B) df[['Sales']].agg(['mean', 'median',
'std'])
C) df.groupby('Product').mean()
D) df.pivot_table(values='Sales',
aggfunc=['mean', 'median', 'std'])
E) df.agg({'Sales': ['mean', 'median',
'std']})
```

QUESTION 16

You are building a report and need to calculate the cumulative sum of sales for each month using a loop. Which code structures correctly calculate this cumulative sum using Python? (Select 2 answers)

```
A) df['Cumulative_Sales'] =
df['Sales'].cumsum()
B) cumulative_sales = 0 for i, row in
df.iterrows(): cumulative_sales +=
row['Sales'] df.at[i, 'Cumulative_Sales'] =
cumulative_sales
C) df['Cumulative_Sales'] =
df.apply(lambda x: x['Sales'].cumsum())
D) df['Cumulative_Sales'] =
[sum(df['Sales'][:i+1]) for i in
range(len(df))]
E) df['Cumulative_Sales'] =
df['Sales'].rolling(window=len(df),
min_periods=1).sum()
```

QUESTION 17

You are importing several Python libraries to perform data analysis, including Pandas, NumPy, and Scikit-learn. However, the libraries are not installed in your Python environment. How can you install and manage these packages effectively? (Select 2 answers)

```
A) !pip install pandas numpy scikit-learn
B) import pandas as pd;
pd.install(['numpy', 'scikit-learn'])
C) !conda install pandas numpy scikit-
learn
D) import os; os.system('pip install
pandas numpy scikit-learn')
E) from pandas import install;
install('numpy', 'scikit-learn')
```

QUESTION 18

You are implementing error handling in your data acquisition script to ensure it runs smoothly when accessing an external API. What are the best practices for handling potential errors in your script? (Select 2 answers)

```
A) try: data = get_data(api_url) except:
pass
B) try: data = get_data(api_url) except
Exception as e: print(E)   C) try: data =
get_data(api_url) except Exception:
print("Error fetching data.")
D) try: data = get_data(api_url) except
```

```
KeyError: print("KeyError encountered.")
 E) try: data = get_data(api_url) except
(KeyError, ValueError): print("An error
occurred.")
```

QUESTION 19

Your Python script connects to an API, and you want
to implement exception handling to retry the
request if it fails due to network issues. How would
you implement this functionality? (Select 2 answers)

```
A) for i in range(3):
try:
response = get_api_data()
break
except ConnectionError:
print("Retrying...")

 B) attempts = 0
while attempts < 3:
try:
response = get_api_data()
break
except ConnectionError:
attempts += 1
print("Retrying...")

 C) for attempt in range(3):
try:
response = get_api_data()
except ConnectionError:
if attempt == 2:
raise

 D) try:
response = get_api_data()
except ConnectionError:
print("Retrying request...")
raise

 E) attempts = 0
while attempts < 3:
try:
response = get_api_data()
attempts += 1
except ConnectionError:
print("Retrying...")
```

QUESTION 20

You need to delete a record from the customers
table where the customer_id is 101. Which SQL
query correctly removes the record? (Select 2
answers)

```
A) DELETE FROM customers
WHERE customer_id = 101;

 B) DELETE FROM customers
```

```
WHERE total_purchase = 200.00;

 C) DELETE customers
WHERE customer_id = 101;

 D) DELETE FROM customers
WHERE customer_name = 'John Doe';

 E) DELETE FROM customers
WHERE customer_id IN (SELECT customer_id
FROM orders
WHERE total_purchase > 100);
```

QUESTION 21

You are creating a Python script to retrieve customer
records from the customers table, but the query is
dynamic and depends on user input for both
customer_name and total_purchase. Which Python
code correctly handles this scenario with
parameterized queries? (Select 2 answers)

```
A) import sqlite3
conn = sqlite3.connect('database.db')
cursor = conn.cursor()
cursor.execute("SELECT * FROM customers
WHERE customer_name = ? AND total_purchase
> ?", (customer_name, total_purchase))
rows = cursor.fetchall()

 B) import sqlite3
conn = sqlite3.connect('database.db')
cursor = conn.cursor()
query = "SELECT * FROM customers WHERE
customer_name = '" + customer_name + "' AND
total_purchase > " + str(total_purchase)
cursor.execute(query)
rows = cursor.fetchall()

 C) import sqlite3
conn = sqlite3.connect('database.db')
cursor = conn.cursor()
cursor.execute("SELECT * FROM customers
WHERE customer_name = :name AND
total_purchase > :purchase", {'name':
customer_name, 'purchase': total_purchase})
rows = cursor.fetchall()

 D) import sqlite3
conn = sqlite3.connect('database.db')
cursor = conn.cursor()
cursor.execute("SELECT * FROM customers
WHERE customer_name = ? AND total_purchase
> ?", [customer_name, total_purchase])
rows = cursor.fetchall()

 E) import sqlite3
conn = sqlite3.connect('database.db')
cursor = conn.cursor()
query = f"SELECT * FROM customers WHERE
customer_name = '{customer_name}' AND
```

```
total_purchase > {total_purchase}"
cursor.execute(query)
rows = cursor.fetchall()
```

QUESTION 22

You are encrypting data in an SQL database using
Python to protect sensitive information. Which
techniques help ensure data confidentiality when
using SQL databases? (Select 2 answers)

A) Use parameterized queries to handle encrypted
data.
B) Enable encryption at rest in the database settings.
C) Use basic SQL commands to store plain-text
sensitive data.
D) Ensure encryption during data transmission (e.g.,
using SSL/TLS).
E) Rely on hashed values for storing sensitive fields,
like passwords.

QUESTION 23

You are tasked with implementing polymorphism
using method overriding. Which code snippets
demonstrate valid polymorphism in Python? (Select
2 answers)

```
A) class Employee:
def get_info(self):
return "Employee Info"
class Manager(Employee):
def get_info(self):
return "Manager Info"

B) class Employee:
def get_info(self):
return "Employee Info"
class Manager(Employee):
def get_details(self):
return "Manager Details"

C) class Employee:
def get_info(self):
return "Employee Info"
class Manager(Employee):
pass

D) class Employee:
def get_info(self):
return "Employee Info"
class Manager(Employee):
def get_info(self):
return super().get_info()

E) class Employee:
def get_info(self):
return "Employee Info"
```

```
class Manager(Employee):
def get_info(self, extra_info):
return "Manager Info: " + extra_info
```

QUESTION 24

You need to manipulate directories in a Python script
by checking if a directory exists and creating it if not.
Which of the following is the correct code to handle
this?

```
A) import os os.mkdir('data_folder')
B) import os if not
os.path.exists('data_folder'):
os.mkdir('data_folder')
C) import os os.makedirs('data_folder')
D) import os if
os.path.exists('data_folder'):
os.mkdir('data_folder')
E) import os if
os.path.isdir('data_folder'):
os.mkdir('data_folder')
```

QUESTION 25

In a data preprocessing pipeline, you need to raise a
custom exception when a required column is missing
in the dataset. How would you handle this using
Python's custom exception handling? (Select 2
correct answers)

```
A) class MissingColumnError(Exception):
def __init__(self, column):
super().__init__(f'Missing column:
{column}')
raise MissingColumnError('age')

B) class MissingColumnError(KeyError):
def __init__(self, column):
self.column = column
raise MissingColumnError('name')

C) try:
raise MissingColumnError('salary')
except KeyError:
print('Key missing')

D) class MissingColumnError(Exception):
raise MissingColumnError()
E) raise KeyError('Missing column').
```

QUESTION 26

You need to write a query to find employees who
have made more than 10 sales from the employees
and sales tables. What is the correct query? (Select 2
correct answers)

```
A) SELECT e.employee_name, COUNT(s.sale_id)
FROM employees e JOIN sales s ON
e.employee_id = s.employee_id GROUP BY
e.employee_id HAVING COUNT(s.sale_id) > 10;

B) SELECT e.employee_name FROM employees e
WHERE (SELECT COUNT(*) FROM sales s WHERE
s.employee_id = e.employee_id) > 10;

C) SELECT e.employee_name, s.sale_id FROM
employees e LEFT JOIN sales s ON
e.employee_id = s.employee_id WHERE
COUNT(s.sale_id) > 10;

D) SELECT e.employee_name, s.sale_id FROM
employees e INNER JOIN sales s ON
e.employee_id = s.employee_id WHERE
COUNT(s.sale_id) > 10;

E) SELECT e.employee_name FROM employees e
INNER JOIN sales s ON e.employee_id =
s.employee_id GROUP BY e.employee_id HAVING
COUNT(s.sale_id) > 10;
```

QUESTION 27

The projects table has a start_date column that should not allow any value in the future. Which SQL constraint would you apply? (Select 1 correct answer)

```
A) ALTER TABLE projects ADD CONSTRAINT
start_date_check CHECK (start_date <=
CURDATE());
B) ALTER TABLE projects ADD PRIMARY KEY
(start_date);
C) ALTER TABLE projects ADD FOREIGN KEY
(start_date) REFERENCES
calendar(start_date);
D) ALTER TABLE projects ADD DEFAULT
start_date = CURDATE();
E) ALTER TABLE projects ADD CONSTRAINT
UNIQUE (start_date);
```

QUESTION 28

When should you avoid creating an index on a table column? (Select 2 correct answers)

A) When the table has frequent UPDATE and DELETE operations.
B) When the column has high cardinality and is queried often.
C) When the column is frequently modified and is not used for filtering queries.
D) When the table has high query performance requirements.
E) When the column is frequently part of aggregate

queries.

QUESTION 29

When analyzing customer ages in a shopping dataset, you discover that the mean age is significantly higher than the median. What does this indicate about the distribution? (Select 1 correct answer)

A) Right-skewed distribution
B) Left-skewed distribution
C) Symmetric distribution
D) Normal distribution
E) Uniform distribution

QUESTION 30

In a manufacturing dataset, you have the processing times for two different production lines. If one line has higher variability than the other, what does this imply? (Select 1 correct answer)

A) The production times are more consistent in the line with higher variability
B) The production line with higher variability is more unpredictable
C) Both lines have similar consistency
D) The line with lower variability has less consistency
E) Variability has no impact on consistency

QUESTION 31

A data scientist is comparing two datasets: one representing a bootstrapped sample and the other representing the original data. What is the primary difference in the statistical properties of these two datasets? (Select 1 correct answer)

A) The bootstrapped sample has the same mean but a slightly higher variance
B) The bootstrapped sample has a lower mean and variance
C) The bootstrapped sample has a higher mean and variance
D) The bootstrapped sample has the same mean and variance
E) There is no difference between the bootstrapped sample and the original data

QUESTION 32

You are comparing logistic and linear regression models for a dataset. In which scenario is logistic regression preferred over linear regression? (Select 2 correct answers)

A) When predicting binary outcomes
B) When the relationship between variables is non-linear
C) When the dependent variable is continuous
D) When you are modeling the probability of an event occurring
E) When the dataset contains categorical predictors

QUESTION 33

You need to reshape a DataFrame 'df' that has columns for 'region', 'product', and 'sales'. You want to create a pivot table where 'region' is the index, 'product' is the columns, and 'sales' is the values. Which is the correct way to generate this pivot table? (Select 1 correct answer)

```
A) df.pivot(index='region',
columns='product', values='sales')
B) df.pivot(index='product',
columns='region', values='sales')
C) pd.pivot_table(df, index='region',
columns='product', values='sales',
aggfunc='sum')
D) df.groupby(['region',
'product'])['sales'].sum().unstack()
E) df.pivot_table(index='region',
columns='product', values='sales',
aggfunc='mean')
```

QUESTION 34

You have two large datasets, and you want to use NumPy for element-wise comparison between two arrays. Which of the following options demonstrates a correct comparison operation using NumPy? (Select 2 correct answers)

```
A) comparison = a == b
B) comparison = np.equal(a, b)
C) comparison = a >= b
D) comparison = a is b
E) comparison = np.logical_or(a, b)
```

QUESTION 35

You need to calculate variance and standard deviation of a numerical dataset using NumPy.

Which code correctly calculates these statistics? (Select 2 correct answers)

```
A) np.var(arr)
B) np.std(arr)
C) np.statistics(arr)
D) arr.variance()
E) np.calculate_variance(arr)
```

QUESTION 36

When training a logistic regression model in Python, how can you handle an imbalanced dataset to improve model performance? (Select 2 correct answers)

A) Use the class_weight='balanced' parameter
B) Reduce the number of instances from the majority class
C) Use a linear regression model instead
D) Oversample the minority class
E) Remove features until the dataset becomes balanced

QUESTION 37

Which is NOT a correct code for performing linear regression in Python using scikit-learn?

```
A) from sklearn.linear_model import
LinearRegression
 model = LinearRegression()
 model.fit(X_train, y_train)

 B) from sklearn.metrics import
mean_squared_error
 mse = mean_squared_error(y_test, y_preD)

C) from sklearn.linear_model import
LogisticRegression
 model = LogisticRegression()
 model.fit(X_train, y_train)

 D) from sklearn.metrics import r2_score
 r2 = r2_score(y_test, y_preD)

E) y_pred = model.predict(X_test)
```

QUESTION 38

You are tasked with grouping sales data by product category and calculating the sum of sales. However, one of the following approaches is incorrect. Which is NOT a valid method for grouping and aggregating?

```
A) df.groupby('category')['sales'].sum()
B) df.groupby('category').sum('sales')
```

```
 C)
df.groupby('category').agg({'sales':'sum'})
 D) df.groupby('category').apply(lambda x:
x['sales'].sum())
 E)
df.groupby('category')['sales'].agg('sum')
```

QUESTION 39

You are applying Ridge regression to a dataset to avoid overfitting. However, you want to find the optimal value of the regularization parameter alpha. Which method would NOT be a correct way to achieve this?

```
A) from sklearn.model_selection import
GridSearchCV; ridge = Ridge(); parameters =
{'alpha':[0.1, 1.0, 10.0]}; clf =
GridSearchCV(ridge, parameters); clf.fit(X,
y)
B) from sklearn.model_selection import
RandomizedSearchCV; ridge = Ridge();
parameters = {'alpha':[0.1, 1.0, 10.0]};
clf = RandomizedSearchCV(ridge,
parameters); clf.fit(X, y)
C) from sklearn.linear_model import Ridge;
ridge = Ridge(alpha=1.0); ridge.fit(X, y)
D) from sklearn.linear_model import
RidgeCV; ridge_cv = RidgeCV(alphas=[0.1,
1.0, 10.0]); ridge_cv.fit(X, y)
E) using cross_val_score with Ridge
regression and multiple alpha values`
```

QUESTION 40

You are creating a bar plot to compare the total sales of different products. Which of the following options is NOT a valid Matplotlib command for creating or enhancing a bar plot?

```
A) plt.bar(df['Product'], df['Sales'])
B) plt.title('Total Sales per Product')
C) plt.ylabel('Sales in USD')
D) plt.xticks(df['Product'])
E) plt.legend(loc='upper right')
```

QUESTION 41

You are visualizing the distribution of a categorical variable (Product Category) in a bar plot using Matplotlib. Which of the following commands is NOT a valid option for generating this plot?

```
A) plt.bar(df['Category'], df['Sales'])
B) plt.hist(df['Category'], bins=10)
C) plt.barh(df['Category'], df['Sales'])
D) plt.bar(df['Product'], df['Category'])`
```

QUESTION 42

You are creating a multi-line plot and need to adjust the size of the plot for better readability by setting its dimensions to 10x6 inches. How would you adjust the plot's size? (Select 2 answers)

```
A) plt.size(10, 6)
B) plt.figure(figsize=(10, 6))
C) plt.figure(dimensions=(10, 6))
D) plt.set_size_inches(10, 6)
E) plt.subplots(figsize=(10, 6))
```

QUESTION 43

You are preparing a scatter plot of sales versus profit for a report. To make the plot accessible to a non-technical audience, which two customizations would enhance readability and interpretation? Select two correct answers.

```
A) plt.scatter(df['Sales'], df['Profit'],
s=50)
B) plt.title('Sales vs. Profit')
C) plt.annotate('Outlier', xy=(3000, 400))
D) plt.scatter(df['Sales'], df['Profit'],
color='red')
E) plt.xlabel('Sales in USD');
plt.ylabel('Profit in USD')
```

QUESTION 44

You need to structure a Python visualization narrative that communicates customer churn over time and highlights periods with the highest churn rates. Which approach achieves this using Matplotlib or Seaborn? Select two correct answers.

```
A) plt.plot(dates, churn)
 plt.title('Customer Churn Over Time')

B) sns.lineplot(x=dates, y=churn)
 plt.text(dates[8], churn[8], 'High Churn',
fontsize=12)

C) plt.scatter(dates, churn) without
additional labels
D) sns.barplot(x=dates, y=churn)
E) plt.pie(churn, labels=dates)
```

QUESTION 45

You are tasked with summarizing the performance of two marketing campaigns using a concise visual. Campaign A generated consistent conversions, while Campaign B showed varying performance. Which plot would best summarize and compare these campaigns?

A) sns.barplot(x="Campaign", y="Conversions", data=campaign_df)

B) plt.scatter(conversions_A, conversions_B) C) plt.boxplot([conversions_A, conversions_B]); plt.title("Campaign Performance")

D) sns.heatmap(data=campaign_df)

E) plt.pie([conversions_A, conversions_B], labels=["Campaign A", "Campaign B"], explode=[0, 0.1])

PRACTICE TEST 4 - ANSWERS ONLY

QUESTION 1

Answer - A

A) Correct – This is the most direct way to calculate the mean order_amount for each customer_type using Pandas' groupby functionality.
B) Incorrect – This code calculates the sum of order_amount for each customer type, not the mean.
C) Incorrect – While the pivot table option works, it is more complex than necessary for this basic task.
D) Incorrect – agg() works, but using it here adds unnecessary complexity compared to the simpler groupby method.
E) Incorrect – df.mean('order_amount') will not work because mean requires grouping to apply the aggregation by customer_type.

EXAM FOCUS	Grouping in Pandas with groupby() is highly efficient for aggregating data. Stick to simple functions like mean() unless more complex operations are necessary.
CAUTION ALERT	Confusing agg() and groupby() can lead to unnecessary complexity. Use the most straightforward function for clarity and performance.

QUESTION 2

Answer - A, C

A) Correct – This converts the date format from MM/DD/YYYY to a datetime object for easy formatting.
B) Incorrect – While this can convert dates from DD-MM-YYYY, it doesn't standardize it to the final format YYYY-MM-DD.
C) Correct – This standardizes dates to the YYYY-MM-DD format using Pandas.
D) Incorrect – This code replaces the date separators but does not convert the date format.
E) Incorrect – Casting the date column as datetime64 may not handle different date formats consistently.

EXAM FOCUS	Use pd.to_datetime() to standardize date formats for consistency in analysis. Always aim for a common format like YYYY-MM-DD.
CAUTION ALERT	Be careful with string replacements like str.replace(). It won't correctly handle date formats or convert them into datetime objects.

QUESTION 3

Answer - B

A) Correct – Data lakes are designed to handle both structured and unstructured data, making them ideal for hybrid use cases.
B) Incorrect – Traditional relational databases are optimized for structured data but are not suited for storing and querying unstructured data such as text or multimedia files.
C) Correct – Cloud object storage solutions like Amazon S3 are ideal for storing large amounts of unstructured data, such as images and videos, in addition to structured data.
D) Correct – Data warehouses optimized for SQL queries can store structured data and run analytics efficiently.
E) Correct – Hybrid storage solutions allow combining the strengths of relational and NoSQL databases to store both structured and unstructured data effectively.

EXAM FOCUS	Data lakes and hybrid storage solutions excel at handling both structured and unstructured data,

| CAUTION ALERT | making them ideal for modern data architectures. |
| | Traditional relational databases are not designed to store or query unstructured data like text or multimedia, limiting their scalability for such tasks. |

QUESTION 4

Answer - D

A) Correct – Z-score is a common method for detecting outliers based on how many standard deviations a data point is from the mean.

B) Correct – IQR is another common method used for identifying outliers by comparing values to the interquartile range.

C) Correct – Removing rows with outliers can prevent them from distorting analysis results.

D) Incorrect – Min-Max scaling is not a recommended approach for directly handling outliers, as it does not reduce the influence of extreme values.

E) Correct – Imputing outliers with the mean value can reduce their impact on the dataset.

| EXAM FOCUS | Z-score and IQR are standard methods for detecting outliers. Handle them either by removal or imputation based on their impact on your model. |
| CAUTION ALERT | Min-Max scaling is for normalizing values, not for handling or mitigating outliers. Always use Z-score or IQR methods for outlier detection. |

QUESTION 5

Answer - D

A) Correct – pd.merge() is useful for cross-referencing the tables to validate matching department_id values.

B) Correct – SQL JOINs allow you to cross-reference the tables and check for matching IDs.

C) Correct – isin() validates that the values in department_id exist in the other table's column.

D) Incorrect – Filling missing department_id values with 'Unknown' does not validate data integrity and may introduce invalid data.

E) Incorrect – The validate() function does not exist in Pandas for this specific purpose.

| EXAM FOCUS | Use pd.merge() or SQL JOINs to cross-reference data across tables. These are the most effective methods for validating integrity across multiple datasets. |
| CAUTION ALERT | Avoid filling invalid department_id values with generic placeholders like 'Unknown' as it introduces potential data integrity issues. |

QUESTION 6

Answer - B

A) Correct – This query uses DISTINCT to retrieve unique job_title values.

B) Incorrect – This query doesn't retrieve distinct values but filters out rows where job_title is NULL.

C) Correct – Grouping by job_title will return unique values of job_title.

D) Correct – This query retrieves distinct values while also applying a condition (job_title = 'Manager').

E) Correct – This query groups by job_title, which will return unique titles along with their counts.

| EXAM FOCUS | Use DISTINCT or GROUP BY in SQL to fetch unique column values. Both methods efficiently retrieve distinct records. |
| CAUTION | Using IS NOT NULL only filters out null values; it doesn't retrieve distinct values. Understand the |

QUESTION 7

Answer - A

A) Correct – regplot() is used to create a scatter plot with a regression line in Seaborn.
B) Incorrect – lineplot() is for line plots, not scatter plots with regression lines.
C) Incorrect – lmplot() is similar but is more suitable for faceted data rather than simple scatter plots.
D) Incorrect – While this creates a scatter plot, it doesn't include a regression line.
E) Incorrect – boxplot() visualizes the distribution of data but is not used for scatter plots with regression lines.

EXAM FOCUS	Use sns.regplot() for creating scatter plots with regression lines. It's ideal for visualizing linear relationships in datasets.
CAUTION ALERT	Avoid using lineplot() when plotting regression relationships. It's meant for time series or trend data, not scatter plot regression analysis.

QUESTION 8

Answer - A

A) Correct – This correctly drops duplicate rows based on 'Column1' and keeps the first occurrence.
B) Incorrect – drop() removes rows entirely, not duplicates.
C) Incorrect – It drops all duplicate rows but not based on a specific column.
D) Incorrect – While it drops duplicates, it does not explicitly specify whether to keep the first or last occurrence.
E) Incorrect – The syntax is wrong for drop(), which is not meant for removing duplicates this way.

EXAM FOCUS	To drop duplicates in Pandas, use drop_duplicates(subset=column) to specify the column and keep='first' to retain the first occurrence.
CAUTION ALERT	Avoid using drop() to remove duplicates; it removes rows or columns entirely, not duplicates. Use drop_duplicates() for this task.

QUESTION 9

Answer - B, D

B) Correct: Setting random_state ensures that empty clusters don't appear due to random initializations.
D) Correct: n_init helps by running the algorithm multiple times to prevent empty clusters.
A) Incorrect: Increasing the number of iterations won't solve empty clusters.
C) Incorrect: Random initialization might worsen the issue.
E) Incorrect: More clusters might lead to more empty ones.

EXAM FOCUS	Use random_state to maintain consistent clustering across runs, and increase n_init to rerun K-Means multiple times for better clustering stability.
CAUTION ALERT	Increasing n_clusters may lead to unnecessary empty clusters. Instead, run multiple initializations (n_init) to improve the model's robustness.

QUESTION 10

Answer - A, C

A) Correct: This is the standard syntax for box plots in Seaborn, where x is categorical and y is numerical data.

B) Incorrect: Switching x and y here would lead to an invalid box plot, as the axis interpretation would be incorrect.

C) Correct: Using catplot with kind="box" is a valid method for plotting box plots, offering additional flexibility for faceting and customization.

D) Incorrect: This lacks the y axis parameter, which is crucial for visualizing distributions properly in a box plot.

E) Incorrect: y alone cannot determine the categories to visualize the distribution of values, so the box plot will fail.

EXAM FOCUS	Use sns.boxplot(x="category", y="value", data=df) to plot categorical vs numerical data. Use catplot() with kind="box" for flexible and faceted plots.
CAUTION ALERT	Don't confuse the x and y axis roles when plotting a box plot. The x-axis should hold categorical data, and the y-axis numerical.

QUESTION 11

Answer - A, C

A) Interpolation helps fill missing data points in a meaningful way.

B) Removing duplicates addresses redundancy but not missing data.

C) Dropping rows with missing data in key columns maintains the integrity of important columns.

D) Backfilling (bfill) fills data backward, which can lead to inconsistencies.

E) Converting data to numeric may lead to errors if applied improperly.

EXAM FOCUS	Interpolation can be useful to fill missing data in a meaningful way, especially for time-series data. Use dropna for key columns to maintain data quality.
CAUTION ALERT	Avoid using backfilling (bfill) unless the data naturally progresses backward, as it can introduce inaccuracies in the dataset.

QUESTION 12

Answer - A, B

A) GDPR requires explicit consent before collecting personal data, so Python-based forms help ensure compliance.

B) Users must be able to access, modify, or delete their personal data to comply with GDPR's right to erasure.

C) Collecting data without notifying users violates GDPR's transparency requirements.

D) Transferring data without consent is a breach of GDPR's consent rules.

E) Encryption protects data security, but GDPR also requires transparency and user control over their data.

EXAM FOCUS	A Python-based form for obtaining explicit consent before collecting personal data is crucial for GDPR compliance. Allow users to request data deletion via a portal.
CAUTION ALERT	Avoid collecting or sharing data without user consent and transparency regarding its use, as this violates fundamental GDPR rules.

QUESTION 13

Answer - A, C

A) Correct, df.fillna(df.mean()) fills missing values with the mean.

B) Interpolation works differently and isn't required here.

C) Using median is acceptable but doesn't meet the "mean" requirement.

D) Forward fill isn't based on mean, which is incorrect.
E) Drops rows with missing values, but doesn't fill them.

EXAM FOCUS	*Filling missing values with the mean (df.fillna(df.mean())) is a common practice for numeric data, ensuring consistent handling of NaNs.*
CAUTION ALERT	*Avoid using forward fill (ffill) when filling missing values with specific statistics like the mean or median. It may not provide accurate results.*

QUESTION 14

Answer - A, C

A) Correct: This custom function calculates percentage of total sales.
B) Incorrect: apply used incorrectly for scalar output.
C) Correct: transform is appropriate for element-wise transformations.
D) Incorrect: apply after sum() doesn't provide expected results.
E) Incorrect: agg is misused for this transformation.

EXAM FOCUS	*Use apply() for custom transformations like calculating percentages of total sales per region; it's versatile for lambda functions.*
CAUTION ALERT	*Be cautious using apply() where transform() or agg() would suffice. Each has its distinct use case for operations.*

QUESTION 15

Answer - B, E

Option A: Incorrect – describe() does not include the median.
Option B: Correct – This calculates the mean, median, and standard deviation for the 'Sales' column.
Option C: Incorrect – Only calculates the mean.
Option D: Incorrect – Pivot tables are not required here.
Option E: Correct – Aggregates the 'Sales' column using the specified functions.

EXAM FOCUS	*Use agg() or describe() to compute key statistics like mean, median, and standard deviation, which provide a comprehensive summary of data.*
CAUTION ALERT	*describe() does not include the median by default. Use agg() for a more detailed summary with custom metrics.*

QUESTION 16

Answer - A, B

Option A: Correct – cumsum() is the most efficient way to calculate the cumulative sum in Pandas.
Option B: Correct – Uses a loop with iterrows() to compute the cumulative sum row by row.
Option C: Incorrect – apply() with cumsum() does not work as expected here.
Option D: Incorrect – Uses an inefficient list comprehension method.
Option E: Incorrect – rolling() calculates a moving sum, not a cumulative sum.

EXAM FOCUS	*Use cumsum() for cumulative sums in Pandas, and ensure you use efficient vectorized operations to avoid unnecessary loops over rows.*
CAUTION ALERT	*Avoid list comprehensions or rolling sums for cumulative operations as they are inefficient compared to Pandas' cumsum().*

QUESTION 17

Answer - A, C

Option A: Correct – Using pip is the standard method for installing packages in Python environments.
Option B: Incorrect – Pandas does not provide an installation method through its API.
Option C: Correct – conda is a popular alternative package manager for Python and works similarly to pip.
Option D: Incorrect – While this works, it is not the recommended or clean way to install Python packages.
Option E: Incorrect – Pandas does not include an install function for package management.

EXAM FOCUS	*Use pip or conda to manage Python package installations efficiently in your environment for a smoother workflow.*
CAUTION ALERT	*Avoid using custom methods or non-standard installation commands like using os.system(), as these might create version control issues.*

QUESTION 18

Answer - B, E

Option A: Incorrect – Silently passing errors with pass leads to undetected failures.
Option B: Correct – Catching general exceptions and printing the error message is a good practice for debugging.
Option C: Incorrect – While this provides a message, it does not specify the error, making debugging harder.
Option D: Incorrect – While it catches a KeyError, it's better to catch a broader range of exceptions.
Option E: Correct – This approach catches multiple exception types, which is useful for handling multiple potential issues.

EXAM FOCUS	*Catch specific exceptions: It's good practice to catch multiple relevant exceptions to handle different errors in your data acquisition scripts.*
CAUTION ALERT	*Avoid generic exception handling: Using a general except: pass block can mask underlying issues in your code, making debugging difficult.*

QUESTION 19

Answer - A, B

Option A: Correct – Implements retry logic using a for loop with a break on success.
Option B: Correct – Uses a while loop with a retry counter and stops on success.
Option C: Incorrect – Retries only twice without handling the final attempt correctly.
Option D: Incorrect – No retry logic is implemented.
Option E: Incorrect – Increments the retry counter even if the request succeeds, leading to incorrect logic.

EXAM FOCUS	*Implement retry logic: Use loops to retry API calls in the case of network issues, with proper limits to avoid infinite retries in case of repeated failures.*
CAUTION ALERT	*Avoid retrying endlessly: Always limit retry attempts to prevent your script from getting stuck in an infinite loop due to persistent connection failures.*

QUESTION 20

Answer - A, E

Option A: Correct – This query correctly deletes the record where customer_id = 101.
Option B: Incorrect – Deletes based on total_purchase, which is not a unique identifier.

Option C: Incorrect – Missing FROM in the DELETE statement.
Option D: Incorrect – Deletes based on customer_name, which is less reliable than using the customer_id.
Option E: Correct – Deletes the record where customer_id meets a condition in a subquery, though more complex than necessary.

EXAM FOCUS	Use DELETE with caution: Always use a unique identifier like customer_id in the WHERE clause to avoid deleting unintended records.
CAUTION ALERT	Watch the DELETE syntax: Missing the FROM keyword in a DELETE query is a common mistake that results in syntax errors.

QUESTION 21

Answer - A, C

Option A: Correct – This uses a parameterized query with ? placeholders and passes a tuple, making it secure.
Option B: Incorrect – Concatenating strings in SQL queries is vulnerable to SQL injection.
Option C: Correct – Uses named placeholders (:name, :purchase) and a dictionary, ensuring security.
Option D: Incorrect – While using ? is correct, passing a list instead of a tuple is less common and non-standard.
Option E: Incorrect – String interpolation (f-strings) for SQL queries exposes the script to SQL injection risks.

EXAM FOCUS	Dynamic queries with parameters: When querying based on multiple inputs, always pass those inputs securely with placeholders, never as concatenated strings.
CAUTION ALERT	Risk of SQL injection: Avoid building SQL queries dynamically by inserting user input directly into the query. Use parameterization instead.

QUESTION 22

Answer - B, D

Option A: Incorrect – Parameterized queries handle input securely but do not encrypt data itself.
Option B: Correct – Enabling encryption at rest protects data stored in the database files.
Option C: Incorrect – Storing plain-text sensitive data without encryption increases security risks.
Option D: Correct – SSL/TLS ensures data is protected during transmission between the application and the database.
Option E: Incorrect – Hashing is good for passwords but is not the same as encrypting other sensitive fields.

EXAM FOCUS	Data encryption is crucial: Use encryption at rest and ensure encrypted data transmission (SSL/TLS) to maintain confidentiality of sensitive data stored in SQL databases.
CAUTION ALERT	Do not store sensitive data in plain text: Storing sensitive fields like passwords or credit card data in plain text is highly insecure. Always encrypt.

QUESTION 23

Answer - A, D

Option A: Correct – This shows polymorphism through method overriding where Manager overrides get_info.
Option B: Incorrect – The method get_details() is not overriding any method from the parent class.
Option C: Incorrect – The Manager class does not override get_info, so no polymorphism occurs.
Option D: Correct – This demonstrates overriding with a call to the parent class's method using super().
Option E: Incorrect – Overloading is not supported in Python in this manner; polymorphism occurs through overriding.

EXAM FOCUS	*Polymorphism is done through overriding: Method overriding allows subclasses to provide specific implementations, making it a key part of polymorphism in object-oriented programming.*
CAUTION ALERT	*Don't confuse with overloading: Python does not support function overloading (multiple methods with the same name). Focus on overriding for polymorphism.*

QUESTION 24

Answer - B

Option A: Incorrect – This will raise an error if the directory already exists.
Option B: Correct – It checks if the directory exists and only creates it if it doesn't, which is ideal.
Option C: Incorrect – os.makedirs() can create nested directories but doesn't check if the directory already exists.
Option D: Incorrect – This creates a directory only if it already exists, which is logically flawed.
Option E: Incorrect – Using os.path.isdir() checks if it is a directory but does not create one if it doesn't exist.

EXAM FOCUS	*Check existence before creating directories: Always check if a directory exists before creating it to avoid unnecessary exceptions using os.path.exists() and os.mkdir().*
CAUTION ALERT	*Avoid using os.mkdir() directly: Calling os.mkdir() without checking for the existence of a directory can raise an error if the directory already exists.*

QUESTION 25

Answer - A, B

A) Correct: This defines and raises a custom exception when a column is missing, with a specific error message.
B) Correct: Inheriting from KeyError is a reasonable approach since missing columns are typically related to key errors.
C) Incorrect: The exception raised is a custom one, but the code is catching a KeyError instead.
D) Incorrect: The exception is raised without defining a meaningful error message or context.
E) Incorrect: While KeyError is valid, it's not specific to the custom exception required for missing columns.

EXAM FOCUS	*Key-based errors need specificity: When dealing with missing columns in datasets, using custom exceptions like MissingColumnError offers clarity about the issue.*
CAUTION ALERT	*Avoid generic KeyError: Though missing columns may technically raise a KeyError, using a more specific custom exception improves code readability.*

QUESTION 26

Answer - A, E

Option A: Correct, this query uses JOIN and HAVING COUNT to filter employees with more than 10 sales.
Option B: Incorrect, the subquery logic is correct but inefficient.
Option C: Incorrect, the WHERE clause is incorrect because COUNT cannot be used here.
Option D: Incorrect, WHERE cannot filter aggregate results like COUNT.
Option E: Correct, this also correctly filters with JOIN and HAVING COUNT.

EXAM FOCUS	*Use JOIN and GROUP BY for counting relationships: JOIN the tables and use GROUP BY with HAVING to filter based on the count of related records, such as sales per employee.*
CAUTION ALERT	*COUNT() can't be used in WHERE: COUNT() is an aggregate function that must be filtered using HAVING, not WHERE. Be careful with this distinction.*

QUESTION 27

Answer - A

Option A: Correct, CHECK (start_date <= CURDATE()) ensures no future dates are allowed.
Option B: Incorrect, PRIMARY KEY does not restrict future dates.
Option C: Incorrect, adding a FOREIGN KEY doesn't enforce date restrictions.
Option D: Incorrect, DEFAULT sets an initial value but doesn't enforce date checks.
Option E: Incorrect, UNIQUE ensures no duplicate dates but doesn't restrict future dates.

EXAM FOCUS	*CHECK constraints prevent invalid data: A CHECK (start_date <= CURDATE()) constraint ensures that dates cannot be set in the future, preventing potential data inconsistencies.*
CAUTION ALERT	*DEFAULT doesn't enforce constraints: DEFAULT sets an initial value but does not enforce data validation like a CHECK constraint.*

QUESTION 28

Answer - A, C

Option A: Correct, frequent UPDATE/DELETE operations will suffer from performance degradation due to index maintenance.
Option B: Incorrect, high cardinality columns benefit from indexes if they are queried often.
Option C: Correct, frequently modified columns not used in queries should avoid indexes due to overhead.
Option D: Incorrect, high-performance requirements often justify indexing, especially on filterable columns.
Option E: Incorrect, aggregate queries can benefit from indexed columns if properly designed.

EXAM FOCUS	*Avoid indexes on frequently modified columns: Avoid indexing columns that are frequently updated or deleted, as indexes can slow down these operations due to maintenance overhead.*
CAUTION ALERT	*High cardinality is ideal for indexing: Columns with high cardinality (many unique values) benefit most from indexing when frequently queried.*

QUESTION 29

Answer - A

Option A: Correct, when the mean is greater than the median, it indicates a right-skewed (positively skewed) distribution.
Option B: Incorrect, a left-skewed distribution occurs when the mean is less than the median.
Option C: Incorrect, symmetric distributions have the mean and median approximately equal.
Option D: Incorrect, normal distributions are symmetric.
Option E: Incorrect, uniform distributions have all values equally likely, not skewed.

EXAM FOCUS	*Right-skewed means higher mean: When the mean is greater than the median, it often indicates a right-skewed distribution, which means there are high outliers pulling the mean upwards.*
CAUTION ALERT	*Mean can be misleading in skewed data: When the distribution is skewed, relying on the mean alone may lead to incorrect conclusions about the data's central tendency.*

QUESTION 30

Answer - B

Option A: Incorrect, higher variability indicates less consistency.

Option B: Correct, higher variability suggests more unpredictability.
Option C: Incorrect, higher variability suggests inconsistency between the lines.
Option D: Incorrect, lower variability indicates higher consistency.
Option E: Incorrect, variability directly impacts consistency.

EXAM FOCUS	*Higher variability means more unpredictability: In data analysis, higher variability indicates less predictability and more fluctuations in the data, especially in time-based data like production times.*
CAUTION ALERT	*Lower variability implies consistency: The dataset with lower variability reflects more consistent behavior, crucial for assessing process reliability.*

QUESTION 31

Answer - A

Option A: Correct, bootstrapped samples usually have the same mean but may have slightly higher variance due to resampling with replacement.
Option B: Incorrect, bootstrapped samples do not generally have lower means.
Option C: Incorrect, bootstrapped samples may have higher variance but not necessarily a higher mean.
Option D: Incorrect, variance tends to differ slightly.
Option E: Incorrect, there is always some difference due to resampling.

EXAM FOCUS	*Bootstrapped samples have higher variance: Bootstrapped samples maintain the same mean as the original dataset but generally exhibit slightly higher variance due to repeated sampling.*
CAUTION ALERT	*Don't expect identical variance: Bootstrapping increases variability, so don't expect the bootstrapped sample to have the exact variance as the original data.*

QUESTION 32

Answer - A, D

Option A: Correct, logistic regression is suitable for binary outcome predictions.
Option B: Incorrect, logistic regression assumes linear relationships between variables.
Option C: Incorrect, continuous outcomes should use linear regression.
Option D: Correct, logistic regression is ideal for modeling probabilities.
Option E: Incorrect, logistic regression can handle categorical predictors, but this isn't its primary distinguishing feature from linear regression.

EXAM FOCUS	*Logistic regression for probability modeling: Logistic regression is best when predicting probabilities for binary outcomes, especially in scenarios like customer churn or purchase behavior.*
CAUTION ALERT	*Linear regression cannot model probabilities: Always choose logistic regression for binary outcomes to avoid misleading results from inappropriate probability modeling.*

QUESTION 33

Answer - A

A) Correct: Creates a pivot table with 'region' as the index, 'product' as the columns, and 'sales' as the values
B) Incorrect: This swaps the index and column roles, which is incorrect
C) Incorrect: This uses pivot_table with an aggregation function, which isn't necessary here
D) Incorrect: This approach is similar to pivot but not as straightforward as A
E) Incorrect: Similar to C, it applies an unnecessary aggregation function

| EXAM FOCUS | Pivot table simplifies reshaping data: Use the .pivot() method in Pandas to quickly reshape your data into a new format where rows become columns based on specified keys. |
| CAUTION ALERT | GroupBy is not always a substitute for pivot: Although groupby() can achieve similar results, .pivot() is more efficient for creating a quick table format without extra aggregation. |

QUESTION 34

Answer - A, B

A) Correct: The == operator is supported by NumPy for element-wise comparison between two arrays, returning an array of boolean values indicating where the condition is true.

B) Correct: np.equal(a, b) is the functionally equivalent way to perform element-wise comparison between arrays a and b and returns a boolean array.

C) Incorrect: While >= can be used for element-wise comparison, the context asks for equality comparison, making this option irrelevant to the specific question.

D) Incorrect: a is b checks for object identity, not element-wise comparison, which is not what is needed for comparing values between arrays in NumPy.

E) Incorrect: np.logical_or() is used for boolean operations on arrays, not for element-wise comparison, and would require the input arrays to be boolean.

| EXAM FOCUS | Efficient element-wise comparison: Use == or np.equal() to compare two arrays element-wise. Both methods return a boolean array with the comparison result. |
| CAUTION ALERT | Avoid object identity checks: Using a is b checks if two variables point to the same object, not if their elements are equal. Use == for comparison. |

QUESTION 35

Answer - A, B

A) Correct: np.var() correctly calculates the variance of the array arr.
B) Correct: np.std() correctly computes the standard deviation of arr.
C) Incorrect: There is no np.statistics() function in NumPy; this would raise an error.
D) Incorrect: arr.variance() is not a valid function for arrays; this would raise an AttributeError.
E) Incorrect: np.calculate_variance() does not exist in NumPy and would result in an error.

| EXAM FOCUS | NumPy handles statistical calculations: Use np.var() and np.std() for variance and standard deviation calculations in NumPy arrays. |
| CAUTION ALERT | Correct function names matter: Functions like np.statistics() and arr.variance() are not valid in NumPy. Ensure you're using the proper NumPy functions. |

QUESTION 36

Answer - A, D

A) Correct: Setting class_weight='balanced' adjusts weights to account for class imbalance.
B) Incorrect: Simply reducing the number of majority class instances could lead to loss of valuable data.
C) Incorrect: Logistic regression is for classification, and using linear regression will not address class imbalance.
D) Correct: Oversampling the minority class helps balance the dataset by creating synthetic instances.
E) Incorrect: Removing features does not balance the classes and may degrade model performance.

| EXAM FOCUS | Handle imbalanced data: Use class_weight='balanced' and oversampling techniques to address class |

imbalance in datasets when training logistic regression models.

QUESTION 37

Answer - C

A) Correct – Linear regression is correctly instantiated and fitted here.
B) Correct – Mean squared error is a valid metric for evaluating regression models.
C) Incorrect – Logistic regression is not appropriate for regression tasks as it is used for classification.
D) Correct – R-squared is a common evaluation metric for regression models.
E) Correct – Prediction is done using the predict() method of the fitted model.

EXAM FOCUS	*Evaluate regression correctly: Use mean_squared_error and r2_score for regression model evaluation. Ensure you generate predictions with model.predict() before evaluation.*
CAUTION ALERT	*Wrong model for regression: Logistic regression is for classification, not regression. Don't use LogisticRegression for continuous variable prediction tasks.*

QUESTION 38

Answer - B

A) Correct – This is the proper way to group by category and calculate the sum of sales.
B) Incorrect – The sum method does not accept arguments in this form.
C) Correct – Using the agg function with a dictionary is valid.
D) Correct – The apply function with a lambda expression is also correct for aggregation.
E) Correct – The agg function can be passed with 'sum' to calculate the total sales.

EXAM FOCUS	*Use agg() for flexibility: When aggregating by multiple metrics like sum or mean, agg() offers flexibility. Make sure you apply it to the grouped DataFrame.*
CAUTION ALERT	*Watch for incorrect method parameters: Methods like sum() do not take column arguments directly. Use correct syntax when performing aggregation to avoid errors.*

QUESTION 39

Answer - C

A) Correct because GridSearchCV is an appropriate method to tune hyperparameters like alpha in Ridge regression.
B) Correct because RandomizedSearchCV is another valid method for tuning alpha in Ridge regression, though it samples fewer values than GridSearchCV.
C) Incorrect because this directly applies Ridge regression with a fixed alpha=1.0 without tuning or optimizing the alpha value, which does not fulfill the requirement to find the optimal alpha.
D) Correct because RidgeCV is designed to find the best value of alpha using cross-validation.
E) Correct because using cross_val_score with different alpha values for Ridge regression is a valid approach to determine the best regularization parameter.

EXAM FOCUS	*Finding Optimal Alpha: Use techniques like GridSearchCV, RandomizedSearchCV, or RidgeCV to tune and optimize regularization parameters like alpha in Ridge regression.*
CAUTION	*Fixed Alpha Values: Applying a Ridge model with a fixed alpha without tuning it can lead to suboptimal*

performance. Use cross-validation methods to find the best alpha.

QUESTION 40

Answer - D

A) Correct because plt.bar() is the correct function to generate a bar plot.
B) Correct because plt.title() adds a title to the plot, enhancing its clarity and presentation.
C) Correct because plt.ylabel() labels the y-axis, which is an important element of plot customization.
D) Incorrect because plt.xticks() requires a list of positions, not just the values from a column. Therefore, this is not a valid option.
E) Correct because plt.legend() adds a legend to the plot, which is valid for bar plots.

EXAM FOCUS	*Bar Plot Tip: plt.bar() is ideal for comparing categories, such as sales per product. Customize the plot with plt.title(), plt.ylabel(), and plt.xticks() for clarity.*
CAUTION ALERT	*Axis Labels in Bar Plot: plt.xticks() needs a list of positions and labels, not direct DataFrame columns. Failing to do so will cause an error or incorrect labeling.*

QUESTION 41

Answer - B

A) Correct because plt.bar() is used to generate bar plots and can visualize categorical variables like product categories.
B) Incorrect because plt.hist() is used for continuous numerical variables, not categorical ones, making it unsuitable for visualizing categories.
C) Correct because plt.barh() generates a horizontal bar plot, which is a valid approach to visualize categorical data.
D) Correct because using plt.bar() with Product as the x-axis and Category as the y-axis is valid.

EXAM FOCUS	*Bar Plot for Categories: Use plt.bar() or plt.barh() for visualizing categorical data like product categories. Bar plots are perfect for comparing different categories.*
CAUTION ALERT	*Histogram Caution: Avoid using plt.hist() for categorical data. It is designed for numerical data distribution, and won't produce meaningful results with categories.*

QUESTION 42

Answer - B, E

A) Incorrect because plt.size() is not a valid Matplotlib function to adjust plot size.
B) Correct because plt.figure(figsize=(10, 6)) correctly adjusts the figure's size to 10x6 inches.
C) Incorrect because plt.figure(dimensions=(10, 6)) is not a valid function; the correct parameter is figsize.
D) Incorrect because plt.set_size_inches() is not a valid function; it works with figure objects but not directly with plt.
E) Correct because plt.subplots(figsize=(10, 6)) is also a valid way to set the figure size, especially when creating subplots.

EXAM FOCUS	*Plot Size Tip: Use plt.figure(figsize=(10, 6)) or plt.subplots(figsize=(10, 6)) to set plot size and improve readability, especially for multi-line plots.*
CAUTION ALERT	*Sizing Error: Avoid using plt.size() or plt.figure(dimensions=(10, 6))—they are not valid for setting plot dimensions in Matplotlib.*

QUESTION 43

Answer - B, E

A) Incorrect because adjusting point size doesn't help non-technical audiences interpret the data.
B) Correct because adding a title gives context to the plot and helps non-technical audiences understand what is being visualized.
C) Incorrect because annotating a single outlier does not enhance the overall readability of the plot for the general audience.
D) Incorrect because changing the color to red does not improve interpretation, as the audience might still struggle to understand the plot's purpose.
E) Correct because labeling the axes with units of measure (USD) makes the data more understandable for a non-technical audience.

EXAM FOCUS	Scatter Plot Labels: Always include informative titles and axis labels like plt.title() and plt.xlabel() to help non-technical audiences understand scatter plots effectively.
CAUTION ALERT	Unreadable Scatter: Merely adjusting scatter point sizes or changing colors does not aid readability for non-technical audiences. Always include context and labels.

QUESTION 44

Answer - A, B

A) Correct because using a line plot and providing a title ensures the narrative of churn over time is communicated clearly.
B) Correct because using Seaborn's lineplot and annotating the highest churn point emphasizes the key insight and drives the narrative effectively.
C) Incorrect because a scatter plot without additional labels won't effectively convey the time-based churn narrative.
D) Incorrect because bar plots aren't optimal for visualizing churn over time compared to line plots.
E) Incorrect because pie charts are unsuitable for representing changes over time.

EXAM FOCUS	Churn Narrative: Use line plots with plt.text() to annotate periods of high customer churn, which provides clarity and reinforces the story of churn over time.
CAUTION ALERT	Avoid Pie for Time-Series: Pie charts are not suited for time-based data like churn. Use line plots or bar plots to clearly represent changes over time.

QUESTION 45

Answer - C

A) Incorrect because a bar plot doesn't effectively summarize the varying performance of Campaign B.
B) Incorrect because a scatter plot doesn't provide a clear comparison of overall performance trends.
C) Correct because a box plot visually summarizes the consistent conversions of Campaign A and the varying performance of Campaign B, providing clear insights for comparison.
D) Incorrect because a heatmap is not appropriate for comparing performance between two discrete campaigns.
E) Incorrect because a pie chart only shows proportions, not the variation in performance between the campaigns.

EXAM FOCUS	Box Plot for Variability: Box plots effectively summarize variability between two campaigns, highlighting differences in performance consistency (Campaign A vs. Campaign B).
CAUTION ALERT	Bar Plot Limitation: Bar plots are less effective at showing variability in performance over time or between different campaigns. Use box plots for clearer comparisons.

PRACTICE TEST 5 - QUESTIONS ONLY

QUESTION 1

A dataset has been scraped from multiple web sources. You are tasked with merging two dataframes df1 and df2 on a common column user_id, but some users may only appear in one dataframe. Which Python code will perform a full outer join on the user_id column?

```
A) pd.merge(df1, df2, on='user_id',
how='outer')
B) pd.concat([df1, df2])
C) pd.join(df1, df2, on='user_id')
D) df1.append(df2)
E) df1.merge(df2, how='inner')
```

QUESTION 2

You are analyzing a dataset where some of the values in the salary column are missing. Which of the following approaches would NOT be appropriate for handling these missing values?

A) Impute missing values using the column's median
B) Impute missing values using the column's mean
C) Remove rows with missing salary values
D) Fill missing values with a constant, e.g., 0
E) Leave the missing values as they are

QUESTION 3

You are conducting sentiment analysis on a set of unstructured text data. Which of the following is NOT an appropriate method for processing unstructured data in Python?

A) Use nltk for text processing and analysis
B) Use pd.read_sql() to load text data into a DataFrame
C) Use TextBlob for basic sentiment analysis
D) Use re for text pattern matching and extraction
E) Use json.loads() to parse JSON-formatted text data

QUESTION 4

You have detected outliers in a dataset of employee salaries. After handling the outliers, you want to visualize the distribution of the salary data. Which Python code snippets would correctly visualize this data? (Select 2 answers)

```
A) sns.boxplot(x='salary', data=df)
B) plt.scatter(df['salary'])
C) sns.histplot(df['salary'], bins=20)
D) df['salary'].plot(kind='bar')
E) plt.plot(df['salary'])
```

QUESTION 5

You are performing data validation on a dataset of product prices. Which of the following code snippets would correctly apply range checks to ensure all price values are between $0 and $1000? (Select 2 answers)

```
A) df[(df['price'] >= 0) & (df['price'] <=
1000)]
B) df.query('price >= 0 and price <=
1000')
C) df['price'].apply(lambda x: 0 <= x <=
1000)
D) df.filter('price', lambda x: 0 <= x <=
1000)
E) df.validate_range('price', 0, 1000)
```

QUESTION 6

You are working with a large dataset and want to retrieve data from a SQL database in batches to avoid memory overload. Which Python method can be used to fetch rows incrementally after running the SQL query? (Select 2 answers)

```
A) cursor.fetchmany(size)
B) cursor.fetchall()
C) cursor.fetchbatch(size)
D) cursor.fetchone()
E) cursor.fetch_chunk()
```

QUESTION 7

You need to calculate the range of a dataset and visualize it using a boxplot. Which of the following Python code snippets accurately computes the range and creates a boxplot using Seaborn? (Select 2 answers)

```
A) import numpy as np
range_val = np.ptp(data)
sns.boxplot(data=data)

B) import numpy as np
range_val = np.max(data) - np.min(data)
sns.boxplot(data=data)

C) import statistics
range_val = max(data) - min(data)
sns.boxplot(data=data)

D) import seaborn as sns
range_val = sns.boxplot(data=data).range()

E) import pandas as pd
range_val = pd.DataFrame(data).range()
```

QUESTION 8

You need to handle missing data in a Pandas DataFrame by dropping any rows that have NaN values. Which of the following code snippets accomplishes this task? (Select 2 answers)

```
A) import pandas as pd
df = df.dropna()

B) import pandas as pd
df.dropna(inplace=True)

C) import pandas as pd
df.fillna(method='ffill')

D) import pandas as pd
df.dropna(axis=1)

E) import pandas as pd
df = df.drop(df.isna())
```

QUESTION 9

You are applying cross-validation to evaluate a machine learning model in Python. What are the correct steps for cross-validation? Select 2 correct options.

```
) from sklearn.model_selection import
cross_val_score
scores = cross_val_score(model, X, y, cv=5)

) from sklearn.model_selection import
KFold
```

```
C) train_test_split(X, y, test_size=0.3)
D) cross_val_score(model, X_test, y_test,
cv=5)
E) model.fit(X_train, y_train)
```

QUESTION 10

You need to customize Seaborn plot aesthetics for a presentation. Which steps are correct for modifying the style and color palette? Select 2 correct options.

```
A) sns.set_style("whitegrid")
B) sns.set_palette("pastel")
C) sns.set_context("talk")
D) sns.barplot(x="category", y="value",
palette="pastel")
E) sns.set_style("ticks", palette="dark")
```

QUESTION 11

You are conducting a structured interview and want to preprocess the collected textual data for analysis. Which Python commands can be used to clean and preprocess the text data? (Select 2 correct answers)

```
A) df['text'].str.lower()
B) df['text'].apply(lambda x: '
'.join(x.split()))
C) df.replace(df['text'], 'Unknown')
D) df['text'] = df['text'].apply(lambda x:
x.strip())
E) df['text'] = None
```

QUESTION 12

A global company using a Python-based system collects data for analysis. To ensure compliance with GDPR, what are the essential measures that need to be implemented? (Select 2 correct answers)

A) Use Python's ssl module to enforce secure transmission of sensitive data

B) Automatically export user data to third-party servers located outside the EU without explicit user consent

C) Provide users with a Python-based interface to withdraw consent for data processing at any time

D) Store user data indefinitely without informing them about how long it will be kept

E) Implement a system for users to request data portability through a Python script

QUESTION 13

You need to merge two DataFrames, df1 and df2, on a common column 'ID' but only keep the rows present in both DataFrames. Which of the following merge options would you choose?

```
 A) pd.merge(df1, df2, on='ID',
how='inner')
 B) pd.concat([df1, df2])
 C) pd.merge(df1, df2, on='ID',
how='left')
 D) pd.merge(df1, df2, on='ID',
how='right')
 E) pd.merge(df1, df2, on='ID',
how='outer')
```

QUESTION 14

You are asked to merge two datasets on multiple keys, such as 'region' and 'product_id'. Which scripts would correctly perform this operation? Select 2 correct answers.

```
 A) pd.merge(df1, df2, on=['region',
'product_id'])
 B) pd.merge(df1, df2, how='left',
on=['region', 'product_id'])
 C) df1.merge(df2, left_on=['region',
'product_id'], right_on=['region',
'product_id'])
 D) df1.join(df2, on=['region',
'product_id'])
 E) df1.merge(df2, left_on='region',
right_on='product_id')
```

QUESTION 15

While preparing a performance report, you need to generate a line plot using Seaborn to display revenue trends over time and save the plot as an image. What is the correct way to implement this? (Select 2 answers)

```
 A) sns.lineplot(x='Date', y='Revenue',
data=df); plt.savefig('revenue_trend.png')
 B) plt.plot(df['Date'], df['Revenue']);
plt.savefig('revenue_trend.png')
 C) sns.lineplot(data=df, x='Date',
y='Revenue').savefig('revenue_trend.png')
 D) sns.lineplot(df['Date'],
df['Revenue']); plt.show()
 E) plt.savefig('revenue_trend.jpg',
format='png')
```

QUESTION 16

You are working with a dataset where a function processes the total revenue from each product category. You want to ensure that variables used inside the function remain local and don't affect global variables. What are the correct ways to manage this using Python? (Select 2 answers)

```
 A) def process_revenue(revenue): total = 0
for rev in revenue: total += rev return
total
 B) def process_revenue(revenue): global
total total = 0 for rev in revenue: total
+= rev return total
 C) def process_revenue(revenue): for rev
in revenue: total = 0 total += rev return
total
 D) def process_revenue(revenue):
local_total = 0 for rev in revenue:
local_total += rev return local_total
 E) def process_revenue(revenue): global
total total = sum(revenue) return total
```

QUESTION 17

You need to create a correlation matrix for your dataset using the Pandas library and then visualize it using Seaborn's heatmap function. What are the correct steps to perform this task? (Select 3 answers)

```
A) import seaborn as sns;
sns.heatmap(df.corr(), annot=TruE)
B) import matplotlib.pyplot as plt;
plt.imshow(df.corr())
C) corr = df.corr(); sns.heatmap(corr,
cmap='coolwarm')
D) df.corr().plot(kind='heatmap')
E) sns.heatmap(df.corr(), cmap='viridis',
linewidths=0.5)
```

QUESTION 18

You are collaborating with other data analysts and want to ensure your Python code is readable and easy to maintain. What are the best practices to follow for writing readable and maintainable Python scripts? (Select 2 answers)

 A) Write long descriptive variable names and avoid abbreviations
 B) Use single-letter variable names like 'x' and 'y' for all variables
 C) Break long functions into smaller, reusable functions
 D) Write all code in a single function for simplicity

E) Use meaningful comments to explain complex sections of code

QUESTION 19

You are debugging a Python script and want to raise a custom exception if the script encounters a specific condition. What is the correct way to define and raise a custom exception? (Select 2 answers)

```
A) class CustomError(Exception):
pass
raise CustomError("Custom error occurred.")

B) raise Exception("Custom error message.")

C) class CustomError:
pass
raise CustomError("Custom error occurred.")

D) class CustomError(Exception):
def __init__(self, message):
self.message = message
raise CustomError("Custom error occurred.")

E) class CustomError(BaseException):
pass
raise CustomError("Custom error occurred.")
```

QUESTION 20

You want to retrieve all customer names and total purchases from the customers table, where the total purchase is greater than $100. How should you structure this SQL query? (Select 2 answers)

```
A) SELECT customer_name, total_purchase
FROM customers
WHERE total_purchase > 100;

B) SELECT customer_name, total_purchase
FROM customers
HAVING total_purchase > 100;

C) SELECT customer_name, total_purchase
FROM customers
WHERE total_purchase >= 100;

D) SELECT customer_name, total_purchase
FROM customers
WHERE total_purchase BETWEEN 100 AND 500;

E) SELECT customer_name, total_purchase
FROM customers
WHERE total_purchase != 100;
```

QUESTION 21

You are tasked with writing a Python function that deletes a record from the customers table based on a user-supplied customer_id. How would you structure this function using parameterized SQL to avoid SQL injection? (Select 2 answers)

```
A) def delete_customer(customer_id):
conn = sqlite3.connect('database.db')
cursor = conn.cursor()
cursor.execute("DELETE FROM customers WHERE
customer_id = ?", (customer_id,))
conn.commit()

B) def delete_customer(customer_id):
conn = sqlite3.connect('database.db')
cursor = conn.cursor()
cursor.execute(f"DELETE FROM customers
WHERE customer_id = {customer_id}")
conn.commit()

C) def delete_customer(customer_id):
conn = sqlite3.connect('database.db')
cursor = conn.cursor()
cursor.execute("DELETE FROM customers WHERE
customer_id = :id", {'id': customer_id})
conn.commit()

D) def delete_customer(customer_id):
conn = sqlite3.connect('database.db')
cursor = conn.cursor()
query = "DELETE FROM customers WHERE
customer_id = '" + customer_id + "'"
cursor.execute(query)
conn.commit()

E) def delete_customer(customer_id):
conn = sqlite3.connect('database.db')
cursor = conn.cursor()
cursor.execute("DELETE FROM customers WHERE
customer_id = ? AND customer_name = ?",
(customer_id,))
conn.commit()
```

QUESTION 22

You are developing a Python script that interacts with a database containing customer credit card information. What practices will ensure secure handling of this data? (Select 2 answers)

A) Store credit card information in plain text.
B) Use parameterized SQL queries to avoid injection attacks.
C) Enable database encryption to protect sensitive information at rest.
D) Log credit card numbers for auditing purposes.
E) Secure the connection using SSL/TLS to protect data in transit.

QUESTION 23

You are implementing a class where you want to provide a utility method that doesn't depend on class instance data. How can you implement a static method? (Select 2 answers)

```
A) class Employee:
@staticmethod
def calculate_tax(income):
return income * 0.1
 B) class Employee:
def calculate_tax(self, income):
return income * 0.1
 C) class Employee:
@staticmethod
def calculate_tax():
return 0.1
 D) class Employee:
@classmethod
def calculate_tax(cls, income):
return income * 0.1
 E) class Employee:
@staticmethod
def calculate_tax(self, income):
return income * 0.1
```

QUESTION 24

You need to write multiple lines to a text file and ensure that it is closed properly after writing. Which approach is best for handling this?

```
 A) f = open('file.txt', 'w')
f.writelines(['Line 1', 'Line 2'])
f.close()
 B) with open('file.txt', 'w') as f:
f.writelines(['Line 1', 'Line 2'])
 C) f = open('file.txt', 'a')
f.writelines(['Line 1', 'Line 2'])
f.close()
 D) with open('file.txt', 'r+') as f:
f.writelines(['Line 1', 'Line 2'])
 E) f = open('file.txt', 'w+')
f.writelines(['Line 1', 'Line 2'])
```

QUESTION 25

You are writing a script that processes data from a SQL database and raises an exception if a query fails. What is the best way to define and use a custom exception for this? (Select 3 correct answers)

```
A) class QueryError(Exception):
def __init__(self, query):
```

```
self.query = query
raise QueryError('SELECT * FROM users')
 B) class QueryError(Exception):
raise QueryError()
 C) try:
raise QueryError('SELECT * FROM data')
except QueryError:
print('Database query failed')
 D) class QueryError(Exception):
def __init__(self, query):
self.query = query
super().__init__('Query failed')
raise QueryError('SELECT * FROM orders')
 E) raise Exception('QueryError').
```

QUESTION 26

You are given the orders and customers tables. You need to retrieve all customers who have placed at least one order. Which query is correct? (Select 1 correct answer)

```
A) SELECT c.customer_name FROM customers c
LEFT JOIN orders o ON c.customer_id =
o.customer_id;

B) SELECT c.customer_name FROM customers c
INNER JOIN orders o ON c.customer_id =
o.customer_id;

C) SELECT c.customer_name FROM customers c
RIGHT JOIN orders o ON c.customer_id =
o.customer_id;

D) SELECT c.customer_name FROM customers c
FULL JOIN orders o ON c.customer_id =
o.customer_id;

E) SELECT c.customer_name FROM customers c
LEFT JOIN orders o ON c.customer_id =
o.customer_id WHERE o.order_id IS NOT NULL;
```

QUESTION 27

You are asked to apply a DEFAULT value for the status column in the orders table where the default value should be 'Pending'. Which SQL statement is appropriate? (Select 1 correct answer)

```
A) ALTER TABLE orders ADD DEFAULT 'Pending'
FOR status;
B) ALTER TABLE orders ADD CONSTRAINT
default_status DEFAULT 'Pending';
C) ALTER TABLE orders ADD CONSTRAINT CHECK
(status = 'Pending');
D) ALTER TABLE orders ADD COLUMN status
DEFAULT 'Pending';
```

E) ALTER TABLE orders ADD DEFAULT status = 'Pending';

QUESTION 28

You are analyzing a query execution plan, and you notice an index scan instead of an index seek. How can you optimize this query to use an index seek instead? (Select 1 correct answer)

A) Rewrite the query to include a WHERE clause that filters on the indexed column.
B) Add more indexes to the table.
C) Rebuild the existing index on the table.
D) Change the index to a clustered index.
E) Drop and recreate the table with fewer columns.

QUESTION 29

You have collected monthly sales data for a retail store and noticed an outlier that is disproportionately affecting the average. Which measure of central tendency will minimize the impact of the outlier? (Select 2 correct answers)

```
A) statistics.mean(sales)
B) statistics.median(sales)
C) statistics.mode(sales)
D) np.mean(sales)
E) statistics.median_grouped(sales)
```

QUESTION 30

You are comparing the spread of prices across different markets. Which Python functions would you use to compute the standard deviation and variance to analyze this data? (Select 2 correct answers)

```
A) statistics.stdev(prices)
B) np.var(prices)
C) prices.stdev()
D) np.std(prices)
E) statistics.mean(prices)
```

QUESTION 31

You are working with a dataset containing sales data. How would you apply bootstrapping to estimate the mean sales over 1000 iterations using the pandas and numpy libraries? (Select 2 correct answers)

```
A) import pandas as pd; import numpy as np;
means = [np.mean(df['sales'].sample(frac=1,
replace=True)) for _ in range(1000)]
```

```
B) import pandas as pd; import numpy as np;
means =
[np.median(df['sales'].sample(frac=1,
replace=False)) for _ in range(1000)]
```

```
C) np.mean(np.random.choice(df['sales'],
size=len(df['sales']), replace=True))
D) import numpy as np;
np.percentile(df['sales'], [2.5, 97.5])
E) import pandas as pd;
pd.bootstrap(df['sales'], size=1000)
```

QUESTION 32

You have fitted a logistic regression model and want to assess its accuracy. Which of the following steps should be taken to ensure the model is not overfitting? (Select 2 correct answers)

A) Split the data into training and test sets before fitting the model
B) Calculate the model's accuracy on the training set
C) Regularize the model using techniques like L1 or L2 regularization
D) Use only a small subset of the available features to fit the model
E) Perform feature scaling using StandardScaler

QUESTION 33

While working on a dataset, you notice missing values in the 'income' column. You decide to replace missing values with the median income. Which methods correctly perform this task? (Select 2 correct answers)

```
A) df['income'] =
df['income'].fillna(df['income'].mean())
B)
df['income'].fillna(df['income'].median(),
inplace=True)
C) df['income'] =
df['income'].fillna(df['income'].median())
D) df.fillna({'income':
df['income'].mean()}, inplace=True)
E) df['income'] = df['income'].fillna(0)
```

QUESTION 34

You have a large dataset and want to apply the broadcasting mechanism to perform element-wise multiplication between an array a with shape (3, 1) and an array b with shape (1, 3). Which of the following shows correct use of broadcasting in NumPy? (Select 2 correct answers)

```
A) result = a * b
B) result = np.multiply(a, b)
C) result = np.dot(a, b)
D) result = np.matmul(a, b)
E) result = np.outer(a, b)
```

QUESTION 35

You are tasked with generating a histogram to visualize the distribution of a column age in a Pandas DataFrame. Which commands will correctly generate this histogram? (Select 2 correct answers)

```
A) plt.hist(df['age'])
B) df['age'].plot(kind='hist')
C) sns.distplot(df['age'])
D) plt.plot(df['age'], kind='hist')
E) df.histogram('age')
```

QUESTION 36

You are implementing a linear regression model to predict salary based on years of experience. Which steps should you follow to ensure the model is trained correctly? (Select 2 correct answers)

A) Split the dataset into training and test sets
B) Scale the feature values using StandardScaler
C) Train the model using the test set first
D) Use LinearRegression() from Scikit-learn to fit the model
E) Normalize the target variable (salary)

QUESTION 37

What steps can you take to improve the fit of a linear regression model? (Select 3 correct answers)

A) Add more features
B) Use polynomial features
C) Reduce the training dataset size
D) Add interaction terms between features
E) Scale the features using StandardScaler

QUESTION 38

You are given a dataset of products and their corresponding prices. You are required to group by product type and calculate both the mean and maximum prices per product type. Which of the following methods will correctly achieve this? Select THREE correct answers.

```
A)
df.groupby('product_type').agg({'price':['m
ean', 'max']})
B)
df.groupby('product_type')['price'].agg(['m
ean', 'max'])
C)
df.groupby('product_type')['price'].mean().
agg(['max'])
D)
df.price.groupby('product_type').apply(['me
an', 'max'])
E)
df.groupby('product_type').price.agg(['mean
', 'max'])
```

QUESTION 39

A team is working on a regression model and suspects that overfitting is occurring. To reduce overfitting, they decide to apply Lasso regression and tune the regularization strength. Which of the following scripts correctly implements this? Select two answers.

```
A) from sklearn.linear_model import Lasso;
lasso = Lasso(alpha=0.5);
lasso.fit(X_train, y_train)

B) from sklearn.linear_model import Ridge;
ridge = Ridge(alpha=0.5);
ridge.fit(X_train, y_train)

C) from sklearn.linear_model import
LassoCV; lasso_cv = LassoCV(alphas=[0.1,
0.5, 1.0]); lasso_cv.fit(X_train, y_train)

D) from sklearn.linear_model import
ElasticNet; enet = ElasticNet(alpha=0.5,
l1_ratio=0.8); enet.fit(X_train, y_train)

E) from sklearn.model_selection import
cross_val_score; lasso = Lasso(alpha=0.5);
cross_val_score(lasso, X_train, y_train,
cv=5)`
```

QUESTION 40

You are visualizing two numerical variables from a dataset using Matplotlib and you want to improve the clarity of your scatter plot by adding axis labels and a title. Which of the following scripts will accomplish this task? Select two answers.

```
A) plt.scatter(df['x'], df['y'])
B) plt.xlabel('X-axis')
C) plt.title('Scatter Plot of X and Y')
D) plt.ylabel('Y-axis')
E) plt.bar(df['x'], df['y'])
```

QUESTION 41

You need to visualize the comparison between product sales and profit in a bar plot using Matplotlib. Which of the following scripts will help you achieve this visualization? Select two correct answers.

```
A) plt.bar(df['Product'], df['Sales'])
B) plt.bar(df['Product'], df['Profit'])
C) plt.plot(df['Sales'], df['Profit'])
D) plt.scatter(df['Product'], df['Sales'])
E) plt.bar(df['Sales'], df['Profit'])
```

QUESTION 42

You are visualizing a dataset with a scatter plot and want to set different colors for different categories. Which method would allow you to color the scatter plot points based on a categorical variable in the dataset? Select two correct answers.

```
A) plt.scatter(df['x'], df['y'],
color='blue')
B) plt.scatter(df['x'], df['y'],
c=df['Category'])
C) plt.scatter(df['x'], df['y'],
color=plt.cm.get_cmap('Category'))
D) plt.scatter(df['x'], df['y'],
c=df['Category'], cmap='viridis')
E) plt.scatter(df['x'], df['y'],
group=df['Category'])
```

QUESTION 43

You are creating a visual summary of quarterly earnings for a management meeting. Which choice would NOT be an effective way to simplify the chart for a non-technical audience?

```
A) plt.bar(df['Quarter'], df['Earnings'],
color='blue')
```

```
B) plt.bar(df['Quarter'], df['Earnings'],
hatch='//')
C) plt.annotate('Peak earnings', xy=(1,
500), xytext=(1.2, 600),
arrowprops=dict(facecolor='black'))
D) plt.bar(df['Quarter'], df['Earnings'],
color='blue', label='Quarterly Earnings')
E) plt.legend()
```

QUESTION 44

During a sales review presentation, you are asked to create a narrative showing how different marketing campaigns influenced product sales. How do you best visualize and narrate this with Python using Seaborn or Matplotlib? Select two correct answers.

```
A) sns.lineplot(x=dates, y=sales,
hue=campaigns)
  plt.title('Campaign Impact on Sales')

B) plt.bar(dates, sales)
C) plt.scatter(dates, sales) without
specifying campaigns
D) sns.boxplot(x=campaigns, y=sales)
E) plt.pie(sales, labels=campaigns)
```

QUESTION 45

After analyzing product sales, you need to present a concise summary that shows which products are driving the most revenue. Which visualization approach would help you best summarize these key insights in a management report?

```
A) plt.pie(revenue, labels=products,
autopct="%1.1f%%")
B) plt.scatter(products, revenuE)
C) sns.heatmap(revenuE)
D) plt.barh(products, revenue);
plt.title("Revenue by Product")
E) sns.lineplot(x=products, y=revenue)
```

PRACTICE TEST 5 - ANSWERS ONLY

QUESTION 1

Answer - A

A) Correct – pd.merge(df1, df2, on='user_id', how='outer') performs a full outer join, including all users, even if they appear in only one dataframe.
B) Incorrect – concat() appends the dataframes without merging on a common column.
C) Incorrect – join() doesn't accept this form of merge syntax in Pandas.
D) Incorrect – append() adds one dataframe to another but does not perform a merge on the user_id column.
E) Incorrect – An inner merge only keeps rows where user_id exists in both dataframes, excluding unique users from either dataframe.

EXAM FOCUS	Full outer joins (how='outer') preserve all records from both datasets, even when keys don't match. This is vital for combining datasets with missing rows.
CAUTION ALERT	Avoid using concat() or append() when merging by a key. These methods won't join based on common columns and may result in incorrect data.

QUESTION 2

Answer - E

A) Correct – Imputing missing values with the median is a common technique when data is skewed.
B) Correct – Imputing missing values with the mean works when the data distribution is approximately normal.
C) Correct – Removing rows is a valid approach, but it may lead to data loss.
D) Correct – Filling missing values with a constant is a viable strategy but may not always be appropriate.
E) Incorrect – Leaving missing values unhandled can lead to errors during analysis and modeling, making this an inappropriate choice.

EXAM FOCUS	For missing values, constant imputation is only suitable when there's a valid reason. Use median or mean when dealing with skewed or normal data.
CAUTION ALERT	Leaving missing values unhandled can break your analysis pipeline. Always choose a strategy that fits your dataset and model requirements.

QUESTION 3

Answer - B

A) Correct – nltk is a natural language processing library commonly used for processing and analyzing unstructured text data.
B) Incorrect – pd.read_sql() is designed for structured SQL queries and is not applicable for loading unstructured text data directly.
C) Correct – TextBlob is a simple Python library used for basic sentiment analysis and text processing.
D) Correct – re can extract structured information from text by searching for patterns using regular expressions.
E) Correct – json.loads() parses JSON data (a common unstructured format) into a Python dictionary, making it easier to work with.

EXAM FOCUS	Natural language processing libraries like nltk and TextBlob are essential tools for handling unstructured text data and performing sentiment analysis.
CAUTION	pd.read_sql() is for structured data retrieval and cannot process unstructured text, making it unsuitable

QUESTION 4

Answer - A, C

A) Correct – A boxplot is ideal for visualizing data distributions and detecting outliers.
B) Incorrect – A scatter plot is better for comparing two variables, not for visualizing a single variable distribution.
C) Correct – A histogram is useful for visualizing the distribution of a single variable like salary.
D) Incorrect – A bar plot is not suitable for visualizing continuous variables like salary.
E) Incorrect – plt.plot() is used for time series data and not ideal for visualizing data distributions or outliers in a single variable.

EXAM FOCUS	Use boxplots and histograms to visually inspect outliers and understand the distribution of your data. This helps in spotting skewness.
CAUTION ALERT	Avoid scatter plots for a single variable's distribution; use histograms or boxplots to get a clear view of data spread and outliers.

QUESTION 5

Answer - A, B

A) Correct – This code uses Boolean indexing to filter rows where the price values are within the valid range.
B) Correct – The query() function allows filtering the dataset based on the given condition, ensuring prices are within the range.
C) Incorrect – This lambda function is not applied correctly for this use case and will return a Boolean for each row, rather than filtering the rows directly.
D) Incorrect – filter() does not work with a lambda function in this context.
E) Incorrect – There is no validate_range() function in Pandas for range validation.

EXAM FOCUS	Use df.query() and Boolean indexing to apply range checks on numeric columns like price. They ensure efficient filtering of data within specified ranges.
CAUTION ALERT	Methods like apply() with lambda functions aren't as efficient for range validation. Stick to Boolean indexing for cleaner and faster filtering.

QUESTION 6

Answer - A, D

A) Correct – fetchmany(size) retrieves the specified number of rows at a time.
B) Incorrect – fetchall() retrieves all rows, which may lead to memory overload with large datasets.
C) Incorrect – There is no fetchbatch() method in sqlite3.
D) Correct – fetchone() retrieves a single row at a time, which can be used to process data incrementally.
E) Incorrect – fetch_chunk() is not a valid method in the sqlite3 library.

EXAM FOCUS	Use fetchmany() for batch data retrieval and fetchone() for one row at a time. These help prevent memory overload with large datasets.
CAUTION ALERT	fetchall() retrieves all rows at once, which can overload memory for large datasets. Avoid it when working with very large data.

QUESTION 7

Answer - A, B

A) Correct – np.ptp() calculates the range, and sns.boxplot() creates a boxplot.
B) Correct – This manually calculates the range by subtracting the minimum value from the maximum, and sns.boxplot() is correctly used.
C) Incorrect – While the range is calculated correctly, the function sns.boxplot() doesn't have a range() method.
D) Incorrect – There is no range() method in Seaborn for boxplots.
E) Incorrect – The range is incorrectly calculated using pd.DataFrame().range(), which doesn't directly compute the data range.

EXAM FOCUS	Use np.ptp() or subtract max and min values to calculate the range. sns.boxplot() visualizes data spread and outliers effectively.
CAUTION ALERT	sns.boxplot() does not have a .range() method. Stick to manual calculations or numpy functions for the range.

QUESTION 8

Answer - A, B

A) Correct – This drops rows with NaN values and returns the result.
B) Correct – This drops rows with NaN values in-place, meaning the DataFrame is updated.
C) Incorrect – This forward fills missing values instead of dropping them.
D) Incorrect – This drops columns with NaN values, not rows.
E) Incorrect – The syntax is incorrect for dropping rows based on NaN values.

EXAM FOCUS	Use df.dropna() to remove rows with missing data in Pandas. Adding inplace=True updates the DataFrame directly.
CAUTION ALERT	Be clear about whether you want to drop rows or columns. axis=0 drops rows, while axis=1 drops columns.

QUESTION 9

Answer - A, B

A) Correct: cross_val_score is the main method to apply cross-validation.
B) Correct: KFold provides an advanced way of customizing cross-validation splits.
C) Incorrect: train_test_split is for one-time train-test split, not cross-validation.
D) Incorrect: cross_val_score should not be used with test data.
E) Incorrect: Fit is part of training but not relevant for cross-validation.

EXAM FOCUS	Cross-validation splits data into multiple folds, training and testing on each fold. Use cross_val_score() to evaluate the model's performance across the folds.
CAUTION ALERT	Don't confuse train_test_split() with cross-validation; they are different techniques. Cross-validation offers a more reliable estimate of model performance.

QUESTION 10

Answer - A, B

A) Correct: sns.set_style("whitegrid") is commonly used to set the background style to a white grid, which is ideal for clean presentations.
B) Correct: Setting the palette to pastel ensures that the colors are soft and non-intrusive, which is appropriate for professional visualizations.
C) Incorrect: set_context("talk") modifies the scaling for larger plots, not for changing the color palette or style.
D) Incorrect: While setting a color palette in individual plots is possible, this would not set it globally for all plots in Seaborn.
E) Incorrect: set_style and palette are handled separately; you cannot set both in the same function call.

EXAM FOCUS	Use sns.set_style("whitegrid") and sns.set_palette("pastel") for professional presentation aesthetics. Style and palette adjustments help clarify plots.
CAUTION ALERT	Don't attempt to modify set_style() and set_palette() in the same function call. These are handled independently in Seaborn.

QUESTION 11

Answer - A, D

A) Converting text to lowercase is a basic text preprocessing step.
B) This removes extra spaces but is less relevant for core text cleaning.
C) Replacing the text with "Unknown" can remove valuable data.
D) Stripping whitespace ensures clean, well-formatted text.
E) Setting text to None removes the data entirely, which is not preprocessing.

EXAM FOCUS	Text preprocessing steps like converting to lowercase (str.lower()) and removing whitespace (strip()) are essential to standardize and clean text data.
CAUTION ALERT	Ensure that you do not remove or replace too much of the data. Over-cleaning text can lead to loss of valuable information for analysis.

QUESTION 12

Answer - A, C

A) Secure transmission via SSL ensures sensitive data is transferred securely under GDPR requirements.
B) Exporting data outside the EU without consent is against GDPR's cross-border data transfer rules.
C) GDPR gives users the right to withdraw consent, and providing this option via Python ensures compliance.
D) GDPR requires informing users about how long data will be retained, so indefinite storage without notice is a violation.
E) Providing data portability ensures users can retrieve their data, a key requirement under GDPR.

EXAM FOCUS	Use Python's ssl module to encrypt sensitive data during transmission and provide users with the ability to withdraw consent for data processing.
CAUTION ALERT	Never transfer data to non-EU servers without user consent. This can breach GDPR's data protection rules regarding international transfers.

QUESTION 13

Answer - A

A) Correct, 'inner' merge keeps only rows common in both DataFrames.
B) Concat combines DataFrames without merging on 'ID'.
C) Left join keeps all rows from the left DataFrame, not both.
D) Right join keeps rows from the right DataFrame.
E) Outer merge keeps all rows from both DataFrames.

EXAM FOCUS	For merging data on a common key (e.g., ID), use an inner join (pd.merge(..., how='inner')) to retain only matched rows.
CAUTION ALERT	Don't use concatenation (pd.concat()) when you need to merge DataFrames based on keys, as it simply stacks the DataFrames without aligning columns.

QUESTION 14

Answer - A, B

A) Correct: This merges on multiple keys using on.
B) Correct: A left join on multiple keys ensures complete data from df1.
C) Incorrect: Redundant use of left_on and right_on for identical columns.
D) Incorrect: join is based on the index, not columns.
E) Incorrect: Keys do not match between left_on and right_on.

EXAM FOCUS	Use pd.merge() with multiple keys (on=['region', 'product_id']) to join datasets, ensuring relationships across columns are retained.
CAUTION ALERT	Avoid using join() when you need to merge by multiple columns. It's better suited for index-based joins.

QUESTION 15

Answer - A, B

Option A: Correct – Uses Seaborn's lineplot and saves the image properly.
Option B: Correct – A basic Matplotlib plot and saving it with plt.savefig().
Option C: Incorrect – The savefig() method is incorrectly attached to Seaborn.
Option D: Incorrect – plt.show() displays the plot but does not save it.
Option E: Incorrect – Incorrect format specified (PNG should be used).

EXAM FOCUS	Save Seaborn or Matplotlib plots using plt.savefig(). Ensure the format is specified correctly when exporting, such as PNG for images.
CAUTION ALERT	Calling savefig() directly on Seaborn objects won't work; it must be done through Matplotlib's plt.savefig().

QUESTION 16

Answer - A, D

Option A: Correct – total is a local variable, ensuring no global variable conflict.
Option B: Incorrect – Uses the global keyword, making total a global variable, which is not desired.
Option C: Incorrect – total is reset to 0 inside the loop, producing incorrect results.

Option D: Correct – local_total ensures the variable is local to the function.
Option E: Incorrect – Uses global, making the variable accessible outside the function.

EXAM FOCUS	Ensure variables are local within functions by avoiding global declarations. Use local variables to keep scope confined within the function.
CAUTION ALERT	Resetting a variable inside a loop can lead to incorrect results. Declare and maintain variable scope outside the loop where needed.

QUESTION 17

Answer - A, C, E

Option A: Correct – Generates a heatmap using Seaborn with annotations.
Option B: Incorrect – plt.imshow() is not a recommended way to visualize correlation matrices.
Option C: Correct – This correctly calculates the correlation and creates a heatmap using Seaborn.
Option D: Incorrect – There is no kind='heatmap' option in Pandas' plot().
Option E: Correct – Creates a heatmap with Seaborn, using a specific color map and linewidths for clarity.

EXAM FOCUS	Combine Pandas and Seaborn for insightful visualizations. First calculate correlations with df.corr(), then use Seaborn's heatmap() for easy visualization.
CAUTION ALERT	Avoid using imshow() for correlation heatmaps, as it doesn't provide the same level of customization and clarity as Seaborn.

QUESTION 18

Answer - A, C

Option A: Correct – Descriptive variable names improve readability and make the code self-explanatory.
Option B: Incorrect – Single-letter variable names can confuse others and reduce readability.
Option C: Correct – Breaking long functions into smaller functions improves reusability and simplifies testing and debugging.
Option D: Incorrect – Writing all code in one function makes it harder to debug and maintain.
Option E: Incorrect – While comments can be useful, over-reliance on comments indicates code that is not self-explanatory.

EXAM FOCUS	Descriptive names are crucial: Long, descriptive variable names make your code more readable and reduce the need for excessive comments.
CAUTION ALERT	Single-letter variables are risky: Avoid using single-letter variable names like 'x' and 'y' for complex logic; it confuses future readers of your code.

QUESTION 19

Answer - A, D

Option A: Correct – Defines a custom exception inheriting from Exception and raises it with a custom message.
Option B: Incorrect – This uses a general Exception, not a custom one.
Option C: Incorrect – The custom exception class does not inherit from Exception.
Option D: Correct – Properly defines a custom exception with an __init__ method for custom error messages.
Option E: Incorrect – BaseException is the top-level class, but Exception is the recommended base class for custom errors.

EXAM FOCUS	Custom exceptions help: Define and use custom exceptions for specific error conditions to make your code cleaner and error handling more understandable.

QUESTION 20

Answer - A, C

Option A: Correct – This query retrieves customer names where total_purchase is greater than $100.
Option B: Incorrect – HAVING is used after GROUP BY and is not applicable here.
Option C: Correct – Retrieves records where total_purchase is greater than or equal to $100.
Option D: Incorrect – Although correct, the question only asks for totals greater than $100, not for a range.
Option E: Incorrect – Excludes records where the purchase is exactly $100, which does not meet the requirement

EXAM FOCUS	*HAVING vs WHERE: Use HAVING with aggregate functions like SUM() or COUNT() and WHERE for row-based filtering.*
CAUTION ALERT	*Don't misuse HAVING: HAVING is meant for filtering results after aggregation, not for simple filtering on row values.*

QUESTION 21

Answer - A, C

Option A: Correct – Uses a ? placeholder to parameterize the customer_id, ensuring SQL injection protection.
Option B: Incorrect – Direct string interpolation in SQL queries opens the door to SQL injection.
Option C: Correct – Uses a named placeholder (:id) in the query and passes a dictionary to avoid SQL injection.
Option D: Incorrect – Concatenating user input into SQL queries is vulnerable to SQL injection.
Option E: Incorrect – The query structure is incorrect; placeholders must be provided for all parameters in the query.

EXAM FOCUS	*Delete safely with parameters: When deleting records based on user input, always use parameterized queries to avoid SQL injection risks.*
CAUTION ALERT	*No direct string interpolation: Avoid using Python's f-strings or concatenation with SQL queries. It leads to serious vulnerabilities.*

QUESTION 22

Answer - B, C

Option A: Incorrect – Storing sensitive information like credit card data in plain text is highly insecure.
Option B: Correct – Parameterized queries prevent SQL injection attacks, ensuring secure query execution.
Option C: Correct – Database encryption protects sensitive data at rest, especially important for credit card information.
Option D: Incorrect – Logging sensitive information like credit card numbers is a security risk.
Option E: Incorrect – While SSL/TLS protects data in transit, it is important but not one of the two best answers for secure data handling.

EXAM FOCUS	*Secure sensitive data: Always use parameterized queries to avoid SQL injection and enable encryption for sensitive data like credit card information to ensure data safety.*
CAUTION ALERT	*Never store sensitive data in plain text: Credit card information and other sensitive data must always be encrypted to prevent exposure in case of data breaches.*

QUESTION 23

Answer - A, C

Option A: Correct – This is a valid static method where @staticmethod decorator is used, and it doesn't rely on instance data.
 Option B: Incorrect – This is a regular instance method because self is passed.
 Option C: Correct – This is another valid static method that doesn't require instance or class reference.
 Option D: Incorrect – This is a class method, not a static method, because @classmethod is used.
 Option E: Incorrect – Static methods should not have self in their parameters as they do not interact with instance attributes.

EXAM FOCUS	Static methods don't need self or cls: Use @staticmethod for methods that don't depend on class or instance data, ensuring cleaner class design.
CAUTION ALERT	Watch for unnecessary parameters: Static methods should not include self or cls, as they don't interact with instance or class-level data.

QUESTION 24

Answer - B

Option A: Incorrect – Although the lines are written, not using a context manager can lead to issues if the file is not closed properly.
 Option B: Correct – This uses a context manager, ensuring the file is properly closed after writing.
 Option C: Incorrect – This appends the lines rather than writing them as new content.
 Option D: Incorrect – r+ mode is used for reading and writing, which is not needed in this case.
 Option E: Incorrect – w+ opens the file for both reading and writing, which is unnecessary when only writing is required.

EXAM FOCUS	Context managers ensure file closure: Use with open() to ensure the file is closed automatically, even if an error occurs during writing.
CAUTION ALERT	Manually closing files is risky: Forgetting to call file.close() can leave files open, leading to resource leaks and issues in concurrent file access scenarios.

QUESTION 25

Answer - A, C, D

A) Correct: This defines a custom exception for query errors and raises it with a specific query.
 B) Incorrect: This raises the exception without any useful context, such as the query that failed.
 C) Correct: This code raises and catches the custom QueryError with proper exception handling.
 D) Correct: This is another valid approach to raising and handling a custom QueryError with a clear message.
 E) Incorrect: Raising a generic Exception with a string doesn't define a custom exception, losing the benefit of having specific exception handling.

EXAM FOCUS	Include query context in errors: Custom exceptions related to SQL queries should include the query string itself to help identify which part of the SQL failed.
CAUTION ALERT	Avoid over-reliance on Exception: Directly raising generic exceptions such as Exception misses the advantage of custom error handling.

QUESTION 26

Answer - E

Option A: Incorrect, LEFT JOIN would include customers who have not placed any orders.
Option B: Incorrect, INNER JOIN excludes customers without orders, but does not filter properly.
Option C: Incorrect, RIGHT JOIN is unnecessary and focuses on orders rather than customers.
Option D: Incorrect, FULL JOIN retrieves all customers, even those without orders.
Option E: Correct, this correctly uses LEFT JOIN and filters out customers without orders.

EXAM FOCUS	*Use WHERE with IS NOT NULL: When checking for records with at least one order, a LEFT JOIN with a WHERE clause checking IS NOT NULL ensures unmatched rows are excluded.*
CAUTION ALERT	*LEFT JOIN without filter may include unwanted rows: Without filtering for non-NULL values, LEFT JOIN may return customers who have placed no orders.*

QUESTION 27

Answer - A

Option A: Correct, DEFAULT 'Pending' FOR status sets the default value for new records in the status column.
Option B: Incorrect, DEFAULT is not typically applied via CONSTRAINT.
Option C: Incorrect, CHECK enforces conditions, not default values.
Option D: Incorrect, adding a column is unnecessary if it already exists.
Option E: Incorrect, this syntax is invalid.

EXAM FOCUS	*DEFAULT sets initial values: The ALTER TABLE statement with DEFAULT 'Pending' FOR status sets an initial value of 'Pending' for new rows in the status column.*
CAUTION ALERT	*CHECK constraints don't set defaults: They only enforce conditions, while DEFAULT assigns a starting value to new records.*

QUESTION 28

Answer - A

Option A: Correct, filtering on the indexed column with a WHERE clause encourages the optimizer to use an index seek.
Option B: Incorrect, adding more indexes won't necessarily improve query performance if the query doesn't filter on them.
Option C: Incorrect, rebuilding the index doesn't guarantee that the query will use a seek.
Option D: Incorrect, changing to a clustered index won't directly affect the query's index usage pattern.
Option E: Incorrect, dropping and recreating the table does not directly address the query optimization issue.

EXAM FOCUS	*Ensure WHERE clause matches indexed columns: To switch from an index scan to an index seek, the query must filter on the indexed column using an appropriate WHERE clause.*
CAUTION ALERT	*Index rebuilding doesn't always help: Rebuilding or reorganizing indexes doesn't guarantee that an index seek will occur unless the query is optimized to use it.*

QUESTION 29

Answer - B, E

Option A: Incorrect, the mean is sensitive to outliers.
Option B: Correct, the median is resistant to outliers and better reflects the central tendency.
Option C: Incorrect, the mode doesn't consider numerical distribution effectively for continuous data.
Option D: Incorrect, np.mean() is influenced by outliers, like statistics.mean().
Option E: Correct, median_grouped() can minimize the effect of an outlier in grouped data.

EXAM FOCUS	Outliers distort the mean: Use the median or grouped median to reduce the impact of outliers in your analysis of central tendency.
CAUTION ALERT	Avoid using mean in the presence of outliers: The mean is affected by outliers and can give a false representation of the dataset's central tendency.

QUESTION 30

Answer - A, D

Option A: Correct, statistics.stdev() computes standard deviation.
Option B: Incorrect, while np.var() calculates variance, the question asks for both variance and standard deviation.
Option C: Incorrect, prices.stdev() is not a valid method.
Option D: Correct, np.std() computes the standard deviation.
Option E: Incorrect, mean is not a measure of spread.

EXAM FOCUS	Standard deviation and variance measure data spread: Use statistics.stdev() or np.std() for standard deviation and np.var() for variance to analyze the spread of values in a dataset.
CAUTION ALERT	Mean doesn't indicate spread: Remember, the mean only provides central tendency, not variability. Use standard deviation and variance to assess spread.

QUESTION 31

Answer - A, C

Option A: Correct, this uses pandas and numpy for bootstrapping correctly.
Option B: Incorrect, replace=False prevents bootstrapping.
Option C: Correct, np.random.choice() can be used for bootstrapping.
Option D: Incorrect, percentile does not apply bootstrapping, just confidence intervals.
Option E: Incorrect, pandas does not have a bootstrap method.

EXAM FOCUS	Use pandas.sample() and numpy for bootstrapping: Resample your data with replacement using df.sample() or np.random.choice() to generate bootstrapped means in Python.
CAUTION ALERT	pandas has no bootstrap() method: Be cautious—pandas does not have a direct bootstrap() method; rely on sample() with replace=True.

QUESTION 32

Answer - A, C

Option A: Correct, splitting the data helps evaluate the model on unseen data, preventing overfitting.
Option B: Incorrect, calculating accuracy on training data alone can mislead about overfitting.
Option C: Correct, regularization controls overfitting by penalizing large coefficients.

Option D: Incorrect, using fewer features does not necessarily prevent overfitting.
Option E: Incorrect, scaling features helps with convergence but does not directly address overfitting.

EXAM FOCUS	Split data and regularize to prevent overfitting: Always split your data into training and test sets and apply regularization (L1 or L2) to reduce overfitting in logistic regression models.
CAUTION ALERT	Training accuracy isn't enough: Relying solely on training accuracy can mislead you. Always validate your model on unseen test data to check for overfitting.

QUESTION 33

Answer - B, C

A) Incorrect: This uses the mean instead of the median
B) Correct: Fills missing values with the median and modifies the DataFrame in place
C) Correct: Fills missing values with the median and assigns the result to the 'income' column
D) Incorrect: This uses the mean instead of the median
E) Incorrect: This fills missing values with 0, not the median.

EXAM FOCUS	In-place operations improve efficiency: Using inplace=True while filling missing values directly modifies the DataFrame, which is efficient when memory usage is a concern.
CAUTION ALERT	Check your aggregation strategy: Avoid replacing missing values with means or arbitrary values (like 0) without checking whether it is appropriate for your dataset.

QUESTION 34

Answer - A, B

A) Correct: Using * for element-wise multiplication works with broadcasting, and the arrays with shapes (3, 1) and (1, 3) are compatible for broadcasting.
B) Correct: np.multiply() performs element-wise multiplication and supports broadcasting between arrays of compatible shapes like (3, 1) and (1, 3).
C) Incorrect: np.dot() performs matrix multiplication, not element-wise multiplication, so it does not apply to this context of broadcasting.
D) Incorrect: np.matmul() is used for matrix multiplication, which is different from element-wise multiplication. Broadcasting is not relevant here.
E) Incorrect: np.outer() computes the outer product, which is not the same as element-wise multiplication. The shapes of the arrays do not align for broadcasting.

EXAM FOCUS	Broadcasting for multiplication: NumPy broadcasting supports element-wise multiplication for arrays with compatible shapes. Learn how to handle different array shapes for broadcasting.
CAUTION ALERT	Differentiate from matrix multiplication: Element-wise multiplication using * or np.multiply() is not the same as matrix multiplication, which requires np.dot() or np.matmul().

QUESTION 35

Answer - A, B

A) Correct: plt.hist() creates a histogram using Matplotlib for the age column.
B) Correct: Pandas' plot(kind='hist') is a quick way to create a histogram directly from a DataFrame.
C) Incorrect: sns.distplot() is deprecated in recent versions of Seaborn, and is no longer recommended.
D) Incorrect: plt.plot() is used for line plots and would raise an error when used with kind='hist'.

E) Incorrect: df.histogram() is not a valid function in Pandas and would raise an AttributeError.

EXAM FOCUS	*Visualize data distributions: Use plt.hist() or df.plot(kind='hist') to create histograms and observe data distributions in your dataset.*
CAUTION ALERT	*Deprecated functions: Avoid using deprecated Seaborn functions like sns.distplot(). Instead, use updated methods like sns.histplot().*

QUESTION 36

Answer - A, D

A) Correct: Splitting the dataset ensures that the model is evaluated on unseen data.
B) Incorrect: Scaling may not be necessary for linear regression unless features vary greatly in magnitude.
C) Incorrect: The test set should only be used for evaluation, not for training.
D) Correct: Using LinearRegression() from Scikit-learn is the correct approach to train a linear regression model.
E) Incorrect: The target variable (salary) should not typically be normalized in regression tasks.

EXAM FOCUS	*Split datasets and use correct models: Always split your dataset into training and test sets. Use LinearRegression() from Scikit-learn to train your model correctly.*
CAUTION ALERT	*Train on training data only: Do not train models on test sets. Ensure proper train-test splits for effective evaluation and generalization.*

QUESTION 37

Answer - A, B, D

A) Correct – Adding more relevant features can improve the model's ability to capture relationships in the data.
B) Correct – Polynomial features can capture non-linear relationships, improving model fit.
C) Incorrect – Reducing the dataset size may limit the model's learning capacity and lead to underfitting.
D) Correct – Interaction terms between features can help the model capture more complex relationships.
E) Incorrect – While scaling can improve convergence, it doesn't directly improve the model's fit for linear regression.

EXAM FOCUS	*Add features thoughtfully: Adding more features and interaction terms can improve model fit, but ensure that these features are relevant and not adding noise.*
CAUTION ALERT	*Reducing data leads to underfitting: Avoid reducing the training dataset size, as this limits the model's learning ability and may result in underfitting.*

QUESTION 38

Answer - A, B, E

A) Correct – This uses the agg method to calculate both the mean and maximum in a grouped DataFrame.
B) Correct – This method is also valid for calculating both metrics within a single groupby operation.
C) Incorrect – The agg function should be applied at the groupby level, not after applying mean().
D) Incorrect – Apply() cannot be used this way; agg() is needed here.
E) Correct – Similar to A and B, this groups and applies both aggregation methods properly.

EXAM FOCUS	*Group by and aggregate multiple functions: Use agg() to apply more than one aggregation (e.g., mean, max) on grouped data. It's especially useful when analyzing across categories like product types.*
CAUTION ALERT	*Don't use apply() for simple aggregations: Functions like apply() are not efficient for basic aggregations like mean or max. Stick to agg() for these tasks.*

QUESTION 39

Answer - A, C

A) Correct because Lasso(alpha=0.5) correctly applies Lasso regression with the specified regularization parameter to reduce overfitting.
B) Incorrect as it applies Ridge regression, which uses L2 regularization, not L1 regularization as required by Lasso regression.
C) Correct because LassoCV performs cross-validation for Lasso regression and tunes the alpha value to reduce overfitting.
D) Incorrect as ElasticNet combines L1 and L2 regularization, which is not purely Lasso regression.
E) Incorrect because although cross-validation is valid, it lacks tuning for alpha values and only applies a fixed alpha=0.5.

EXAM FOCUS	*Lasso Regression for Feature Selection: Lasso regression (L1) is useful for both preventing overfitting and performing feature selection, especially in datasets with many irrelevant features.*
CAUTION ALERT	*Don't confuse Ridge and Lasso: Ridge (L2) reduces overfitting by penalizing large coefficients, but it does not perform feature selection like Lasso (L1).*

QUESTION 40

Answer - B, D

A) Incorrect because while plt.scatter() generates the plot, it does not address the requirement of adding labels and a title.
B) Correct because plt.xlabel() adds a label to the x-axis, which improves the clarity of the plot.
C) Incorrect because while it adds a title, the question asks for labels as well, and this does not fulfill all the requirements.
D) Correct because plt.ylabel() adds a label to the y-axis, improving the clarity and interpretability of the plot.
E) Incorrect because plt.bar() generates a bar plot, which is not appropriate for the given task.

EXAM FOCUS	*Axis Labels: Always add axis labels with plt.xlabel() and plt.ylabel() to improve the interpretability of scatter plots, especially when visualizing two numerical variables.*
CAUTION ALERT	*Incorrect Plot Type: Bar plots (plt.bar()) should not be used when the task is to visualize numerical relationships. Stick to plt.scatter() for continuous data.*

QUESTION 41

Answer - A, B

A) Correct because plt.bar() creates a valid bar plot, with Product as the categorical variable on the x-axis and Sales as the numerical variable on the y-axis.
B) Correct because this is another valid bar plot, with Product on the x-axis and Profit on the y-axis.
C) Incorrect because plt.plot() creates a line plot, which is not ideal for comparing categorical data like product names with numerical values.
D) Incorrect because plt.scatter() is used for scatter plots, not for comparing categorical data with bar plots.
E) Incorrect because using plt.bar() with Sales and Profit as axes will not give the correct comparison.

EXAM FOCUS	*Bar Plot Tip: Use plt.bar() to compare sales and profit across categories. Bar plots work best when comparing numerical values across different categories like products.*
CAUTION ALERT	*Avoid Scatter and Line Plots: plt.scatter() and plt.plot() are not appropriate for comparing categorical data like products with numerical values. Stick to bar plots.*

QUESTION 42

Answer - B, D

A) Incorrect because setting color='blue' applies a single color to all points and does not differentiate between categories.

B) Correct because c=df['Category'] correctly applies different colors to the points based on the values in the 'Category' column.

C) Incorrect because color=plt.cm.get_cmap('Category') is not the correct syntax; colormap objects need to be used directly with cmap or c parameters.

D) Correct because this correctly maps the categories using the 'viridis' colormap for color coding the points based on the categorical variable.

E) Incorrect because group=df['Category'] is not a valid argument in plt.scatter().

EXAM FOCUS	*Scatter Plot Tip: Use c=df['Category'] and cmap='viridis' in plt.scatter() to color points based on a categorical variable. This enhances clarity in the visualization.*
CAUTION ALERT	*Incorrect Syntax: Avoid using color=plt.cm.get_cmap('Category') or group=df['Category']—these aren't valid in plt.scatter() for color-coding categories.*

QUESTION 43

Answer - E

A) Suitable because a simple bar plot with a single color keeps the visualization clear and easy to interpret for non-technical audiences.

B) Suitable because adding a pattern (hatch) makes the bars visually distinct without adding complexity to the plot.

C) Suitable because annotating a key point helps emphasize important information for the audience.

D) Suitable because adding a label clarifies the meaning of the bars without adding unnecessary complexity.

E) Least effective because adding a legend without multiple categories might confuse the audience, making the chart more complex than necessary.

EXAM FOCUS	*Simplification for Non-Tech Audiences: Use annotations (plt.annotate()) to highlight peaks or key data points without overloading the audience with complex legends or multiple visuals.*
CAUTION ALERT	*Legend Overuse: Avoid adding legends if they aren't needed (e.g., in simple bar plots). This can clutter the chart and confuse non-technical viewers unnecessarily.*

QUESTION 44

Answer - A, D

A) Correct because using a Seaborn line plot and differentiating sales by campaigns with the hue parameter emphasizes the impact of marketing efforts on sales over time.

B) Incorrect because a bar chart lacks the granularity needed to show campaign differentiation effectively.

C) Incorrect because using a scatter plot without campaign differentiation weakens the narrative's focus on campaign impact.

D) Correct because a boxplot can visually compare the sales distribution for each campaign, helping to narrate which campaign had the most significant influence.

E) Incorrect because pie charts are not effective in showing time-based sales comparisons across campaigns.

EXAM FOCUS	*Marketing Impact: Use Seaborn's hue parameter in sns.lineplot() to differentiate campaigns. It's ideal for showing how different marketing efforts influence product sales over time.*
CAUTION ALERT	*Scatter Plot Limitations: Avoid using scatter plots without specifying categories or campaigns. This weakens the narrative when differentiating marketing impacts.*

QUESTION 45

Answer - D

A) Incorrect because a pie chart may show the distribution of revenue but doesn't clearly summarize which products are driving the most revenue, especially if there are many products.

B) Incorrect because a scatter plot doesn't summarize the data concisely for a management report.

C) Incorrect because a heatmap is not suitable for summarizing individual product revenue data.

D) Correct because a horizontal bar chart clearly shows which products are driving the most revenue, making it easy to summarize for a management report.

E) Incorrect because a line plot is not ideal for summarizing discrete product categories.

EXAM FOCUS	*Horizontal Bar for Revenue: When showing products driving the most revenue, horizontal bar charts help present the data clearly, especially for reports with many categories.*
CAUTION ALERT	*Pie Chart Limitations: A pie chart with too many segments becomes difficult to read and doesn't clearly show which products generate the most revenue.*

PRACTICE TEST 6 - QUESTIONS ONLY

QUESTION 1

You need to integrate customer data from two different APIs, one in JSON and the other in XML. What is the correct Python code to read these data sources and combine them into a single Pandas DataFrame? (Select 3 answers)

```
 A) df_json = pd.read_json('api_data.json')
 B) df_xml = pd.read_xml('api_data.xml')
 C) combined_df = pd.concat([df_json,
df_xml], axis=1)
 D) df_xml = pd.read_csv('api_data.xml')
 E) combined_df = pd.merge(df_json, df_xml)
```

QUESTION 2

You are tasked with storing large volumes of unstructured data collected from IoT devices. The data needs to be scalable and accessed for machine learning analysis. Which storage solution would be most appropriate for this use case?

A) Data warehouse
B) Data lake
C) CSV files stored in cloud
D) Relational database
E) Local Excel files

QUESTION 3

You have a dataset with numerical features that range from 0 to 1000, and you need to apply Min-Max scaling to normalize the data for machine learning. Which Python code would correctly implement Min-Max scaling? (Select 2 answers)

```
 A) from sklearn.preprocessing import
MinMaxScaler
 B) scaler = MinMaxScaler()
 C) df_scaled = scaler.fit_transform(df)
 D) df_scaled = df.apply(MinMaxScaler)
 E) df_scaled = scaler.scale(df)
```

QUESTION 4

You are working with a dataset of customer transactions and want to split it into training and testing sets for machine learning. What Python code would you use to correctly split the dataset into training and testing sets? (Select 2 answers)

```
 A) from sklearn.model_selection import
train_test_split
 B) train_test_split(df, test_size=0.3,
random_state=42)
 C) df.split(test_size=0.3)
 D) train_test_split(df)
 E) df.sample(0.7)
```

QUESTION 5

You are writing a function to find the sum of all numbers in a list. Which Python code snippets correctly implement this functionality using a for loop? (Select 2 answers)

```
A) def sum_list(lst): total = 0
for num in lst: total += num
return total

 B) def sum_list(lst): total = 0
lst.forEach(lambda x: total += x)
return total

 C) def sum_list(lst):
return sum(lst)

 D) def sum_list(lst): total = 0
for num in lst: total += num
print(total)

 E) def sum_list(lst):
return sum([i for i in lst])
```

QUESTION 6

You need to establish a connection to an SQLite database using Python. Which of the following Python code snippets correctly establishes the connection? (Select 2 answers)

```
A) import sqlite3
conn = sqlite3.connect('database.db')

 B) import sqlite3
conn = sqlite3.connect('localhost')

 C) import sqlite3
conn = sqlite3.connect(':memory:')

 D) import sqlite
conn = sqlite3.connect('db_file')

 E) import sqlite
conn = sqlite3.create('db_file')
```

QUESTION 7

You are performing a hypothesis test in Python using

the scipy.stats library. Which of the following snippets correctly conducts a two-tailed t-test to compare the means of two independent samples? (Select 2 answers)

```
A) import scipy.stats as stats
t_stat, p_val = stats.ttest_ind(sample1,
sample2)

 B) from scipy import stats
t_stat, p_val = stats.ttest_1samp(sample1,
sample2)

 C) from scipy import stats
t_stat, p_val = stats.ttest_rel(sample1,
sample2)

 D) import statsmodels.api as sm
t_stat, p_val = sm.ttest(sample1, sample2)

 E) from scipy.stats import ttest_ind
t_stat, p_val = ttest_ind(sample1, sample2)
```

QUESTION 8

You are tasked with creating a 2D NumPy array and slicing a subarray from it. Which of the following snippets correctly creates an array and slices the first two rows and first two columns?

```
A) import numpy as np
arr = np.array([[1, 2], [3, 4], [5, 6]])
subarr = arr[:2, :2]

 B) import numpy as np
arr = np.array([[1, 2, 3], [4, 5, 6], [7,
8, 9]])
subarr = arr[1:, :2]

 C) import numpy as np
arr = np.arange(6).reshape(2, 3)
subarr = arr[:, :1]

 D) import numpy as np
arr = np.array([1, 2, 3, 4, 5, 6])
subarr = arr.reshape(2, 3)[1:, 1:]

 E) import numpy as np
arr = np.array([[1, 2, 3], [4, 5, 6], [7,
8, 9]])
subarr = arr[:2, :2]
```

QUESTION 9

You are tasked with creating a basic line plot using Matplotlib to visualize the sales data over the months. Which of the following steps are correct to customize the plot with title, labels, and legends? Select 2 correct options.

```
A) import matplotlib.pyplot as plt
plt.plot(months, sales)
plt.title('Monthly Sales')
plt.xlabel('Months')
plt.ylabel('Sales')

B) plt.legend(['Sales'])
plt.show()

C) plt.legend(loc='upper right')
plt.grid(True)

D) plt.scatter(months, sales)
plt.title('Sales Scatter Plot')

E) plt.bar(months, sales)
plt.title('Sales Bar Plot')
```

QUESTION 10

A data analyst is tasked with visualizing the distribution of a dataset using Seaborn. The dataset contains a column "age" and they want to create a box plot to display the distribution. Which of the following Python scripts will accomplish this? (Select 2 correct answers)

```
A) import seaborn as sns
sns.boxplot(x='age', data=df)

 B) import seaborn as sns
sns.histplot(data=df, x='age')

 C) import seaborn as sns
sns.boxplot(x='age', y='gender', data=df)

 D) import seaborn as sns
sns.scatterplot(x='age', y='salary',
data=df)

 E) import seaborn as sns
sns.boxplot(data=df)
```

QUESTION 11

You are collecting data from users for an online survey. How do you ensure compliance with GDPR when collecting personally identifiable information (PII)? (Select 2 correct answers)

 A) Ensure that users provide informed consent before collecting their data
 B) Store user data without encryption
 C) Allow users to withdraw consent and delete their data on request
 D) Transfer user data internationally without safeguards
 E) Make data retention policies transparent to users

QUESTION 12

You are tasked with gathering customer data to help improve business strategies. You have collected raw data with missing values and irregular formats. How would you clean the data using Python to ensure its readiness for analysis? (Select 2 correct answers)

```
A) df.fillna(df.mean())
B) df.dropna()
C) df.replace('', 'Unknown')
D) df.to_numeric(df['age'],
errors='coerce')
E) df.remove_duplicates()
```

QUESTION 13

You are tasked with processing a list of customer transactions to identify all transactions over $5000 using a loop. Which control structures would efficiently help you achieve this? Select 2 correct answers.

```
A) for transaction in transactions:
if transaction > 5000:
high_transactions.append(transaction)

B) i = 0
while i < len(transactions):
if transactions[i] > 5000:
high_transactions.append(transactions[i])
i += 1

C) for transaction in transactions:
high_transactions.append(transaction)

D) for transaction in transactions:
if transaction > 5000:
high_transactions.append(transaction)
if len(high_transactions) == 10:
break

E) for transaction in transactions:
if transaction < 5000:
continue
```

QUESTION 14

You have a DataFrame containing sales data, and you need to reshape it from wide to long format using melt(). Which of the following Python scripts accomplish this task correctly? Select 2 correct answers.

```
A) pd.melt(df, id_vars=['product'],
value_vars=['sales_jan', 'sales_feb'])
B) df.melt(id_vars=['product'],
value_vars=['sales_jan', 'sales_feb'])
```

```
C) df.melt(['product'], var_name='month',
value_name='sales')
D) df.pivot(id_vars=['product'],
columns=['month'], values=['sales'])
E) pd.pivot(df, index=['product'],
columns=['month'], values='sales')
```

QUESTION 15

You are working with a dataset containing product prices in various currencies. To prepare this data for machine learning, you need to standardize the prices to USD and scale them using StandardScaler from sklearn. What steps will correctly perform this operation in Python? (Select 2 answers)

```
A) df['Price_USD'] = df['Price'] *
exchange_rate; from sklearn.preprocessing
import StandardScaler; df[['Price_USD']] =
StandardScaler().fit_transform(df[['Price_U
SD']])

B) df['Price'] = df['Price'] /
exchange_rate; from sklearn.preprocessing
import MinMaxScaler; df[['Price']] =
MinMaxScaler().fit_transform(df[['Price']])

C) df['Price'] = df['Price'] /
exchange_rate; from sklearn.preprocessing
import StandardScaler; df[['Price']] =
StandardScaler().fit_transform(df[['Price']
])

D) df['Price'] = df['Price'] /
exchange_rate; df['Price'] =
df['Price'].apply(lambda x: (x -
df['Price'].mean()) / df['Price'].std())

E) df['Price_USD'] = df['Price'] *
exchange_rate; df['Price_USD'] =
(df['Price_USD'] - df['Price_USD'].mean())
/ df['Price_USD'].std()
```

QUESTION 16

You are writing a Python function that calculates the sum of squares of a list of numbers. The function should accept a list as the first argument and a boolean flag square (default is True). If square is set to False, the function should return the sum without squaring the numbers. What is the correct implementation? (Select 2 answers)

```
A) def sum_of_squares(nums, square=True):
return sum([n**2 for n in nums]) if square
else sum(nums)
B) def sum_of_squares(nums, square=False):
if square: return sum([n**2 for n in nums])
```

```
else: return sum(nums)
 C) def sum_of_squares(nums, square=True):
return sum([n if not square else n**2 for n
in nums])
 D) def sum_of_squares(nums, square=True):
result = 0 for n in nums: result += n**2 if
square else n return result
 E) def sum_of_squares(nums, square=False):
return sum([n**2 for n in nums]) if square
else sum([n for n in nums])
```

QUESTION 17

You are working with customer data and need to
store customer IDs and their corresponding purchase
totals. Which Python data structure is best suited for
this task, considering efficient lookups of purchase
totals based on customer IDs? (Select 2 answers)

```
 A) customer_data = []
 B) customer_data = {}
 C) customer_data = {'cust_1': 200.50,
'cust_2': 100.75}
 D) customer_data = {('cust_1', 200.50),
('cust_2', 100.75)}
 E) customer_data = [('cust_1', 200.50),
('cust_2', 100.75)]
```

QUESTION 18

You are tasked with writing a Python script to
preprocess customer data. As part of the script, you
want to ensure that your code follows the PEP 8 style
guide for readability and best practices. Which of the
following code snippets adheres to PEP 8 standards?
(Select 2 answers)

```
A) def process_data():
total=0
for i in range(10):
total+=i
return total

 B) def process_data():
total = 0
for i in range(10):
total += i
return total

 C) def processData():
total=0
for i in range(10):
total+=i
return total

 D) def process_data():
total = 0
for i in range(10):
```

```
total+=i
return total

 E) def process_data():
total = 0
for i in range(10):
total += i
return total
```

QUESTION 19

You are asked to write a SQL query to retrieve the
customer_name and total_purchase from a table
customers. Only customers who have made more
than $500 in purchases should be included in the
result. Which SQL query correctly retrieves this
information? (Select 2 answers)

```
A) SELECT customer_name, total_purchase
FROM customers
WHERE total_purchase > 500;

 B) SELECT customer_name, total_purchase
FROM customers
WHERE total_purchase >= 500;

 C) SELECT customer_name, total_purchase
FROM customers
WHERE total_purchase > 500
ORDER BY total_purchase DESC;

 D) SELECT customer_name
FROM customers
WHERE total_purchase > 500;

 E) SELECT *
FROM customers
WHERE total_purchase > 500;
```

QUESTION 20

You are tasked with connecting to a SQLite database
in Python to retrieve customer data. Which Python
code snippet correctly establishes the connection to
the database and retrieves the data? (Select 2
answers)

```
A) import sqlite3
conn = sqlite3.connect('database.db')
cursor = conn.cursor()
cursor.execute("SELECT * FROM customers")
rows = cursor.fetchall()
conn.close()

 B) import sqlite3
conn = sqlite3.connect('database.db')
with conn.cursor() as cursor:
cursor.execute("SELECT * FROM customers")
rows = cursor.fetchall()
```

```
 C) import sqlite3
with sqlite3.connect('database.db') as
conn:
cursor = conn.cursor()
cursor.execute("SELECT * FROM customers")
rows = cursor.fetchall()

 D) import sqlite3
conn = sqlite3.connect('database.db')
cursor = conn.execute("SELECT * FROM
customers")
rows = cursor.fetchall()

 E) import sqlite3
conn = sqlite3.connect('database.db')
cursor = conn.cursor()
rows = cursor.fetch_all("SELECT * FROM
customers")
conn.close()
```

QUESTION 21

You are extracting data from a SQL table where
date_of_purchase is stored as VARCHAR. You need
to convert it to a Python datetime object. Which
Python code handles the conversion correctly?
(Select 2 answers)

```
A) conn = sqlite3.connect('db.db')
cur = conn.cursor()
cur.execute("SELECT date_of_purchase FROM
purchases")
for r in cur.fetchall():
print(datetime.strptime(r[0], '%Y-%m-%d'))

 B) conn = sqlite3.connect('db.db')
cur = conn.cursor()
cur.execute("SELECT date_of_purchase FROM
purchases")
for r in cur.fetchall():
print(datetime(r[0]))

 C) cur.execute("SELECT strftime('%Y-%m-
%d', date_of_purchase) FROM purchases")
print(cur.fetchall())
 D) cur.execute("SELECT date_of_purchase
FROM purchases")
for r in cur.fetchall():
print(r[0].strftime('%Y-%m-%d'))

 E) cur.execute("SELECT date_of_purchase
FROM purchases")
for r in cur.fetchall():
print(r[0].strptime('%Y-%m-%d'))
```

QUESTION 22

You are tasked with creating a recursive function in
Python to calculate the factorial of a number. Which
of the following implementations is correct? (Select

2 answers)

```
A) def factorial(n):
return 1 if n == 0 else n * factorial(n -
1)

 B) def factorial(n):
if n == 0:
return 1
else:
return n * factorial(n)

 C) def factorial(n):
if n == 1:
return 1
else:
return n * factorial(n - 1)

 D) def factorial(n):
return n * factorial(n - 1)

 E) def factorial(n):
for i in range(n):
return n * factorial(n - 1)
```

QUESTION 23

You are working on a Python project and want to
organize the codebase into modules and packages.
How can you import a function calculate from a file
math_operations.py located in the utilities folder?
(Select 2 answers)

A) from utilities.math_operations import calculate
B) import utilities.calculate
C) from utilities import math_operations.calculate
D) import utilities.math_operations as mo
E) import calculate from utilities.math_operations

QUESTION 24

You are tasked with parsing a JSON response from an
API that contains nested structures. You need to
extract data from nested keys and write the result
back into a new JSON file. Which Python code would
accomplish this task? (Select 2 correct answers)

```
A) import json
data = {'name': 'John', 'details': {'age':
30, 'city': 'New York'}}
with open('output.json', 'w') as file:
json.dump(data, filE)

B) import json
with open('data.json') as file:
data = json.load(file)
print(datA)

C) import json
```

```
data = json.loads('{"name": "John"}')
print(data['details']['age'])

D) import json
data = {'name': 'John', 'details': {'age':
30}}
print(data['details']['age'])

E) import json
json_str = '{"name": "John", "age": 30}'
print(json.loads(json_str)['age'])
```

QUESTION 25

You are working with a large dataset in a SQL database, and you need to extract the sales data of employees who have made more than 5 sales in a month. You want to write a nested query to calculate the total sales per employee and then filter the employees with more than 5 sales. Which of the following SQL queries will correctly achieve the task? (Select 2 correct answers)

```
A) SELECT employee_id, COUNT(sale_id) FROM
sales GROUP BY employee_id HAVING
COUNT(sale_id) > 5;
SELECT * FROM sales WHERE employee_id IN
(SELECT employee_id FROM sales GROUP BY
employee_id HAVING COUNT(sale_id) > 5);

 B) SELECT employee_id FROM (SELECT
employee_id, COUNT(sale_id) FROM sales
GROUP BY employee_id HAVING COUNT(sale_id)
> 5);

 C) WITH TotalSales AS (SELECT employee_id,
COUNT(sale_id) AS sales_count FROM sales
GROUP BY employee_id) SELECT * FROM
TotalSales WHERE sales_count > 5;

 D) SELECT employee_id, COUNT(sale_id) FROM
sales HAVING COUNT(sale_id) > 5;
 E) SELECT * FROM employees e JOIN sales s
ON e.employee_id = s.employee_id WHERE
sales_count > 5;
```

QUESTION 26

You are given a large table sales_data with millions of records. The performance of your SQL query to retrieve records is very slow. Which indexing strategy would improve the performance? (Select 2 correct answers)

```
A) CREATE INDEX idx_sales_date ON
sales_data(sale_date);
B) CREATE INDEX idx_sales_customer ON
sales_data(customer_id);
C) CREATE INDEX idx_sales_price ON
```

```
sales_data(sale_price);
D) CREATE FULLTEXT INDEX idx_sales_comments
ON sales_data(comments);
E) CREATE INDEX idx_sales_amount ON
sales_data(sale_amount);
```

QUESTION 27

You have a view employee_view that simplifies access to employee data by joining multiple tables. How can you update the salary of an employee through this view? (Select 2 correct answers)

```
A) UPDATE employee_view SET salary = 50000
WHERE employee_id = 101;
B) ALTER VIEW employee_view AS SELECT
employee_id, salary FROM employees;
C) CREATE OR REPLACE VIEW employee_view AS
SELECT employee_id, salary FROM employees;
D) DROP VIEW employee_view;
E) INSERT INTO employee_view (employee_id,
salary) VALUES (102, 55000);
```

QUESTION 28

You are implementing a system where multiple users perform financial transactions on the same dataset. To ensure consistency and avoid conflicts, how can you manage SQL transactions effectively? (Select 2 correct answers)

```
A) BEGIN TRANSACTION
B) USE SAVEPOINT
C) COMMIT TRANSACTION
D) ROLLBACK TO SAVEPOINT
E) SET TRANSACTION READ ONLY
```

QUESTION 29

You are analyzing the distribution of a company's annual sales data. How would you calculate the variance and standard deviation of this data using Python? (Select 2 correct answers)

```
A) import statistics;
statistics.variance(sales)
B) import statistics;
statistics.stdev(sales)
C) import numpy as np; np.var(sales)
D) sales.variance()
E) import statistics;
statistics.mean(sales)
```

QUESTION 30

A retail company wants to find the correlation between the number of sales calls and the revenue generated. How would you calculate the Pearson correlation coefficient in Python using pandas? (Select 2 correct answers)

```
A) import pandas as pd;
df['sales_calls'].corr(df['revenue'])
B) df.corr(method='pearson')
C) import statistics;
statistics.correlation(df['sales_calls'],
df['revenue'])
D) np.corrcoef(df['sales_calls'],
df['revenue'])
E) df['sales_calls'].cov(df['revenue'])
```

QUESTION 31

You are tasked with fitting a linear regression model to predict house prices based on the square footage of houses. The dataset has been loaded into a Pandas DataFrame df. Which code snippets below will correctly fit a linear regression model in Python using the scikit-learn library? (Select 2 correct answers)

```
A) from sklearn.linear_model import
LinearRegression; model =
LinearRegression(); X =
df[['square_footage']]; y = df['price'];
model.fit(X, y)
B) import statsmodels.api as sm; X =
df['square_footage']; y = df['price']; X =
sm.add_constant(X); model = sm.OLS(y,
X).fit()
C) from sklearn.model_selection import
train_test_split; X_train, X_test, y_train,
y_test =
train_test_split(df[['square_footage']],
df['price']); model = LinearRegression();
model.fit(X_train, y_train)
D) import numpy as np; model =
np.polyfit(df['square_footage'],
df['price'], 1)
E) from sklearn.preprocessing import
StandardScaler; scaler = StandardScaler();
X =
scaler.fit_transform(df[['square_footage']]
); y = df['price']; model =
LinearRegression(); model.fit(X, y)
```

QUESTION 32

You are tasked with detecting outliers in a dataset of house prices using the Z-score method in Python. Which of the following Python scripts will correctly

identify outliers? (Select 2 correct answers)

```
A) from scipy import stats; z =
np.abs(stats.zscore(df['price']));
df_outliers = df[z > 3]
B) z = np.abs(stats.norm(df['price']));
outliers = df[z > 1.96]
C) import numpy as np; df['z'] =
(df['price'] - np.mean(df['price'])) /
np.std(df['price']); df_outliers =
df[df['z'] > 3]
D) outliers = df[df['price'] > 3 *
df['price'].std()]
E) outliers = df[df['price'] <
df['price'].mean() - 3 * df['price'].std()]
```

QUESTION 33

You have a Pandas DataFrame 'df' and a Pandas Series 'ser'. Which of the following options demonstrate the differences between DataFrame and Series handling in Python? (Select 2 correct answers)

```
A) df.iloc[0]
B) ser.iloc[0]
C) df['column1']
D) ser.loc[0]
E) df[['column1', 'column2']]
```

QUESTION 34

You are working with a large dataset of employee records and want to group them by the department and calculate the mean salary per department using Pandas. Which of the following options correctly implements this? (Select 2 correct answers)

```
A)
df.groupby('department')['salary'].mean()
B)
df['salary'].groupby(df['department']).mean
()
C) df.pivot_table(values='salary',
index='department', aggfunc='mean')
D)
df.groupby('salary')['department'].mean()
E)
df.groupby(['department'])['salary'].agg('m
ean')
```

QUESTION 35

You are training a supervised learning model and want to split your dataset into training and testing sets using Scikit-learn. Which of the following methods will correctly achieve this? (Select 2 correct answers)

```
A) train_test_split(X, y, test_size=0.2)
B) train_test_split(X, y, test_size=0.2,
random_state=42)
C) X_train, X_test, y_train, y_test =
split(X, y)
D) train_test_split(X, y,
validation_size=0.2)
E) X_train, y_train = train(X, y)
```

QUESTION 36

You are building a logistic regression model to predict customer churn based on customer features. Which Python script is NOT appropriate for this task?

```
A) from sklearn.linear_model import
LogisticRegression
 clf = LogisticRegression()
 clf.fit(X_train, y_train)

 B) from sklearn.metrics import
accuracy_score
 y_pred = clf.predict(X_test)
 accuracy = accuracy_score(y_test, y_preD)

C) from sklearn.linear_model import
LinearRegression
 model = LinearRegression()
 model.fit(X_train, y_train)

D) from sklearn.model_selection import
train_test_split
 X_train, X_test, y_train, y_test =
train_test_split(X, y, test_size=0.2)

E) from sklearn.metrics import
confusion_matrix
 cm = confusion_matrix(y_test, y_pred)
```

QUESTION 37

You are tasked with building a logistic regression model to classify whether a customer will purchase a product based on age and income. Which of the following is the correct way to implement and fit the logistic regression model using scikit-learn?

```
A) from sklearn.linear_model import
LogisticRegression
 model = LogisticRegression()
 model.fit(X_train, y_train)

 B) from sklearn.linear_model import
LinearRegression
 model = LinearRegression()
```

```
model.fit(X_train, y_train)

 C) from sklearn.ensemble import
RandomForestClassifier
 model = RandomForestClassifier()
 model.fit(X_train, y_train)

 D) from sklearn.naive_bayes import
GaussianNB
 model = GaussianNB()
 model.fit(X_train, y_train)

 E) from sklearn.svm import SVC
 model = SVC()
 model.fit(X_train, y_train)
```

QUESTION 38

You are analyzing the sales data of a company. Using Pandas, create a pivot table that shows the total sales (sales) for each product (product) and each region (region). Which of the following scripts will achieve this? Select two answers.

```
A) pd.pivot_table(df, values='sales',
index='product', columns='region',
aggfunc='sum')
B) pd.pivot_table(df, values='product',
index='sales', columns='region',
aggfunc='sum')
C) df.pivot(index='product',
columns='region', values='sales',
aggfunc='sum')
D) pd.pivot_table(df, values='sales',
index='region', columns='product',
aggfunc='sum')
E) df.groupby(['product',
'region'])['sales'].sum().unstack()
```

QUESTION 39

A classifier model is evaluated on test data, and the confusion matrix is generated. Which metrics can be derived from the confusion matrix to evaluate model performance? Select three correct metrics.

```
A) Precision
B) Recall
C) F1-score
D) AUC (Area Under the Curve)
E) R-squared
```

QUESTION 40

You are tasked with creating a boxplot to visualize the distribution of sales data across different product categories using Seaborn. Which of the following scripts will help you achieve this? Select two correct answers.

```
A) sns.boxplot(x='Product_Category',
y='Sales', data=df)
B) sns.histplot(x='Product_Category',
y='Sales', data=df)
C) sns.scatterplot(x='Product_Category',
y='Sales', data=df)
D) sns.boxplot(y='Product_Category',
x='Sales', data=df)
E) sns.barplot(x='Product_Category',
y='Sales', data=df)
```

QUESTION 41

You are visualizing the sales data using a line plot in Matplotlib. How would you label the x-axis as "Months" and y-axis as "Sales" while adding a title "Sales Over Time"?

```
A) plt.xlabel('Months') plt.ylabel('Sales')
plt.title('Sales Over Time')
B) plt.xlabel='Months' plt.ylabel='Sales'
plt.title='Sales Over Time'
C) plt.set_xlabel('Months')
plt.set_ylabel('Sales')
plt.set_title('Sales Over Time')
D) plt.label('Months', 'Sales')
E) plt.add_labels('Months', 'Sales', 'Sales
Over Time')
```

QUESTION 42

You are presenting a sales data visualization to a non-technical audience. The plot should highlight the total sales and make it easy to interpret key figures. What is the best way to annotate the bar plot with the sales values?

```
A) plt.bar(df['Region'], df['Sales']);
plt.text(df['Sales'], ha='right')
B) plt.bar(df['Region'], df['Sales']); for
i, v in enumerate(df['Sales']): plt.text(i,
v, str(v), ha='center')
C) plt.bar(df['Region'], df['Sales']);
plt.annotate(df['Sales'], ha='right')
D) plt.bar(df['Region'], df['Sales'],
label='Sales Values')
```

QUESTION 43

You are preparing a data-driven presentation about sales growth in different regions. To effectively balance visuals and text, what is the best approach for presenting key insights alongside a bar chart? Select two correct answers.

```
A) plt.bar(df['Region'], df['Sales']);
plt.text(df['Region'], df['Sales'],
fontsize=12)
B) Add key insights in the chart as
annotations using plt.annotate()
C) plt.title('Regional Sales') and include
detailed text analysis on a separate slide
D) Present only text-based insights and
avoid visuals altogether
```

QUESTION 44

You are tasked with visualizing the distribution of customer age groups in your dataset. To ensure accessibility for individuals with color vision deficiencies, which color palette would you select using Seaborn?

```
A) sns.histplot(data=ages, color="green")
B) sns.histplot(data=ages,
palette="colorblind")
C) sns.histplot(data=ages, color="magenta")
D) sns.histplot(data=ages, palette="deep")
E) sns.histplot(data=ages, color="cyan")
```

QUESTION 45

You are tasked with analyzing customer churn data and must present your findings to show that high customer churn is linked to a specific subscription type. Which visualization would best provide evidence for this claim?

```
A) plt.scatter(customer_churn,
subscription_type);
plt.xlabel('Subscription Type');
plt.ylabel('Customer Churn')
B) sns.barplot(x='subscription_type',
y='customer_churn', data=churn_datA)

C) plt.hist(customer_churn, bins=10)
D) sns.boxplot(x='subscription_type',
y='customer_churn', data=churn_datA)

E) plt.pie(customer_churn,
labels=subscription_type)
```

PRACTICE TEST 6 - ANSWERS ONLY

QUESTION 1

Answer - A, B, C

A) Correct – pd.read_json() correctly reads JSON data into a Pandas DataFrame, enabling data manipulation and integration.

B) Correct – pd.read_xml() is the appropriate method to read XML files and convert them to Pandas DataFrames.

C) Correct – Using pd.concat([df_json, df_xml], axis=1) combines both DataFrames side by side by columns, which is suitable for combining these datasets.

D) Incorrect – pd.read_csv() cannot read XML data because it is designed for CSV files, not hierarchical data formats like XML.

E) Incorrect – pd.merge() is unnecessary because merging requires a common key column, which is not mentioned in the scenario.

EXAM FOCUS	*When working with both JSON and XML formats, ensure you use appropriate readers like read_json() and read_xml(). Combining them is made easy with concat().*
CAUTION ALERT	*Be cautious about using read_csv() on XML files. CSV is a flat format, while XML is hierarchical, requiring distinct handling methods.*

QUESTION 2

Answer - B

A) Incorrect – Data warehouses are better suited for structured data rather than unstructured IoT data.

B) Correct – Data lakes are ideal for storing large volumes of unstructured data and allow for scalability and analytics.

C) Incorrect – CSV files, while useful for small datasets, are not ideal for handling unstructured data at scale.

D) Incorrect – Relational databases are structured and not suitable for unstructured, large-scale IoT data.

E) Incorrect – Local Excel files are not scalable and not suitable for handling massive unstructured datasets.

EXAM FOCUS	*Data lakes are better for storing unstructured data at scale, making them ideal for IoT data and machine learning workloads.*
CAUTION ALERT	*Avoid storing large unstructured data in traditional relational databases or local files like Excel. They lack the scalability and flexibility of data lakes.*

QUESTION 3

Answer - A, C

A) Correct – MinMaxScaler is imported from sklearn.preprocessing to implement Min-Max scaling.

B) Correct – This initializes the Min-Max scaler object.

C) Correct – fit_transform() applies the Min-Max scaling to the dataset.

D) Incorrect – You cannot apply MinMaxScaler directly using the .apply() method; fit_transform() is required.

E) Incorrect – scale() is not a method used in this context for scaling data.

EXAM FOCUS	*MinMaxScaler() from sklearn is a highly efficient method to normalize data by transforming numerical features into a 0 to 1 range.*
CAUTION ALERT	*Avoid using .apply() for scaling numerical data directly; use fit_transform() with MinMaxScaler() for best results in machine learning preprocessing.*

QUESTION 4

Answer - A, B

A) Correct – train_test_split is a function from sklearn.model_selection used to split data into training and testing sets.

B) Correct – This code splits the dataset with 70% for training and 30% for testing, using a random state for reproducibility.

C) Incorrect – split() is not a valid Pandas function for splitting datasets; train_test_split() is used instead.

D) Incorrect – train_test_split(df) requires additional parameters like test_size to function properly.

E) Incorrect – sample() is used to randomly sample rows, but it does not specifically split the dataset into training and testing sets.

EXAM FOCUS	Always use train_test_split() from sklearn to split datasets for machine learning. Ensure reproducibility by setting random_state in your split.
CAUTION ALERT	Don't use sample() or split() from Pandas to divide datasets for machine learning. They don't provide the flexibility and reliability of train_test_split().

QUESTION 5

Answer - A, C

A) Correct – This code uses a for loop to iterate through the list and add each number to total, returning the correct sum.

B) Incorrect – There is no forEach() method in Python for lists, and the syntax for lambda is incorrect.

C) Correct – sum(lst) is the most efficient method to sum a list, though it doesn't explicitly use a for loop.

D) Incorrect – This code prints the sum instead of returning it, which is not the expected behavior for a function.

E) Incorrect – This uses list comprehension, which is less efficient than using sum(lst) directly.

EXAM FOCUS	A for loop or sum(lst) are the most efficient ways to calculate the sum of numbers in a list. List comprehension with sum works, but it's less efficient.
CAUTION ALERT	Avoid using non-existent methods like forEach() on lists in Python. Python lists don't have this method, so make sure to use valid alternatives.

QUESTION 6

Answer - A, C

) Correct – This code establishes a connection to a local SQLite database file named database.db.

B) Incorrect – SQLite doesn't use the localhost format for connections; it's file-based.

C) Correct – This code establishes an in-memory SQLite database which is useful for testing purposes.

D) Incorrect – The import statement is wrong (sqlite instead of sqlite3), and the file reference is incomplete.

E) Incorrect – There is no create() method for establishing a database connection in sqlite3.

EXAM FOCUS	Use sqlite3.connect('database.db') to connect to an SQLite database. For testing, use ':memory:' for an in-memory database.
CAUTION ALERT	SQLite uses file-based databases, so avoid using the localhost format, which is for client-server databases like MySQL.

QUESTION 7

Answer - A, E

A) Correct – ttest_ind() performs a two-sample t-test for independent samples.
B) Incorrect – ttest_1samp() is for one-sample t-tests, not two-sample tests.
C) Incorrect – ttest_rel() is for paired t-tests, which compares means of related samples.
D) Incorrect – There is no ttest() method in statsmodels.api for independent t-tests.
E) Correct – This is an alternate syntax for performing a two-sample t-test using ttest_ind().

EXAM FOCUS	ttest_ind() compares the means of two independent samples. Import from scipy.stats for performing common statistical tests.
CAUTION ALERT	Don't confuse ttest_ind() with ttest_rel()—the latter is for paired or dependent samples, while the former is for independent ones.

QUESTION 8

Answer - A

A) Correct – This creates a 2D array and slices the first two rows and two columns.
B) Incorrect – The slice starts at row 1, which is not what the question asks.
C) Incorrect – It slices only the first column, not a 2x2 subarray.
D) Incorrect – The shape and slicing do not match the question.
E) Correct – This is also a correct option, as it achieves the correct 2x2 slice from the array.

EXAM FOCUS	In NumPy, use slicing like arr[:2, :2] to extract specific subarrays from a 2D array. It efficiently slices multi-dimensional arrays.
CAUTION ALERT	Be cautious when reshaping arrays. Ensure the new shape is compatible with the number of elements in the array.

QUESTION 9

Answer - A, B

A) Correct: This is the proper way to set titles, labels, and legends.
B) Correct: This shows the plot with a legend.
C) Incorrect: Adding a grid is optional and unrelated to the core task.
D) Incorrect: This is for scatter plots, not a line plot.
E) Incorrect: A bar plot is not relevant in this scenario.

EXAM FOCUS	Always include plot customization in Matplotlib, such as adding titles, axis labels, and legends for clarity. plt.legend() is key for distinguishing multiple plots.
CAUTION ALERT	Be cautious when using gridlines. While useful, they may clutter simple plots like line charts if overused without consideration for the context.

QUESTION 10

Answer - A, C

A) Correct. This creates a box plot to display the distribution of "age".
B) Incorrect. This creates a histogram, not a box plot.
C) Correct. A box plot by "age" and "gender" is valid.
D) Incorrect. This creates a scatter plot, not a box plot.
E) Incorrect. No column is specified, so the plot will fail.

EXAM FOCUS	*Use sns.boxplot(x='age', data=df) for quick visualization of age distribution. This works well when displaying single-variable data.*
CAUTION ALERT	*If comparing multiple variables, include categorical features in your box plot (e.g., sns.boxplot(x='age', y='gender')) to avoid skewed interpretations.*

QUESTION 11

Answer - A, C

A) Ensuring informed consent is a GDPR requirement.
B) Storing data without encryption violates GDPR.
C) Users must have the right to withdraw consent and request data deletion.
D) International data transfers must have safeguards under GDPR.
E) Transparency about data retention is a must for GDPR compliance.

EXAM FOCUS	*Ensure that you obtain explicit user consent when collecting personally identifiable information (PII) to comply with GDPR and other privacy regulations.*
CAUTION ALERT	*Never store sensitive data without encryption or transfer it internationally without adequate legal safeguards in place to avoid compliance issues.*

QUESTION 12

Answer - B, D

A) Replacing missing values with the mean is not suitable for all data types.
B) Dropping rows with missing values ensures data integrity.
C) Replacing empty strings with "Unknown" might obscure valuable data.
D) Converting invalid data to NaN ensures compatibility in numeric analysis.
E) Removing duplicates is helpful but not a solution for data cleaning.

EXAM FOCUS	*Drop missing values with dropna() to ensure clean datasets. For converting invalid data, use to_numeric() with errors='coerce' to handle improper values.*
CAUTION ALERT	*Avoid using mean imputation for categorical data or where it's inappropriate. Filling values arbitrarily can introduce bias into the analysis.*

QUESTION 13

Answer - A, B

A) Correct: A for loop with if condition checks transactions efficiently.
B) Correct: A while loop with a counter and if condition allows traversal through the list with conditions.
C) Incorrect: This will append all transactions without any filtering.
D) Incorrect: Breaking after 10 ignores additional transactions above $5000.
E) Incorrect: continue skips transactions under $5000 but does not solve the full problem.

EXAM FOCUS	*Use a for or while loop with a condition to efficiently filter transactions over $5000. Loops are ideal for conditional operations on lists.*
CAUTION ALERT	*Avoid breaking the loop early unless necessary (e.g., after processing 10 transactions). This can lead to incomplete processing of valid entries.*

QUESTION 14

Answer - A, B

A) Correct: Uses pd.melt with id_vars and value_vars.
B) Correct: This also reshapes the DataFrame using melt.
C) Incorrect: Syntax issue; missing argument names in melt.
D) Incorrect: pivot reshapes from long to wide, opposite of melt.
E) Incorrect: pivot cannot be used for melting data.

EXAM FOCUS	pd.melt() is ideal for reshaping data from wide to long format, making it useful for preparing data for visualization or further analysis.
CAUTION ALERT	Don't confuse pivot() and melt(). pivot() reshapes from long to wide, while melt() does the reverse.

QUESTION 15

Answer - A, C

Option A: Correct – Multiplies the price by the exchange rate and uses StandardScaler to scale the prices correctly.
Option B: Incorrect – Uses MinMaxScaler instead of StandardScaler, and scales the price incorrectly without converting to USD.
Option C: Correct – Converts the price to USD and applies StandardScaler as required.
Option D: Incorrect – Manually standardizes the values but doesn't follow the best practice of using StandardScaler.
Option E: Incorrect – Uses manual scaling instead of StandardScaler, which is not recommended.

EXAM FOCUS	Convert prices to USD before scaling them with StandardScaler. Ensure currency conversion is consistent for machine learning model inputs.
CAUTION ALERT	Don't use manual scaling methods when StandardScaler or MinMaxScaler are available; they ensure consistent results.

QUESTION 16

Answer - A, C

Option A: Correct – Uses list comprehension and the ternary operator to conditionally square the numbers.
Option B: Incorrect – The default value for square is set incorrectly.
Option C: Correct – Applies the logic directly in the list comprehension.
Option D: Incorrect – Misplaces the else clause inside the loop, leading to incorrect logic.
Option E: Incorrect – Default value for square is set incorrectly, and sum is redundant.

EXAM FOCUS	Use list comprehensions and ternary operations to control whether numbers should be squared based on a condition in Python functions.
CAUTION ALERT	Ensure the correct default value is set for flags like square=True. Avoid manual loops when list comprehensions are available.

QUESTION 17

Answer - B, C

Option A: Incorrect – A list is not efficient for key-value lookups based on customer IDs.

Option B: Correct – A dictionary is ideal for key-value pairs where you need to look up purchase totals by customer ID.

Option C: Correct – This uses a dictionary to store customer IDs as keys and purchase totals as values, ideal for fast lookups.

Option D: Incorrect – A set does not support key-value pairs and would not allow efficient lookups.

Option E: Incorrect – A list of tuples is less efficient for lookups compared to a dictionary.

EXAM FOCUS	A dictionary is ideal for storing key-value pairs, such as customer IDs and purchase totals, allowing for fast lookups.
CAUTION ALERT	Avoid using lists or sets for this task; lists are inefficient for lookups, and sets do not support key-value pairings.

QUESTION 18

Answer - B, E

Option A: Incorrect – Missing spaces around operators (total+=i).

Option B: Correct – Follows proper indentation and spacing per PEP 8.

Option C: Incorrect – The function name processData does not follow PEP 8 naming conventions (should use underscores).

Option D: Incorrect – Missing space after +=.

Option E: Correct – Proper spacing, indentation, and naming conventions as per PEP 8.

EXAM FOCUS	Separate logic by function: Breaking your code into smaller, reusable functions is a great way to improve both readability and testability in Python.
CAUTION ALERT	Long functions reduce clarity: Writing all logic in a single function makes it harder to understand and increases the chance of bugs or errors.

QUESTION 19

Answer - A, C

Option A: Correct – This retrieves the correct columns and filters for customers with total_purchase > 500.

Option B: Incorrect – The query includes customers with exactly $500, which does not meet the condition of "more than $500".

Option C: Correct – Retrieves customers with total_purchase > 500 and orders them by purchase amount in descending order.

Option D: Incorrect – This query omits the total_purchase column, which is required.

Option E: Incorrect – The query retrieves all columns, which is not required and can lead to performance issues.

EXAM FOCUS	Query for exact conditions: Use conditions like > 500 or >= 500 in SQL depending on whether you want to include or exclude the boundary value in results.
CAUTION ALERT	Don't query all columns unless needed: Using SELECT * is inefficient and can degrade performance; always query for specific columns.

QUESTION 20

Answer - A, C

Option A: Correct – This code correctly establishes the connection, creates a cursor, executes the query, and closes the connection.

Option B: Incorrect – conn.cursor() cannot be used directly in a with block.

Option C: Correct – Uses a context manager to automatically close the connection after the block.

Option D: Incorrect – conn.execute() is not a valid method for creating a cursor; cursor() is required.

Option E: Incorrect – fetch_all() is not a valid method; it should be fetchall().

EXAM FOCUS	*Use context managers: When working with databases, using with blocks automatically closes connections, improving reliability and reducing the risk of memory leaks.*
CAUTION ALERT	*Cursor management: conn.cursor() cannot be used directly within a with block without proper context management (like contextlib).*

QUESTION 21

Answer - A, C

Option A: Correct – Uses strptime to convert a string into a datetime object using the specified format. This method ensures proper parsing of string dates.

Option B: Incorrect – Calling datetime(r[0]) without providing a format string results in an error as the format is required for conversion.

Option C: Correct – SQL strftime converts the date to a string in the correct format, making it compatible with datetime in Python.

Option D: Incorrect – You cannot use strftime on a string as it is a method for datetime objects, not for strings directly.

Option E: Incorrect – strptime is used incorrectly; it should be applied on a datetime object, not directly on a string.

EXAM FOCUS	*Use strptime for date conversion: Convert date strings from SQL into Python datetime objects using strptime, ensuring correct format handling.*
CAUTION ALERT	*Don't misuse strftime: strftime is for formatting datetime objects, not strings. Ensure you're using it appropriately in conversions.*

QUESTION 22

Answer - A, C

Option A: Correct – This is a concise implementation of the recursive factorial function with a base case of n == 0.

Option B: Incorrect – The recursive call lacks proper termination due to n * factorial(n), leading to infinite recursion.

Option C: Correct – This is a standard recursive implementation, starting with n == 1 as the base case.

Option D: Incorrect – Lacks the base case, causing an infinite recursive loop.

Option E: Incorrect – A loop inside the recursive function is unnecessary and incorrect, leading to logic errors.

EXAM FOCUS	*Recursive functions need base cases: Always include a base case in recursive functions, like factorial, to prevent infinite recursion and stack overflow errors.*
CAUTION ALERT	*Avoid infinite recursion: Forgetting the base case (e.g., n == 0) leads to infinite recursion, which will crash your Python program.*

QUESTION 23

Answer - A, D

Option A: Correct – This is the proper syntax for importing a function from a module in a subdirectory.

Option B: Incorrect – The syntax is incorrect as calculate is not directly in the utilities package.
Option C: Incorrect – This is an invalid syntax for importing a function nested inside a module.
Option D: Correct – This imports the module math_operations and allows access using the alias mo.
Option E: Incorrect – The import keyword cannot be used like this; it has a syntax error.

EXAM FOCUS	Use from to import specific functions: Use from <module> import <function> to keep your imports efficient and reduce clutter in your namespace.
CAUTION ALERT	Be cautious with wildcards: Avoid using import * unless absolutely necessary, as it can lead to namespace conflicts and unexpected behavior.

QUESTION 24

Answer - A, E

A) Correct: The code successfully writes a nested JSON structure to a file using json.dump().
B) Incorrect: This only reads data from a file, but doesn't handle nested keys.
C) Incorrect: The key details is missing in the JSON string.
D) Incorrect: While this accesses a nested structure, it doesn't write back to a new JSON file.
E) Correct: This parses the string and accesses the age key correctly.

EXAM FOCUS	Use json.dump() for writing JSON files: When working with JSON data in Python, use json.dump() to serialize Python objects and write them directly to files.
CAUTION ALERT	Watch out for missing keys: Always ensure that keys you're accessing in nested JSON structures exist to avoid KeyErrors. Handle missing keys gracefully using .get().

QUESTION 25

Answer - A, C

Option A: Correct, it correctly uses a nested query with HAVING COUNT(sale_id) > 5.
Option B: Incorrect, the syntax of the query is incorrect and results in an error.
Option C: Correct, uses the WITH clause to create a common table expression for filtering employees.
Option D: Incorrect, the HAVING clause is used improperly as it misses grouping.
Option E: Incorrect, there is no defined sales_count in the query.

EXAM FOCUS	Nested SQL queries aid filtering: Using HAVING in SQL helps filter aggregated results efficiently, such as when filtering based on total sales or counts.
CAUTION ALERT	Grouping and filtering mistakes: Ensure that HAVING is only used after GROUP BY and only applies to aggregate functions like COUNT().

QUESTION 26

Answer - A, B

Option A: Correct, indexing on sale_date will speed up queries filtering by date.
Option B: Correct, indexing customer_id will improve lookups for specific customers.
Option C: Incorrect, sale price is not commonly queried directly, making this less efficient.
Option D: Incorrect, FULLTEXT indexing is for text-based search and irrelevant here.
Option E: Incorrect, sale amount may not be a frequent filter criterion in large datasets.

EXAM FOCUS	Indexing improves query performance: Creating indexes on columns frequently used in filters or joins, such as sale_date or customer_id, can significantly speed up queries.

QUESTION 27

Answer - A, C

Option A: Correct, you can update the salary through an updatable view.
Option B: Incorrect, this alters the view definition but doesn't update data.
Option C: Correct, replacing a view can restructure it to allow updates.
Option D: Incorrect, dropping the view does not update data.
Option E: Incorrect, inserting data into a view depends on the base table's ability to accept inserts.

| EXAM FOCUS | *Updatable views allow direct changes: Some views, like employee_view, allow updates if they are simple enough and reflect only one table, making it possible to update through the view.* |
| CAUTION ALERT | *Inserts depend on the underlying table: Inserting into a view may fail if the underlying table structure does not support it. Make sure your base table is configured for inserts.* |

QUESTION 28

Answer - A, C

Option A: Correct, starting a transaction ensures that all operations are treated as a single unit.
Option B: Incorrect, using SAVEPOINT alone does not manage the entire transaction effectively.
Option C: Correct, committing the transaction ensures the changes are saved permanently.
Option D: Incorrect, ROLLBACK to SAVEPOINT is useful but not sufficient for overall transaction management.
Option E: Incorrect, SET TRANSACTION READ ONLY is for non-modifying queries, not managing transaction conflicts.

| EXAM FOCUS | *Start and commit transactions: Use BEGIN TRANSACTION and COMMIT TRANSACTION to ensure all related operations are treated as a single unit and changes are finalized only when committed.* |
| CAUTION ALERT | *ROLLBACK undoes changes: Keep in mind that ROLLBACK reverts changes made during the transaction, which helps avoid partial updates but doesn't replace a proper commit.* |

QUESTION 29

Answer - A, C

Option A: Correct, statistics.variance() calculates the variance of the dataset.
Option B: Correct, statistics.stdev() is used to compute the standard deviation of the dataset.
Option C: Correct, np.var() computes the variance using NumPy.
Option D: Incorrect, sales.variance() is not a valid method.
Option E: Incorrect, mean is not a measure of spread.

| EXAM FOCUS | *Use statistics or NumPy for variance and standard deviation: Both libraries are excellent for calculating variance and standard deviation, key measures for understanding data variability.* |
| CAUTION ALERT | *Variance and standard deviation measure spread: Remember that while they both measure spread, variance is in squared units, making it less intuitive than standard deviation.* |

QUESTION 30

Answer - A, D

Option A: Correct, .corr() in pandas computes the Pearson correlation.
Option B: Incorrect, while df.corr() works, it does not specify the specific columns.
Option C: Incorrect, statistics module does not have a correlation() function.
Option D: Correct, np.corrcoef() from NumPy calculates the Pearson correlation coefficient.
Option E: Incorrect, covariance is not the same as correlation.

EXAM FOCUS	*Pearson correlation shows linear relationship: Use pandas.corr() or np.corrcoef() to calculate the Pearson correlation coefficient for understanding relationships between continuous variables.*
CAUTION ALERT	*Correlation isn't the same as covariance: Covariance measures direction, but correlation standardizes it, making it easier to understand relationships between variables.*

QUESTION 31

Answer - A, B

Option A: Correct, this is the basic implementation of fitting a linear regression model using scikit-learn.
Option B: Correct, statsmodels also fits an OLS model for linear regression.
Option C: Incorrect, this splits the dataset but doesn't complete the prediction.
Option D: Incorrect, np.polyfit fits a polynomial model but isn't linear regression.
Option E: Incorrect, scaling is used but doesn't explicitly call for fitting.

EXAM FOCUS	*Linear regression in sklearn and statsmodels: Use LinearRegression in sklearn or OLS in statsmodels for fitting linear regression models in Python.*
CAUTION ALERT	*Scaling isn't always necessary: StandardScaler is helpful but not required unless your data has varying scales. Don't confuse scaling with fitting the model.*

QUESTION 32

Answer - A, C

Option A: Correct, the script uses Z-scores from scipy.stats and selects values greater than 3.
Option B: Incorrect, stats.norm does not compute Z-scores.
Option C: Correct, the Z-score calculation is done manually and outliers are selected.
Option D: Incorrect, this uses a threshold but does not apply Z-score logic.
Option E: Incorrect, this only captures lower outliers and misses upper ones.

EXAM FOCUS	*Z-score for outlier detection: Use Z-scores to identify outliers effectively by filtering values greater than 3 or less than -3 standard deviations from the mean.*
CAUTION ALERT	*Ensure correct Z-score threshold: A Z-score threshold of ±3 is typically used to detect extreme outliers. Using a lower threshold may capture non-outlier points.*

QUESTION 33

Answer - C, E

) Incorrect: .iloc[0] returns the first row in both DataFrame and Series. It does not demonstrate the difference between them since both can return a single element.
) Incorrect: Similar to A, ser.iloc[0] fetches the first element from the Series, and this doesn't showcase how

Series differs from a DataFrame.

C) Correct: When accessing a single column with df['column1'], a Series is returned, showing how selecting a single column can yield a Series instead of a DataFrame.

D) Incorrect: Using .loc in a Series works similarly to a DataFrame, retrieving a single element based on the label, which doesn't demonstrate the distinction between the two.

E) Correct: Selecting multiple columns from a DataFrame returns another DataFrame, highlighting the difference between DataFrame and Series.

EXAM FOCUS	Series vs. DataFrame: Pandas Series behaves like a 1D array, while a DataFrame is a 2D table. Accessing one column from a DataFrame returns a Series.
CAUTION ALERT	Ambiguity in element access: Be mindful that selecting a single column or row in a DataFrame returns a Series, which can behave differently from DataFrame slices.

QUESTION 34

Answer - A, C

A) Correct: This is the most straightforward way to group by department and calculate the mean of salary.

B) Incorrect: This option does not follow Pandas' correct grouping syntax; it would result in an error.

C) Correct: The pivot_table function in Pandas also allows aggregation, and this option calculates the mean salary by department.

D) Incorrect: Grouping by salary and calculating the mean of department does not make sense for this context and would result in an error.

E) Incorrect: Although close, the additional agg('mean') is unnecessary when only one column (salary) is being aggregated.

EXAM FOCUS	Grouping and aggregation in Pandas: Use groupby() and pivot_table() to group data and calculate aggregated statistics, such as mean salary by department.
CAUTION ALERT	Ensure correct aggregation columns: Make sure you're grouping by the correct column, such as department, and calculating statistics on the appropriate column like salary.

QUESTION 35

Answer - A, B

A) Correct: This is the correct syntax to split a dataset using train_test_split.
B) Correct: Including random_state ensures reproducibility, making this a valid choice.
C) Incorrect: There is no split() function like this in Scikit-learn.
D) Incorrect: The correct parameter is test_size, not validation_size.
E) Incorrect: train() is not a valid method in Scikit-learn for splitting data.

EXAM FOCUS	Split data efficiently: Use train_test_split() with proper parameters like test_size and random_state to split your data for training and testing.
CAUTION ALERT	Correct parameter names: There's no validation_size parameter in train_test_split(). Use test_size for controlling test set size.

QUESTION 36

Answer - C

A) Correct – Logistic Regression is used to solve binary classification problems like customer churn prediction.

B) Correct – The accuracy_score is used to evaluate the model's performance by comparing predicted and actual values.
C) Incorrect – Linear Regression is used for continuous target variables, not for classification problems.
D) Correct – The train_test_split function is used to split the dataset for training and testing.
E) Correct – Confusion matrix helps evaluate classification models by summarizing predictions.

EXAM FOCUS	Correct models for classification tasks: Logistic regression (LogisticRegression) is used for binary classification tasks like churn prediction, not linear regression.
CAUTION ALERT	Linear regression not suitable for classification: Always use logistic regression for classification problems. Linear regression should not be applied to binary outcomes.

QUESTION 37

Answer - A

A) Correct – Logistic regression is appropriate for classification tasks with binary or categorical outputs.
B) Incorrect – Linear regression is used for predicting continuous variables, not for classification.
C) Incorrect – RandomForestClassifier is another classification model, but it is not logistic regression.
D) Incorrect – Naive Bayes is a classification algorithm, but it is not logistic regression.
E) Incorrect – Support Vector Classifier is another classifier but does not use logistic regression.

EXAM FOCUS	Logistic regression is for classification: Use LogisticRegression() for binary or categorical outcomes like customer purchases, not for continuous predictions.
CAUTION ALERT	Don't use linear regression for classification: Linear regression is inappropriate for classification tasks. Stick to LogisticRegression for classifying data.

QUESTION 38

Answer - A, E

A) Correct because it uses pd.pivot_table with the correct parameters: values='sales', index='product', columns='region', and aggfunc='sum'. This will create the desired pivot table.
B) Incorrect as it mixes up the index and values parameters, using sales as the index and product as the value, which does not meet the requirement.
C) Incorrect since pivot() does not have an aggfunc argument. It is not used for aggregation.
D) Incorrect because it reverses the index and column requirements. The prompt asks for product as the index and region as the column, but this option uses region as the index.
E) Correct as it uses groupby() with ['product', 'region'] and performs sum(), followed by unstack() to reshape the data in the required format.

EXAM FOCUS	Pivot tables for cross-dimensional data: Use pivot_table() for multi-dimensional data summaries, especially when comparing metrics across categories like products and regions.
CAUTION ALERT	Avoid confusing index and column: Ensure the correct assignment of index and columns in pivot tables. Confusing them can lead to incorrect or misaligned outputs.

QUESTION 39

Answer - A, B, C

A) Correct because precision measures the proportion of positive identifications that are actually correct, derived from the confusion matrix.

B) Correct because recall measures the proportion of actual positives identified correctly, which is calculated using the confusion matrix. C) Correct because F1-score is a harmonic mean of precision and recall, derived directly from the confusion matrix. D) Incorrect because AUC is derived from the ROC curve, not directly from the confusion matrix. E) Incorrect because R-squared is a metric for regression models, not classification models.

EXAM FOCUS	Confusion Matrix Metrics: Metrics such as precision, recall, and F1-score are all derived from confusion matrices. These help evaluate different aspects of classifier performance.
CAUTION ALERT	AUC and R-squared Misuse: AUC is derived from the ROC curve, not the confusion matrix. R-squared is a regression metric and should not be used for classification evaluation.

QUESTION 40

Answer - A, D

A) Correct because sns.boxplot() is used to create a boxplot, and x and y define the categorical and numerical variables, respectively.
B) Incorrect because sns.histplot() is used for histograms, not boxplots.
C) Incorrect because sns.scatterplot() is used for scatter plots, not for visualizing distributions like boxplots.
D) Correct because switching x and y will still generate a boxplot, just with reversed axes, which is valid.
E) Incorrect because sns.barplot() is used for bar charts, not for visualizing distributions like boxplots.

EXAM FOCUS	Boxplot Visualization: Use Seaborn's sns.boxplot() to display distributions and detect outliers across categories. Boxplots help you understand spread and variability.
CAUTION ALERT	Boxplot vs. Bar Plot: Don't confuse sns.boxplot() with sns.barplot(). Bar plots compare averages, while boxplots display the data distribution, median, and outliers.

QUESTION 41

Answer - A

A) Correct because plt.xlabel(), plt.ylabel(), and plt.title() are the valid functions to add labels and a title to the plot in Matplotlib. B) Incorrect because the syntax uses an assignment operator (=) instead of the valid function calls.
C) Incorrect because .set_xlabel() and .set_ylabel() are used with axes objects, not directly with plt.
D) Incorrect because plt.label() does not exist in Matplotlib; labels must be set separately for x and y axes.
E) Incorrect because plt.add_labels() is not a valid Matplotlib function.

EXAM FOCUS	Labeling Tip: Always use plt.xlabel(), plt.ylabel(), and plt.title() to label your plots properly. This enhances clarity and helps readers understand your visualizations.
CAUTION ALERT	Incorrect Syntax: Be careful not to use assignment syntax (=) for labeling axes. Always use functions like plt.xlabel() and plt.ylabel() for labeling.

QUESTION 42

Answer - B

A) Incorrect because plt.text() is not used properly to place the labels at the sales values.
B) Correct because the loop correctly positions the text annotation at the center of each bar to show the sales values. C) Incorrect because plt.annotate() is not the correct method for this context; it's more suitable for pointing to specific data points rather than general bar values. D) Incorrect because label='Sales Values' adds a label to the plot legend, not to the bars themselves.

EXAM FOCUS	*Annotating Tip: Use a loop to annotate bar plots with values. For example, for i, v in enumerate(df['Sales']): plt.text(i, v, str(v), ha='center') works best.*
CAUTION ALERT	*Annotation Mistake: Avoid using plt.annotate() for simple bar labeling—it's better suited for pointing out specific data points rather than labeling all bars.*

QUESTION 43

Answer - B, C

A) Incorrect because directly adding text over the bar chart can clutter the visualization. B) Correct because using plt.annotate() to highlight key insights allows you to combine visuals and text effectively without overwhelming the chart. C) Correct because combining visual data with a simple title and offering detailed insights on a separate slide balances clarity and avoids clutter. D) Incorrect because excluding visuals diminishes the effectiveness of the presentation.

EXAM FOCUS	*Visual & Text Balance: Combine simple visuals with concise text summaries using plt.annotate() or place key insights beside the chart for clear presentations.*
CAUTION ALERT	*Text Overload: Avoid placing long text directly inside charts or overloading visuals with too many annotations. It detracts from the clarity of your message.*

QUESTION 44

Answer - B

A) Incorrect because using green may be difficult for individuals with red-green color vision deficiencies. B) Correct because the colorblind palette is specifically designed for accessibility, making the plot more inclusive. C) Incorrect because magenta might pose readability issues for those with color vision deficiencies and does not guarantee accessibility. D) Incorrect because the "deep" palette, while aesthetically pleasing, is not explicitly designed for accessibility. E) Incorrect because using cyan alone does not account for accessibility and may not provide enough contrast for all viewers.

EXAM FOCUS	*Accessible Visuals: When visualizing distributions, use the "colorblind" palette in Seaborn (palette="colorblind") to ensure accessibility for individuals with color vision deficiencies.*
CAUTION ALERT	*Avoid Bright Colors: Using color combinations like red and green or magenta can make visualizations difficult for individuals with color vision impairments.*

QUESTION 45

Answer - B

A) Incorrect because scatter plots are not ideal for comparing categorical data (subscription types) with a target variable. B) Correct because bar plots are effective for showing categorical data relationships and summarizing the evidence linking subscription type with customer churn. C) Incorrect because a histogram doesn't provide a clear comparison between subscription types and churn rates. D) Incorrect because box plots show data distributions, but they are not ideal for summarizing categorical comparisons needed to prove the claim. E) Incorrect because a pie chart doesn't display the direct comparison between subscription types and churn data.

EXAM FOCUS	*Use Bar Plots for Categorical Data: Bar plots are best for showing the relationship between categorical data (like subscription type) and a numeric variable (like customer churn).*
CAUTION ALERT	*Scatter Plot Limitation: Scatter plots are not ideal for comparing categorical data against a continuous variable, such as subscription types against churn rates.*

PRACTICE TEST 7 - QUESTIONS ONLY

QUESTION 1

When aggregating data from a data warehouse and a data lake, what are the key considerations to ensure consistency and accuracy? (Select 3 answers)

A) Validate data types across both sources
B) Ensure consistent naming conventions
C) Concatenate datasets without checking formats
D) Use schema-on-read for unstructured data
E) Directly append the datasets without validation

QUESTION 2

A team is working with customer data stored across multiple formats (CSV, Excel, and a cloud-based database). They need to load this data into Python for further analysis. Which steps should they take to efficiently load and integrate this data? (Select 2 answers)

```
 A) Use pd.read_csv() for CSV files
 B) Use pd.read_sql() for the cloud
database
 C) Use pd.read_excel() for Excel files
 D) Use df.merge() to concatenate all data
sources
 E) Use pandas.concat() to join data along
axis 1
```

QUESTION 3

A company wants to standardize their sales data using Z-score normalization to remove the impact of outliers. What Python code and steps should they follow to achieve Z-score normalization? (Select 2 answers)

```
 A) Use from sklearn.preprocessing import
StandardScaler
 B) Use df.mean() and df.std() for manual
Z-score calculation
 C) Use df_normalized = (df - df.mean()) /
df.std()
 D) Use from sklearn.preprocessing import
Normalizer
 E) Use StandardScaler to scale categorical
variables
```

QUESTION 4

You have a dataset that contains missing values in several columns. Which Python functions can be used to filter out rows or columns that contain missing data? (Select 2 answers)

```
 A) df.dropna()
 B) df.fillna()
 C) df.isnull()
 D) df.replace()
 E) df.drop_duplicates()
```

QUESTION 5

You are given a Python list of customer names and need to store it in a dictionary where the keys are the indices of the names. Which of the following methods correctly converts the list into a dictionary? (Select 2 answers)

```
A) names = ['John', 'Alice']
dict_names = {i: names[i] for i in
range(len(names))}

 B) names = ['John', 'Alice']
dict_names = dict(enumerate(names))

 C) names = ['John', 'Alice']
dict_names = {i: name for i, name in
enumerate(names)}

 D) names = ['John', 'Alice']
dict_names = list(enumerate(names))

 E) names = ['John', 'Alice']
dict_names = {names: i for i in
range(len(names))}
```

QUESTION 6

You are running a SQL query in Python using the sqlite3 library and need to execute the query to fetc all the rows. Which functions correctly execute the query and retrieve the results? (Select 2 answers)

```
 A) cursor.execute('SELECT * FROM
employees')
 B) cursor.fetchone()
 C) cursor.fetchall()
 D) cursor.execute('SELECT * FROM
```

```
employees')
results = cursor.fetchall()
 E) cursor.run_query('SELECT * FROM
employees')
```

QUESTION 7

You are conducting a simple linear regression
analysis using Python's statsmodels library. Which of
the following code snippets correctly fits a linear
regression model and prints the summary of the
results?

```
A) import statsmodels.api as sm
X = sm.add_constant(X)
model = sm.OLS(Y, X)
results = model.fit()
print(results.summary())

 B) import statsmodels.api as sm
model = sm.OLS(Y, X)
results = model.summary()

 C) import statsmodels.api as sm
model = sm.fit(Y, X)
print(model.summary())

 D) import statsmodels.api as sm
model = sm.OLS(X, Y)
print(results.fit())

 E) import statsmodels as sm
model = sm.regression(Y, X)
results = model.fit()
print(results.summary())
```

QUESTION 8

You need to perform element-wise addition between
two NumPy arrays. Which of the following code
snippets will add two arrays element-wise and store
the result in a new array? (Select 2 answers)

```
A) import numpy as np
arr1 = np.array([1, 2, 3])
arr2 = np.array([4, 5, 6])
arr_sum = np.add(arr1, arr2)

 B) import numpy as np
arr1 = np.array([1, 2])
arr2 = np.array([[3], [4]])
arr_sum = np.add(arr1, arr2)

 C) import numpy as np
arr1 = np.array([1, 2, 3])
arr2 = np.array([4, 5])
arr_sum = np.add(arr1, arr2)

 D) import numpy as np
arr1 = np.array([1, 2, 3])
```

```
arr2 = np.array([4, 5, 6])
arr_sum = arr1 + arr2
```

QUESTION 9

You want to create subplots comparing sales data
across three regions. Which steps are correct for
creating subplots in Matplotlib? Select 2 correct
options.

```
A) import matplotlib.pyplot as plt
fig, axs = plt.subplots(3)
axs[0].plot(region1)
axs[1].plot(region2)
axs[2].plot(region3)

B) fig, ax = plt.subplots()
ax.plot(region1, region2, region3)

C) plt.subplot(3, 1, 1)
plt.plot(region1)
plt.subplot(3, 1, 2)
plt.plot(region2)
plt.subplot(3, 1, 3)
plt.plot(region3)

D) plt.plot(region1)
plt.plot(region2)
plt.plot(region3)

E) fig, ax = plt.subplots(3, figsize=(10,
5))
ax[0].plot(region1)
ax[1].plot(region2)
ax[2].plot(region3)
```

QUESTION 10

A Python script needs to create a heatmap showing
correlations between numerical variables in a
dataset. Which of the following scripts would
correctly generate this heatmap? (Select 3 correct
answers)

```
A) import seaborn as sns
sns.heatmap(df)

 B) import seaborn as sns
sns.heatmap(df.corr())

 C) import seaborn as sns
sns.heatmap(data=df)

 D) import seaborn as sns
sns.heatmap(df.corr(), annot=True)

 E) import seaborn as sns
sns.heatmap(df.corr(), cmap='coolwarm')
```

QUESTION 11

A company wants to anonymize customer data before analysis. Which Python-based approaches could they use to ensure data privacy? (Select 2 correct answers)

```
A) df['email'] = df['email'].apply(lambda
x: hash(x))
B) df.drop(columns=['email'])
C) df['name'] = df['name'].apply(lambda x:
x[:2] + '****')
D) df['email'] = 'hidden'
E) df.replace({'email': 'masked'})
```

QUESTION 12

You need to prepare a dataset for market analysis, which includes categorical and numerical data. Which steps would you take using Python to encode categorical data for machine learning models? (Select 2 correct answers)

```
A) pd.get_dummies(df['region'])
B) df['region'].factorize()
C) df['age'].astype(str)
D)
LabelEncoder().fit_transform(df['region'])
E) df['age'] = df['age'].apply(lambda x:
x.upper())
```

QUESTION 13

In a dataset containing multiple types of sales transactions, you are asked to separate them based on regions using nested loops and if-else conditions. Write the appropriate loop structure to categorize the data. Select 3 correct answers.

```
A) for transaction in transactions:
if transaction['region'] == 'North':
north_sales.append(transaction)

B) while i < len(transactions):
if transactions[i]['region'] == 'West':
west_sales.append(transactions[i])
i += 1

C) for transaction in transactions:
if 'region' in transaction:
region_sales.append(transaction)

D) for region in regions:
for transaction in transactions:
if transaction['region'] == region:
region_sales[region].append(transaction)

E) for region in regions:
```

```
if region not in transaction.keys():
continue
```

QUESTION 14

You are tasked with filling missing values in a DataFrame using forward fill and backward fill. Which of the following scripts will correctly perform this task? Select 2 correct answers.

```
A) df.fillna(method='ffill')
B) df.fillna(method='bfill')
C) df.fillna(axis=1, method='ffill')
D) df.fillna(method='forward', axis=1)
E) df.replace(np.nan, method='ffill')
```

QUESTION 15

A dataset contains date-time information in multiple formats. You need to standardize the 'Order_Date' column to a consistent format: YYYY-MM-DD. What are the correct ways to achieve this in Python using Pandas? (Select 2 answers)

A) df['Order_Date'] = pd.to_datetime(df['Order_Date'], format='%Y-%m-%d')

B) df['Order_Date'] = pd.to_datetime(df['Order_Date']).dt.strftime('%Y-%m-%d')

C) df['Order_Date'] = pd.to_datetime(df['Order_Date'], infer_datetime_format=TruE) D) df['Order_Date'] = pd.to_datetime(df['Order_Date']).dt.date

E) df['Order_Date'] = df['Order_Date'].apply(lambda x: datetime.strptime(x, '%Y-%m-%d'))

QUESTION 16

You need to write a function that accepts variable-length arguments and returns their average. The function should also accept a keyword argument round_result which, if set to True, rounds the result to 2 decimal places. What is the correct implementation? (Select 2 answers)

```
A) def average(*args, round_result=False):
avg = sum(args) / len(args) return
round(avg, 2) if round_result else avg

B) def average(*args, round_result=False):
return round(sum(args) / len(args), 2) if
round_result else sum(args) / len(args)

C) def average(round_result=False, *args):
```

```
avg = sum(args) / len(args) return
round(avg, 2) if round_result else avg

D) def average(*args, round_result=True):
if round_result: return round(sum(args) /
len(args), 2) else: return sum(args) /
len(args)

E) def average(*args, round_result=False):
avg = sum(args) / len(args) return
round(avg) if round_result else avg
```

QUESTION 17

You need to count the occurrence of each word in a large text dataset. Which Python data structure and method combination would be most efficient for this task? (Select 2 answers)

```
A) word_count = {}; for word in text:
word_count[word] = word_count.get(word, 0)
+ 1
B) from collections import Counter;
word_count = Counter(text)
C) word_count = {word: text.count(word)
for word in set(text)}
D) word_count = dict(); for word in text:
word_count[word] = text.count(worD)   E)
word_count = {}
```

QUESTION 18

You are documenting your Python functions with docstrings to improve code readability and maintainability. Which of the following examples follows the PEP 257 conventions for docstrings? (Select 2 answers)

```
) def calculate_mean(data):
""Calculate the mean of a list of
numbers."""
return sum(data) / len(datA)

) def calculate_mean(data):
""Calculates the mean of the numbers."""
return sum(data) / len(datA)

) def calculate_mean(data):
""Calculate the mean of a list of numbers.
rgs:
ata (list): A list of numeric values.
eturns:
loat: The mean of the list."""
eturn sum(data) / len(datA)

) def calculate_mean(data):
""Calculates the mean of the numbers
rgs:
ata (list): A list of numeric values.
```

```
Returns:
float: The mean."""
return sum(data) / len(datA)

E) def calculate_mean(data):
"""Calculate the mean.
Args: list:
Returns: float."""
return sum(data) / len(data)
```

QUESTION 19

You have two tables: orders (with columns order_id, customer_id, and order_total) and customers (with columns customer_id and customer_name). You need to write a query that retrieves each customer_name along with their order_total. Which SQL query correctly implements this join? (Select 2 answers)

```
A) SELECT customer_name, order_total
FROM customers
INNER JOIN orders
ON customers.customer_id =
orders.customer_id;

 B) SELECT customer_name, order_total
FROM customers
LEFT JOIN orders
ON customers.customer_id =
orders.customer_id;

 C) SELECT customer_name, order_total
FROM orders
JOIN customers
ON orders.customer_id =
customers.customer_id;

 D) SELECT customer_name, order_total
FROM customers
RIGHT JOIN orders
ON orders.customer_id =
customers.customer_id;

 E) SELECT customer_name, order_total
FROM customers
FULL JOIN orders
ON customers.customer_id =
orders.customer_id;
```

QUESTION 20

You are writing a Python script that connects to a MySQL database using pymysql. Which code snippet correctly connects to the database and retrieves data securely? (Select 2 answers)

```
A) import pymysql
conn = pymysql.connect(host='localhost',
```

```
user='root',
password='password',
database='sales')
cursor = conn.cursor()
cursor.execute("SELECT * FROM customers")
rows = cursor.fetchall()
conn.close()

 B) import pymysql
conn = pymysql.connect('localhost', 'root',
'password', 'sales')
cursor = conn.cursor()
cursor.execute("SELECT * FROM customers")
rows = cursor.fetchall()
conn.close()

 C) import pymysql
conn = pymysql.connect(host='localhost',
user='root',
password='password',
database='sales')
with conn.cursor() as cursor:
cursor.execute("SELECT * FROM customers")
rows = cursor.fetchall()

 D) import pymysql
conn = pymysql.connect(host='localhost',
user='root',
password='password',
db='sales')
with conn.cursor() as cursor:
cursor.execute("SELECT * FROM customers")
rows = cursor.fetchall()

 E) import pymysql
with pymysql.connect(host='localhost',
user='root',
password='password',
database='sales') as conn:
cursor = conn.cursor()
cursor.execute("SELECT * FROM customers")
rows = cursor.fetchall()
```

QUESTION 21

You need to load customer data from MySQL into a
Pandas DataFrame, and total_purchase is stored as
DECIMAL. What is the correct way to handle the
conversion of DECIMAL to float in Python? (Select 2
answers)

```
A) conn = pymysql.connect()
df = pd.read_sql("SELECT * FROM customers",
conn)
df['total'] = df['total'].astype(float)

 B) conn = pymysql.connect()
df = pd.read_sql("SELECT * FROM customers",
conn)
```

```
 C) df = pd.read_sql("SELECT CAST(total AS
FLOAT) FROM customers", conn)
 D) df['total'] = df['total'].apply(lambda
x: float(x))
 E) df['total'] = df['total'].map(float)
```

QUESTION 22

You need to apply a lambda function to square a list
of numbers in Python. Which code snippets correctly
implement this requirement? (Select 2 answers)

```
 A) squared = map(lambda x: x**2, [1, 2, 3,
4])
 B) squared = [lambda x: x**2 for x in [1,
2, 3, 4]]
 C) squared = list(map(lambda x: x**2, [1,
2, 3, 4]))
 D) squared = [x**2 for x in [1, 2, 3, 4]]
 E) squared = map(x**2, [1, 2, 3, 4])
```

QUESTION 23

You are managing a large project using virtual
environments to keep dependencies isolated. Which
statements are correct regarding virtual
environments? (Select 2 answers)

A) Virtual environments allow you to install packages
specific to a project without affecting the global
Python environment.
 B) A virtual environment can be created using the
command: python3 -m venv myenv
 C) After creating a virtual environment, it is
automatically activated.
 D) To install packages into a virtual environment,
you must activate it first using source
myenv/bin/activate
 E) The command to deactivate a virtual environment
is deactivate myenv

QUESTION 24

You need to serialize a Python dictionary into a JSON
string and then deserialize it back to a Python object.
Which of the following code snippets would achieve
this? (Select 3 correct answers)

```
A) import json
data = {"name": "Alice", "age": 25}
json_str = json.dumps(data)
print(json_str)

 B) import json
data = {"name": "Alice", "age": 25}
```

```
json_str = json.dumps(data)
new_data = json.loads(json_str)
print(new_datA)

C) import json
json_str = '{"name": "Alice", "age": 25}'
print(json_str)

D) import json
data = {"name": "Alice", "age": 25}
print(json.load(data))

E) import json
data = {"name": "Alice"}
json_str = json.dumps(data)
new_data = json.loads(json_str)
print(new_data)
```

QUESTION 25

You are tasked with performing a SQL query to calculate the average sales for each product, but you want to filter products that have an average sale amount above $1000. Which of the following options correctly retrieves the required result? (Select 1 correct answer)

```
A) SELECT product_id, AVG(sale_amount) FROM
sales GROUP BY product_id HAVING
AVG(sale_amount) > 1000;

 B) WITH SalesAverage AS (SELECT
product_id, AVG(sale_amount) AS avg_sales
FROM sales GROUP BY product_id) SELECT *
FROM SalesAverage WHERE avg_sales > 1000;

 C) SELECT * FROM sales WHERE sale_amount >
1000;
 D) SELECT product_id, sale_amount FROM
sales GROUP BY product_id HAVING
AVG(sale_amount) > 1000;
 E) SELECT product_id FROM sales WHERE
sale_amount > 1000;
```

QUESTION 26

You are tasked with optimizing a query that retrieves all orders placed by customers from orders and customers tables. The performance is slow. What is the best way to analyze and improve the query? (Select 1 correct answer)

A) Use EXPLAIN to analyze the query execution plan;
B) Create indexes on all columns in the tables;
C) Use a subquery to reduce the number of joins;
D) Increase the memory allocated to the database;
E) Add an index only on the order_date column;

QUESTION 27

You want to create a view that shows the total sales from the orders table for each customer. Which SQL statement is appropriate? (Select 1 correct answer)

```
A) CREATE VIEW sales_view AS SELECT
customer_id, SUM(sales) FROM orders GROUP
BY customer_id;
B) CREATE VIEW sales_view AS SELECT
SUM(sales) FROM orders;
C) CREATE VIEW sales_view AS SELECT
customer_id, COUNT(sales) FROM orders GROUP
BY customer_id;
D) CREATE OR REPLACE VIEW sales_view AS
SELECT sales FROM orders;
E) CREATE VIEW sales_view AS SELECT sales,
customer_id FROM orders;
```

QUESTION 28

A banking application processes multiple transfers at the same time. How can you prevent partial updates in case of a failure? (Select 1 correct answer)

```
A) BEGIN TRANSACTION
B) ROLLBACK TRANSACTION
C) SET TRANSACTION ISOLATION LEVEL
SERIALIZABLE
D) CREATE SAVEPOINT
E) COMMIT TRANSACTION
```

QUESTION 29

You have a dataset with exam scores for two different classes. How would you compare the variability of scores between the two classes? (Select 2 correct answers)

```
A) np.std(class1) > np.std(class2)
B) statistics.stdev(class1) >
statistics.stdev(class2)
C) max(class1) - min(class1) > max(class2)
- min(class2)
D) np.mean(class1) > np.mean(class2)
E) import pandas as pd;
pd.DataFrame.std([class1, class2])
```

QUESTION 30

You are analyzing the correlation between advertising spend and product sales. The scatter plot reveals a strong negative correlation. What can be inferred from this? (Select 1 correct answer)

A) The more you spend on advertising, the fewer products you sell

B) More advertising leads to more product sales
C) There is no relationship between advertising and sales
D) The correlation indicates outliers are skewing results
E) Advertising spend is irrelevant to product sales

QUESTION 31

You are analyzing the performance of a linear regression model you have built to predict sales figures. After fitting the model, how would you interpret the R-squared value in the context of the model's performance? (Select 1 correct answer)

A) An R-squared value of 0.85 indicates that the model explains 85% of the variability in sales
B) An R-squared value of 0.85 means the model is 85% accurate
C) An R-squared value of 0.85 indicates that the sales predictions have an error margin of 15%
D) An R-squared value of 0.85 suggests that the model is underfitting the data
E) An R-squared value of 0.85 means that 85% of the predictions are correct

QUESTION 32

You are analyzing a dataset with significant outliers that skew the mean. Which measure of central tendency should be preferred in this scenario to avoid the impact of outliers? (Select 1 correct answer)

A) Mean
B) Median
C) Mode
D) Standard Deviation
E) Variance

QUESTION 33

You want to use .loc and .iloc in Pandas to retrieve data. Which options demonstrate proper usage of these functions? (Select 3 correct answers)

```
A) df.loc[1:3, ['column1', 'column2']]
B) df.iloc[1, 2]
C) df.loc['row_label', 'column_label']
D) df.iloc[0]
E) df.iloc[1:3, [0, 2]]
```

QUESTION 34

You are tasked with finding missing values in a DataFrame df and filling them with the median of the respective column. Which of the following is the correct method to achieve this? (Select 2 correct answers)

```
A) df.fillna(df.median(), inplace=True)
B) df.fillna(method='median', inplace=True)
C) df.apply(lambda x: x.fillna(x.median()))
D) df.fillna(df.mean(), inplace=True)
E) df.replace(np.nan, df.median(),
inplace=True)
```

QUESTION 35

In the context of avoiding overfitting, which techniques can be used to ensure a model generalizes well on test data? (Select 2 correct answers)

A) Using a larger training dataset
B) Applying cross-validation
C) Reducing test dataset size
D) Fitting the model only on the test dataset
E) Ignoring feature selection

QUESTION 36

You are tasked with performing linear regression using Python to predict housing prices based on square footage. Which of the following steps are necessary to implement linear regression? (Select 2 correct answers)

```
A) from sklearn.linear_model import
LinearRegression
model = LinearRegression()
model.fit(X_train, y_train)

B) from sklearn.linear_model import
LogisticRegression
model = LogisticRegression()
model.fit(X_train, y_train)

C) model.predict(X_test)
D) import matplotlib.pyplot as plt
plt.scatter(X, y)

E) from sklearn.preprocessing import
StandardScaler
X_train_scaled =
StandardScaler().fit_transform(X_train)
```

QUESTION 37

What are the steps to evaluate the accuracy of a logistic regression model using a confusion matrix? (Select 2 correct answers)

```
A) from sklearn.metrics import
confusion_matrix
confusion_matrix(y_test, y_preD)

B) model.predict(X_test)
C) model.intercept_
D) from sklearn.metrics import
mean_squared_error
mse = mean_squared_error(y_test, y_preD)

E) model.coef_
```

QUESTION 38

A dataset of employee details (df) includes columns for Department and Gender. You want to calculate the count of employees for each gender across all departments using a cross table. Which script will do this correctly? (Select 2 answers)

```
A) pd.crosstab(df['Department'],
df['Gender'])
B) pd.pivot_table(df, values='Department',
index='Gender', aggfunc='count')
C) pd.pivot_table(df, index='Department',
columns='Gender', aggfunc='count')
D) pd.crosstab(df['Gender'],
df['Department'])
E) df.groupby(['Department',
'Gender']).size().unstack()
```

QUESTION 39

You are working with a binary classifier and want to improve the recall of your model. Which of the following strategies can help you achieve this? Select two answers.

A) Adjust the decision threshold to lower values
B) Increase the regularization term to reduce overfitting
C) Use SMOTE (Synthetic Minority Over-sampling Technique) to balance the classes
D) Apply PCA to reduce the dimensionality of the data
E) Use a confusion matrix to evaluate model performance

QUESTION 40

You need to visualize the correlation between multiple variables in a dataset using Seaborn. Which of the following commands will help you generate a heatmap to display the correlation matrix? Select one answer.

```
A) sns.heatmap(df.corr())
B) sns.pairplot(df)
C) sns.boxplot(x='variable', y='value',
data=df)
D) sns.histplot(df['variable'])
E) sns.scatterplot(x='var1', y='var2',
data=df)
```

QUESTION 41

You need to emphasize a specific sales peak in a line plot by annotating the peak value. Which of the following commands will help you correctly annotate the peak on the plot? Select two correct answers.

```
A) plt.annotate('Peak', xy=(max_x, max_y),
xytext=(max_x+1, max_y+500),
arrowprops=dict(facecolor='black',
shrink=0.05))
B) plt.label('Peak', max_x, max_y)
C) plt.annotate_peak(max_x, max_y)
D) plt.annotate('Peak', xy=(max_x, max_y),
xytext=(max_x+1, max_y),
arrowprops=dict(facecolor='blue'))
E) plt.annotate('Peak', max_x)
```

QUESTION 42

You have created a time-series plot but are presenting to a non-technical team. You want to simplify the visualization by reducing axis tick frequency and adding descriptive labels to the x-axis. Which commands would best achieve this? Select two correct answers.

```
A) plt.xticks(rotation=45)
B) plt.locator_params(axis='x', nbins=6)
C) plt.xaxis.set_tick_params(labelsize=10)
D) plt.xlabel('Date')
E) plt.xlabel_font('Date', size=14)
```

QUESTION 43

You are tasked with presenting quarterly revenue data using both visuals and text. What are the two most effective methods to structure your presentation slides to ensure clarity and engagement? Select two correct answers.

A) Place the visualizations in the center of the slide, with concise bullet points summarizing the main insights beside them.
B) Use multiple charts on the same slide to present all quarterly data at once.
C) Avoid text and rely only on visuals to show trends.
D) Break down data by quarters with one key chart per slide and a text summary below each visualization.

QUESTION 44

You are visualizing sales data using a bar chart and want to ensure that the color palette used remains consistent across multiple charts for clarity. Which Seaborn function allows you to set a consistent color palette globally in your analysis?

```
A) sns.set_palette("muted")
```

```
B) sns.set_context("paper")
C) sns.palplot(sales)
D) sns.color_palette("viridis")
E) plt.set_color_palette("coolwarm")
```

QUESTION 45

After analyzing sales performance over two years, you need to present evidence that the company's new marketing strategy has led to increased revenue. Which Python code would best show this growth?

```
A) plt.plot(years, revenuE)

B) sns.lineplot(x='months', y='revenue',
hue='strategy', data=sales_data);
plt.title('Revenue Growth with Strategy')
C) plt.bar(years, revenuE)

D) plt.pie(revenue, labels=years)
E) plt.scatter(years, revenue)
```

PRACTICE TEST 7 - ANSWERS ONLY

QUESTION 1

Answer - A, B, D

A) Correct – Validating data types between the warehouse and lake ensures that you can aggregate data without encountering type mismatch errors.

B) Correct – Consistent naming conventions across both sources are essential for clean and accurate integration, especially when merging data.

C) Incorrect – Concatenating datasets without checking formats can lead to misaligned data or incorrect aggregations.

D) Correct – Schema-on-read allows processing unstructured data without forcing it into a predefined structure, making it ideal for data lakes.

E) Incorrect – Directly appending datasets without validation can result in inaccurate data and inconsistencies during analysis.

EXAM FOCUS	*Validating data types and ensuring consistent schemas are crucial when integrating data from different sources, especially between data lakes and warehouses.*
CAUTION ALERT	*Never concatenate datasets without first validating formats. It could lead to mismatches and errors during aggregation or further analysis.*

QUESTION 2

Answer - A, C

A) Correct – pd.read_csv() is the standard method to load CSV files into a DataFrame for analysis in Python.

B) Incorrect – While pd.read_sql() is used to load data from databases, this option is valid only for structured SQL databases, which may not apply to a cloud-based database unless specifically configured.

C) Correct – pd.read_excel() is the proper method for loading data from Excel files into a DataFrame.

D) Incorrect – df.merge() is used to combine DataFrames based on a common key, but concatenation isn't the same as merging based on a key.

E) Incorrect – concat() is a viable option for joining data along an axis, but it's not the most efficient when dealing with different formats like CSV, Excel, and databases.

EXAM FOCUS	*Use pd.read_csv() and pd.read_excel() for loading respective formats efficiently into DataFrames for analysis.*
CAUTION ALERT	*Be mindful when merging or concatenating different formats. Ensure consistent data types and handle nulls or discrepancies before integration.*

QUESTION 3

Answer - A, C

A) Correct – StandardScaler from sklearn.preprocessing standardizes features by removing the mean and scaling to unit variance (Z-score normalization).

B) Incorrect – While this can calculate Z-scores manually, it is not the preferred method in Python due to the availability of automated libraries.

C) Correct – This code manually calculates Z-scores by subtracting the mean and dividing by the standard deviation.

D) Incorrect – The Normalizer is not used for Z-score normalization; it normalizes row-wise data.

E) Incorrect – StandardScaler should not be applied to categorical variables, as Z-score normalization only applies to numerical data.

EXAM FOCUS	Z-score normalization centers data around the mean and standard deviation, which helps reduce the impact of outliers on the dataset.
CAUTION ALERT	StandardScaler should not be applied to categorical variables. Z-score normalization is strictly for numerical data in machine learning contexts.

QUESTION 4

Answer - A, C

A) Correct – dropna() is used to remove rows or columns that contain missing values.
B) Incorrect – fillna() is used to fill missing values with a specified value, not to filter out missing data.
C) Correct – isnull() identifies missing data and can be combined with filtering functions to remove rows or columns.
D) Incorrect – replace() substitutes specified values and is not used for filtering missing data.
E) Incorrect – drop_duplicates() is used for removing duplicate rows, not for handling missing data.

EXAM FOCUS	dropna() filters out rows/columns with missing values; combine it with isnull() to identify where missing values occur in your dataset.
CAUTION ALERT	replace() changes specific values, not missing data. Use fillna() for filling and dropna() for filtering out missing values.

QUESTION 5

Answer - A, B

A) Correct – This uses dictionary comprehension to assign list elements to dictionary keys based on their indices.
B) Correct – dict(enumerate(names)) converts the list to a dictionary with index-value pairs.
C) Incorrect – The syntax is invalid because the dictionary keys and values are reversed.
D) Incorrect – This creates a list of tuples instead of a dictionary, which doesn't fulfill the requirement.
E) Incorrect – This code reverses the order of keys and values, trying to assign list elements as dictionary keys.

EXAM FOCUS	Use dictionary comprehension or enumerate() to convert lists into dictionaries. These are common Pythonic methods that maintain clarity and efficiency.
CAUTION ALERT	Be careful not to reverse keys and values when using dictionary comprehension. Incorrect order will result in an unusable or illogical structure.

QUESTION 6

Answer - A, D

A) Correct – This function executes the SQL query in Python.
B) Incorrect – fetchone() retrieves only one row, and it doesn't execute the query.
C) Incorrect – fetchall() is used to retrieve results after the query is executed but doesn't execute the query itself.
D) Correct – This code executes the query and retrieves all rows from the result set using fetchall().
E) Incorrect – run_query() is not a valid method in sqlite3.

EXAM FOCUS	Always pair cursor.execute() with fetchall() or fetchone() to retrieve results from a SQL query in Python.

QUESTION 7

Answer - A

A) Correct – This correctly adds the constant, fits the OLS regression model, and prints the summary.
B) Incorrect – model.summary() doesn't execute the model fitting; it only returns a summary without fitting the model.
C) Incorrect – There is no fit() method directly called on sm; the model must be created using OLS() first.
D) Incorrect – The model incorrectly swaps X and Y, and the fit method syntax is wrong.
E) Incorrect – sm.regression() is not a valid function in the statsmodels library.

EXAM FOCUS	*Use sm.OLS() for fitting regression models in Python. Always add a constant term using*
	sm.add_constant() for a proper linear regression setup.
CAUTION	*Avoid calling summary() before fitting the model. Use .fit() first to ensure the model is properly*
ALERT	*constructed before generating the summary.*

QUESTION 8

Answer - A, D

A) Correct – This correctly adds two NumPy arrays element-wise using the np.add() method.
B) Incorrect – The arrays have incompatible shapes for element-wise addition.
C) Incorrect – This results in an error due to differing array sizes.
D) Correct – This uses the + operator to add arrays element-wise, which works equivalently.

EXAM FOCUS	*Element-wise operations like np.add(arr1, arr2) or arr1 + arr2 add corresponding elements of two*
	NumPy arrays. They work best when arrays have the same shape.
CAUTION	*Ensure the arrays have compatible shapes for element-wise operations. Mismatched shapes will lead to*
ALERT	*broadcasting errors.*

QUESTION 9

Answer - A, E

) Correct: This is the correct method for subplots.
) Incorrect: This does not use subplots properly.
) Incorrect: Although valid, it's more cumbersome and lacks flexibility.
) Incorrect: This overlaps the plots without subplots.
) Correct: Another way to handle subplots and set figure size.

EXAM FOCUS	*Use plt.subplots() for creating multiple subplots in one figure. Each subplot can be customized*
	individually by referencing axs[] for each plot.
CAUTION	*Avoid overlapping plots without using subplots. Overlap makes data comparison difficult and visually*
ALERT	*unclear. Use subplots for distinct data sets.*

QUESTION 10

Answer - B, D, E

A) Incorrect. Correlation matrix is missing.
B) Correct. This generates a heatmap using correlation values.
C) Incorrect. The argument "data=" is unnecessary here.
D) Correct. Annotating the heatmap with values is appropriate.
E) Correct. The heatmap with a custom color map works.

EXAM FOCUS	*Always compute a correlation matrix (df.corr()) before generating a heatmap. Use cmap='coolwarm' for visually distinct color contrast.*
CAUTION ALERT	*Be sure to include only numerical variables in your correlation matrix to avoid unwanted errors when generating heatmaps.*

QUESTION 11

Answer - A, C

A) Hashing sensitive data is a valid method of anonymization.
B) Dropping the email column will remove valuable information.
C) Masking part of the name is a common practice in anonymization.
D) Replacing with 'hidden' doesn't protect the original data properly.
E) Using 'masked' for all entries removes differentiation in the data.

EXAM FOCUS	*Hashing sensitive fields like emails or partially masking names are valid anonymization techniques for privacy protection without losing data utility.*
CAUTION ALERT	*Dropping important columns or replacing sensitive data with generic placeholders like 'masked' may render the dataset less useful for analysis.*

QUESTION 12

Answer - A, D

A) One-hot encoding using pd.get_dummies() is an effective way to convert categorical data.
B) Factorizing provides numeric representation but is not recommended for modeling.
C) Converting numbers to strings does not contribute to encoding.
D) Label encoding is another method to convert categories into numbers.
E) Converting numeric data to uppercase is irrelevant in this context.

EXAM FOCUS	*For encoding categorical data, use pd.get_dummies() for one-hot encoding or LabelEncoder for numerical encoding suitable for machine learning models.*
CAUTION ALERT	*Avoid converting numeric columns to strings without a clear purpose, as this will disrupt your analysis and model performance.*

QUESTION 13

Answer - A, B, D

A) Correct: A for loop with if condition works for segregating based on region.
B) Correct: A while loop with if condition helps traverse based on a region.
C) Incorrect: This adds all transactions without checking region values.
D) Correct: This nested loop method helps filter by region and append appropriately.
E) Incorrect: continue does not solve region filtering in this context.

QUESTION 14

Answer - A, B

A) Correct: Uses forward-fill (ffill) method.
B) Correct: Uses backward-fill (bfill) method.
C) Incorrect: axis specification not necessary here.
D) Incorrect: Incorrect method name, should be 'ffill'.
E) Incorrect: replace is used for value substitution, not for fillna.

QUESTION 15

Answer - A, B

Option A: Correct – Converts the column to datetime and ensures the format is standardized.
Option B: Correct – Converts the date column and formats it to YYYY-MM-DD.
Option C: Incorrect – Infers the datetime format but does not enforce a consistent format like YYYY-MM-DD.
Option D: Incorrect – Converts to Python date objects, which may not retain the desired format.
Option E: Incorrect – Uses a manual approach but may not handle multiple date formats well.

QUESTION 16

Answer - A, B

Option A: Correct – Handles both positional arguments and the round_result flag correctly.
Option B: Correct – Implements the same logic as Option A in a compact form.
Option C: Incorrect – Keyword arguments should come after positional arguments when using *args.
Option D: Incorrect – Incorrect default value for round_result.
Option E: Incorrect – Rounds the value without specifying the number of decimal places.

QUESTION 17

Answer - A, B

Option A: Correct – Uses a dictionary with the get() method for efficient word counting.
Option B: Correct – Counter from collections is specifically optimized for counting elements in an iterable.
Option C: Incorrect – Although correct, it is less efficient as text.count() will iterate over the text for each word.
Option D: Incorrect – This method is inefficient due to the repeated calls to text.count().
Option E: Incorrect – A dictionary is created but not populated with any counting logic.

EXAM FOCUS	Use the Counter class from collections to efficiently count word occurrences in text datasets, avoiding manual counting loops.
CAUTION ALERT	Avoid using text.count() inside loops as it will cause performance issues with large datasets due to repeated iterations.

QUESTION 18

Answer - A, C

Option A: Correct – Single-line docstring that is simple and concise, following PEP 257.
Option B: Incorrect – The verb "Calculates" should be in the imperative ("Calculate").
Option C: Correct – Follows proper multi-line docstring format with clear description, arguments, and return type.
Option D: Incorrect – Improper punctuation and format for the docstring.
Option E: Incorrect – Incorrect argument and return type formatting.

EXAM FOCUS	Avoid silent failures: Always print or log specific error messages when catching exceptions to understand what went wrong and improve troubleshooting.
CAUTION ALERT	Catching broad exceptions is risky: Catching broad exceptions without specifying types (like Exception) may hide important error details that help in debugging.

QUESTION 19

Answer - A, C

Option A: Correct – Performs an INNER JOIN between the customers and orders tables based on customer_id.
Option B: Incorrect – A LEFT JOIN would include customers without orders, which may result in NULL values for order_total.
Option C: Correct – A JOIN (same as INNER JOIN) retrieves the necessary data by matching the customer_id in both tables.
Option D: Incorrect – A RIGHT JOIN would include orders without matching customers, which is not required.
Option E: Incorrect – A FULL JOIN includes both unmatched customers and orders, which is unnecessary here.

EXAM FOCUS	Join tables effectively: Use INNER JOIN to fetch matching records across tables. Ensure proper JOIN clauses to avoid missing or duplicated records.
CAUTION ALERT	Avoid null values with joins: If null values are not needed, avoid using LEFT or RIGHT JOIN; these can result in partial data.

QUESTION 20

Answer - A, D

Option A: Correct – This code correctly uses pymysql to connect to the MySQL database and retrieves data.

Option B: Incorrect – The parameters are incorrectly passed; they should be passed using named arguments like host, user, etc.

Option C: Incorrect – conn.cursor() cannot be directly used in a with block; it requires a contextlib manager.

Option D: Correct – Uses db for the database name and retrieves data with a with block that automatically closes the cursor.

Option E: Incorrect – pymysql.connect cannot be directly used in a with block for the connection.

EXAM FOCUS	*Named arguments improve readability: When connecting to databases, use named arguments like host, user, and password for clarity and maintainability.*
CAUTION ALERT	*Avoid incorrect syntax: Ensure you pass arguments like host, user, and db properly to avoid runtime errors in database connections.*

QUESTION 21

Answer - A, D

Option A: Correct – Converts the DECIMAL column to a float using the astype() method in Pandas, which is a reliable and common method for type conversion.

Option B: Incorrect – While the data is loaded correctly, no conversion of the DECIMAL type to float is performed, making this incomplete for the task.

Option C: Incorrect – SQL's CAST can convert the DECIMAL type to FLOAT, but this may lead to precision loss in certain scenarios. Handling the conversion in Python is preferred.

Option D: Correct – The apply() function allows you to apply a function (in this case, float()) to each element, ensuring the conversion is done correctly.

Option E: Incorrect – Although map(float) works, it's not the most efficient or preferred method for handling large datasets in Pandas.

EXAM FOCUS	*Convert DECIMAL to float safely: When working with DECIMAL data types in Pandas, use astype(float) or apply(float) to convert them to float for analysis.*
CAUTION ALERT	*Be cautious with SQL CAST: Converting to FLOAT within SQL may cause precision loss. Handle type conversions in Python for better accuracy.*

QUESTION 22

Answer - A, C

Option A: Correct – This correctly applies the lambda function using map, but the result is an iterator that needs conversion to a list.

Option B: Incorrect – Lambda function inside a list comprehension is incorrect as the lambda isn't applied to the values directly.

Option C: Correct – map() combined with list() properly converts the map object into a list.

Option D: Incorrect – While list comprehension is correct, this isn't using a lambda function.

Option E: Incorrect – The syntax map(x**2, [1, 2, 3, 4]) is invalid as x**2 is not a callable function.

EXAM FOCUS	*Lambda functions with map: Use map(lambda x: x**2, ...) to apply a function across a list, or convert the map object to a list for immediate access.*
CAUTION ALERT	*Don't use lambda inside comprehensions: A lambda function inside a list comprehension isn't necessary and adds complexity. Use list comprehensions directly.*

QUESTION 23

Answer - A, B

Option A: Correct – Virtual environments isolate dependencies for specific projects.
Option B: Correct – This is the correct syntax to create a virtual environment using the venv module.
Option C: Incorrect – Virtual environments must be manually activated after creation.
Option D: Incorrect – The command source myenv/bin/activate is correct for activation, but the explanation is missing the reason it is not related to installation.
Option E: Incorrect – The correct command to deactivate a virtual environment is simply deactivate, not deactivate myenv.

EXAM FOCUS	*Activate virtual environments manually: After creating a virtual environment, remember to activate it using source myenv/bin/activate for the environment to take effect.*
CAUTION ALERT	*Virtual environment is not auto-activated: Virtual environments do not activate automatically upon creation, so you must activate them manually before use.*

QUESTION 24

Answer - A, B, E

A) Correct: This serializes a Python dictionary into a JSON string.
B) Correct: This performs both serialization and deserialization correctly.
C) Incorrect: This does not deserialize the JSON string back into a Python object.
D) Incorrect: json.load() expects a file object, not a Python dictionary.
E) Correct: This also serializes and deserializes a Python dictionary correctly.

EXAM FOCUS	*Serialize and deserialize with json: To convert Python dictionaries to JSON and back, use json.dumps() for serialization and json.loads() for deserialization.*
CAUTION ALERT	*Avoid json.load() on non-file objects: json.load() expects a file object, not a Python dictionary. For string-based JSON, use json.loads().*

QUESTION 25

Answer - A

Option A: Correct, it uses HAVING to filter products with average sales greater than $1000.
Option B: Incorrect, this is close but unnecessarily complex for the given task.
Option C: Incorrect, this query filters individual sales but not average sales per product.
Option D: Incorrect, this incorrectly includes sale_amount without aggregation.
Option E: Incorrect, this filters individual products but not by average sale amount.

EXAM FOCUS	*Use HAVING with aggregates: To filter on aggregates such as AVG(), use the HAVING clause rather than WHERE, which cannot handle aggregated data.*
CAUTION ALERT	*Avoid complex solutions: Avoid unnecessary complexity—use HAVING directly when filtering aggregate results like average sales.*

QUESTION 26

Answer - A

Option A: Correct, EXPLAIN reveals how the query is executed and helps optimize it.

Option B: Incorrect, indexing all columns can worsen performance.
Option C: Incorrect, using a subquery does not necessarily optimize performance.
Option D: Incorrect, increasing memory might not address the root issue.
Option E: Incorrect, indexing only order_date may not improve performance if other columns are used in filtering.

EXAM FOCUS	Use EXPLAIN to optimize queries: Running the EXPLAIN command on a slow query helps you understand how the database is executing it, providing insights for optimization.
CAUTION ALERT	Avoid indexing every column: Blindly indexing all columns can backfire, leading to slower inserts and updates. Only index columns frequently used in queries.

QUESTION 27

Answer - A

Option A: Correct, this query summarizes sales by customer using SUM and GROUP BY.
Option B: Incorrect, this query lacks GROUP BY to total sales per customer.
Option C: Incorrect, COUNT counts rows, not sales.
Option D: Incorrect, this query only selects sales, not total per customer.
Option E: Incorrect, this just lists sales without summarizing them.

EXAM FOCUS	Use GROUP BY for aggregated results in views: When creating a view like sales_view, GROUP BY helps in summarizing data, such as total sales per customer.
CAUTION ALERT	COUNT and SUM are different: Be sure to use SUM when calculating totals rather than COUNT, which counts rows instead of summing values.

QUESTION 28

Answer - B

Option A: Incorrect, BEGIN TRANSACTION starts a transaction but does not prevent partial updates.
Option B: Correct, rolling back a transaction reverts changes if a failure occurs, preventing partial updates.
Option C: Incorrect, setting the isolation level ensures read consistency but does not prevent partial updates.
Option D: Incorrect, SAVEPOINT allows partial rollback, but does not prevent partial updates.
Option E: Incorrect, COMMIT finalizes the transaction, but does not prevent issues if a failure occurs.

EXAM FOCUS	ROLLBACK prevents partial updates: Using ROLLBACK TRANSACTION ensures that changes are reverted if a failure occurs, maintaining data integrity in critical systems like banking applications.
CAUTION ALERT	COMMIT does not handle failures: COMMIT TRANSACTION finalizes changes but won't protect against partial updates in case of failure during the transaction.

QUESTION 29

Answer - A, B

Option A: Correct, comparing standard deviations gives insight into variability.
Option B: Correct, using statistics.stdev() is also valid for comparing variability.
Option C: Incorrect, range does not give as much insight into variability as standard deviation.
Option D: Incorrect, comparing means does not address variability.
Option E: Incorrect, the syntax for calculating standard deviation is wrong here.

EXAM FOCUS	Standard deviation for variability comparison: Use standard deviation to compare the spread or variability between datasets—it's an essential metric in statistical analysis.

QUESTION 30

Answer - A

Option A: Correct, a strong negative correlation indicates as advertising increases, sales decrease.
Option B: Incorrect, positive correlation would suggest this.
Option C: Incorrect, a strong negative correlation suggests a relationship.
Option D: Incorrect, the correlation does not suggest outliers but an inverse relationship.
Option E: Incorrect, the correlation clearly shows a relationship.

EXAM FOCUS	Negative correlation means inverse relationship: In a scatter plot, a negative correlation means that as one variable increases, the other decreases.
CAUTION ALERT	Don't confuse correlation with causation: A negative correlation doesn't imply that one variable causes the other to decrease; they are just related inversely.

QUESTION 31

Answer - A

Option A: Correct, R-squared explains the percentage of variance in the dependent variable explained by the independent variables.
Option B: Incorrect, R-squared is not a measure of model accuracy.
Option C: Incorrect, R-squared does not indicate error margin directly.
Option D: Incorrect, R-squared is not used to determine underfitting.
Option E: Incorrect, R-squared does not reflect prediction correctness.

EXAM FOCUS	R-squared indicates explained variance: An R-squared value of 0.85 means that 85% of the variability in the dependent variable is explained by the independent variables.
CAUTION ALERT	R-squared isn't accuracy: Avoid mistaking R-squared for model accuracy—it only explains the variance, not how often the predictions are correct.

QUESTION 32

Answer - B

Option A: Incorrect, mean is sensitive to outliers and may not represent the central tendency accurately.
Option B: Correct, the median is robust against outliers and provides a better measure of central tendency.
Option C: Incorrect, the mode is not appropriate for continuous numerical data.
Option D: Incorrect, standard deviation measures spread, not central tendency.
Option E: Incorrect, variance is also a measure of spread, not central tendency.

EXAM FOCUS	Median is robust against outliers: When data is skewed or contains outliers, prefer the median over the mean, as it better reflects central tendency.
CAUTION ALERT	Mean is affected by outliers: The mean can be skewed by extreme values, giving an inaccurate representation of central tendency in datasets with outliers.

QUESTION 33

Answer - A, B, E

A) Correct: This usage of .loc is proper for selecting specific rows and columns in a DataFrame using both row and column labels, which is an essential feature of .loc.

B) Correct: The .iloc function retrieves data based on integer-location-based indexing, so this is a valid way to select the element at the first row and second column.

C) Incorrect: This would work only if both row_label and column_label are present in the DataFrame. It's not demonstrated here whether labels exist or not, making it ambiguous.

D) Incorrect: This returns the entire first row using .iloc[0], but it's not relevant for selecting a specific element, which is typically expected in data retrieval operations.

E) Correct: This demonstrates how to retrieve a slice of rows and specific columns by index using .iloc. It efficiently combines both row slicing and specific column retrieval.

EXAM FOCUS	Use .iloc[] for integer indexing: .iloc[] allows you to select rows and columns by position. It's particularly useful when you don't know the labels.
CAUTION ALERT	Label vs. integer indexing: .loc[] is for label-based access, while .iloc[] is for position-based access. Using them interchangeably can lead to errors.

QUESTION 34

Answer - A, C

A) Correct: This fills missing values with the median of each column using fillna() and df.median().

B) Incorrect: There is no method='median' parameter in fillna(); this would raise an error.

C) Correct: Using apply() with a lambda function allows filling missing values with the median for each column.

D) Incorrect: This fills missing values with the mean, not the median, which is not what the question asks.

E) Incorrect: While replace() can replace values, it is not the typical way to fill missing values in Pandas, and f.median() is not correctly used here.

EXAM FOCUS	Fill missing data using the median: fillna() and apply() are powerful methods to handle missing values in Pandas, especially for filling with the median.
CAUTION ALERT	Check method compatibility: fillna(method='median') is not valid. Ensure you use the correct approach like fillna(df.median()).

QUESTION 35

Answer - A, B

A) Correct: A larger training set helps models generalize better and avoid overfitting.

B) Correct: Cross-validation helps by using different subsets of data, thus improving model generalization.

C) Incorrect: Reducing the test set size may lead to biased evaluation and does not prevent overfitting.

D) Incorrect: Fitting a model only on the test dataset defeats the purpose of training.

E) Incorrect: Ignoring feature selection may introduce irrelevant features, increasing overfitting.

EXAM FOCUS	Prevent overfitting: Techniques like cross-validation and increasing the training data size help models generalize better and prevent overfitting.
CAUTION ALERT	Avoid shrinking the test set: Reducing test data size may lead to biased evaluation and doesn't prevent overfitting.

QUESTION 36

Answer - A, C

A) Correct – Linear regression uses the LinearRegression() class to create the model.
B) Incorrect – Logistic Regression is used for classification, not regression.
C) Correct – After fitting the model, predictions are made using model.predict().
D) Incorrect – While plotting a scatter plot is useful for visualization, it is not mandatory for linear regression implementation.
E) Incorrect – Scaling is helpful, but not a required step for basic linear regression.

EXAM FOCUS	*Prediction and regression steps: After training the model, use model.predict() to generate predictions. Linear regression can be effectively implemented with Scikit-learn.*
CAUTION ALERT	*Avoid incorrect scaling requirements: While scaling can improve convergence in certain models, it is not mandatory for basic linear regression tasks.*

QUESTION 37

Answer - A, B

A) Correct – Confusion matrix is used to evaluate classification model accuracy.
B) Correct – The predict() method must be used to generate predictions for evaluation.
C) Incorrect – Model intercept is a parameter of the model, not a performance evaluation metric.
D) Incorrect – Mean squared error is for regression tasks, not classification.
E) Incorrect – Coefficients represent the weights of features but do not directly evaluate the accuracy of the model.

EXAM FOCUS	*Use confusion_matrix for classification evaluation: Confusion matrix provides detailed insight into a classifier's performance, especially for imbalanced datasets.*
CAUTION ALERT	*Avoid using regression metrics for classification: Don't use metrics like mean squared error for classification models; confusion matrices and accuracy are better suited.*

QUESTION 38

Answer - A, D

A) Correct because pd.crosstab is designed to calculate cross tables between categorical variables, making this a valid solution.
B) Incorrect because it uses pivot_table() and mistakenly assigns Department to values instead of indexing both Department and Gender for cross tabulation.
C) Incorrect as it sets Department as the index instead of using the proper cross-tabulation.
D) Correct as it performs a cross-tabulation with the correct parameters to get the employee count by gender and department.
E) Incorrect because the .size() method returns the correct grouping but it doesn't give the structure required for cross table.

EXAM FOCUS	*Cross-tabulate categorical variables: Use pd.crosstab() to summarize counts of categorical variables, such as employee counts by gender and department. It simplifies comparison across categories.*
CAUTION ALERT	*Avoid using incorrect aggregation functions: Don't mistakenly assign categorical data to values in pivot tables or use aggregation functions like mean or sum for categorical analysis.*

QUESTION 39

Answer - A, C

A) Correct because lowering the decision threshold increases the number of positive predictions, which can improve recall.
B) Incorrect because increasing regularization typically helps with generalization but does not directly improve recall.
C) Correct because SMOTE addresses class imbalance, improving the recall for minority classes.
D) Incorrect because applying PCA helps reduce data complexity but does not directly improve recall.
E) Incorrect because the confusion matrix is used to evaluate performance, not to improve recall.

EXAM FOCUS	*Improving Recall: Adjusting the decision threshold to lower values or using techniques like SMOTE can improve recall, especially in imbalanced datasets.*
CAUTION ALERT	*Thresholds and Regularization: Changing the decision threshold directly affects recall but may also lower precision. Regularization doesn't directly influence recall improvement.*

QUESTION 40

Answer - A

A) Correct because sns.heatmap() is the right function to visualize a correlation matrix using a heatmap, making it ideal for showing relationships between variables.
B) Incorrect because sns.pairplot() creates scatter plots between pairs of variables, not a heatmap of correlations.
C) Incorrect because sns.boxplot() visualizes the distribution of data, not correlations.
D) Incorrect because sns.histplot() generates a histogram, not a heatmap of correlations.
E) Incorrect because sns.scatterplot() generates a scatter plot, not a heatmap.

EXAM FOCUS	*Correlation Heatmaps: To visualize correlations between multiple variables, use Seaborn's sns.heatmap() with the .corr() method to generate a correlation matrix.*
CAUTION ALERT	*Pairplot vs. Heatmap: While sns.pairplot() helps visualize pairwise relationships, it doesn't show correlations between variables. Use heatmaps for correlation matrices.*

QUESTION 41

Answer - A, D

A) Correct because plt.annotate() is the right function, and the syntax includes xy for the peak point, xytext for the annotation position, and arrowprops for a pointing arrow, which is valid for highlighting a peak.
B) Incorrect because plt.label() is not a valid Matplotlib function for annotating points.
C) Incorrect because plt.annotate_peak() is not a valid function in Matplotlib.
D) Correct because it correctly uses plt.annotate(), and while arrowprops uses a different color, the structure is valid for annotating a peak.
E) Incorrect because plt.annotate() requires both xy coordinates for placement, not just max_x.

EXAM FOCUS	*Annotation Tip: Use plt.annotate() to highlight important data points like peaks in a plot. Adjust the position of the annotation and add arrows for clarity.*
CAUTION ALERT	*Common Error: plt.annotate() requires both xy coordinates for placement. Avoid functions like plt.label() or plt.annotate_peak()—these don't exist in Matplotlib.*

QUESTION 42

Answer - B, D

A) Incorrect because plt.xticks(rotation=45) only rotates the labels, but does not reduce the tick frequency.
B) Correct because plt.locator_params(axis='x', nbins=6) reduces the number of x-axis ticks for clarity.
C) Incorrect because plt.xaxis.set_tick_params() is not a valid function in this context.
D) Correct because plt.xlabel('Date') adds a descriptive label to the x-axis, making it clearer to the audience.
E) Incorrect because plt.xlabel_font() is not a valid function.

EXAM FOCUS	*Tick Frequency Tip: Use plt.locator_params(axis='x', nbins=6) to reduce x-axis tick frequency. Add plt.xlabel() for descriptive labels, especially in time-series plots.*
CAUTION ALERT	*Tick Error: Avoid using functions like plt.xticks(rotation=45) or plt.xaxis.set_tick_params()—these only adjust label rotation or tick appearance, not frequency.*

QUESTION 43

Answer - A, D

A) Correct because summarizing insights beside visuals ensures a clear, concise presentation that enhances audience understanding.
B) Incorrect because too many visuals on a single slide can overwhelm the audience, reducing clarity.
C) Incorrect because relying only on visuals can lead to misinterpretation of trends by a non-technical audience.
D) Correct because using one chart per slide with a text summary maintains focus and clarity for each point presented.

EXAM FOCUS	*Slide Structure Tip: Use one chart per slide with a concise summary below or beside the visual to maintain clarity. Focus on one key message per slide.*
CAUTION ALERT	*Too Many Visuals: Avoid using multiple charts per slide. Overloading visuals reduces the impact and can confuse your audience, especially if they are non-technical.*

QUESTION 44

Answer - A

A) Correct because sns.set_palette("muted") allows you to set a consistent color palette across multiple visualizations, ensuring clarity and consistency.
B) Incorrect because sns.set_context("paper") adjusts the plot aesthetics for publication but does not specifically set a color palette.
C) Incorrect because sns.palplot(sales) is used to plot a color palette, not to set it globally.
D) Incorrect because this only specifies a color palette, but does not set it for multiple charts.
E) Incorrect because plt.set_color_palette() is not a valid Matplotlib or Seaborn function for setting a global color palette.

EXAM FOCUS	*Consistent Colors: Use sns.set_palette("muted") to set a consistent color palette across multiple charts for readability and consistency in reports or presentations.*
CAUTION ALERT	*Color Overload: Avoid using overly vibrant color palettes like "bright" in complex visualizations. These can overwhelm the viewer and obscure key insights.*

QUESTION 45

Answer - B

A) Incorrect because a simple line plot doesn't differentiate between the revenue increase before and after implementing the strategy. B) Correct because this line plot clearly compares revenue growth over time, separated by strategy type, offering evidence of the marketing strategy's effect on revenue. C) Incorrect because a bar plot doesn't offer the nuance required to compare before and after the strategy. D) Incorrect because pie charts are unsuitable for showing growth over time. E) Incorrect because scatter plots are not effective for summarizing time-series growth data.

EXAM FOCUS	*Show Growth with Comparison: Use Seaborn's hue parameter in line plots to differentiate before and after a strategy implementation, clearly showing revenue growth over time.*
CAUTION ALERT	*Avoid Simple Line Plots: Simple line plots without context or comparison (e.g., strategy vs. no strategy) fail to clearly convey the impact of marketing strategies on revenue.*

PRACTICE TEST 8 - QUESTIONS ONLY

QUESTION 1

You are tasked with analyzing sales data stored in a CSV file. After loading the data, you notice several missing values in the sales_amount column. Which Python code snippet will correctly replace the missing values with the column's median value?

```
A) df['sales_amount'].fillna(df['sales_amount'].mean(), inplace=True)
B) df['sales_amount'].fillna(df['sales_amount'].median(), inplace=True)
C) df['sales_amount'].replace(np.nan, df['sales_amount'].median(), inplace=True)
D) df['sales_amount'].dropna()
```

QUESTION 2

You are analyzing financial data stored in multiple CSV files. Before loading the data into Python, you want to ensure that it is stored in the correct format. Which of the following is NOT an appropriate best practice for file-based storage?

A) Store CSV files in cloud storage
B) Standardize column headers before loading
C) Store large files in Excel format
D) Use consistent delimiters across CSV files
E) Ensure CSV files are compressed for efficiency

QUESTION 3

You are working with a dataset containing categorical features like country and gender. To include these in a machine learning model, you need to convert the categorical variables into a format the model can process. Which methods can be used to encode these variables? (Select 3 answers).

A) Use one-hot encoding to convert categorical variables into binary columns
B) Use label encoding to assign numerical values to categorical variables
C) Use pd.get_dummies() to implement one-hot encoding in Pandas
D) Use Min-Max scaling on categorical variables

QUESTION 4

You are cleaning a dataset and need to ensure that the date column is in a consistent format (YYYY-MM-DD). Which Python functions can be used to standardize the date format across the entire dataset? (Select 2 answers).

```
A) Use pd.to_datetime() to convert the column to a datetime object
B) Use df['date'].apply(lambda x: datetime.strptime(x, '%Y-%m-%d'))
C) Use pd.read_csv() to automatically parse dates into the desired format
D) Use df['date'] = df['date'].strftime('%Y-%m-%d')
```

QUESTION 5

You are tasked with handling errors in your code when dividing two numbers. Which Python code properly uses a try-except block to catch division-by-zero errors? (Select 2 answers).

```
A) try: result = a / b
except: print('Error: Division by zero')
```

```
 B) try: result = a / b
except ZeroDivisionError: print('Error: Division by zero')

 C) try: result = a / b
except ZeroDivisionError as e: print(e)

 D) try: result = a // b
except: print('Error: Division by zero')
```

QUESTION 6

You are retrieving data from a MySQL database using Python. Which Python library and method are typically used to establish a connection to a MySQL database? (Select 2 answers).

```
A) import pymysql
conn = pymysql.connect(host='localhost', user='user', password='pass', db='database')

 B) import mysql
conn = mysql.connect(host='localhost', user='user', password='pass', db='database')

 C) import mysql.connector
conn = mysql.connector.connect(host='localhost', user='user', password='pass',
database='database')

 D) import mysqldb
conn = mysqldb.connect(host='localhost', user='user', password='pass', db='database')
```

QUESTION 7

You are testing the statistical significance of the mean difference between two groups using a p-value. If the p-value is less than 0.05, the null hypothesis is rejected. True or False?

A) True
B) False

QUESTION 8

You want to find the mean of a NumPy array. Which of the following correctly calculates the mean of a 2D array along the first axis (rows)? (Select 2 answers)

```
A) import numpy as np
arr = np.array([[1, 2, 3], [4, 5, 6]])
mean_value = np.mean(arr, axis=1)

 B) import numpy as np
arr = np.array([[1, 2], [3, 4]])
mean_value = np.mean(arr, axis=0)

 C) import numpy as np
arr = np.array([1, 2, 3, 4])
mean_value = arr.mean(axis=1)

 D) import numpy as np
arr = np.array([[1, 2], [3, 4], [5, 6]])
mean_value = np.mean(arr, axis=0)

 E) import numpy as np
arr = np.array([1, 2, 3])
mean_value = np.mean(arr)
```

QUESTION 9

You need to visualize sales data over time using a time-series plot in Matplotlib. Which steps are correct for handling time-series data? Select 2 correct options.

```
A) import matplotlib.dates as mdates
plt.gca().xaxis.set_major_formatter(mdates.DateFormatter('%Y-%m-%d'))
plt.plot(dates, sales)

B) plt.plot(dates, sales)
plt.title('Sales Over Time')

C) plt.xaxis.set_major_locator(mdates.MonthLocator())
D) plt.plot(dates, sales, linestyle='--')

E) plt.xticks(rotation=45)
plt.grid(True)
```

QUESTION 10

You are visualizing pairwise relationships in a dataset using Seaborn. What script can you use to generate pair plots of numerical columns? (Select 2 correct answers)

```
A) import seaborn as sns
sns.pairplot(df)

 B) import seaborn as sns
sns.catplot(data=df)

 C) import seaborn as sns
sns.pairplot(df, hue='category')

 D) import seaborn as sns
sns.pairplot(df, vars=['age', 'income'])

 E) import seaborn as sns
sns.lmplot(x='age', y='income', data=df)
```

QUESTION 11

You are collecting data from customers, and some sensitive data is required. What steps should you take to protect sensitive data during transmission? (Select 2 correct answers)

A) Encrypt the data using SSL/TLS
B) Send sensitive data over HTTP without encryption
C) Use a secure API for data transmission
D) Store the data in plain text
E) Send data directly without using a secure method

QUESTION 12

You are conducting a data-driven market research analysis. After querying the database using Python, you receive a dataset with 1,000,000 rows. How would you optimize memory usage and handle such a large dataset effectively? (Select 2 correct answers)

```
 A) df.astype({'column_name': 'float32'})
 B) df.astype({'column_name': 'object'})
 C) Use df.memory_usage(deep=True) to monitor memory usage
 D) Split the dataset into smaller parts using np.split(df, 4)
 E) df.copy(deep=True)
```

QUESTION 13

A retail company wants to run a script that processes customer orders and adds an additional fee if the order value exceeds a certain threshold. You are asked to implement this using if-else within a loop. What is the best approach? Select 2 correct answers.

```
A) for order in orders:
if order['value'] > 100:
order['value'] += fee

B) for order in orders:
if order['value'] < 100:
continue
else:
order['value'] += fee

C) for order in orders:
if order['value'] > 100:
continue
else:
order['value'] += fee

D) i = 0
while i < len(orders):
if orders[i]['value'] > 100:
orders[i]['value'] += fee
i += 1

E) for order in orders:
if order['value'] < 100:
break
else:
order['value'] += fee
```

QUESTION 14

You have a large dataset containing date-time values, and you need to convert the 'date' column from string format to date-time format for further analysis. Which of the following Python scripts achieves this? Select 2 correct answers.

```
A) df['date'] = pd.to_datetime(df['date'])
B) df['date'] = df['date'].astype('datetime64[ns]')
C) df['date'] = pd.to_datetime(df['date'], format='%Y-%m-%d')
D) df['date'] = df['date'].strftime('%Y-%m-%d')
E) df['date'] = pd.read_csv(df, parse_dates=['date'])
```

QUESTION 15

You need to normalize a feature in your dataset using the Min-Max scaling technique. Which of the following methods in Python will correctly achieve this normalization? (Select 2 answers)

```
A) from sklearn.preprocessing import MinMaxScaler; df[['Feature']] =
MinMaxScaler().fit_transform(df[['Feature']])

B) df['Feature'] = (df['Feature'] - df['Feature'].min()) / (df['Feature'].max() -
df['Feature'].min())

C) df['Feature'] = df['Feature'] / df['Feature'].max()

D) from sklearn.preprocessing import StandardScaler; df[['Feature']] =
StandardScaler().fit_transform(df[['Feature']])
```

```
E) df['Feature'] = df['Feature'] / df['Feature'].std()
```

QUESTION 16

You need to create a reusable function that accepts a function as an argument and applies it to each element in a list. The function should also handle optional arguments for the passed function. What is the correct way to implement this in Python? (Select 2 answers)

```
A) def apply_func(func, data, **kwargs): return [func(d, **kwargs) for d in data]
B) def apply_func(data, func, *args): return [func(d, *args) for d in data]
C) def apply_func(func, data, *args, **kwargs): return [func(d, *args, **kwargs) for d in
data]
D) def apply_func(data, func): return [func(d) for d in data]
E) def apply_func(func, *args, **kwargs): return func(*args, **kwargs)
```

QUESTION 17

You are tasked with removing duplicate entries from a list of customer email addresses. Which Python data structure and method would efficiently help you achieve this? (Select 2 answers)

```
A) unique_emails = list(set(email_list))
B) unique_emails = [] for email in email_list: if email not in unique_emails:
unique_emails.append(email)
C) from collections import OrderedDict; unique_emails =
list(OrderedDict.fromkeys(email_list))
D) unique_emails = email_list.copy()
E) unique_emails = {email for email in email_list}
```

QUESTION 18

You are writing a Python script to analyze sales data. Your manager has asked you to organize your code into modules to improve maintainability. Which of the following approaches represents best practices for organizing the code into modules? (Select 2 answers)

A) Create a single script sales_analysis.py for all processing tasks
B) Create separate modules: data_processing.py, data_visualization.py, and model_building.py
C) Create a module sales_data.py that handles everything including data processing, visualization, and modeling
D) Create a main script sales_main.py that calls functions from data_processing.py, data_visualization.py, and model_building.py
E) Create a single script sales.py and import all libraries at the top of the file

QUESTION 19

You need to write a SQL query that groups the total sales (order_total) by customer_name and only includes customers whose total sales exceed $1000. Which SQL query accomplishes this task? (Select 2 answers)

```
A) SELECT customer_name, SUM(order_total) as total_sales
FROM orders
GROUP BY customer_name
HAVING SUM(order_total) > 1000;

B) SELECT customer_name, total_sales
FROM orders
GROUP BY customer_name
WHERE SUM(order_total) > 1000;

C) SELECT customer_name, SUM(order_total) as total_sales
```

```
FROM orders
GROUP BY customer_name
HAVING total_sales > 1000;

 D) SELECT customer_name, SUM(order_total) as total_sales
FROM orders
WHERE SUM(order_total) > 1000
GROUP BY customer_name;

 E) SELECT customer_name, SUM(order_total) as total_sales
FROM orders
GROUP BY customer_name
HAVING SUM(order_total) >= 1000;
```

QUESTION 20

Your script is required to handle database connection errors securely and retry connecting three times before raising an exception. Which Python code correctly implements this functionality? (Select 2 answers)

```
A) import sqlite3
for i in range(3):
try:
conn = sqlite3.connect('database.db')
break
except sqlite3.Error:
print("Connection failed. Retrying...")
raise

B) import sqlite3
for i in range(3):
try:
conn = sqlite3.connect('database.db')
break
except sqlite3.Error:
print("Connection failed. Retrying...")
if i == 2:
raise

C) import pymysql
attempts = 0
while attempts < 3:
try:
conn = pymysql.connect(host='localhost',
user='root',
password='password',
database='sales')
break
except pymysql.MySQLError:
attempts += 1
print("Retrying connection...")
if attempts == 3:
raise

D) import sqlite3
for i in range(3):
try:
conn = sqlite3.connect('database.db')
except sqlite3.Error:
raise

E) import pymysql
```

```
for attempts in range(3):
try:
conn = pymysql.connect(host='localhost',
user='root',
password='password',
database='sales')
except pymysql.MySQLError:
if attempts == 2:
raise
```

QUESTION 21

You are working with a SQL table where birth_date is stored as DATETIME. When loading this data into Python using Pandas, what is the correct way to convert it to a Pandas datetime object? (Select 2 answers)

```
A) df = pd.read_sql("SELECT birth_date FROM customers", conn)
df['birth'] = pd.to_datetime(df['birth'])

 B) df = pd.read_sql("SELECT birth_date FROM customers", conn)
df['birth'] = df['birth'].astype('datetime64')

 C) df = pd.read_sql("SELECT birth_date FROM customers", conn)
df['birth'] = pd.to_datetime(df['birth'], format='%Y-%m-%d')

 D) df['birth'] = df['birth'].apply(pd.datetimE)  E) df['birth'] =
pd.to_datetime(df['birth']).strftime('%Y-%m-%d')
```

QUESTION 22

You are working with a higher-order function that takes another function as an argument and applies it to a list. Which of the following implementations will work? (Select 2 answers)

```
 A) def apply_func(f, lst):
return [f(x) for x in lst]

 B) def apply_func(f, lst):
return f(lst)

 C) def apply_func(f, lst):
for x in lst:
return f(x)

 D) def apply_func(f, lst):
return map(f, lst)

 E) def apply_func(f, lst):
return [f(lst)]
```

QUESTION 23

You need to organize several modules within a package. What is the best way to initialize a Python package and import all its modules? (Select 2 answers)

A) Create an __init__.py file inside the package folder to make it a Python package.
B) Use from package import * to import all modules in a package.
C) There is no need for __init__.py, as Python automatically treats folders as packages.
D) Import modules one by one from the package without needing an __init__.py file.
E) To import specific modules, the __init__.py file must explicitly list all modules inside the package.

QUESTION 24

You are working with XML data using the xml.etree.ElementTree library. You need to parse an XML file and extract specific elements by their tag name. Which code snippets are valid approaches to extract the data? (Select 2 correct answers)

```
A) import xml.etree.ElementTree as ET
tree = ET.parse('data.xml')
root = tree.getroot()
for elem in root.findall('item'):
print(elem.text)

B) import xml.etree.ElementTree as ET
root = ET.Element('data')
tree = ET.parse('data.xml')
print(root.find('item').text)

C) import xml.etree.ElementTree as ET
tree = ET.ElementTree(file='data.xml')
for elem in tree.findall('item'):
print(elem.text)

D) import xml.etree.ElementTree as ET
tree = ET.ElementTree(ET.parse('data.xml'))
print(tree.getroot().find('item').text)
E) import xml.etree.ElementTree as ET
tree = ET.ElementTree().
```

QUESTION 25

You need to retrieve the total number of sales for each product and customer, ensuring that only customers with at least 3 total sales are included in the result. Which of the following queries will achieve the desired result? (Select 1 correct answer)

```
A) SELECT product_id, customer_id, COUNT(sale_id) FROM sales GROUP BY product_id,
customer_id HAVING COUNT(sale_id) >= 3;

B) SELECT customer_id, COUNT(sale_id) FROM sales WHERE COUNT(sale_id) >= 3 GROUP BY
customer_id;

C) WITH CustomerSales AS (SELECT customer_id, COUNT(sale_id) AS total_sales FROM sales GROUP
BY customer_id) SELECT * FROM CustomerSales WHERE total_sales >= 3;

D) SELECT customer_id FROM sales GROUP BY customer_id HAVING COUNT(sale_id) >= 3;
E) SELECT customer_id, product_id FROM sales WHERE COUNT(sale_id) >= 3;
```

QUESTION 26

You are running a query that uses multiple joins across several large tables. The query is taking a long time to execute. What can you do to optimize the query? (Select 2 correct answers)

) Use indexes on the columns being used in JOINs;
) Use subqueries instead of joins;
) Break down the query into smaller parts;
) Use appropriate WHERE clauses to filter data early;
) Remove indexes to reduce overhead;

QUESTION 27

You have created a view project_view to encapsulate project data. How can you ensure the view remains up-to-date when the base table projects is altered? (Select 1 correct answer)

```
A) CREATE OR REPLACE VIEW project_view AS SELECT * FROM projects;
B) ALTER TABLE projects ADD COLUMN new_field;
C) ALTER VIEW project_view;
D) DROP VIEW project_view;
E) INSERT INTO project_view (project_id, project_name) VALUES (5, 'New Project');
```

QUESTION 28

What is the purpose of a savepoint in SQL transactions? (Select 1 correct answer)

A) Savepoint allows partial rollback of a transaction.

B) Savepoint commits the entire transaction.

C) Savepoint marks the beginning of a transaction.

D) Savepoint prevents other transactions from accessing data.

E) Savepoint increases the transaction isolation level.

QUESTION 29

You have two datasets: one with salaries and one with house prices. Both datasets are skewed. What measure of spread would you use to compare their variability? (Select 1 correct answer)

```
A) statistics.mean(salaries)
B) statistics.stdev(salaries)
C) statistics.variance(house_prices)
D) max(house_prices) - min(house_prices)
E) np.mean(salaries)
```

QUESTION 30

A dataset shows the number of study hours and test scores of students. You suspect an outlier affecting the correlation between the two variables. What technique can you use to identify this in Python? (Select 1 correct answer)

```
A) sns.scatterplot(data=df, x='hours', y='score')
B) sns.histplot(data=df, x='hours', y='score')
C) np.var(df['hours'])
D) df.corr(method='kendall')
E) sns.boxplot(data=df, x='hours', y='score')
```

QUESTION 31

A linear regression model has been fit on a dataset, but you suspect multicollinearity between two independent variables: age and experience. What is an effective way to detect multicollinearity in Python? (Select 1 correct answer)

```
A) from statsmodels.stats.outliers_influence import variance_inflation_factor; vif =
variance_inflation_factor(df[['age', 'experience']], i)

B) from sklearn.preprocessing import StandardScaler; vif = scaler.fit_transform(df[['age',
'experience']])
C) from statsmodels.api import OLS; vif = OLS(df[['age']], df[['experience']]).fit()
D) import numpy as np; vif = np.corrcoef(df['age'], df['experience'])
E) vif = np.linalg.det(df[['age', 'experience']])
```

QUESTION 32

You are tasked with identifying outliers using the Interquartile Range (IQR) method. Which Python code correctly applies this technique? (Select 2 correct answers)

```
A) Q1 = df['age'].quantile(0.25); Q3 = df['age'].quantile(0.75); IQR = Q3 - Q1; df_outliers =
df[(df['age'] < Q1 - 1.5 * IQR) | (df['age'] > Q3 + 1.5 * IQR)]

B) IQR = np.percentile(df['age'], 75) - np.percentile(df['age'], 25); df_outliers =
df[df['age'] > np.percentile(df['age'], 75) + 1.5 * IQR]

C) df_outliers = df[df['age'] > df['age'].mean() + 3 * df['age'].std()]
D) IQR = np.median(df['age']); df_outliers = df[df['age'] < IQR]
E) outliers = df[df['age'] > df['age'].median() * 1.5]
```

QUESTION 33

You are tasked with identifying outliers in a dataset based on the 'age' column. Which of the following options correctly implement the IQR (Interquartile Range) method to filter outliers? (Select 2 correct answers)

```
A) IQR = Q3 - Q1; df_outliers = df[df['age'] > Q3 + 1.5 * IQR]
B) IQR = np.percentile(df['age'], 75) - np.percentile(df['age'], 25); df_outliers =
df[df['age'] > np.percentile(df['age'], 75) + 1.5 * IQR]
C) df_outliers = df[df['age'] > df['age'].mean() + 3 * df['age'].std()]
D) IQR = np.median(df['age']); df_outliers = df[df['age'] < IQR]
E) outliers = df[df['age'] > df['age'].median() * 1.5]
```

QUESTION 34

You need to reshape a dataset in Pandas by converting long-form data into wide format using a pivot table. How would you correctly accomplish this? (Select 2 correct answers)

```
A) df.pivot(index='department', columns='year', values='salary')
B) df.pivot_table(index='department', columns='year', values='salary')
C) pd.pivot_table(df, index='department', columns='year', values='salary')
D) df.unstack('salary')
E) df.melt(id_vars=['department'], value_vars=['salary'])
```

QUESTION 35

After splitting your dataset into training and test sets, you realize your model is overfitting. Which of the following actions can help address overfitting? (Select 2 correct answers)

A) Regularization (e.g., L2)
B) Using a simpler model
C) Reducing the training data size
D) Removing the test set entirely
E) Increasing the complexity of the model

QUESTION 36

In supervised learning, overfitting can result in a model that performs well on the training data but poorly on new data. Reducing the number of features can help prevent overfitting in machine learning models.

A) True
B) False

QUESTION 37

You are working as a data analyst at a retail company. You have been tasked with predicting whether customers will purchase a product based on their age and income. You decide to use logistic regression as your model. After training the model, you observe an R-squared value of 0.85. The R-squared value indicates that your logistic regression model fits the data well and explains 85% of the variance.

A) True
B) False

QUESTION 38

You are asked to summarize a sales dataset by showing the mean (avg_sales) for each product in different regions using a pivot table in Pandas. The following script will achieve this. pd.pivot_table(df, values='sales', index='product', columns='region', aggfunc='mean')

A) True
B) False`

QUESTION 39

A binary classifier shows a high precision but low recall. This model is successfully identifying most of the positive cases.

A) True
B) False

QUESTION 40

You want to customize a Seaborn plot to add labels to the axes and a title. In Seaborn, you can use plt.xlabel(), plt.ylabel(), and plt.title() from Matplotlib to customize the appearance of the plot.

A) True
B) False

QUESTION 41

You have generated a scatter plot to compare sales and profit. You are asked to add a legend for "Sales" and "Profit". The following code will add a correct legend: plt.legend(['Sales', 'Profit'])

A) True
B) False

QUESTION 42

You are visualizing revenue data and need to adapt the chart for an audience unfamiliar with revenue numbers. You want to make it easier to understand the revenue amounts by converting values to thousands. Which approach is best? Select two correct answers.

```
A) plt.bar(df['Month'], df['Revenue'])
B) df['Revenue'] = df['Revenue'] / 1000; plt.bar(df['Month'], df['Revenue'])
C) plt.bar(df['Month'], df['Revenue']/1000)
D) df['Revenue'] = df['Revenue'] / 1000; plt.annotate('Revenue (in thousands)', xy=(0.5, 0.5))
```

QUESTION 43

You are presenting trends in customer spending across various product categories using a combination of a line plot and a text summary. Which two actions can improve the clarity and impact of your presentation? Select two correct answers.

A) Use concise text to summarize the key trend for each product category directly above the plot.
B) Present the chart without any text and explain the trends verbally.
C) Annotate the chart using plt.annotate() to highlight key turning points.
D) Use a multiline chart for all categories but avoid adding any text for clarity.

QUESTION 44

You want to differentiate between multiple data series in a line chart representing sales across different regions. Which color palette should you use to avoid overwhelming the viewer with too many contrasting colors?

```
A) sns.lineplot(x="time", y="sales", hue="region", palette="bright")
B) sns.lineplot(x="time", y="sales", hue="region", palette="pastel")
C) sns.lineplot(x="time", y="sales", hue="region", palette="dark")
D) sns.lineplot(x="time", y="sales", hue="region", palette="coolwarm")
E) sns.lineplot(x="time", y="sales", hue="region", palette="deep")
```

QUESTION 45

Your company needs to justify an increase in production due to rising customer demand. What visual evidence would best demonstrate the correlation between rising demand and production needs?

```
A) sns.heatmap(data=demand_production_df)
B) plt.plot(customer_demand, production_needs); plt.xlabel('Customer Demand');
plt.ylabel('Production Needs')
C) sns.lineplot(x='months', y='production_needs', data=demand_datA)   D)
plt.pie(production_needs, labels=months)
E) plt.scatter(customer_demand, production_needs, color='green')
```

PRACTICE TEST 8 - ANSWERS ONLY

QUESTION 1

Answer - B

A) Incorrect – This replaces missing values with the mean instead of the median, which is not what the question asked for.

B) Correct – df['sales_amount'].fillna(df['sales_amount'].median(), inplace=True) correctly replaces missing values with the median of the column, which is what the question requires.

C) Incorrect – While replace works for NaNs, fillna() is more appropriate for replacing missing values with specific statistics like the median.

D) Incorrect – Dropping missing values will remove rows entirely, which can lead to data loss rather than imputing the values.

EXAM FOCUS	*Always consider the data distribution when imputing missing values. For skewed distributions, using the median may yield more accurate imputation than the mean.*
CAUTION ALERT	*Dropping rows with missing values can significantly reduce your dataset. Only use it if you're sure the data is non-essential or outliers.*

QUESTION 2

Answer - C

A) Correct – Storing CSV files in cloud storage is a good practice to ensure scalability and accessibility.

B) Correct – Standardizing column headers before loading ensures consistent data handling and merging.

C) Incorrect – Excel format is not suited for large datasets due to limitations in row count and processing power.

D) Correct – Consistent delimiters across CSV files prevent parsing errors when loading the data into Python.

E) Correct – Compressing CSV files reduces storage requirements and speeds up data transfer.

EXAM FOCUS	*Standardizing column headers and using consistent delimiters prevent parsing issues when loading CSV files into Python for analysis.*
CAUTION ALERT	*Avoid using Excel for large files. Excel has row limitations and isn't optimized for handling large datasets, especially in financial data analysis.*

QUESTION 3

Answer - A, B, C

A) Correct – One-hot encoding converts categorical variables into binary columns, making them compatible with machine learning models.

B) Correct – Label encoding assigns numerical values to categories, which is useful when there is a natural order in the categories.

C) Correct – pd.get_dummies() is a Pandas function that creates dummy variables for categorical features, implementing one-hot encoding.

D) Incorrect – Min-Max scaling applies only to numerical data, not categorical data.

EXAM FOCUS	*Use one-hot encoding for non-ordinal categorical features and label encoding when the categories have an inherent order (like low, medium, high).*
CAUTION ALERT	*Avoid applying Min-Max scaling to categorical variables. It's meant for numerical data and doesn't make sense for non-numeric categories.*

QUESTION 4

Answer - A, B

A) Correct – pd.to_datetime() is used to convert a column to a datetime object, allowing easy formatting and manipulation.
B) Correct – This lambda function can convert strings to datetime objects in the desired format using strptime.
C) Incorrect – pd.read_csv() does not automatically parse dates into a specific format; the parse_dates parameter is used for automatic detection, but formatting requires additional steps.
D) Incorrect – strftime() is used for formatting a datetime object to a string, not for converting a column of strings into datetime objects.

EXAM FOCUS	Use pd.to_datetime() to easily standardize date columns. This function converts strings into datetime objects, allowing for easier manipulation.
CAUTION ALERT	pd.read_csv() doesn't automatically format dates. Make sure you explicitly use pd.to_datetime() or a similar function to convert date columns.

QUESTION 5

Answer - B, C

A) Incorrect – The syntax is incorrect as the except block must be indented, and no specific exception type is mentioned.
B) Correct – This catches ZeroDivisionError when division by zero occurs and prints an error message.
C) Correct – This catches the error and assigns it to the variable e, which is printed.
D) Incorrect – This uses floor division (//), but the error handling is not structured correctly, and except is not indented.

EXAM FOCUS	Use try-except with specific error handling like ZeroDivisionError to catch common runtime errors. Always specify exceptions for more controlled debugging.
CAUTION ALERT	Don't use a bare except clause without specifying the error. It can mask important errors and make debugging more difficult later.

QUESTION 6

Answer - A, C

A) Correct – pymysql.connect() is commonly used for connecting to MySQL databases.
B) Incorrect – mysql.connect() is not a valid method in this context, as the correct module is mysql.connector.
C) Correct – mysql.connector.connect() is the official MySQL connector method for Python.
D) Incorrect – mysqldb is not commonly used anymore, and this method lacks support for modern Python versions.

EXAM FOCUS	Use libraries like pymysql or mysql.connector to connect to MySQL databases from Python, as these are standard connectors.
CAUTION ALERT	mysqldb is deprecated in modern Python versions. Stick to pymysql or mysql.connector for stable MySQL connections.

QUESTION 7

Answer - A

A) Correct – If the p-value is less than 0.05, it indicates strong evidence against the null hypothesis, and it is rejected.

B) Incorrect – This statement is false because a p-value less than 0.05 suggests that the null hypothesis should be rejected.

EXAM FOCUS	*A p-value less than 0.05 suggests strong evidence against the null hypothesis, prompting its rejection. This is a fundamental threshold in hypothesis testing.*
CAUTION ALERT	*Failing to reject the null hypothesis when the p-value is greater than 0.05 means the evidence isn't strong enough to claim a significant difference.*

QUESTION 8

Answer - A, D

A) Correct – This calculates the mean across rows (axis=1) in a 2D array.

B) Incorrect – This calculates the mean along columns (axis=0), but the question asks for rows.

C) Incorrect – The array is 1D, so axis=1 will cause an error.

D) Correct – This calculates the mean across rows, which is correct based on the question.

E) Incorrect – The array is 1D and doesn't involve axis-specific mean calculation.

EXAM FOCUS	*Use np.mean(arr, axis=0) or axis=1 to compute the mean across specific dimensions of a 2D array. Axis defines the direction of computation.*
CAUTION ALERT	*Watch for errors when applying axis-specific calculations on 1D arrays. A 1D array does not support axis=1, which is for multi-dimensional arrays.*

QUESTION 9

Answer - A, E

A) Correct: Proper method to handle and format time-series data.

B) Incorrect: This does not handle time-specific formatting.

C) Incorrect: Missing plt.gca() to use xaxis.

D) Incorrect: No time-series specific formatting here.

E) Correct: Rotating xticks and adding grid is helpful for time-series.

EXAM FOCUS	*Use matplotlib.dates for time-series formatting, and rotate the x-axis ticks (plt.xticks(rotation=45)) for better readability when dealing with date labels.*
CAUTION ALERT	*Ensure that time-series data is handled with date-specific formatting like mdates.DateFormatter. Without this, dates may be misinterpreted in the plot.*

QUESTION 10

Answer - A, C

A) Correct. Generates pair plots of numerical variables.

B) Incorrect. This creates categorical plots, not pair plots.

C) Correct. Pair plot with categorical differentiation is valid.

D) Incorrect. While valid, the question doesn't specify variable selection.

E) Incorrect. This creates a linear regression plot, not pair plots.

EXAM FOCUS	*Use pairplot() for quick visual analysis of relationships among numerical variables in your dataset. Leverage hue to differentiate based on categories.*

Avoid using catplot() or lmplot() for tasks requiring pairwise relationships. These are better suited for categorical and regression plots.

QUESTION 11

Answer - A, C

A) SSL/TLS encryption protects sensitive data during transmission.
B) Sending data over HTTP is insecure.
C) Using a secure API ensures safe data transmission.
D) Storing data in plain text is not secure.
E) Sending data without secure methods is a security risk.

EXAM FOCUS	*Use SSL/TLS encryption and secure APIs to transmit sensitive customer data to avoid exposing it during transfer and ensure end-to-end security.*
CAUTION ALERT	*Never send sensitive data over unencrypted HTTP or store it in plain text, as this exposes your data to significant security risks.*

QUESTION 12

Answer - A, C

A) Converting column data types to float32 optimizes memory.
B) Converting to object increases memory usage.
C) Monitoring memory usage helps detect inefficiencies.
D) Splitting the dataset is not necessary if memory optimization is achieved.
E) Copying the dataframe increases memory consumption.

EXAM FOCUS	*Reducing memory usage by converting data types (float32) and using memory_usage(deep=True) to monitor data efficiency is critical when handling large datasets.*
CAUTION ALERT	*Avoid unnecessary memory duplication (e.g., deep copying) as it increases resource usage. Optimize data types to conserve memory.*

QUESTION 13

Answer - A, D

A) Correct: Simple loop with a conditional to add the fee efficiently.
B) Incorrect: This will skip orders above 100 incorrectly.
C) Incorrect: The condition is inverted, skipping orders over 100.
D) Correct: A while loop effectively traverses orders and adds the fee.
E) Incorrect: Breaking the loop prematurely misses valid orders.

EXAM FOCUS	*Use if-else in loops to add a fee to orders exceeding a certain value. Always ensure you properly condition the fee addition.*
CAUTION ALERT	*Avoid using continue incorrectly in your loop structure. It may skip important processing logic for orders exceeding the threshold.*

QUESTION 14

Answer - A, C

A) Correct: pd.to_datetime() converts string to date-time.
B) Incorrect: This is valid but unnecessary for common scenarios.
C) Correct: to_datetime() with specified format works.
D) Incorrect: strftime() is used for formatting, not conversion.
E) Incorrect: read_csv is incorrect for DataFrame transformation.

EXAM FOCUS	*Convert string dates to datetime with pd.to_datetime() to enable date-based operations and efficient date filtering or manipulation.*
CAUTION ALERT	*Avoid using strftime() for conversion; it's used for formatting datetime objects, not for converting strings.*

QUESTION 15

Answer - A, B

Option A: Correct – This is the proper method using MinMaxScaler from sklearn.
Option B: Correct – Manually applies Min-Max scaling by calculating the min and max values of the feature.
Option C: Incorrect – Only divides by the max, which does not correctly implement Min-Max scaling.
Option D: Incorrect – StandardScaler performs Z-score normalization, not Min-Max scaling.
Option E: Incorrect – Dividing by the standard deviation is not the correct approach for Min-Max scaling.

EXAM FOCUS	*MinMaxScaler() is ideal for scaling data between 0 and 1, ensuring uniformity across features in machine learning models.*
CAUTION ALERT	*Dividing by max values alone doesn't achieve true Min-Max scaling. Always subtract the min before dividing by the max.*

QUESTION 16

Answer - A, C

Option A: Correct – Handles both positional data and keyword arguments properly.
Option B: Incorrect – Arguments are misordered; func should come first.
Option C: Correct – Handles both positional and keyword arguments, as required.
Option D: Incorrect – Does not handle optional arguments for func.
Option E: Incorrect – Does not loop through the data, only applies the function once.

EXAM FOCUS	*Use higher-order functions in Python, such as passing functions as arguments, to build flexible and reusable code that processes lists efficiently.*
CAUTION ALERT	*Ensure optional arguments are handled properly when passed into a function, especially when using **kwargs to add flexibility.*

QUESTION 17

Answer - A, C

Option A: Correct – Converting a list to a set removes duplicates automatically, and converting it back to a list preserves the structure.
Option B: Incorrect – This is inefficient since it checks each email against the list for every iteration.
Option C: Correct – OrderedDict.fromkeys() removes duplicates while maintaining order, which can be important in some cases.
Option D: Incorrect – Simply copying the list does not remove duplicates.

Option E: Incorrect – While sets remove duplicates, this creates a set and not a list, which may not be the desired output format.

EXAM FOCUS	*Use sets or OrderedDict to remove duplicates while preserving order in a list, depending on whether you need to maintain the original sequence.*
CAUTION ALERT	*Avoid manual loops for checking and removing duplicates; they are inefficient compared to using sets or OrderedDict.*

QUESTION 18

Answer - B, D

Option A: Incorrect – A single script may lead to poor maintainability as the project grows.
Option B: Correct – Organizing code into specific modules based on functionality is a best practice for maintainability and clarity.
Option C: Incorrect – Combining all tasks in one module defeats the purpose of modularity.
Option D: Correct – Having a main script that calls functions from well-separated modules follows best practices for Python projects.
Option E: Incorrect – A single script approach can become unmanageable as the project scales.

EXAM FOCUS	*Follow the single responsibility principle: Each module should have a specific responsibility like data processing, visualization, or modeling, rather than doing everything in one script.*
CAUTION ALERT	*Don't overload one module: Combining too many functionalities in one module reduces code clarity and maintainability, making debugging more difficult as your project grows.*

QUESTION 19

Answer - A, E

Option A: Correct – Uses GROUP BY to group by customer and HAVING to filter out customers with sales below $1000.
Option B: Incorrect – The WHERE clause cannot filter on aggregate functions like SUM(); HAVING must be used instead.
Option C: Incorrect – The HAVING clause must contain the aggregate function, not a derived column like total_sales.
Option D: Incorrect – The WHERE clause is incorrectly placed before the GROUP BY clause, and aggregate functions cannot be used here.
Option E: Correct – Same as Option A but includes customers with exactly $1000 in total sales.

EXAM FOCUS	*Filter with HAVING: When using aggregate functions like SUM(), apply filters using HAVING instead of WHERE to get correct results for grouped data.*
CAUTION ALERT	*GROUP BY with aggregate functions: Always use GROUP BY in combination with aggregate functions, and apply conditions in the HAVING clause for filtering results.*

QUESTION 20

Answer - B, C

Option A: Incorrect – The raise is outside the retry block, which would raise an exception on the first failure.
Option B: Correct – Correctly handles retry logic with three attempts and raises an exception on the third failure.
Option C: Correct – Implements while loop retry logic with a pymysql.MySQLError and breaks upon success.

Option D: Incorrect – Missing retry logic; this will raise the error on the first failure.
Option E: Incorrect – The logic does not retry correctly after the second attempt.

EXAM FOCUS	*Retry mechanisms are critical: Implement retry logic when handling database connections to avoid failures due to intermittent network issues. Limit retry attempts to avoid infinite loops.*
CAUTION ALERT	*Handle retries carefully: Without limiting retries, your script can get stuck in an endless loop. Always include a maximum retry count.*

QUESTION 21

Answer - A, C

Option A: Correct – pd.to_datetime is the standard and efficient way to convert strings to Pandas datetime objects, preserving date formats.
Option B: Incorrect – Using astype('datetime64') can work, but it is not the best practice for converting DATETIME strings in SQL to Pandas.
Option C: Correct – By explicitly defining the format, pd.to_datetime ensures accurate conversion, especially when the format is known.
Option D: Incorrect – pd.datetime is deprecated and should not be used for datetime conversions.
Option E: Incorrect – strftime converts datetime objects back into strings, which is not what is required here.

EXAM FOCUS	*Use pd.to_datetime for date conversion: This is the most efficient method for converting strings into Pandas datetime objects when loading data from SQL.*
CAUTION ALERT	*Avoid deprecated functions: Don't use outdated methods like pd.datetime. Use pd.to_datetime for reliability and accuracy.*

QUESTION 22

Answer - A, D

Option A: Correct – This is a higher-order function that correctly applies the function f to each element of lst.
Option B: Incorrect – It applies the function f to the entire list, not element-wise.
Option C: Incorrect – It returns prematurely in the loop after processing only the first element of the list.
Option D: Correct – Using map() is an efficient way to apply a function to each element in the list.
Option E: Incorrect – It passes the entire list to f instead of applying it to individual elements.

EXAM FOCUS	*Higher-order functions are powerful: They can take functions as arguments and return new functions, simplifying repetitive tasks like applying operations to a list.*
CAUTION ALERT	*Don't return prematurely in loops: Returning inside a loop without completing all iterations results in partial or incorrect processing of the data.*

QUESTION 23

Answer - A, B

Option A: Correct – The presence of __init__.py makes a folder recognizable as a Python package.
Option B: Correct – Using from package import * imports all the modules defined in the package.
Option C: Incorrect – Without __init__.py, Python does not recognize the folder as a package in versions older than Python 3.3.
Option D: Incorrect – While possible, importing modules one by one is not best practice for managing large packages.

Option E: Incorrect – The __init__.py file does not need to explicitly list all modules.

EXAM FOCUS	*Packages need __init__.py: Always include __init__.py in your package directory to ensure it is treated as a Python package. This is essential for older Python versions.*
CAUTION ALERT	*Avoid missing __init__.py: Without an __init__.py file, Python may not recognize your folder as a package in versions prior to Python 3.3.*

QUESTION 24

Answer - A, D

A) Correct: This parses the XML and retrieves elements by their tag name.
B) Incorrect: The root element is incorrectly initialized; it should come from tree.getroot().
C) Incorrect: The ET.ElementTree constructor requires an Element, not a file path.
D) Correct: This correctly parses and accesses elements.
E) Incorrect: This does not load or parse any XML data.

EXAM FOCUS	*Use xml.etree.ElementTree for XML parsing: For XML data, ElementTree provides a simple way to parse, find, and modify elements by tag name.*
CAUTION ALERT	*Ensure proper XML structure: Always ensure the XML file is well-formed and accessible before parsing to avoid common parsing errors.*

QUESTION 25

Answer - A

Option A: Correct, it groups by both product and customer, and filters by having at least 3 sales.
Option B: Incorrect, COUNT(sale_id) cannot be used in the WHERE clause directly.
Option C: Incorrect, this query introduces unnecessary complexity for the task.
Option D: Incorrect, it does not include product information as required.
Option E: Incorrect, it uses WHERE improperly and does not perform aggregation.

EXAM FOCUS	*Group by multiple fields: When calculating counts for customers and products, group by both fields to avoid incorrect results due to missing relationships.*
CAUTION ALERT	*COUNT() with WHERE issue: You cannot use COUNT() directly in a WHERE clause—aggregate functions must be filtered using HAVING.*

QUESTION 26

Answer - A, D

Option A: Correct, indexing JOIN columns improves join performance.
Option B: Incorrect, subqueries are usually slower than joins.
Option C: Incorrect, breaking the query might not resolve performance issues.
Option D: Correct, applying WHERE clauses early filters data efficiently.
Option E: Incorrect, removing indexes would make the query slower.

EXAM FOCUS	*Index JOIN columns for performance: When using multiple JOINs, indexing the columns involved in the JOIN conditions speeds up the matching process.*
CAUTION ALERT	*Filter early to reduce data: Applying WHERE clauses early reduces the data being processed, making queries more efficient and faster.*

QUESTION 27

Answer - A

Option A: Correct, replacing the view ensures the view reflects the current structure of the base table.
Option B: Incorrect, altering the table does not automatically update the view.
Option C: Incorrect, altering a view without replacement doesn't affect the view's structure.
Option D: Incorrect, dropping the view removes it but does not help with updating.
Option E: Incorrect, inserting data into a view depends on the base table's ability to accept inserts.

EXAM FOCUS	*Keep views updated with table changes: Replacing a view (CREATE OR REPLACE VIEW) ensures that your view reflects the latest structure of the base table after any alterations.*
CAUTION ALERT	*Views don't auto-update with table changes: You must manually replace or alter views when the base table's structure is modified.*

QUESTION 28

Answer - A

Option A: Correct, a SAVEPOINT enables you to rollback to a specific point in the transaction, allowing partial undo of operations.
Option B: Incorrect, SAVEPOINT does not commit transactions; COMMIT does.
Option C: Incorrect, BEGIN TRANSACTION marks the start of a transaction.
Option D: Incorrect, SAVEPOINT does not prevent access by other transactions.
Option E: Incorrect, SAVEPOINT has no effect on isolation level.

EXAM FOCUS	*Savepoints enable partial rollbacks: SAVEPOINT allows you to mark points in a transaction and rollback to specific points without undoing the entire transaction, useful for complex processes.*
CAUTION ALERT	*Savepoints don't commit transactions: Remember, SAVEPOINT only marks points for partial rollbacks— it doesn't commit or finalize a transaction.*

QUESTION 29

Answer - C

Option A: Incorrect, the mean is not a measure of spread.
Option B: Incorrect, standard deviation alone may not provide enough insight in skewed data.
Option C: Correct, variance is a good measure of spread to compare skewed distributions.
Option D: Incorrect, range does not consider the shape of the data.
Option E: Incorrect, mean does not represent spread.

EXAM FOCUS	*Variance for comparing skewed data: Variance gives a better understanding of spread, especially in skewed datasets, where other measures of spread may not be sufficient.*
CAUTION ALERT	*Standard deviation might not tell the full story: Be cautious with only using standard deviation, especially in skewed datasets—it may not fully capture the distribution's spread.*

QUESTION 30

Answer - A

Option A: Correct, a scatter plot is the best way to visually identify outliers affecting correlation.
Option B: Incorrect, histogram is not ideal for finding outliers.

Option C: Incorrect, variance measures spread, not outliers.

Option D: Incorrect, kendall correlation does not help detect outliers.

Option E: Incorrect, boxplot is more suited for distribution than correlation outliers.

EXAM FOCUS	*Scatter plots help identify outliers: A scatter plot is the most effective visual tool for detecting outliers, especially when analyzing correlations between variables.*
CAUTION ALERT	*Variance doesn't identify outliers: Use visual tools like scatter plots, not variance or standard deviation, to easily spot outliers in a dataset.*

QUESTION 31

Answer - A

Option A: Correct, variance_inflation_factor is used to check for multicollinearity in linear regression.

Option B: Incorrect, StandardScaler is used for scaling data, not detecting multicollinearity.

Option C: Incorrect, OLS is for fitting models, not detecting multicollinearity directly.

Option D: Incorrect, correlation is a step but not the correct method for detecting multicollinearity.

Option E: Incorrect, the determinant of a matrix doesn't measure multicollinearity.

EXAM FOCUS	*Detect multicollinearity with VIF: Variance Inflation Factor (VIF) from statsmodels helps detect multicollinearity between independent variables in linear regression.*
CAUTION ALERT	*Correlation isn't enough to detect multicollinearity: A high correlation does not confirm multicollinearity. Use VIF for a more accurate assessment.*

QUESTION 32

Answer - A, B

Option A: Correct, the IQR method is applied using quantiles and 1.5 times the IQR to filter outliers.

Option B: Correct, uses the percentile function, which is another valid method to calculate IQR and detect outliers based on the upper threshold.

Option C: Incorrect, it applies the Z-score method rather than IQR.

Option D: Incorrect, this incorrectly uses median instead of the IQR range.

Option E: Incorrect, multiplying the median by 1.5 is not a valid outlier detection technique.

EXAM FOCUS	*IQR method for robust outlier detection: Use the Interquartile Range (IQR) method to identify outliers by calculating Q1, Q3, and filtering values beyond 1.5 times the IQR.*
CAUTION ALERT	*Avoid relying solely on standard deviation for outliers: Standard deviation-based methods might not detect outliers in skewed data as effectively as the IQR method.*

QUESTION 33

Answer - A, B

A) Correct: This option calculates the IQR (Q3 - Q1) and applies the standard method to filter out values greater than Q3 + 1.5 * IQR, which is the correct approach for identifying outliers using IQR.

B) Correct: This uses NumPy's percentile function to calculate Q3 and Q1 and correctly applies the IQR method to filter outliers based on the upper threshold (Q3 + 1.5 * IQR).

C) Incorrect: This approach calculates outliers based on the standard deviation, not the IQR method, which makes it unsuitable for this question. It uses the z-score method instead.

D) Incorrect: The median is not used in the IQR method for identifying outliers. IQR is based on percentiles (Q1 and Q3), not the median, making this option invalid.

E) Incorrect: This uses the median multiplied by 1.5 as the threshold, which is incorrect for outlier detection with IQR. The correct approach should use percentiles, not the median.

EXAM FOCUS	*IQR method for identifying outliers: Use IQR with the 1.5 * IQR rule to identify outliers that are significantly above or below the middle 50% of the data.*
CAUTION ALERT	*Don't misuse the median: The IQR method is based on percentiles (Q1 and Q3), not the median. Using the median for outlier detection can lead to incorrect conclusions.*

QUESTION 34

Answer - A, B

A) Correct: pivot() is used to reshape data based on unique values in columns, here for department and year.

B) Correct: pivot_table() is similar to pivot() but provides more functionality, such as handling missing values.

C) Incorrect: The syntax is mostly correct, but the use of pd.pivot_table() here is redundant, as it can be directly applied on df.

D) Incorrect: unstack() is used to convert a level of a MultiIndex into columns, which is not the goal in this case.

E) Incorrect: melt() does the opposite of pivoting; it converts wide-format data into long-format, which is not what is being asked here.

EXAM FOCUS	*Pivot table for reshaping data: Use .pivot() or .pivot_table() to transform long data into wide format based on categories, such as department and year.*
CAUTION ALERT	*Avoid unstacking when pivoting: unstack() is used for hierarchical indices, not for reshaping data like pivot() or pivot_table().*

QUESTION 35

Answer - A, B

A) Correct: Regularization adds a penalty term to the loss function, helping to reduce overfitting.

B) Correct: A simpler model is less likely to memorize training data, improving generalization.

C) Incorrect: Reducing the training size may lead to underfitting instead.

D) Incorrect: Removing the test set does not address overfitting and compromises evaluation.

E) Incorrect: Increasing model complexity can worsen overfitting rather than help.

EXAM FOCUS	*Combat overfitting with regularization: Use regularization techniques like L2 to prevent overfitting by controlling the complexity of your model.*
CAUTION ALERT	*Avoid removing the test set: Removing the test set will hinder proper evaluation and make it impossible to detect overfitting.*

QUESTION 36

Answer - A

A) Correct – Reducing the number of features (dimensionality reduction) can help avoid overfitting by simplifying the model and reducing noise.

B) Incorrect – Reducing features is a common strategy to prevent overfitting.

EXAM FOCUS	*Feature reduction prevents overfitting: Reducing the number of features can simplify your model and prevent overfitting by focusing on the most important attributes.*

QUESTION 37

Answer - B

A) Incorrect – R-squared is a metric used for linear regression, not for logistic regression. Logistic regression uses other metrics like accuracy, precision, recall, or AUC-ROC for evaluating model performance.
B) Correct – Logistic regression is evaluated using classification metrics, and R-squared is not appropriate for interpreting logistic regression results. Instead, metrics like accuracy, precision, and recall should be considered.

EXAM FOCUS	*Logistic regression doesn't use R-squared: Metrics like accuracy, precision, recall, or AUC-ROC should be used for logistic regression model evaluation.*
CAUTION ALERT	*R-squared is not suitable for classification: Don't evaluate logistic regression using R-squared. It's designed for linear regression, not for classification models.*

QUESTION 38

Answer - A

A) Correct as this script uses the correct syntax for creating a pivot table, where values='sales' is aggregated by mean across product and region. This matches the prompt's requirements.
B) Incorrect because the provided script meets the requirement and correctly summarizes sales data using mean() aggregation.

EXAM FOCUS	*Pivot for summarized data: Use pivot_table() with proper aggregation functions to create summaries like average sales across categories and regions. Always choose an appropriate aggfunc.*
CAUTION ALERT	*Choose the right index/column: Ensure that you are not swapping the roles of index and columns in your pivot tables, as this can lead to misaligned summaries.*

QUESTION 39

Answer - B

A) Incorrect because high precision means that when the model predicts a positive class, it is correct, but it does not indicate that the model is identifying all the actual positive cases.
B) Correct because low recall means the model is missing many positive cases, even though its precision is high, indicating that the model is conservative in its positive predictions.

EXAM FOCUS	*Precision and Recall Trade-Off: High precision doesn't mean high recall. A model can be highly precise while missing many true positives, leading to low recall.*
CAUTION ALERT	*Don't Misinterpret High Precision: A model with high precision might still miss a lot of positive cases, reflected in low recall, which measures sensitivity.*

QUESTION 40

Answer - A

A) Correct because Seaborn integrates with Matplotlib, allowing you to use plt.xlabel(), plt.ylabel(), and plt.title() customize the appearance of Seaborn plots.

B) Incorrect because Matplotlib functions like plt.xlabel(), plt.ylabel(), and plt.title() are compatible with Seaborn, so this statement is not false.

EXAM FOCUS	*Plot Customization: Seaborn plots can be customized with Matplotlib functions like plt.xlabel(), plt.ylabel(), and plt.title() for improved clarity and presentation.*
CAUTION ALERT	*Seaborn Customization: Don't forget that Seaborn integrates smoothly with Matplotlib, allowing you to use Matplotlib commands for further customization of plots.*

QUESTION 41

Answer - A

A) Correct because plt.legend() with a list of labels ['Sales', 'Profit'] will correctly add a legend for the plotted data, assuming the plot has two series of data.
B) Incorrect because the code correctly adds the legend with plt.legend() and provides the required labels.

EXAM FOCUS	*Legend Tip: Use plt.legend() to add labels to your plot for clarity. This is crucial when visualizing multiple data series, like sales and profit, in a single plot.*
CAUTION ALERT	*Label Mismatch: Ensure that the number of labels in plt.legend() matches the data series plotted. Otherwise, the legend won't correspond correctly to the plot.*

QUESTION 42

Answer - B, C

A) Incorrect because this does not scale the revenue values to thousands, making it harder for the non-technical audience to interpret large numbers.
B) Correct because this scales the revenue to thousands directly in the DataFrame before plotting.
C) Correct because dividing df['Revenue'] by 1000 directly in the plot ensures the data is displayed in thousands.
D) Incorrect because although it adds a label, it does not address the revenue scaling issue for easier interpretation.

EXAM FOCUS	*Scaling Tip: When displaying large numbers, scale values for clarity. For revenue, divide by 1000: df['Revenue']/1000 and label it as "Revenue (in thousands)".*
CAUTION ALERT	*Scaling Mistake: Avoid displaying large numbers without scaling—this may confuse non-technical audiences. Scale appropriately and update axis labels for context.*

QUESTION 43

Answer - A, C

A) Correct because summarizing key trends using concise text placed above the chart ensures that the audience grasps the essential points.
B) Incorrect because a visual presentation without accompanying text might confuse the audience and reduce engagement.
C) Correct because annotating key points on the chart improves clarity and emphasizes critical moments in the trends.
D) Incorrect because failing to provide context with text could hinder comprehension, especially with a multiline chart.

EXAM FOCUS	*Effective Presentation: Summarize trends concisely above the plot and use plt.annotate() to point out key turning points for an easy-to-understand executive presentation.*

QUESTION 44

Answer - B

A) Incorrect because palette="bright" might create visual overload with vibrant contrasting colors, which can be overwhelming in a multi-series chart.
B) Correct because palette="pastel" uses muted colors that effectively differentiate between regions without overwhelming the viewer with contrast.
C) Incorrect because palette="dark" emphasizes deeper tones, which might not be as visually soothing when multiple series are compared.
D) Incorrect because palette="coolwarm" introduces heavy contrasts, which could lead to visual overload.
E) Incorrect because palette="deep" focuses on richer colors, which may be too strong for a multi-series comparison.

| EXAM FOCUS | Pastel Palettes: When differentiating between multiple series, use palette="pastel" for subtle colors that avoid overwhelming the viewer in multi-line charts. |
| CAUTION ALERT | Overwhelming Contrast: Avoid using high-contrast palettes like "bright" or "coolwarm" in multi-line charts; they may cause visual overload. |

QUESTION 45

Answer - B

A) Incorrect because a heatmap doesn't offer a clear representation of trends between customer demand and production. B) Correct because a line plot showing customer demand and production needs over time would provide clear evidence of how rising customer demand justifies increased production. C) Incorrect because a single-line plot doesn't directly compare customer demand to production needs. D) Incorrect because a pie chart isn't suitable for time-series or correlation data. E) Incorrect because while scatter plots can show correlation, they are not ideal for demonstrating the trend over time in this context.

| EXAM FOCUS | Correlation with Line Plot: For demonstrating how demand correlates with production needs, use a line plot with clear labels on both axes to make the relationship easy to interpret. |
| CAUTION ALERT | Scatter Plot Confusion: Scatter plots can be less intuitive in showing trends over time, especially when illustrating correlations between variables like demand and production. |

PRACTICE TEST 9 - QUESTIONS ONLY

QUESTION 1

You are integrating data from two databases using SQL. One dataset comes from a relational database, and the other is stored in a NoSQL database. What is NOT a best practice for integrating these datasets?

A) Use SQL queries to extract structured data
B) Use Python's pymongo to extract data from NoSQL
C) Directly concatenate relational and NoSQL data without cleaning
D) Normalize NoSQL data to match relational schema
E) Use Python's pandas to join the two datasets

QUESTION 2

Your organization is transitioning from a traditional data warehouse to a cloud-based data lake. Which of the following advantages does a data lake offer over a data warehouse? (Select 2 answers)

A) Data lakes store both structured and unstructured data
B) Data lakes are optimized for SQL queries
C) Data lakes are more scalable for large datasets
D) Data lakes require schema-on-write processing

QUESTION 3

You are scaling data for a linear regression model and want to reduce dimensionality for computational efficiency. Which of the following is NOT a recommended approach for dimensionality reduction?

A) Use Principal Component Analysis (PCA)
B) Use t-distributed Stochastic Neighbor Embedding (t-SNE)
C) Use Label Encoding to reduce feature dimensions
D) Drop features with low variance
E) Use Feature Selection methods to reduce irrelevant features

QUESTION 4

You are working with a dataset that contains categorical variables. To prepare the dataset for a machine learning model, you need to convert these categorical variables into numerical format. Which of the following methods is NOT a recommended approach for encoding categorical variables?

A) Use one-hot encoding
B) Use label encoding for ordinal variables
C) Use Min-Max scaling for categorical variables
D) Use pd.get_dummies() to convert categorical variables into dummy variables
E) Use sklearn.preprocessing.LabelEncoder() for label encoding

QUESTION 5

Which of the following code snippets is NOT a valid way to write a clean and efficient Python for loop?

```
A) for i in range(10):
print(i)

 B) for i in range(10):
i = i + 1
print(i)

 C) for i in [1, 2, 3, 4]:
print(i)

 D) for i in enumerate([1, 2, 3]):
print(i)

 E) for i, val in enumerate([1, 2, 3]):
print(i, val)
```

QUESTION 6

Which of the following Python code snippets is NOT appropriate for handling errors during a database connection in Python?

```
A) try: conn =
sqlite3.connect('database.db')
except sqlite3.Error as e:
print('Error:', e)

 B) try: conn =
sqlite3.connect('database.db')
except Exception as e:
```

```
print('Connection failed')

C) try: conn =
sqlite3.connect('database.db')
except sqlite3.Error:
print('Failed to connect')

D) try: conn =
sqlite3.connect('database.db')
except:
print('General error')

E) try: conn =
sqlite3.connect('database.db')
f conn:
print('Connection successful')
```

QUESTION 7

You need to calculate a 95% confidence interval for
the mean of a dataset using Python. Which of the
following code snippets correctly computes this?
(Select 2 answers)

```
) import numpy as np
ean = np.mean(data)
td = np.std(data)
 = len(data)
i = (mean - 1.96 * std / np.sqrt(n), mean
 1.96 * std / np.sqrt(n))

B) from scipy import stats
i = stats.norm.interval(0.95,
oc=np.mean(data), scale=stats.sem(data))

C) import pandas as pd
i =
d.DataFrame(data).confidence_interval()

D) import numpy as np
i = (np.mean(data) - 1.96 * np.std(data),
p.mean(data) + 1.96 * np.std(data))

E) from scipy import stats
i = stats.norm.interval(0.95,
oc=np.mean(data),
cale=np.std(data)/np.sqrt(len(data)))
```

QUESTION 8

ou are working with a large dataset and need to
ompute the sum of all elements in a NumPy array
ficiently. Which of the following options will
ompute the sum correctly? (Select 2 answers)

```
) import numpy as np
r = np.array([[1, 2, 3], [4, 5, 6]])
otal_sum = np.sum(arr)

) import numpy as np
r = np.array([1, 2, 3])
```

```
total_sum = sum(arr)

C) import numpy as np
arr = np.array([1, 2, 3])
total_sum = arr.sum(axis=0)

D) import numpy as np
arr = np.array([[1, 2], [3, 4], [5, 6]])
total_sum = arr.sum(axis=1)

E) import numpy as np
arr = np.array([1, 2, 3])
total_sum = np.sum(arr, axis=1)
```

QUESTION 9

You are exporting your Matplotlib plots as high-
resolution images for a report. What are the correct
steps to export the plot? Select 2 correct options.

```
A) plt.savefig('sales_plot.png', dpi=300)
B) plt.show()
plt.savefig('sales_plot.png')
C) plt.savefig('sales_plot.png',
transparent=True)
D) plt.savefig('sales_plot.png',
bbox_inches='tight')
E) plt.savefig('sales_plot.pdf',
quality=95)
```

QUESTION 10

A data analyst is generating a bar plot to visualize the
count of different categories in the "region" column
of a dataset. Which of the following Python scripts
will achieve this? (Select 2 correct answers)

```
A) import seaborn as sns
sns.countplot(x='region', data=df)

B) import seaborn as sns
sns.barplot(x='region', y='sales', data=df)

C) import seaborn as sns
sns.countplot(data=df)

D) import seaborn as sns
sns.barplot(x='sales', y='region', data=df)

E) import seaborn as sns
sns.countplot(y='region', data=df)
```

QUESTION 11

During a data collection process, you want to ensure
ethical data sharing practices. Which actions should
you take to comply with ethical standards? (Select 2
correct answers)

A) Share data only with third parties who follow data

protection policies

B) Sell user data without their consent

C) Give users full control over how their data is shared

D) Store data on shared public servers

E) Use anonymized datasets before sharing data

QUESTION 12

You are tasked with merging two large datasets in Python. Which Python commands would you use to perform this task efficiently? (Select 2 correct answers)

```
A) pd.merge(df1, df2, on='id', how='left')
B) pd.join(df1, df2, on='id')
C) df1.append(df2)
D) df1.concat(df2)
E) df1.merge(df2, left_on='id1',
right_on='id2')
```

QUESTION 13

You are analyzing data in a list where some values are missing. You need to count all non-null values while skipping over None values. Which control structure is most appropriate? Select 2 correct answers.

```
A) for value in data:
if value is not None:
count += 1

B) i = 0
while i < len(data):
if data[i] is not None:
count += 1
i += 1

C) for value in data:
if value == None:
break
count += 1

D) for value in data:
if value is None:
continue
count += 1

E) i = 0
while i < len(data):
if data[i] is None:
break
i += 1
```

QUESTION 14

You need to filter rows from a DataFrame where the

'sales' column values are greater than 500 and the 'region' column is either 'North' or 'South'. Which scripts would work? Select 2 correct answers.

```
A) df[(df['sales'] > 500) &
(df['region'].isin(['North', 'South']))]
B) df.query('sales > 500 and region in
["North", "South"]')
C) df[df.sales > 500 & df.region in
['North', 'South']]
D) df[(df.sales > 500) & (df.region ==
['North', 'South'])]
E) df.loc[(df.sales > 500) & df.region in
['North', 'South']]
```

QUESTION 15

A machine learning model requires all numerical data to be standardized (mean=0, std=1). You are tasked with ensuring this for the columns "Age" and "Salary". What methods will correctly apply Z-score normalization to these columns? (Select 2 answers)

```
A) from sklearn.preprocessing import
StandardScaler; df[['Age', 'Salary']] =
StandardScaler().fit_transform(df[['Age',
'Salary']])

B) df[['Age', 'Salary']] = (df[['Age',
'Salary']] - df[['Age', 'Salary']].mean())
/ df[['Age', 'Salary']].std()

C) from sklearn.preprocessing import
MinMaxScaler; df[['Age', 'Salary']] =
MinMaxScaler().fit_transform(df[['Age',
'Salary']])

D) df[['Age', 'Salary']] = df[['Age',
'Salary']].apply(lambda x: (x - x.mean())
x.std())
E) df[['Age', 'Salary']] = df[['Age',
'Salary']].apply(lambda x: x / x.max())
```

QUESTION 16

You need to write a Python function that accepts two arguments: a list of numbers and a function that will process each number (e.g., multiply by 2, add 5, etc.). It should return a new list with the processed values. Which implementation is correct? (Select 2 answers)

```
A) def process_numbers(numbers, func):
return [func(n) for n in numbers]
B) def process_numbers(func, *numbers):
return [func(n) for n in numbers]
C) def process_numbers(numbers, func):
result = [] for n in numbers:
```

```
result.append(func(n)) return result
 D) def process_numbers(numbers, func):
return list(map(func, numbers))
 E) def process_numbers(func, *numbers):
return map(func, numbers)
```

QUESTION 17

You have two lists: one contains product IDs, and the other contains product prices. You need to match each product ID with its corresponding price. Which data structure should you use for efficient lookup and manipulation? (Select 2 answers)

```
 A) product_info = zip(product_ids,
product_prices)
 B) product_info = dict(zip(product_ids,
product_prices))
 C) product_info = {id: price for id, price
in zip(product_ids, product_prices)}
 D) product_info = list(zip(product_ids,
product_prices))
 E) product_info = [(id, price) for id,
price in zip(product_ids, product_prices)]
```

QUESTION 18

You are implementing error handling in your data acquisition script to ensure it runs smoothly when accessing an external API. What are the best practices for handling potential errors in your script? (Select 2 answers)

```
A) try: data = get_data(api_url)
except: pass

B) try: data = get_data(api_url)
except Exception as e:
print(E)

C) try: data = get_data(api_url)
except Exception:
print("Error fetching data.")

D) try: data = get_data(api_url)
except KeyError:
print("KeyError encountered.")

E) try: data = get_data(api_url)
except (KeyError, ValueError):
print("An error occurred.")
```

QUESTION 19

You are tasked with retrieving the top 5 customers with the highest total purchase values from the customers table. How would you structure your SQL query? (Select 2 answers)

```
A) SELECT customer_name, total_purchase
FROM customers
ORDER BY total_purchase DESC
LIMIT 5;

 B) SELECT customer_name, total_purchase
FROM customers
ORDER BY total_purchase ASC
LIMIT 5;

 C) SELECT customer_name, total_purchase
FROM customers
LIMIT 5
ORDER BY total_purchase DESC;

 D) SELECT customer_name, total_purchase
FROM customers
WHERE total_purchase IN
(SELECT total_purchase
FROM customers
ORDER BY total_purchase DESC
LIMIT 5);

 E) SELECT customer_name, total_purchase
FROM customers
WHERE total_purchase > 500
ORDER BY total_purchase DESC
LIMIT 5;
```

QUESTION 20

You want to connect to a database using SQLAlchemy in Python for ORM (Object-Relational Mapping) purposes. Which Python code correctly establishes a connection using SQLAlchemy and retrieves data? (Select 2 answers)

```
A) from sqlalchemy import create_engine
engine =
create_engine('sqlite:///database.db')
connection = engine.connect()
result = connection.execute("SELECT * FROM
customers")
for row in result:
print(row)

 B) from sqlalchemy import create_engine
engine =
create_engine('mysql+pymysql://root:passwor
d@localhost/sales')
connection = engine.connect()
result = connection.execute("SELECT * FROM
customers")
for row in result:
print(row)

 C) from sqlalchemy import create_engine
engine =
create_engine('mysql://root:password@localh
ost/sales')
```

```
connection = engine.connect()
result = connection.execute("SELECT * FROM
customers")
for row in result:
print(row)

 D) from sqlalchemy import create_engine
engine =
create_engine('mysql+pymysql://root:passwor
d@localhost/sales')
with engine.connect() as connection:
result = connection.execute("SELECT * FROM
customers")
for row in result:
print(row)

 E) from sqlalchemy import create_engine
engine =
create_engine('mysql+mysqlconnector://root:
password@localhost/sales')
connection = engine.connect()
result = connection.execute("SELECT * FROM
customers")
for row in result:
print(row)
```

QUESTION 21

Your Python script is failing due to a mismatch between SQL BIGINT and Python int. What is the best way to handle this conversion in Python? (Select 2 answers)

```
A) cur.execute("SELECT order_value FROM
orders")
for r in cur.fetchall():
print(int(r[0]))

 B) cur.execute("SELECT order_value FROM
orders")
for r in cur.fetchall():
print(int(r[0]))

 C) df = pd.read_sql("SELECT order_value
FROM orders", conn)
df['order'] = df['order'].astype('int64')

 D) df['order'] =
df['order'].astype('BIGINT')

 E) cur.execute("SELECT CAST(order_value AS
INT) FROM orders")
print(cur.fetchall())
```

QUESTION 22

You want to use closures in Python to create a function that remembers an argument. How would you implement a closure that adds a constant n to any given number? (Select 2 answers)

```
A) def make_adder(n):
return lambda x: x + n

 B) def make_adder(n):
def add(x):
return x + n
return add

 C) def make_adder(n):
return add(n + x)

 D) def make_adder(n):
def add(x):
return x + n
add(x)

 E) def make_adder(n):
return lambda x: x * n
```

QUESTION 23

You want to share your Python package with other developers. How can you properly create and distribute it? (Select 2 answers)

A) Use the setup.py file to specify metadata and dependencies for the package.
B) Publish the package directly by copying it into the recipient's Python environment.
C) Create a source distribution with python setup.py sdist
D) Install the package using pip without needing a setup.py file.
E) To distribute the package, simply share the __init__.py file.

QUESTION 24

While managing JSON data, you are asked to handle complex nested structures and extract specific values from them. How would you correctly access nested JSON values? (Select 2 correct answers)

```
A) import json
data = json.loads('{"person": {"name":
"Alice", "age": 25}}')
print(data['person']['name'])

B) import json
data = json.loads('{"person": {"name":
"Alice", "age": 25}}')
print(data['person']['gender'])

C) import json
data = {"person": {"name": "Alice", "age":
25}}
print(data['person']['age'])

D) import json
```

```python
data = json.loads('{"person": {"name":
"Alice", "age": 25}}')
print(data['name'])
E) import json
data = json.loads('{"name": "Alice", "age":
25}')
print(data['age'])
```

QUESTION 25

You are working with hierarchical data that requires the use of a recursive SQL query. The table employees contains a self-referential foreign key manager_id linking employees to their managers. How would you write a query to retrieve all employees under a specific manager, including the manager? (Select 1 correct answer)

```
A) WITH RECURSIVE EmployeeHierarchy AS
(SELECT employee_id, name FROM employees
WHERE manager_id IS NULL UNION ALL SELECT
e.employee_id, e.name FROM employees e JOIN
EmployeeHierarchy eh ON e.manager_id =
eh.employee_id) SELECT * FROM
EmployeeHierarchy;

B) SELECT * FROM employees WHERE manager_id
= (SELECT employee_id FROM employees WHERE
name = 'Manager');

C) WITH EmployeeHierarchy AS (SELECT
employee_id FROM employees WHERE manager_id
IS NULL) SELECT * FROM EmployeeHierarchy;

D) SELECT e.name FROM employees e WHERE
e.manager_id IN (SELECT employee_id FROM
employees WHERE manager_id IS NULL);

E) WITH EmployeeHierarchy AS (SELECT
employee_id FROM employees WHERE manager_id
IS NULL UNION ALL SELECT employee_id FROM
employees WHERE manager_id IS NOT NULL)
SELECT * FROM EmployeeHierarchy;
```

QUESTION 26

You have a query that filters data based on a range of dates from a large dataset. What is the most effective indexing strategy? (Select 1 correct answer)

```
A) CREATE INDEX idx_date_range ON
dataset(order_date);
B) Create an index on all columns in the
dataset;
C) Avoid indexing and increase memory
usage;
D) Use a compound index on order_date and
customer_id;
```

E) Create a hash index for the date column;

QUESTION 27

You need to restrict access to the employee_salary column but allow users to view all other employee data. Which SQL view would you use? (Select 1 correct answer)

```
A) CREATE VIEW employee_view AS SELECT
employee_id, employee_name FROM employees;
B) CREATE VIEW employee_view AS SELECT *
FROM employees;
C) CREATE OR REPLACE VIEW employee_view AS
SELECT employee_id FROM employees;
D) CREATE VIEW employee_view AS SELECT
employee_salary FROM employees;
E) CREATE VIEW employee_view AS SELECT
employee_id, employee_name, employee_salary
FROM employees;
```

QUESTION 28

You have multiple users inserting data into a table. What transaction strategy can ensure atomicity and prevent conflicts between users? (Select 2 correct answers)

```
A) BEGIN TRANSACTION
B) COMMIT TRANSACTION
C) SET TRANSACTION ISOLATION LEVEL
REPEATABLE READ
D) ROLLBACK TRANSACTION
E) CREATE SAVEPOINT
```

QUESTION 29

In a manufacturing dataset, you have the processing times for two different production lines. If one line has higher variability than the other, what does this imply? (Select 1 correct answer)

A) The production times are more consistent in the line with higher variability
B) The production line with higher variability is more unpredictable
C) Both lines have similar consistency
D) The line with lower variability has less consistency
E) Variability has no impact on consistency

QUESTION 30

You want to find out the linear relationship between two continuous variables: temperature and ice cream sales. What Python code would you use to compute the Pearson correlation coefficient? (Select 1 correct answer)

```
A) np.corrcoef(temperature,
ice_cream_sales)
B) statistics.stdev(temperature)
C) df.cov(temperature, ice_cream_sales)
D) df['temperature'].var()
E) df['ice_cream_sales'].mean()
```

QUESTION 31

In a linear regression analysis of house prices based on the number of rooms and neighborhood, you notice that the regression coefficients for neighborhood are significantly large. What could this indicate about the regression model? (Select 1 correct answer)

A) Neighborhood is likely a categorical variable and should be one-hot encoded
B) The model is overfitting the data
C) The relationship between neighborhood and price is non-linear
D) The neighborhood variable is too important and should be removed
E) The model has multicollinearity issues between neighborhood and price

QUESTION 32

After identifying outliers in your dataset, what is a valid approach to handle them? (Select 2 correct answers)

A) Remove the outliers from the dataset
B) Apply log transformation to reduce the impact of the outliers
C) Increase the size of the dataset to dilute the effect of outliers
D) Apply min-max scaling to normalize the dataset
E) Change the datatype of outliers to categorical

QUESTION 33

You are tasked with merging two DataFrames, df1 and df2, on a common column, 'ID'. Which of the following demonstrates a correct way to merge these DataFrames using an inner join? (Select 2 correct answers)

```
A) df_merged = df1.merge(df2, on='ID',
how='inner')
```

```
B) df_merged = pd.merge(df1, df2,
left_on='ID', right_on='ID')
C) df_merged = df1.join(df2, how='inner',
on='ID')
D) df_merged = df1.concat(df2, axis=1,
on='ID')
E) df_merged = pd.concat([df1, df2],
join='inner', axis=1)
```

QUESTION 34

You are asked to calculate the descriptive statistics o a dataset stored in a Pandas DataFrame. Which of the following methods correctly computes the required statistics? (Select 2 correct answers)

```
A) df.describe()
B) df.stats()
C) df.aggregate(['mean', 'std', 'max',
'min'])
D) df.describe(include='all')
E) df.apply(np.stats)
```

QUESTION 35

You have trained a regression model and now need to evaluate it using your test dataset. Which Python scripts would correctly generate evaluation metrics like RMSE and MAE? (Select 2 correct answers)

```
A) from sklearn.metrics import
mean_squared_error, mean_absolute_error;
rmse = mean_squared_error(y_test, y_pred,
squared=False)
B) from sklearn.metrics import rmse, mae;
rmse(y_test, y_pred)
C) mean_absolute_error(y_test, y_pred)
D) mse(y_test, y_pred, squared=True)
E) rmse(y_test, y_pred, squared=False)
```

QUESTION 36

You are evaluating the accuracy of a classification model using Python. Which of the following techniques would NOT be suitable for classification model evaluation?

```
A) accuracy_score(y_test, y_preD)
B) confusion_matrix(y_test, y_preD)
C) precision_score(y_test, y_preD)
D) mean_squared_error(y_test, y_preD)
E) roc_auc_score(y_test, y_pred)
```

QUESTION 37

Which of the following is NOT a correct implementation of logistic regression in Python?

```
A) from sklearn.linear_model import
LogisticRegression
 model = LogisticRegression()
 model.fit(X_train, y_train)

 B) from sklearn.metrics import
confusion_matrix
 confusion_matrix(y_test, y_preD)

 C) from sklearn.linear_model import
LinearRegression
 model = LinearRegression()
 model.fit(X_train, y_train)

 D) y_pred = model.predict(X_test)
 E) from sklearn.metrics import
accuracy_score
 accuracy_score(y_test, y_pred)
```

QUESTION 38

You want to create a pivot table to show the total count of sales (sales_count) for each category (product_category) by month (month) and region (region). Which of the following is NOT a correct script to achieve this? (Select 2 answers)

```
A) df.pivot_table(values='sales',
index='product_category', columns=['month',
'region'], aggfunc='count')
B) pd.pivot_table(df, values='sales',
index='product_category', columns=['month',
'region'], aggfunc='sum')
C) df.pivot_table(values='sales',
index='product_category', columns='month',
aggfunc='count')
D) pd.pivot_table(df, index='month',
values='sales', aggfunc='count')
E) df.pivot_table(values='sales',
columns=['month', 'region'],
aggfunc='count')
```

QUESTION 39

A classification model is evaluated using cross-validation to assess its performance. Which of the following approaches is NOT a correct implementation of cross-validation?

```
A) from sklearn.model_selection import
cross_val_score; cross_val_score(model, X,
y, cv=5)

B) from sklearn.model_selection import
train_test_split; X_train, X_test, y_train,
y_test = train_test_split(X, y,
test_size=0.2)

C) from sklearn.model_selection import
```

```
StratifiedKFold; skf =
StratifiedKFold(n_splits=5); for
train_index, test_index in skf.split(X, y):
X_train, X_test = X[train_index],
X[test_index]; y_train, y_test =
y[train_index], y[test_index]

D) from sklearn.model_selection import
KFold; kf = KFold(n_splits=10);
kf.split(X)`
```

QUESTION 40

You are visualizing the distribution of a numerical variable using Seaborn. Which of the following options is NOT a valid Seaborn command for generating this visualization?

```
A) sns.histplot(df['variable'])
B) sns.kdeplot(df['variable'])
C) sns.scatterplot(df['variable'])
D) sns.boxplot(x='variable', data=df)
E) sns.violinplot(x='variable', data=df)
```

QUESTION 41

You want to customize the font size of your plot's title and axis labels in Matplotlib. Which command is NOT a valid option to achieve this?

```
A) plt.title('Sales Over Time',
fontsize=16)
B) plt.xlabel('Months', fontsize=12)
C) plt.ylabel('Sales', fontsize=12)
D) plt.titlefontsize(16)`
```

QUESTION 42

You are creating a scatter plot and want to enhance readability by making it easier for non-technical audiences to interpret. What methods could be used to achieve this? Select two correct answers.

```
A) plt.scatter(df['x'], df['y'], s=50)
B) plt.title('Relationship between X and
Y')
C) plt.annotate('Important point', xy=(5,
20))
D) plt.scatter(df['x'], df['y'], c='blue',
marker='*')
E) plt.xlabel('X Axis'); plt.ylabel('Y
Axis')
```

QUESTION 43

You are preparing a report on quarterly financial performance and need to present it to a non-technical audience. How would you balance visuals and text effectively to avoid clutter and confusion? Select two correct answers.

A) Use one chart per slide with concise summaries of each quarter's financials directly below each chart.
B) Include text-heavy slides with minimal visuals.
C) Add multiple charts on one slide with all data points listed in a detailed table below.
D) Present each quarter visually with only one key financial takeaway text on the same slide.

QUESTION 44

For an upcoming presentation, you need to highlight significant differences between categories in a pie chart. To ensure the most important segments stand out, which approach would you use?

```
A) plt.pie(sales, labels=categories,
colors=sns.color_palette("colorblind"))
B) plt.pie(sales, labels=categories,
```

```
colors=sns.color_palette("pastel"))
C) plt.pie(sales, labels=categories,
colors=sns.color_palette("dark"))
D) plt.pie(sales, labels=categories,
colors=sns.color_palette("coolwarm"))
E) plt.pie(sales, labels=categories,
colors=sns.color_palette("muted"))
```

QUESTION 45

A stakeholder is skeptical about your claim that shipping delays are correlated with increased sales returns. Which visualization would provide clear evidence to support this claim?

```
A) plt.plot(shipping_delays,
sales_returns)
B) sns.scatterplot(x='shipping_delays',
y='sales_returns', data=shipping_datA)
C) plt.hist(sales_returns)
D) sns.boxplot(x='shipping_delays',
y='sales_returns', data=shipping_datA)
E) plt.pie(sales_returns,
labels=shipping_delays)
```

PRACTICE TEST 9 - ANSWERS ONLY

QUESTION 1

Answer - C

A) Correct – Using SQL queries to extract structured data from relational databases is standard practice for data integration.

B) Correct – Python's pymongo is a common tool for extracting data from NoSQL databases like MongoDB.

C) Incorrect – Concatenating structured relational data and unstructured NoSQL data without cleaning and validation will lead to inconsistencies and data quality issues.

D) Correct – Normalizing NoSQL data to fit into a relational schema is necessary for consistent integration.

E) Correct – Using Pandas to join the datasets allows for flexible and efficient merging of different types of data.

EXAM FOCUS	Integrating relational and NoSQL databases requires careful schema matching. Use tools like pymongo for NoSQL and SQL queries for relational data.
CAUTION ALERT	Direct concatenation of structured and unstructured data leads to chaos. Always clean and normalize data before integration to avoid misalignment.

QUESTION 2

Answer - A, C

A) Correct – Data lakes are capable of storing both structured and unstructured data, making them more flexible than traditional warehouses.

B) Incorrect – Data warehouses, not lakes, are optimized for structured data and SQL queries.

C) Correct – Data lakes offer greater scalability as they can handle larger volumes of data without predefined schemas.

D) Incorrect – Data lakes typically employ schema-on-read processing, allowing more flexibility when handling different types of data.

EXAM FOCUS	Data lakes are built for scalability and can handle both structured and unstructured data, unlike data warehouses, which are optimized for structured data only.
CAUTION ALERT	Don't assume data lakes are optimized for SQL queries. They typically support schema-on-read, offering more flexibility but less optimization for structured queries.

QUESTION 3

Answer - C

A) Correct – PCA is a popular method for dimensionality reduction by transforming features into fewer components while preserving variance.

B) Correct – t-SNE is used for dimensionality reduction, especially for visualization purposes, though not typically used in supervised models.

C) Incorrect – Label encoding is used for encoding categorical variables, not for reducing dimensions.

D) Correct – Dropping low-variance features can help reduce dimensions without losing significant information.

E) Correct – Feature selection techniques help reduce dimensions by eliminating irrelevant or redundant features.

EXAM FOCUS	PCA reduces dimensionality while preserving variance, making it a common technique for improving model performance and reducing computation time.
CAUTION	Label encoding is not a dimensionality reduction technique. It converts categorical variables into

QUESTION 4

Answer - C

A) Correct – One-hot encoding is a common method for converting categorical variables into binary columns for machine learning models.
 B) Correct – Label encoding is recommended for ordinal variables, where the categories have an inherent order.
 C) Incorrect – Min-Max scaling is used for numerical features, not for encoding categorical variables.
 D) Correct – pd.get_dummies() creates dummy variables from categorical columns, implementing one-hot encoding.
 E) Correct – LabelEncoder from sklearn is used to convert categorical variables into numerical labels, useful for algorithms like decision trees.

EXAM FOCUS	*One-hot encoding is standard for categorical variables, and label encoding is used for ordinal variables. Both are necessary for converting categorical data to numerical format.*
CAUTION ALERT	*Min-Max scaling applies to numerical features and is not appropriate for encoding categorical variables. Use encoding methods specific to category data.*

QUESTION 5

Answer - B

A) Correct – This is a standard for loop that iterates over the range and prints each value.
 B) Incorrect – Modifying i inside the loop is inefficient and may lead to unexpected behavior.
 C) Correct – This loop iterates over a list and prints each element.
 D) Correct – This loop uses enumerate() to iterate and print the index and value from the list.
 E) Correct – This loop unpacks the index and value from enumerate(), which is both efficient and clean.

EXAM FOCUS	*Loops should not modify the iterator variable inside the loop, as it leads to unpredictable behavior. Stick to clean, standard iteration practices.*
CAUTION ALERT	*Avoid modifying the iterator (i) inside a for loop. This can break the loop's logic and cause hard-to-find bugs in larger programs.*

QUESTION 6

Answer - E

A) Correct – This is a proper way to handle errors using sqlite3.Error.
 B) Correct – This is valid error handling using a general Exception to catch any errors.
 C) Correct – Catching sqlite3.Error is appropriate for SQLite database connection errors.
 D) Correct – A generic except: block can catch any error, though it's not recommended.
 E) Incorrect – This is not an error-handling block, and it doesn't raise exceptions, just checks if the connection object exists, which does not ensure error handling.

EXAM FOCUS	*Always handle database connection errors using specific exceptions like sqlite3.Error or general Exception for broader error handling.*
CAUTION ALERT	*Avoid using generic except: without specifying the error type. It catches all exceptions, making debugging difficult.*

QUESTION 7

Answer - A, B

A) Correct – This snippet correctly calculates the confidence interval using the formula for a 95% confidence interval.
 B) Correct – This snippet uses scipy.stats.norm.interval() to compute the confidence interval.
 C) Incorrect – Pandas DataFrames do not have a confidence_interval() method.
 D) Incorrect – This formula is incomplete, as it doesn't account for the sample size (n).
 E) Incorrect – While the logic is close, using np.std(data) without normalizing by the sample size produces an incorrect interval.

EXAM FOCUS	Use np.mean() and scipy.stats.sem() for computing confidence intervals. These provide a statistical range in which the true mean likely falls.
CAUTION ALERT	Ensure you account for sample size when computing confidence intervals manually. Using just std() without considering n will lead to incorrect results.

QUESTION 8

Answer - A, C

A) Correct – This correctly calculates the sum of all elements in a 2D array.
 B) Incorrect – While sum() works, it is less efficient than NumPy's sum() for large datasets.
 C) Correct – This calculates the sum along the first axis, which is a valid operation.
 D) Incorrect – This computes the sum along rows (axis=1), not the overall sum.
 E) Incorrect – The axis for a 1D array cannot be axis=1, as it doesn't have that many dimensions.

EXAM FOCUS	Use np.sum(arr) to calculate the sum of all elements in an array. NumPy's sum function is optimized for large datasets.
CAUTION ALERT	While Python's built-in sum() works for small datasets, NumPy's sum() is faster and more efficient for large-scale numerical data.

QUESTION 9

Answer - A, D

A) Correct: Saving the plot with high resolution using dpi.
B) Incorrect: plt.show() does not need to precede save.
C) Incorrect: Transparency is optional and irrelevant here.
D) Correct: bbox_inches ensures all elements are captured in the plot.
E) Incorrect: Quality setting is for JPEGs, not PDFs.

EXAM FOCUS	Use plt.savefig('filename.png', dpi=300) to export high-resolution plots suitable for reports. The bbox_inches='tight' option ensures nothing is cropped in the plot.
CAUTION ALERT	Don't rely on plt.show() before saving the plot. This is not necessary for saving images and can sometimes interfere with layout adjustments.

QUESTION 10

Answer - A, E

A) Correct. This generates a count plot for the "region".

B) Incorrect. A bar plot with "sales" is not specified in the question.
C) Incorrect. The column name is missing.
D) Incorrect. The "region" should be on the x-axis.
E) Correct. A vertical count plot is valid.

EXAM FOCUS	*sns.countplot() is ideal for visualizing the frequency of categorical data. Combine it with the y parameter to visualize count data vertically.*
CAUTION ALERT	*Don't confuse countplot() with barplot(). countplot() is for frequency distribution, whereas barplot() handles aggregation of numerical data.*

QUESTION 11

Answer - A, C

A) Ensuring third-party compliance with data policies is an ethical practice.
B) Selling data without consent violates ethical standards.
C) Users should have control over how their data is shared.
D) Public servers may compromise data security.
E) Anonymization protects user privacy before sharing.

EXAM FOCUS	*Ensure ethical data sharing by only working with third parties who adhere to strict data protection policies, and always obtain consent from users.*
CAUTION ALERT	*Avoid sharing or selling user data without explicit consent, as this violates ethical standards and can lead to legal repercussions.*

QUESTION 12

Answer - A, E

A) Using pd.merge() is the correct method to combine datasets based on a key.
B) pd.join() requires index-based joins, not ideal for key merging.
C) Appending adds rows, not suitable for merging data.
D) concat() is better for concatenating data, not merging.
E) Merging on different columns allows for flexible merging of datasets.

EXAM FOCUS	*Use pd.merge() for dataset merging based on a key, ensuring proper column matching with left_on and right_on. Efficient merging improves data integration.*
CAUTION ALERT	*Avoid using concat() or join() for merging based on column keys. These are better suited for index-based joins or appending data.*

QUESTION 13

Answer - A, B

A) Correct: A for loop with if condition is efficient to filter None values.
B) Correct: A while loop with a condition works well for this scenario.
C) Incorrect: Breaking the loop on None causes loss of valid data.
D) Incorrect: continue incorrectly skips valid data.
E) Incorrect: Breaking the loop prematurely loses valid non-null data.

EXAM FOCUS	*Use a for or while loop with a condition like value is not None to efficiently count non-null entries in a dataset.*

QUESTION 14

Answer - A, B

A) Correct: Uses correct isin() and filtering logic.
B) Correct: Uses query() method to filter rows.
C) Incorrect: Operator precedence error with & and in.
D) Incorrect: == operator should not be used with lists.
E) Incorrect: loc[] method cannot handle list with ==.

EXAM FOCUS	*Use isin() or query() to filter rows based on conditions across multiple columns, ensuring you handle lists correctly.*
CAUTION ALERT	*Be careful with operator precedence in filtering conditions. Misusing & and in can lead to logic errors.*

QUESTION 15

Answer - A, B

Option A: Correct – Uses StandardScaler from sklearn, which standardizes the columns correctly.
Option B: Correct – Manually applies Z-score normalization by subtracting the mean and dividing by the standard deviation.
Option C: Incorrect – MinMaxScaler performs min-max scaling, not Z-score normalization.
Option D: Incorrect – While Z-score is being applied, the method is less efficient than using StandardScaler.
Option E: Incorrect – Dividing by the max is not a correct Z-score normalization technique.

EXAM FOCUS	*Standardize columns like "Age" and "Salary" using StandardScaler() or by applying Z-score normalization to improve machine learning model performance.*
CAUTION ALERT	*Using MinMaxScaler instead of StandardScaler when Z-score normalization is required may lead to inaccurate model performance.*

QUESTION 16

Answer - A, D

Option A: Correct – Applies the function to each element using list comprehension.
Option B: Incorrect – Incorrect parameter order and use of *numbers.
Option C: Incorrect – This implementation works but is less efficient than A or D.
Option D: Correct – Uses map() to apply the function, which is efficient.
Option E: Incorrect – Misuses *numbers and lacks list wrapping around map().

EXAM FOCUS	*map() and list comprehensions are efficient ways to apply a function to each element of a list in Python. They can simplify code and improve readability.*
CAUTION ALERT	*Avoid manual loops when built-in functions like map() or list comprehensions can achieve the same task more efficiently.*

QUESTION 17

Answer - B, C

Option A: Incorrect – zip() alone creates an iterator, but it does not provide a data structure that allows for efficient lookup.
Option B: Correct – Using dict() with zip() creates a dictionary where product IDs are mapped to prices, allowing efficient lookups.
Option C: Correct – This dictionary comprehension achieves the same result as option B but is more explicit.
Option D: Incorrect – This creates a list of tuples, which is not optimal for lookups based on product IDs.
Option E: Incorrect – A list of tuples is not as efficient for lookups as a dictionary.

EXAM FOCUS	Use zip() with dict() or dictionary comprehensions for efficient key-value pairing when matching lists like product IDs and prices.
CAUTION ALERT	Avoid using lists or tuples for matching IDs and prices when lookups are required; they are less efficient than dictionaries.

QUESTION 18

Answer - B, E

Option A: Incorrect – Silently passing errors with pass leads to undetected failures.
Option B: Correct – Catching general exceptions and printing the error message is a good practice for debugging.
Option C: Incorrect – While this provides a message, it does not specify the error, making debugging harder.
Option D: Incorrect – While it catches a KeyError, it's better to catch a broader range of exceptions.
Option E: Correct – This approach catches multiple exception types, which is useful for handling multiple potential issues.

EXAM FOCUS	Use meaningful comments sparingly: While comments can be helpful, over-reliance suggests that your code may not be self-explanatory enough and needs restructuring.
CAUTION ALERT	Avoid over-commenting: Too many comments can make code look cluttered. Instead, write clear, self-explanatory code that needs minimal commentary.

QUESTION 19

Answer - A, D

Option A: Correct – Orders the customers by total_purchase in descending order and limits the result to the top 5
Option B: Incorrect – Orders the results in ascending order, which returns the lowest values instead.
Option C: Incorrect – The LIMIT clause must come after ORDER BY in SQL.
Option D: Correct – Uses a subquery to select the top 5 customers with the highest total_purchase.
Option E: Incorrect – Filters out customers below $500, which is not required by the question.

EXAM FOCUS	Use LIMIT for performance: When fetching top results, use ORDER BY with LIMIT to retrieve only the necessary number of rows, improving query performance.
CAUTION ALERT	Correct clause ordering: Always ensure that ORDER BY comes before LIMIT in SQL queries, as reversing them will lead to syntax errors.

QUESTION 20

Answer - A, B

Option A: Correct – Uses SQLite and SQLAlchemy to establish a connection and retrieve data.
Option B: Correct – Uses SQLAlchemy with the pymysql connector for MySQL to retrieve data.
Option C: Incorrect – The URL format is incorrect; it should use mysql+pymysql for MySQL connections.
Option D: Incorrect – The with block is not necessary when using SQLAlchemy's engine.connect() directly.
Option E: Incorrect – Uses the wrong connector (mysqlconnector) instead of pymysql.

EXAM FOCUS	*SQLAlchemy simplifies ORM: SQLAlchemy allows you to work with databases in an object-oriented way, abstracting raw SQL queries for cleaner code.*
CAUTION ALERT	*Ensure correct connectors: Always use the correct connector like mysql+pymysql for MySQL in SQLAlchemy to avoid connection issues.*

QUESTION 21

Answer - A, C

Option A: Correct – Casting to int ensures the SQL BIGINT type is interpreted as a Python int, handling smaller values properly.
Option B: Incorrect – Same as Option A but does not consider larger values that exceed the limit of Python int.
Option C: Correct – Converting the Pandas column to int64 using astype matches the BIGINT type from SQL, ensuring larger integers are handled.
Option D: Incorrect – Pandas does not support SQL-specific types like BIGINT. The int64 type should be used in Python.
Option E: Incorrect – While casting in SQL can work, it is more efficient to handle the type conversion in Python for greater flexibility.

EXAM FOCUS	*BIGINT to int in Python: Use astype('int64') in Pandas for BIGINT conversion to ensure your data can handle large numbers in Python.*
CAUTION ALERT	*Python int limits: Python's native int can handle large values, but always ensure the type is correctly interpreted to avoid errors.*

QUESTION 22

Answer - A, B

Option A: Correct – This creates a closure using a lambda function, capturing the value of n.
Option B: Correct – This nested function add() also forms a closure that remembers the value of n.
Option C: Incorrect – The syntax is incorrect, as add() is not defined, and the operation is invalid.
Option D: Incorrect – The function doesn't return add, so it will not form a proper closure.
Option E: Incorrect – While it creates a lambda function, it multiplies instead of adding, which isn't the intended behavior.

EXAM FOCUS	*Closures capture variables: When using closures in Python, the inner function can remember variables from its enclosing scope, making the outer function unnecessary afterward.*
CAUTION ALERT	*Check closure behavior: If your closure function doesn't return the inner function, it will not behave as a proper closure, failing to capture values correctly.*

QUESTION 23

Answer - A, C

Option A: Correct – The setup.py file is used to define package details and dependencies.

Option B: Incorrect – Manually copying packages is error-prone and not a best practice.
Option C: Correct – The command python setup.py sdist creates a distributable source package.
Option D: Incorrect – The setup.py file is needed to package and install code using pip.
Option E: Incorrect – The __init__.py file alone is not sufficient for distributing a package.

EXAM FOCUS	*Use setup.py to define your package: A well-defined setup.py file is necessary for creating, managing, and distributing Python packages effectively.*
CAUTION ALERT	*Manual package distribution is risky: Manually copying files into environments is prone to errors; use proper tools like pip and source distributions for package sharing.*

QUESTION 24

Answer - A, C

A) Correct: This accesses the nested name key correctly.
B) Incorrect: The key gender doesn't exist, causing an error.
C) Correct: This accesses the nested age key in a dictionary structure.
D) Incorrect: The key name is not found at the top level, as it's inside the person key.
E) Incorrect: While this works, it's not accessing a nested structure, which the question specifically asks for.

EXAM FOCUS	*Access nested JSON data properly: Use chained indexing like data['key1']['key2'] to access nested structures in JSON, and ensure key existence to avoid KeyErrors.*
CAUTION ALERT	*Handle missing keys safely: Use the .get() method when unsure about key existence in deeply nested JSON structures to prevent runtime errors.*

QUESTION 25

Answer - A

Option A: Correct, it uses a recursive query to fetch all employees under a manager.
Option B: Incorrect, this does not handle recursive relationships to retrieve all employees.
Option C: Incorrect, this query does not perform recursion and only selects the top-level managers.
Option D: Incorrect, this is a basic subquery that does not solve the recursive problem.
Option E: Incorrect, this query does not correctly define recursion for employee hierarchy.

EXAM FOCUS	*Recursive queries for hierarchies: Use recursive CTEs (WITH RECURSIVE) to handle hierarchical relationships like employee-manager structures in databases.*
CAUTION ALERT	*Recursive query pitfalls: Be cautious of infinite loops—ensure the base case is properly defined when using recursive queries.*

QUESTION 26

Answer - A

Option A: Correct, indexing on order_date will optimize range-based queries.
Option B: Incorrect, indexing all columns would add unnecessary overhead.
Option C: Incorrect, increasing memory does not address index optimization.
Option D: Incorrect, compound indexing is unnecessary unless multiple columns are frequently queried together.
Option E: Incorrect, hash indexes are less efficient for range-based queries.

EXAM FOCUS	*Indexing date columns speeds range queries: For queries filtering by date ranges, indexing the date column can significantly improve query performance.*

QUESTION 27

Answer - A

Option A: Correct, this view selects only the employee_id and employee_name, hiding the salary.
Option B: Incorrect, this includes all columns, including the salary.
Option C: Incorrect, this view excludes the employee name.
Option D: Incorrect, this view selects only the salary column, which is not what is needed.
Option E: Incorrect, this view includes the salary, which should be restricted.

EXAM FOCUS	*Views can restrict sensitive data: Use views to control access to specific columns, such as excluding employee_salary while displaying other employee details.*
CAUTION ALERT	*Excluding columns in views hides data: Ensure critical columns, like IDs, are included in views when necessary, while keeping sensitive information hidden.*

QUESTION 28

Answer - A, B

Option A: Correct, BEGIN TRANSACTION ensures that all the operations are treated as a single unit, preserving atomicity.
Option B: Correct, COMMIT TRANSACTION saves the entire operation, preventing conflicts from partial updates.
Option C: Incorrect, REPEATABLE READ ensures read consistency but does not handle atomicity.
Option D: Incorrect, ROLLBACK undoes changes, but does not handle atomicity for multiple users.
Option E: Incorrect, SAVEPOINT does not ensure atomicity across the whole transaction.

EXAM FOCUS	*Ensure atomicity in multi-user environments: Use BEGIN TRANSACTION and COMMIT to group multiple operations, ensuring atomicity and preventing partial updates when multiple users are interacting with the same data.*
CAUTION ALERT	*SET ISOLATION levels don't ensure atomicity: While isolation levels help with read consistency, they don't handle atomicity or protect against conflicts in multi-user environments.*

QUESTION 29

Answer - B

Option A: Incorrect, higher variability indicates less consistency.
Option B: Correct, higher variability suggests more unpredictability.
Option C: Incorrect, higher variability suggests inconsistency between the lines.
Option D: Incorrect, lower variability indicates higher consistency.
Option E: Incorrect, variability directly impacts consistency.

EXAM FOCUS	*Higher variability means less consistency: If a dataset shows higher variability, the values fluctuate more, indicating less consistency in data such as production times.*
CAUTION ALERT	*Low variability means more predictability: A dataset with lower variability shows more predictability and consistency, especially in time-based processes.*

QUESTION 30

Answer - A

Option A: Correct, np.corrcoef() computes the Pearson correlation.
Option B: Incorrect, standard deviation does not measure correlation.
Option C: Incorrect, covariance and correlation are related but different metrics.
Option D: Incorrect, variance alone does not give correlation.
Option E: Incorrect, mean does not represent the correlation.

EXAM FOCUS	np.corrcoef() computes Pearson correlation: This function from NumPy calculates the linear relationship between two continuous variables, perfect for identifying correlations.
CAUTION ALERT	Covariance and correlation are different: Covariance shows direction, but correlation standardizes this, providing clearer insights into the strength of relationships.

QUESTION 31

Answer - A

Option A: Correct, large coefficients for categorical variables often indicate that they need to be one-hot encoded
Option B: Incorrect, large coefficients don't necessarily mean overfitting.
Option C: Incorrect, this doesn't suggest non-linearity without further investigation.
Option D: Incorrect, removing neighborhood isn't a solution without further tests.
Option E: Incorrect, neighborhood-price relationship doesn't indicate multicollinearity here.

EXAM FOCUS	One-hot encode categorical variables: Large coefficients for categorical variables may suggest the need for one-hot encoding. Always check your data type before fitting the model.
CAUTION ALERT	Large coefficients don't imply overfitting: If you see large coefficients for categorical variables, it often means they need encoding, not that the model is overfitting.

QUESTION 32

Answer - A, B

Option A: Correct, removing outliers is a common approach to mitigate their effect.
Option B: Correct, log transformation reduces the influence of extreme values.
Option C: Incorrect, increasing dataset size does not directly address outliers.
Option D: Incorrect, scaling changes the data range but does not handle outliers.
Option E: Incorrect, changing the datatype is not an appropriate handling method for numerical outliers.

EXAM FOCUS	Log transformation reduces outlier impact: Applying a log transformation to features can mitigate the effect of extreme values, making your model more stable.
CAUTION ALERT	Scaling doesn't remove outliers: While normalization adjusts data scales, it doesn't address the issue of outliers, which can still skew results.

QUESTION 33

Answer - A, B

A) Correct: This is the standard syntax for using .merge() to perform an inner join on the 'ID' column in both DataFrames. It is a highly efficient way to merge two DataFrames.
 B) Correct: Using pd.merge() with left_on and right_on correctly merges two DataFrames on the 'ID' column. Thi

is another valid method of merging.

C) Incorrect: The .join() method requires the index to be the same or explicitly set, which is not demonstrated here. It is not the correct approach for merging on a column.

D) Incorrect: .concat() is primarily used for concatenating along the axis and doesn't support on as an argument. It is not suitable for an inner join on a specific column.

E) Incorrect: This option uses .concat() with join='inner', which is incorrect since .concat() is for concatenating along axes, not for merging based on a column.

EXAM FOCUS	Merge DataFrames on a common key: Use pd.merge() with how='inner' to join DataFrames based on matching values from both DataFrames.
CAUTION ALERT	Avoid .concat for merging keys: Use .concat() for combining DataFrames along an axis, not for merging based on a common key column.

QUESTION 34

Answer - A, C

A) Correct: df.describe() provides a quick summary of the descriptive statistics for each column in the DataFrame.

B) Incorrect: df.stats() is not a valid Pandas function and would raise an AttributeError.

C) Correct: The aggregate() function allows for custom statistics like mean, standard deviation, max, and min to be calculated across the DataFrame.

D) Incorrect: While describe(include='all') can work, it includes non-numerical statistics, which may not be what the question is asking for.

E) Incorrect: There is no np.stats function, and applying such a method would result in an error.

EXAM FOCUS	Descriptive statistics in Pandas: Use df.describe() to quickly generate summary statistics, or aggregate() for more custom aggregations.
CAUTION ALERT	Avoid invalid function names: Functions like df.stats() do not exist in Pandas. Use valid methods like describe() or aggregate().

QUESTION 35

Answer - A, C

A) Correct: mean_squared_error() with squared=False gives the RMSE, which is correct.

B) Incorrect: rmse and mae are not direct functions from sklearn; use the proper import.

C) Correct: mean_absolute_error() from sklearn is the right way to calculate MAE.

D) Incorrect: mse() is not a recognized function; mean_squared_error() should be used instead.

E) Incorrect: rmse() does not exist; use mean_squared_error() with squared=False for RMSE.

EXAM FOCUS	Use correct evaluation functions: For regression models, use mean_squared_error() and mean_absolute_error() from sklearn to calculate RMSE and MAE.
CAUTION ALERT	Avoid non-existent functions: Functions like rmse() and mse() don't exist in Scikit-learn. Always use mean_squared_error() for RMSE and MSE.

QUESTION 36

Answer - D

A) Correct – Accuracy is a common metric for evaluating classification models.

B) Correct – Confusion matrix is used to summarize the performance of a classification model.

C) Correct – Precision evaluates the accuracy of positive predictions.
D) Incorrect – Mean Squared Error is used for regression, not classification.
E) Correct – ROC AUC is used to evaluate the performance of a binary classifier.

EXAM FOCUS	*Choose the right evaluation metric: For regression models, use metrics like RMSE or MAE. For classification, rely on accuracy, confusion matrix, precision, and ROC AUC.*
CAUTION ALERT	*MSE is for regression models: Avoid using mean_squared_error() to evaluate classification models; it's designed for regression and not classification performance.*

QUESTION 37

Answer - C

A) Correct – This is the standard way to implement logistic regression in Python.
B) Correct – Confusion matrix is a valid metric for evaluating classification models.
C) Incorrect – LinearRegression is not used for classification and cannot be substituted for logistic regression.
D) Correct – predict() generates predictions for classification tasks in logistic regression.
E) Correct – Accuracy score is a valid evaluation metric for classification tasks.

EXAM FOCUS	*Stick to logistic regression for classification: Ensure you're using LogisticRegression for binary classification problems and avoid using linear regression for such tasks.*
CAUTION ALERT	*Wrong model choice: Avoid using LinearRegression() for classification tasks. Logistic regression (LogisticRegression) is the correct choice for binary classification.*

QUESTION 38

Answer - B, E

A) Correct because this script uses the proper format of pivot_table with count as the aggregation function and matches the prompt.
B) Incorrect because it uses sum() instead of count(), which will not return the number of sales, but the sum of the sales.
C) Correct since it counts sales based on product_category and month, though region is missing, it still meets the requirement.
D) Correct as it counts sales by month, though it does not include all the required dimensions, it is still valid.
E) Incorrect because the index parameter is missing, which is required for grouping by product_category in the pivot table.

EXAM FOCUS	*Count sales in pivot tables: Use pivot_table() with count to summarize data where you want to count occurrences of a variable, like the number of sales across product categories and regions.*
CAUTION ALERT	*Ensure correct aggregation method: Be careful to use aggfunc='count' when counting, rather than sum(), to avoid summing sales values instead of counting them.*

QUESTION 39

Answer - B

A) Correct because cross_val_score(model, X, y, cv=5) implements 5-fold cross-validation, a standard approach for evaluating models.
B) Incorrect because train_test_split divides data into one training and one test set, but it is not a cross-validation method where the data is split into multiple folds.

C) Correct because StratifiedKFold ensures that each fold has a similar distribution of class labels, an appropriate cross-validation method for imbalanced data.
D) Correct because KFold(n_splits=10) is a valid approach to 10-fold cross-validation, ensuring multiple training-test splits.

EXAM FOCUS	*Cross-Validation Importance: Use cross-validation (cross_val_score(), KFold()) to assess model generalization. It helps test models on multiple splits for robust evaluation.*
CAUTION ALERT	*Train-test Split ≠ Cross-Validation: train_test_split() creates one split of data but doesn't offer the benefits of cross-validation, which tests the model on multiple folds.*

QUESTION 40

Answer - C

A) Correct because sns.histplot() is a valid Seaborn command for visualizing the distribution of a numerical variable.
B) Correct because sns.kdeplot() visualizes the distribution of a variable using a kernel density estimate.
C) Incorrect because sns.scatterplot() is used for visualizing relationships between two variables, not distributions.
D) Correct because sns.boxplot() shows the distribution of a numerical variable using quartiles.
E) Correct because sns.violinplot() visualizes the distribution of a numerical variable, combining aspects of boxplots and KDE.

EXAM FOCUS	*Distribution Visualization Tip: Seaborn offers several commands to visualize distributions. Use sns.histplot() or sns.kdeplot() for continuous data, depending on the level of detail needed.*
CAUTION ALERT	*Scatter Plot Misuse: sns.scatterplot() is not suitable for visualizing distributions. Stick to commands like sns.histplot() or sns.boxplot() for that purpose.*

QUESTION 41

Answer - D

A) Correct because plt.title() accepts the fontsize parameter to set the size of the title.
B) Correct because plt.xlabel() can take fontsize as a parameter to set the font size of the x-axis label.
C) Correct because plt.ylabel() accepts fontsize to adjust the y-axis label's font size.
D) Incorrect because plt.titlefontsize() is not a valid function in Matplotlib. Font sizes must be set using the fontsize argument within plt.title().

EXAM FOCUS	*Font Size Customization: You can control the font size of plot titles and labels using the fontsize parameter in Matplotlib. This helps improve readability.*
CAUTION ALERT	*Invalid Command: Don't use plt.titlefontsize(). It's not a valid function. Always use the fontsize parameter inside plt.title() or plt.xlabel().*

QUESTION 42

Answer - B, E

A) Incorrect because increasing point size does not necessarily help with clarity for non-technical audiences.
B) Correct because adding a title helps give context to the plot for non-technical audiences.
C) Incorrect because while annotations can be useful, a single annotation without broader context might not significantly help with overall readability.
D) Incorrect because changing color and marker style alone does not simplify the interpretation for a non-

technical audience.

E) Correct because adding axis labels makes the visualization more informative and easier to understand.

EXAM FOCUS	*Simplifying Visualization Tip: Label your scatter plots with titles and axes labels to ensure clarity for non-technical audiences, like plt.xlabel() and plt.title().*
CAUTION ALERT	*Common Error: Simply adjusting point size or colors in a scatter plot doesn't make it more readable. Always prioritize adding axis labels and titles.*

QUESTION 43

Answer - A, D

A) Correct because this approach ensures clarity by presenting one key chart and supporting it with a concise summary, reducing clutter.
B) Incorrect because text-heavy slides with few visuals can overwhelm or lose the audience's attention.
C) Incorrect because presenting multiple charts and a detailed table on one slide creates clutter and confusion for non-technical audiences.
D) Correct because presenting visuals with one key takeaway ensures that the audience remains focused on core insights without unnecessary details.

EXAM FOCUS	*Chart Simplification: Use one clear chart per slide with a key financial takeaway text. This keeps the presentation focused and reduces unnecessary complexity.*
CAUTION ALERT	*Text-Heavy Slides: Avoid using text-heavy slides with minimal visuals. This reduces engagement and might overwhelm the audience with too much information.*

QUESTION 44

Answer - C

A) Incorrect because palette="colorblind" focuses on accessibility rather than emphasizing significant differences
B) Incorrect because palette="pastel" may fail to make the important differences between categories visually obvious.
C) Correct because palette="dark" uses strong, rich colors that make the differences between significant categories stand out effectively.
D) Incorrect because palette="coolwarm" introduces a spectrum that is more suited for showing gradients rather than distinct categories.
E) Incorrect because palette="muted" uses soft tones that may not provide enough contrast to highlight key segments.

EXAM FOCUS	*Highlighting Pie Segments: Use darker palettes like sns.color_palette("dark") for pie charts to make significant differences between segments stand out effectively.*
CAUTION ALERT	*Pastel Limitation: Avoid using pastel palettes for highlighting important differences in pie charts, as they may not provide enough visual contrast.*

QUESTION 45

Answer - B

A) Incorrect because a simple line plot doesn't effectively demonstrate correlation between two variables like shipping delays and returns. B) Correct because a scatter plot shows the correlation between shipping delays and sales returns, providing clear evidence of the relationship. C) Incorrect because a histogram doesn't effectively show relationships between variables. D) Incorrect because while a box plot shows data distribution, it isn't ideal for demonstrating correlation. E) Incorrect because pie charts don't show correlation between shipping delays and sales returns.

EXAM FOCUS	Scatter Plot for Correlation: Use scatter plots to show correlation between two continuous variables like shipping delays and sales returns. This helps in providing visual evidence.
CAUTION ALERT	Avoid Pie Charts for Correlation: Pie charts are not suitable for showing relationships between variables. They're better for representing proportions rather than trends or correlations.

PRACTICE TEST 10 - QUESTIONS ONLY

QUESTION 1

You are asked to clean a dataset containing customer feedback that has multiple spelling errors in a particular column, feedback_text. How can you programmatically detect and correct these errors using Python? (Select 2 answers)

A) Use Python's re module to detect patterns and correct spelling
B) Use the fuzzywuzzy library to detect similar strings and correct errors
C) Manually inspect and correct spelling errors row by row
D) Use the TextBlob library to perform spell-checking and corrections
E) Drop rows containing errors from the dataset

QUESTION 2

Your team has been tasked with storing sensitive user data collected from an e-commerce website. Which of the following is NOT a best practice for storing this type of data in cloud storage?

A) Encrypt sensitive data before storage
B) Use role-based access control for storage
C) Store sensitive data in unencrypted CSV files
D) Ensure data is regularly backed up
E) Use cloud storage with compliance certifications like SOC 2

QUESTION 3

You are building a machine learning model using a dataset that contains both numerical and categorical variables. Which of the following steps would NOT be appropriate for preparing the data?

A) Apply Min-Max scaling to numerical features
B) Use one-hot encoding for categorical features
C) Apply Z-score normalization to categorical features
D) Impute missing values in numerical columns using the mean
E) Use label encoding for ordinal categorical features

QUESTION 4

You are preparing a dataset for regression analysis and want to structure it in a "long format." Which Python functions will help you convert a wide dataset into long format for analysis? (Select 2 answers)

```
A) pd.melt()
B) pd.pivot()
C) df.transpose()
D) pd.pivot_table()
E) pd.wide_to_long()
```

QUESTION 5

You are asked to iterate through a dictionary of products and their prices and calculate the total price of all products. Which of the following methods correctly calculates the total price? (Select 2 answers)

```
A) total = sum([price for product, price in products.items()])
```

```
B) total = sum(products.values())

C) for price in products:
   total += price

D) total = 0
   for product, price in products.items():
   total += price

E) total = products.sum()
```

QUESTION 6

You want to use SQLAlchemy to manage database connections and execute queries. Which of the following methods in SQLAlchemy are typically used to connect and query a database? (Select 2 answers)

```
A) from sqlalchemy import create_engine
   engine = create_engine('sqlite:///mydb.db')

B) from sqlalchemy import create_connection
   conn = create_connection('sqlite:///mydb.db')

C) from sqlalchemy.orm import sessionmaker
   session = sessionmaker(bind=enginE) session = Session()

D) engine.query('SELECT * FROM employees')
E) session.execute('SELECT * FROM employees')
```

QUESTION 7

You want to perform a chi-squared test for independence between two categorical variables in Python using scipy.stats. Which of the following correctly performs the chi-squared test? (Select 2 answers)

```
A) import scipy.stats as stats
   chi2, p, dof, ex = stats.chi2_contingency(table)

B) from scipy.stats import chi2
   chi2, p, dof, ex = chi2.test_independence(table)

C) import statsmodels.api as sm
   chi2, p, dof = sm.chisq_test(table)

D) from scipy import chi2
   chi2, p = chi2.test_chi_square(table)

E) from scipy.stats import chi2_contingency
   chi2, p, dof, ex = chi2_contingency(table)
```

QUESTION 8

You want to apply a mathematical function to every element in a NumPy array, specifically squaring each element. Which of the following code snippets will accomplish this task? (Select 3 answers)

```
A) import numpy as np
   arr = np.array([1, 2, 3])
   squared_arr = np.square(arr)

B) import numpy as np
   arr = np.array([1, 2, 3])
   squared_arr = arr ** 2

C) import numpy as np
   arr = np.array([1, 2, 3])
```

```
squared_arr = arr * arr

 D) import numpy as np
arr = np.array([1, 2, 3])
squared_arr = np.power(arr, 2)

 E) import numpy as np
arr = np.array([1, 2, 3])
squared_arr = arr ** 3
```

QUESTION 9

You are asked to visualize comparative data using a bar plot for different product categories in Matplotlib. Which steps are correct? Select 2 correct options.

```
A) plt.bar(categories, sales)
plt.xlabel('Categories')
plt.ylabel('Sales')

B) plt.barh(categories, sales)
plt.xlabel('Categories')

C) plt.bar(categories, sales, color='skyblue')

D) plt.hist(sales)
plt.title('Sales Histogram')

E) plt.pie(sales, labels=categories)
plt.title('Sales Pie Chart')
```

QUESTION 10

You need to visualize the distribution of the "sales" column using Seaborn. What scripts can achieve this? (Select correct answers)

```
 A) import seaborn as sns
sns.histplot(x='sales', data=df)

 B) import seaborn as sns
sns.kdeplot(x='sales', data=df)

 C) import seaborn as sns
sns.distplot(df['sales'])

 D) import seaborn as sns
sns.boxplot(x='sales', data=df)

 E) import seaborn as sns
sns.countplot(x='sales', data=df)
```

QUESTION 11

Your company is collecting medical data for research. How should you handle sensitive health data in compliance with privacy laws? (Select 2 correct answers)

A) Encrypt health data before storing it
B) Share identifiable health data without consent
C) Allow participants to access and review their data
D) Sell health data to third parties for marketing
E) Make the health data anonymized before analysis

QUESTION 12

While working on a data collection project, you are asked to anonymize customer data before analysis to comply with GDPR. How can you implement this using Python? (Select 2 correct answers)

```
A) df['customer_id'] = df['customer_id'].apply(lambda x: 'XXXX' + str(x)[-4:])
B) df.drop(columns=['customer_id'])
C) df['customer_id'] = df['customer_id'].replace(df['customer_id'], 'Anon')
D) df['customer_id'] = df['customer_id'].apply(lambda x:
hashlib.md5(str(x).encode()).hexdigest())
E) df['customer_name'] = None
```

QUESTION 13

You are tasked with writing a loop that processes customer data. You want to skip processing any customer with a None value in their order history, but continue with others. Which control structure best suits this? Select 2 correct answers.

```
A) for customer in customers:
if customer['order_history'] is None:
continue

B) for customer in customers:
if customer['order_history'] is not None:
process(customer)

C) i = 0
while i < len(customers):
if customers[i]['order_history'] is None:
i += 1
continue

D) for customer in customers:
if customer['order_history'] is None:
break

E) i = 0
while i < len(customers):
if customers[i]['order_history'] is None:
process(customers[i])
i += 1
```

QUESTION 14

You need to apply a lambda function to a DataFrame column to normalize the 'sales' column by dividing by its maximum value. Which of the following scripts will achieve this? Select 2 correct answers.

```
A) df['sales'] = df['sales'].apply(lambda x: x / df['sales'].max())
B) df['sales'] = df['sales'] / df['sales'].max()
C) df['sales'] = df.apply(lambda x: x['sales'] / df['sales'].max(), axis=1)
D) df.apply(lambda x: x / df['sales'].max(), axis=1)
E) df['sales'] = df.transform(lambda x: x / df['sales'].max())
```

QUESTION 15

You are analyzing a dataset where the range of values in one column significantly exceeds the range in another, which is affecting the performance of your machine learning model. To address this, you decide to scale both columns. Which methods using Python will effectively solve this? (Select 2 answers)

```
A) from sklearn.preprocessing import MinMaxScaler; df[['Col1', 'Col2']] =
MinMaxScaler().fit_transform(df[['Col1', 'Col2']])

 B) from sklearn.preprocessing import StandardScaler; df[['Col1', 'Col2']] =
StandardScaler().fit_transform(df[['Col1', 'Col2']])

 C) df[['Col1', 'Col2']] = df[['Col1', 'Col2']].apply(lambda x: (x - x.min()) / (x.max() -
x.min()))

 D) df[['Col1', 'Col2']] = df[['Col1', 'Col2']].apply(lambda x: x / x.sum())
 E) df[['Col1', 'Col2']] = df[['Col1', 'Col2']].apply(lambda x: x / x.max())
```

QUESTION 16

You are working with data from a CSV file and need to write a Python function that reads the file, processes the data using another passed-in function, and then writes the processed data to a new file. Which function structure is correct? (Select 3 answers)

```
A) def process_csv(input_file, output_file, process_func): import csv with open(input_file)
as f, open(output_file, 'w') as out_f: reader = csv.reader(f) writer = csv.writer(out_f) for
row in reader: writer.writerow(process_func(row))

 B) def process_csv(input_file, output_file, process_func): with open(input_file) as f: data
= f.readlines() with open(output_file, 'w') as out_f: for line in data:
out_f.write(process_func(line))

 C) def process_csv(input_file, output_file, process_func): with open(input_file) as f,
open(output_file, 'w') as out_f: data = f.readlines() out_f.writelines([process_func(line)
for line in data])

 D) def process_csv(input_file, output_file, process_func): with open(input_file) as f: data
= f.read().splitlines() with open(output_file, 'w') as out_f: for line in data:
out_f.write(process_func(line))

 E) def process_csv(input_file, output_file, process_func): import pandas as pd df =
pd.read_csv(input_file) df = df.apply(process_func, axis=1) df.to_csv(output_file,
index=FalsE)
```

QUESTION 17

You need to store a sequence of unique product codes and ensure that the order of insertion is preserved. Which Python data structure should you use to achieve this efficiently? (Select 2 answers)

```
A) product_codes = set()
B) from collections import OrderedDict; product_codes = OrderedDict()
C) product_codes = list()
D) from collections import deque; product_codes = deque()
E) product_codes = set() with manual sorting after insertion
```

QUESTION 18

You are collaborating with other data analysts and want to ensure your Python code is readable and easy to maintain. What are the best practices to follow for writing readable and maintainable Python scripts? (Select 2 answers)

A) Write long descriptive variable names and avoid abbreviations
B) Use single-letter variable names like 'x' and 'y' for all variables
C) Break long functions into smaller, reusable functions
D) Write all code in a single function for simplicity
E) Use meaningful comments to explain complex sections of code

You need to retrieve all order_id and order_total from the orders table where the order_total is above the average order_total for all orders in the table. Which query correctly implements this logic? (Select 2 answers)

```
A) SELECT order_id, order_total
FROM orders
WHERE order_total > (SELECT AVG(order_total)
FROM orders);

B) SELECT order_id, order_total
FROM orders
WHERE order_total >= (SELECT AVG(order_total)
FROM orders);

C) SELECT order_id, order_total
FROM orders
WHERE order_total > AVG(order_total);

D) SELECT order_id, order_total
FROM orders
WHERE order_total > (SELECT AVG(order_total)
FROM orders)
GROUP BY order_total;

E) SELECT order_id, order_total
FROM orders
HAVING order_total > (SELECT AVG(order_total)
FROM orders);
```

QUESTION 20

Your Python script needs to insert new customer records into a SQLite database, and you want to handle errors related to constraints, such as unique keys. Which Python code correctly handles this scenario? (Select 2 answers)

```
A) import sqlite3
conn = sqlite3.connect('database.db')
try:
conn.execute("INSERT INTO customers (customer_id, customer_name)
VALUES (101, 'John Doe')")
conn.commit()
except sqlite3.IntegrityError:
print("Unique key constraint failed.")

B) import sqlite3
conn = sqlite3.connect('database.db')
cursor = conn.cursor()
cursor.execute("INSERT INTO customers (customer_id, customer_name)
VALUES (101, 'John Doe')")
conn.commit()
except sqlite3.IntegrityError:
print("Record already exists.")

C) import sqlite3
conn = sqlite3.connect('database.db')
try:
conn.execute("INSERT INTO customers (customer_id, customer_name)
VALUES (101, 'John Doe')")
conn.commit()
except sqlite3.DatabaseError:
print("Database error occurred.")
```

```
conn.rollback()

 D) import sqlite3
conn = sqlite3.connect('database.db')
try:
conn.execute("INSERT INTO customers (customer_id, customer_name)
VALUES (101, 'John Doe')")
conn.commit()
except sqlite3.OperationalError:
print("Database is locked.")

 E) import sqlite3
conn = sqlite3.connect('database.db')
cursor = conn.cursor()
cursor.execute("INSERT INTO customers (customer_id, customer_name)
VALUES (101, 'John Doe')")
conn.commit()
```

QUESTION 21

You are retrieving DECIMAL(10, 2) product_price from SQL, and you want to store it as float in Python. How would you ensure the conversion while maintaining precision? (Select 2 answers)

```
 A) cur.execute("SELECT product_price FROM products")
for r in cur.fetchall():
print(float(r[0]))

 B) df['price'] = df['price'].apply(float)

 C) cur.execute("SELECT CAST(product_price AS FLOAT) FROM products")
for r in cur.fetchall():

print(r[0])

 D) df['price'] = pd.to_numeric(df['price'], downcast='float')
 E) df['price'] = df['price'].astype(float)
```

QUESTION 22

You need to implement a decorator in Python that prints the name of a function before executing it. Which of the following decorators correctly implements this functionality? (Select 2 answers)

```
A) def decorator(func):
def wrapper():
print(func.__name__)
return func()
return wrapper

 B) def decorator(func):
print(func.__name__)
return func()

 C) def decorator(func):
def wrapper(*args, **kwargs):
print(func.__name__)
return func(*args, **kwargs)
return wrapper

 D) def decorator(func):
def wrapper():
return print(func.__name__)
return wrapper
```

```
  E) def decorator(func):
def wrapper():
print(func.__name__)
return
```

QUESTION 23

You are using a Python package that has conflicting versions across different projects. What is the most effective way to manage this? (Select 2 answers)

A) Use virtual environments to isolate package versions for different projects.
B) Install the conflicting package version globally using pip install --global
C) Create separate virtual environments for each project that use different versions of the package.
D) Remove the package from one project to avoid conflicts.
E) Use the package only with the latest version to avoid version conflicts.

QUESTION 24

You need to write Python code that opens and reads from an XML file and modifies certain elements. Which of the following code snippets would work correctly? (Select 3 correct answers)

```
A) import xml.etree.ElementTree as ET
tree = ET.parse('data.xml')
root = tree.getroot()
for elem in root.findall('item'):
elem.text = 'Updated'
tree.write('data.xml')

 B) import xml.etree.ElementTree as ET
root = ET.Element('data')
tree = ET.parse('data.xml')
for elem in tree.getroot().findall('item'):
elem.text = 'Updated'
tree.write('output.xml')

 C) import xml.etree.ElementTree as ET
tree = ET.parse('data.xml')
for elem in tree.findall('item'):
elem.text = 'Updated'
tree.write('output.xml')

 D) import xml.etree.ElementTree as ET
tree = ET.parse('data.xml')
root = tree.getroot()
tree.write('output.xml')
 E) import xml.etree.ElementTree as ET
root = ET.Element('data')
tree = ET.ElementTree().
```

QUESTION 25

You are tasked with writing a SQL query to combine the results of two different queries: one returning customers who have placed orders, and another returning customers who have registered but not placed any orders. You want to use UNION to combine the results while avoiding duplicates. Which of the following options is correct? (Select 1 correct answer)

```
A) SELECT customer_id FROM orders UNION SELECT customer_id FROM customers WHERE customer_id
NOT IN (SELECT customer_id FROM orders);
```

B) SELECT customer_id FROM orders UNION ALL SELECT customer_id FROM customers WHERE customer_id NOT IN (SELECT customer_id FROM orders);

C) SELECT customer_id FROM customers WHERE customer_id IN (SELECT customer_id FROM orders) UNION SELECT customer_id FROM customers;

D) SELECT customer_id FROM orders UNION DISTINCT SELECT customer_id FROM customers WHERE customer_id IS NOT NULL;

E) WITH CustomerUnion AS (SELECT customer_id FROM orders UNION SELECT customer_id FROM customers) SELECT * FROM CustomerUnion;

QUESTION 26

You notice a query is running slow when filtering on customer_name in the customers table. What is the best way to optimize this query? (Select 1 correct answer)

```
A) CREATE INDEX idx_customer_name ON customers(customer_name);
B) Create a FULLTEXT index on customer_name;
C) Increase database cache size;
D) Rewrite the query using subqueries;
E) Remove the filter on customer_name;
```

QUESTION 27

You are using a view to simplify complex queries in your application. How can you prevent users from modifying data through this view? (Select 1 correct answer)

```
A) CREATE VIEW readonly_view AS SELECT * FROM employees WITH CHECK OPTION;
B) CREATE VIEW readonly_view AS SELECT * FROM employees WITH READ ONLY;
C) CREATE VIEW readonly_view AS SELECT * FROM employees WHERE employee_salary > 50000;
D) ALTER VIEW readonly_view ADD READ ONLY;
E) CREATE VIEW readonly_view AS SELECT employee_id, employee_name FROM employees;
```

QUESTION 28

In a transaction processing system, you want to ensure the ACID properties. Which SQL statement guarantees durability? (Select 1 correct answer)

```
A) COMMIT TRANSACTION
B) ROLLBACK TRANSACTION
C) CREATE SAVEPOINT
D) SET TRANSACTION READ COMMITTED
E) SET TRANSACTION SERIALIZABLE
```

QUESTION 29

You are comparing the spread of prices across different markets. Which Python functions would you use to compute the standard deviation and variance to analyze this data? (Select 2 correct answers)

```
A) statistics.stdev(prices)
B) np.var(prices)
C) prices.stdev()
D) np.std(prices)
E) statistics.mean(prices)
```

QUESTION 30

A marketing analyst wants to know if there is a correlation between social media ad spend and customer acquisition. Which function would help calculate the correlation and visualize the relationship in Python? (Select 2 correct answers)

```
A) df[['ad_spend', 'customers']].corr()
B) sns.heatmap(df.corr(), annot=True)
C) np.mean(df['ad_spend'])
D) sns.boxplot(df['ad_spend'], df['customers'])
E) df['ad_spend'].count()
```

QUESTION 31

You are running a linear regression model on sales data and receive an R-squared value of 0.30. What is the best course of action to improve the model's performance? (Select 2 correct answers)

A) Consider adding more relevant independent variables
B) Increase the number of polynomial terms in the model
C) Use a different type of regression model like logistic regression
D) Check for outliers or influential points in the dataset
E) Randomly shuffle the dependent variable and refit the model

QUESTION 32

You are analyzing the effect of outliers on a linear regression model. What is the primary impact of outliers on regression analysis? (Select 1 correct answer)

A) Outliers increase the accuracy of the model
B) Outliers can distort the regression coefficients
C) Outliers do not impact the linearity of the model
D) Outliers improve the R-squared value of the model
E) Outliers reduce the variance of residuals

QUESTION 33

You have missing values in a Pandas DataFrame. Which of the following demonstrates a proper way to handle missing values using Pandas? (Select 2 correct answers)

```
A) df.fillna(df.mean(), inplace=True)
B) df.dropna(axis=0, how='any')
C) df.fillna(method='ffill')
D) df.replace(np.nan, 0)
E) df.drop_duplicates()
```

QUESTION 34

In NumPy, you want to calculate the sum of all elements in an array arr and find its cumulative sum. Which of the following demonstrates the correct usage of NumPy aggregation functions? (Select 2 correct answers)

```
A) total_sum = np.sum(arr)
B) cumulative_sum = np.cumsum(arr)
C) total_sum = arr.sum(axis=1)
D) cumulative_sum = arr.cumsum()
E) total_sum = arr.total_sum()
```

QUESTION 35

In a machine learning project, you are concerned about your model overfitting and want to reduce its complexity.

What steps can you take to reduce the risk of overfitting? (Select 2 correct answers)

A) Cross-validation
B) Reducing the size of the test dataset
C) Reducing the number of features
D) Ignoring regularization
E) Using early stopping

QUESTION 36

You are building a machine learning model and need to avoid both overfitting and underfitting. What steps can you take? (Select 3 correct answers)

A) Increase the size of the training dataset
B) Use cross-validation techniques
C) Increase the complexity of the model
D) Regularize the model
E) Use fewer training epochs in neural networks

QUESTION 37

What can you do to prevent overfitting in a logistic regression model? (Select 3 correct answers)

A) Add L2 regularization
B) Increase the size of the training data
C) Add irrelevant features to the model
D) Use cross-validation
E) Add more polynomial features to the model

QUESTION 38

A retail company wants to analyze product returns using a pivot table. They want to show the total returns (returns_count) by both product (product) and return reason (reason). Which of the following correctly implements this? Select two answers.

```
A) pd.pivot_table(df, values='returns', index='product', columns='reason', aggfunc='count')
B) df.groupby(['product', 'reason'])['returns'].sum().unstack()
C) pd.pivot_table(df, values='product', columns='returns', index='reason', aggfunc='count')
D) pd.pivot_table(df, index=['product', 'reason'], values='returns', aggfunc='count')
E) df.pivot(index='product', values='returns', columns='reason', aggfunc='count')
```

QUESTION 39

You are evaluating the performance of a model on test data and want to compute the F1-score. Which of the following python scripts will correctly compute the F1-score for a binary classification model? Select two answers.

```
A) from sklearn.metrics import f1_score; f1_score(y_true, y_pred)
B) from sklearn.metrics import precision_score; precision_score(y_true, y_pred)
C) from sklearn.metrics import recall_score; recall_score(y_true, y_pred)
D) from sklearn.metrics import f1_score; f1_score(y_true, y_pred, average='macro')
E) from sklearn.metrics import accuracy_score; accuracy_score(y_true, y_pred)`
```

QUESTION 40

You are tasked with creating a Seaborn line plot to show the trend of sales over time. You want to enhance the plot by adding a title and gridlines for better readability. Which of the following code snippets will achieve this? Select two correct answers.

```
A) sns.lineplot(x='Date', y='Sales', data=df)
B) sns.lineplot(x='Sales', y='Date', data=df)
C) plt.title('Sales Trend Over Time')
D) plt.grid(True)
E) plt.bar(x='Date', y='Sales', data=df)
```

QUESTION 41

You need to create a bar plot and label each bar with its respective height value. Which of the following scripts will help you correctly label the bars? Select two correct answers.

```
A) for i in range(len(df['Sales'])): plt.text(i, df['Sales'][i], df['Sales'][i], ha='center')
B) for i in range(len(df['Sales'])): plt.annotate(df['Sales'][i], (i, df['Sales'][i]))
C) plt.bar_label(df['Sales'])
D) plt.text(df['Sales'])
E) for i in range(len(df['Sales'])): plt.text(i, df['Sales'][i] + 0.2, str(df['Sales'][i]),
ha='center')
```

QUESTION 42

You are preparing a plot for a report, and your audience is unfamiliar with the technical details of the data. You want to keep the visualization simple by reducing the number of visual elements. Which approach would be least suitable for this scenario?

```
A) plt.bar(df['Category'], df['Values'], color='blue')
B) plt.bar(df['Category'], df['Values']); plt.legend(loc='upper left')
C) plt.bar(df['Category'], df['Values'], edgecolor='black')
D) plt.bar(df['Category'], df['Values']); plt.annotate('Max value', xy=(3, 200))
E) plt.bar(df['Category'], df['Values'])
```

QUESTION 43

You are presenting a combined text and visualization slide on sales performance, but you notice the slide feels cluttered. Which is NOT a correct strategy to balance visuals and text for clarity?

A) plt.bar(df['Region'], df['Sales']) and place key sales insights as a concise bullet-point list next to the chart.
B) Present one visualization per slide with a few key takeaways.
C) Minimize text and rely primarily on visuals to explain the data trends.
D) Remove visualizations altogether and present only text-based insights.

QUESTION 44

You are designing a heatmap to show the correlation between various financial metrics. You need to use contrasting colors to highlight high and low correlation values effectively. Which palette should you use to achieve this?

```
A) sns.heatmap(correlation_matrix, cmap="Greys")
B) sns.heatmap(correlation_matrix, cmap="coolwarm")
C) sns.heatmap(correlation_matrix, cmap="Blues")
D) sns.heatmap(correlation_matrix, cmap="viridis")
E) sns.heatmap(correlation_matrix, cmap="Purples")
```

QUESTION 45

The finance department requests evidence of the relationship between marketing spend and overall sales. How would you visually present this relationship using Python?

```
A) plt.scatter(x='marketing_spend', y='sales', data=finance_datA)
B) sns.heatmap(data=finance_datA)
C) sns.barplot(x='marketing_spend', y='sales', data=finance_datA)
D) plt.pie(sales, labels=marketing_spenD)
E) plt.boxplot([marketing_spend, sales])
```

PRACTICE TEST 10 - ANSWERS ONLY

QUESTION 1

Answer - B, D

A) Incorrect – While re is powerful for detecting patterns, it's not designed for spelling correction and would require manual input.
B) Correct – The fuzzywuzzy library allows you to detect similar strings and correct minor spelling mistakes programmatically.
C) Incorrect – Manually inspecting and correcting spelling errors row by row is inefficient and impractical for large datasets.
D) Correct – TextBlob can detect and correct spelling errors efficiently using its built-in NLP tools.
E) Incorrect – Dropping rows with errors would reduce data quality and volume, and is not an appropriate solution.

EXAM FOCUS	Using libraries like fuzzywuzzy and TextBlob simplifies the process of spelling corrections. This is crucial for cleaning unstructured text data efficiently.
CAUTION ALERT	Avoid manual spell-checking for large datasets; it's time-consuming and error-prone. Instead, use libraries built for text analysis and correction.

QUESTION 2

Answer - C

A) Correct – Encrypting sensitive data is essential for protecting user information and preventing unauthorized access.
B) Correct – Role-based access control ensures that only authorized personnel can access the data.
C) Incorrect – Storing sensitive data in unencrypted CSV files exposes it to security risks and is not a best practice.
D) Correct – Regular backups ensure data is not lost and can be recovered in case of incidents.
E) Correct – Using cloud storage providers with compliance certifications ensures that sensitive data is handled according to security standards.

EXAM FOCUS	Encrypt all sensitive data before storing it, and use role-based access controls to restrict who can view or modify it.
CAUTION ALERT	Never store sensitive data in unencrypted CSV files. Doing so makes it vulnerable to data breaches, violating privacy and security protocols.

QUESTION 3

Answer - C

A) Correct – Min-Max scaling is commonly applied to numerical features to scale them within a specific range.
B) Correct – One-hot encoding is used to convert categorical variables into binary features.
C) Incorrect – Z-score normalization is used for numerical features, not for categorical variables.
D) Correct – Imputing missing values with the mean is an appropriate preprocessing step for numerical data.
E) Correct – Label encoding is used for ordinal categorical features, where the categories have a meaningful order (e.g., low, medium, high).

EXAM FOCUS	Min-Max scaling is crucial for normalizing numerical features, while one-hot encoding is used to handle categorical data before feeding it into a model.

QUESTION 4

Answer - A, E

A) Correct – pd.melt() is a function that reshapes a wide-format dataset into long format by unpivoting columns.
B) Incorrect – pd.pivot() is used to convert a long dataset into wide format, the opposite of what is needed here.
C) Incorrect – transpose() swaps rows and columns but does not convert between wide and long formats.
D) Incorrect – pivot_table() is used to create a spreadsheet-style pivot table and is not used for restructuring data into long format.
E) Correct – pd.wide_to_long() is a Pandas function specifically designed to convert a wide dataset into long format for analysis.

EXAM FOCUS	Use pd.melt() and pd.wide_to_long() to convert wide-format data into long format. This is necessary for certain types of statistical analysis.
CAUTION ALERT	Avoid using transpose() for reshaping into long format. It's meant for swapping rows and columns, not restructuring datasets between wide and long formats.

QUESTION 5

Answer - A, D

A) Correct – This list comprehension iterates through the dictionary and sums the prices.
B) Incorrect – products.values() returns the values, but sum() cannot directly sum them without iteration.
C) Incorrect – This code incorrectly iterates over the keys of the dictionary instead of values.
D) Correct – This for loop iterates over the dictionary and sums the price values.
E) Incorrect – Dictionaries do not have a sum() method, so this syntax is invalid.

EXAM FOCUS	Use dictionary methods like .items() to loop through key-value pairs. The sum() function works well with list comprehensions and dictionary values.
CAUTION ALERT	Iterating over dictionary keys when you need values will cause logic errors. Use .items() to ensure you access both key and value for calculations.

QUESTION 6

Answer - A, C

A) Correct – create_engine() is the main method used to establish a connection with SQLAlchemy.
B) Incorrect – There is no create_connection() method in SQLAlchemy.
C) Correct – Using sessionmaker is the standard way to create a session for executing queries in SQLAlchemy.
D) Incorrect – engine objects do not have a query() method; queries are executed through sessions.
E) Incorrect – While session.execute() is valid, it is missing context on how the session is created and executed.

EXAM FOCUS	Use SQLAlchemy's create_engine() to connect to databases and sessionmaker() to create a session for querying.
CAUTION ALERT	SQLAlchemy doesn't support methods like create_connection(). Stick to create_engine() and sessions for database handling.

QUESTION 7

Answer - A, E

A) Correct – This uses chi2_contingency() from scipy.stats to perform the chi-squared test.
B) Incorrect – chi2.test_independence() is not a valid function in scipy.stats.
C) Incorrect – There is no chisq_test() method in statsmodels.api.
D) Incorrect – The chi2.test_chi_square() method doesn't exist in SciPy.
E) Correct – This is another valid syntax for performing the chi-squared test with the correct import statement.

EXAM FOCUS	Use chi2_contingency() from scipy.stats to perform a chi-squared test for independence. It's the go-to method for testing categorical associations.
CAUTION ALERT	Don't confuse chi2 with a function for performing the chi-squared test. Use chi2_contingency() for proper execution of independence tests.

QUESTION 8

Answer - A, B, D

A) Correct – np.square(arr) squares each element in the array.
B) Correct – Using arr ** 2 correctly squares each element.
C) Correct – Element-wise multiplication of arr * arr also squares each element.
D) Correct – np.power(arr, 2) squares each element in the array.
E) Incorrect – This cubes the elements rather than squaring them.

EXAM FOCUS	Use np.square(arr) or arr ** 2 to square each element in a NumPy array. Element-wise operations are essential in mathematical transformations.
CAUTION ALERT	Be careful with exponentiation. arr ** 3 cubes the elements rather than squaring them, which might lead to incorrect results if unintended.

QUESTION 9

Answer - A, C

A) Correct: Standard bar plot creation.
B) Incorrect: This creates a horizontal bar plot, which isn't required.
C) Correct: Adding color to customize the bar plot.
D) Incorrect: A histogram is not relevant to bar plots.
E) Incorrect: A pie chart is not a bar plot.

EXAM FOCUS	Bar plots (plt.bar()) are ideal for comparing categorical data. Customize the plot using colors like color='skyblue' for better visual representation.
CAUTION ALERT	Avoid using pie charts for comparative data where bar charts are better. Pie charts can distort data representation, especially with too many categories.

QUESTION 10

Answer - A, B, D

A) Correct. A histogram shows the distribution.
B) Correct. A KDE plot shows the density distribution.
C) Incorrect. distplot() is deprecated.

D) Correct. A box plot shows distribution and outliers.

E) Incorrect. Count plot is for categorical variables, not numerical.

EXAM FOCUS	Use sns.histplot(x='sales', data=df) for plotting a histogram and sns.kdeplot() for density estimates. boxplot() visualizes the distribution and outliers.
CAUTION ALERT	Avoid using countplot() for continuous variables like sales. It is designed for categorical variables, not numerical distributions.

QUESTION 11

Answer - A, E

A) Encrypting sensitive data ensures security.

B) Sharing identifiable health data without consent breaches privacy.

C) Allowing access to data aligns with privacy regulations.

D) Selling health data for marketing without consent is unethical.

E) Anonymization protects patient privacy during analysis.

EXAM FOCUS	Encrypting health data and anonymizing it before analysis helps maintain compliance with privacy laws while preserving the utility of the data for research.
CAUTION ALERT	Never share identifiable health data without proper consent, and avoid using it for purposes outside of the agreed research scope (e.g., marketing).

QUESTION 12

Answer - A, D

A) Masking part of the customer ID is a valid anonymization technique.

B) Dropping the customer ID removes essential data.

C) Replacing values with a generic string reduces uniqueness in analysis.

D) Hashing the ID ensures the data is anonymized while retaining uniqueness.

E) Setting names to None discards valuable data.

EXAM FOCUS	Anonymize sensitive data using Python methods like masking or hashing with hashlib.md5() to protect user privacy under GDPR guidelines.
CAUTION ALERT	Avoid dropping or setting fields to None unnecessarily, as this can remove valuable data required for further analysis and compliance tracking.

QUESTION 13

Answer - A, B

A) Correct: Using continue skips customers with None and proceeds.

B) Correct: Processing valid data while ignoring None is an efficient solution.

C) Incorrect: Misplaced continue disrupts flow of loop.

D) Incorrect: Breaking on None prematurely stops processing.

E) Incorrect: Processing None values is not the right approach.

EXAM FOCUS	Use continue to skip customers with None order histories and proceed with valid ones. It's a simple way to handle missing data during loops.
CAUTION ALERT	Avoid breaking the loop prematurely when encountering None. This will stop processing, missing valid customer data that follows.

QUESTION 14

Answer - A, B

A) Correct: Applies a lambda function to normalize sales.
B) Correct: Directly divides the 'sales' column by its maximum value.
C) Incorrect: Axis=1 will not work in this context for column-wise operation.
D) Incorrect: apply method should be used for specific columns, not entire DataFrame.
E) Incorrect: transform does not work for single-column lambda functions.

EXAM FOCUS	Normalize a DataFrame column by dividing it by its maximum using a lambda function or direct division for efficiency.
CAUTION ALERT	Avoid using apply() with axis=1 for column-wise operations, as it's slower compared to using vectorized operations directly.

QUESTION 15

Answer - A, B

Option A: Correct – Applies Min-Max scaling to both columns, making them range between 0 and 1.
Option B: Correct – Uses StandardScaler, which standardizes the columns by subtracting the mean and dividing by the standard deviation.
Option C: Incorrect – Manually applies Min-Max scaling, which can be error-prone compared to using MinMaxScaler.
Option D: Incorrect – Normalizing by sum is not a valid approach for general scaling.
Option E: Incorrect – Dividing by the max is not a comprehensive scaling method.

EXAM FOCUS	Use either MinMaxScaler() or StandardScaler() from sklearn to scale features in datasets with varying ranges, ensuring consistency in model training.
CAUTION ALERT	Normalizing by sum or dividing by max values is not an effective method for scaling when ranges vary significantly between features.

QUESTION 16

Answer - A, B, E

Option A: Correct – Uses csv.reader and csv.writer to read and write rows while processing them.
Option B: Correct – Uses basic file operations to read lines, process them, and write the results.
Option C: Incorrect – Inefficient as it processes the entire file into memory at once.
Option D: Incorrect – Uses splitlines() unnecessarily, making it less efficient.
Option E: Correct – Uses pandas to read, process, and write data efficiently for CSV files.

EXAM FOCUS	Use Pandas' read_csv() and apply() for efficient data processing and csv.writer() for writing back processed rows into a new CSV file.
CAUTION ALERT	Avoid reading entire CSV files into memory if the file is large; use chunking or row-by-row processing for better performance.

QUESTION 17

Answer - B, D

Option A: Incorrect – A set ensures uniqueness but does not preserve order.

Option B: Correct – OrderedDict maintains both uniqueness and the order of insertion.

Option C: Incorrect – A list does not guarantee uniqueness.

Option D: Correct – deque is an efficient data structure that preserves order and allows efficient insertion at both ends.

Option E: Incorrect – Sorting manually after using a set is inefficient and defeats the purpose of using an efficient data structure.

EXAM FOCUS	Use OrderedDict or deque when you need to maintain insertion order and ensure uniqueness for sequences like product codes.
CAUTION ALERT	Avoid using plain sets if order preservation is crucial, as sets do not maintain the order of elements.

QUESTION 18

Answer - A, C

Option A: Correct – Descriptive variable names improve readability and make the code self-explanatory.

Option B: Incorrect – Single-letter variable names can confuse others and reduce readability.

Option C: Correct – Breaking long functions into smaller functions improves reusability and simplifies testing and debugging.

Option D: Incorrect – Writing all code in one function makes it harder to debug and maintain.

Option E: Incorrect – While comments can be useful, over-reliance on comments indicates code that is not self-explanatory.

EXAM FOCUS	Use built-in best practices: Python provides try-except for robust error handling. Always include proper error messages or logging in your exception handling.
CAUTION ALERT	Don't skip error messages: Passing errors with no action (pass) is dangerous. You might miss critical runtime issues that could affect your analysis later.

QUESTION 19

Answer - A, B

Option A: Correct – Compares order_total to the average using a subquery.

Option B: Correct – Retrieves orders with totals greater than or equal to the average using a subquery.

Option C: Incorrect – AVG() must be used within a SELECT or subquery, not directly in a WHERE clause.

Option D: Incorrect – GROUP BY is unnecessary here.

Option E: Incorrect – HAVING should be used after GROUP BY, but this query doesn't need grouping.

EXAM FOCUS	Use subqueries effectively: To compare a value with an aggregate, like the average, use a subquery in the WHERE clause for clarity and accuracy.
CAUTION ALERT	Avoid HAVING without grouping: The HAVING clause is meant for filtering after aggregation with GROUP BY. Don't use it if no grouping is applied.

QUESTION 20

Answer - A, C

Option A: Correct – Handles sqlite3.IntegrityError, which is raised when a unique constraint is violated.

Option B: Incorrect – The cursor should be wrapped in a try-except block.

Option C: Correct – Uses DatabaseError for handling more general database-related errors and rolls back the transaction.

Option D: Incorrect – The OperationalError is not relevant to unique key violations in this context.

Option E: Incorrect – Missing error handling for constraint violations.

| EXAM FOCUS | Use transactions for safety: Inserting records within a transaction (conn.commit() and rollback()) ensures that errors do not leave the database in an inconsistent state. |
| CAUTION ALERT | Handle unique constraints: Use IntegrityError to handle unique key violations, such as duplicate primary keys, in SQL inserts. |

QUESTION 21

Answer - A, D

Option A: Correct – Converts DECIMAL to float in Python without losing precision, ensuring correct data handling for further calculations.

Option B: Incorrect – Using apply(float) works, but can cause precision loss when working with large or high-precision decimal values.

Option C: Incorrect – SQL CAST to FLOAT can lead to loss of precision, especially for large values, and it's better handled in Python.

Option D: Correct – pd.to_numeric with downcast='float' efficiently converts to float while minimizing the precision loss, ensuring optimal data handling.

Option E: Incorrect – astype(float) can cause precision loss, and is not as efficient for handling high-precision DECIMAL types.

| EXAM FOCUS | Converting DECIMAL to float: Convert DECIMAL to float carefully using astype(float) or pd.to_numeric to avoid precision loss while handling financial data. |
| CAUTION ALERT | Beware of precision loss: SQL's CAST to FLOAT may lead to precision loss, especially when handling high-precision values like prices. |

QUESTION 22

Answer - A, C

Option A: Correct – This decorator prints the function name and then calls the function.

Option B: Incorrect – It immediately prints and calls the function, losing the benefits of using a wrapper.

Option C: Correct – This is the most general and correct form of a decorator, handling both positional and keyword arguments.

Option D: Incorrect – The function returns the result of print(), which is None, instead of calling the original function.

Option E: Incorrect – It prints the function name but doesn't call the original function, leading to incorrect functionality.

| EXAM FOCUS | Decorators enhance functions: Use decorators to add functionality to existing functions, like printing their names, without altering their original behavior. |
| CAUTION ALERT | Be careful with return values: Ensure your decorator returns the correct result from the original function, or you risk losing its functionality entirely. |

QUESTION 23

Answer - A, C

Option A: Correct – Virtual environments are designed to handle such cases by isolating dependencies.
Option B: Incorrect – Installing packages globally will lead to conflicts between projects using different versions.
Option C: Correct – Separate virtual environments for each project allow you to handle package version conflicts.
Option D: Incorrect – Removing the package from one project is not a solution as both projects may require it.
Option E: Incorrect – Using only the latest version may break compatibility with older projects.

EXAM FOCUS	*Handle version conflicts with virtual environments: Use virtual environments to avoid package version conflicts across different projects, ensuring project stability.*
CAUTION ALERT	*Avoid global package installation: Installing packages globally can create conflicts when different projects require different versions of the same package.*

QUESTION 24

Answer - A, B, C

A) Correct: This code reads the XML, modifies the elements, and writes back to the file.
B) Correct: This approach also modifies XML data and saves to a new file.
C) Correct: This is another correct way to handle reading, modifying, and writing XML data.
D) Incorrect: The XML file is only written without any modifications to the elements.
E) Incorrect: This code doesn't parse any XML data, and thus it cannot be used to modify elements.

EXAM FOCUS	*Use ElementTree to modify and write XML: When working with XML, use ElementTree to parse, modify, and write the updated XML back to a file.*
CAUTION ALERT	*Don't skip parsing steps: Ensure you correctly parse XML data using ElementTree.parse() before attempting to modify it; otherwise, modifications won't work as expected.*

QUESTION 25

Answer - A

Option A: Correct, it uses UNION to combine both queries and avoid duplicates.
Option B: Incorrect, UNION ALL allows duplicates, which is not required here.
Option C: Incorrect, this query returns duplicates as it includes customers unnecessarily.
Option D: Incorrect, UNION DISTINCT is redundant because UNION already removes duplicates.
Option E: Incorrect, the query is overcomplicated and uses unnecessary subqueries.

EXAM FOCUS	*Use UNION for distinct results: To combine results from multiple queries while avoiding duplicates, always use UNION instead of UNION ALL.*
CAUTION ALERT	*Avoid UNION ALL for distinct results: UNION ALL does not remove duplicates—ensure you use just UNION when duplicates should be filtered out.*

QUESTION 26

Answer - A

Option A: Correct, indexing customer_name speeds up lookups and filtering.
Option B: Incorrect, FULLTEXT index is for text search, not name filtering.
Option C: Incorrect, increasing cache size may not help with index optimization.
Option D: Incorrect, subqueries do not necessarily optimize performance.
Option E: Incorrect, removing the filter is not a practical solution.

EXAM FOCUS	Create an index on frequently queried columns: When queries often filter by customer_name, an index on that column will speed up those searches.
CAUTION ALERT	FULLTEXT is for full-text searches: FULLTEXT indexing is not needed for simple name lookups, and using it can unnecessarily complicate query performance.

QUESTION 27

Answer - B

Option B: Correct, WITH READ ONLY prevents users from modifying data through the view.
Option A: Incorrect, WITH CHECK OPTION ensures data adheres to the view conditions but does not restrict updates.
Option C: Incorrect, this is a filter condition but does not prevent updates.
Option D: Incorrect, there is no ADD READ ONLY syntax in SQL.
Option E: Incorrect, while this limits the columns shown, it doesn't prevent data modification.

EXAM FOCUS	WITH READ ONLY makes views non-updatable: Adding WITH READ ONLY prevents users from updating data through views, ensuring the integrity of the underlying data.
CAUTION ALERT	CHECK OPTION doesn't make views read-only: This constraint ensures data follows view conditions but doesn't prevent updates or deletions.

QUESTION 28

Answer - A

Option A: Correct, COMMIT ensures that all changes are made permanent in the database, guaranteeing durability.
Option B: Incorrect, ROLLBACK undoes changes, which does not guarantee durability.
Option C: Incorrect, SAVEPOINT does not ensure the entire transaction's durability.
Option D: Incorrect, READ COMMITTED affects isolation, not durability.
Option E: Incorrect, SERIALIZABLE guarantees isolation but does not directly ensure durability.

EXAM FOCUS	COMMIT guarantees durability: Committing a transaction ensures that changes are permanent and stored on disk, fulfilling the durability aspect of the ACID properties in database transactions.
CAUTION ALERT	ROLLBACK undoes changes: Be aware that ROLLBACK undoes changes made in a transaction, and while important for consistency, it does not ensure durability.

QUESTION 29

Answer - A, D

Option A: Correct, statistics.stdev() computes standard deviation.
Option B: Incorrect, while np.var() calculates variance, the question asks for both variance and standard deviation.
Option C: Incorrect, prices.stdev() is not a valid method.
Option D: Correct, np.std() computes the standard deviation.
Option E: Incorrect, mean is not a measure of spread.

EXAM FOCUS	Standard deviation measures spread: To analyze the spread of data, use statistics.stdev() or np.std() to compute the standard deviation, which shows how much data varies from the mean.
CAUTION ALERT	Don't confuse mean with variability: Remember, mean measures central tendency, not spread—use variance and standard deviation to analyze the data's spread.

QUESTION 30

Answer - A, B

Option A: Correct, .corr() computes the correlation between the specified variables.
Option B: Correct, sns.heatmap() visualizes the correlation matrix.
Option C: Incorrect, mean does not indicate correlation.
Option D: Incorrect, boxplot shows distribution, not correlation.
Option E: Incorrect, .count() counts rows, not correlation.

EXAM FOCUS	*Use heatmaps to visualize correlation matrices: Use sns.heatmap() to visualize correlations between multiple variables easily and interpret relationships.*
CAUTION ALERT	*Boxplot shows distribution, not correlation: While useful for identifying outliers, boxplots do not show relationships between variables like correlation does.*

QUESTION 31

Answer - A, D

Option A: Correct, adding more relevant features may improve the model's performance.
Option B: Incorrect, polynomial terms are more suitable for non-linear relationships.
Option C: Incorrect, logistic regression is used for classification, not regression.
Option D: Correct, outliers can distort model performance and should be checked.
Option E: Incorrect, shuffling the dependent variable will lead to nonsensical results.

EXAM FOCUS	*Improve regression by adding relevant features: Low R-squared values can be improved by adding more independent variables or handling outliers effectively.*
CAUTION ALERT	*Avoid using logistic regression for continuous targets: Logistic regression is for classification, not predicting continuous outcomes like sales.*

QUESTION 32

Answer - B

Option A: Incorrect, outliers often reduce accuracy by skewing the model fit.
Option B: Correct, outliers distort regression coefficients and may lead to a misleading model.
Option C: Incorrect, outliers affect the linear relationship between variables.
Option D: Incorrect, outliers typically reduce R-squared by adding noise to the model.
Option E: Incorrect, outliers increase the variance of residuals.

EXAM FOCUS	*Outliers distort regression coefficients: Outliers can have a disproportionately large influence on the coefficients in linear regression, leading to biased or misleading results.*
CAUTION ALERT	*Outliers increase residual variance: Always check for and handle outliers, as they increase the variance of residuals, reducing model accuracy.*

QUESTION 33

Answer - A, C

A) Correct: This option uses fillna() to replace missing values with the mean of the DataFrame, a common metho for handling missing numerical data. It ensures continuity in the dataset.

B) Incorrect: This drops all rows that contain any missing values. While valid, it is not always the best option as it can lead to significant data loss.

C) Correct: The forward-fill method (ffill) replaces missing values with the previous non-missing value, which is a suitable approach when data continuity is important.

D) Incorrect: Replacing all NaN values with 0 is not recommended in most cases as it can distort data, especially when dealing with numerical datasets where 0 may not be appropriate.

E) Incorrect: Dropping duplicates is unrelated to handling missing values. This operation is for removing duplicate rows, not filling or handling missing data.

EXAM FOCUS	*Handling missing data effectively: Filling missing values with the mean or forward-fill method ensures continuity without drastically altering the dataset.*
CAUTION ALERT	*Be cautious when dropping rows: Dropping rows with missing values (dropna()) can lead to loss of valuable data. Always consider the trade-off between completeness and data loss.*

QUESTION 34

Answer - A, B

A) Correct: np.sum() is a valid function that calculates the sum of all elements in the NumPy array arr.

B) Correct: np.cumsum() calculates the cumulative sum of the elements along a given axis or the entire array.

C) Incorrect: While arr.sum(axis=1) is valid, the axis argument is specific to multidimensional arrays, which may not always be applicable.

D) Incorrect: arr.cumsum() is a valid syntax, but the context suggests the user prefers using np.cumsum(arr) for clarity.

E) Incorrect: There is no total_sum() function in NumPy or on array objects. This would raise an AttributeError.

EXAM FOCUS	*NumPy sum and cumulative sum: Use np.sum(arr) for the total sum and np.cumsum(arr) for the cumulative sum of array elements.*
CAUTION ALERT	*Avoid non-existent functions: Functions like arr.total_sum() don't exist in NumPy. Always use valid functions like np.sum() for aggregation.*

QUESTION 35

Answer - A, C, E

A) Correct: Cross-validation reduces the risk of overfitting by providing more balanced training across data subsets.

B) Incorrect: Reducing the size of the test set doesn't mitigate overfitting; it's essential for evaluation.

C) Correct: Reducing the number of irrelevant features simplifies the model and helps prevent overfitting.

D) Incorrect: Ignoring regularization can lead to more complex models that overfit.

E) Correct: Early stopping prevents overfitting by stopping training when the validation loss stops improving.

EXAM FOCUS	*Cross-validation and feature selection: Both cross-validation and reducing irrelevant features can help prevent overfitting in machine learning models.*
CAUTION ALERT	*Regularization is key: Ignoring regularization can lead to overly complex models that overfit. Always apply proper regularization techniques.*

QUESTION 36

Answer - A, B, D

A) Correct – More training data helps the model generalize better, reducing overfitting.
B) Correct – Cross-validation helps ensure the model generalizes well by testing on multiple subsets of data.
C) Incorrect – Increasing model complexity can lead to overfitting.
D) Correct – Regularization methods like L1/L2 can reduce overfitting by penalizing large coefficients.
E) Incorrect – Using fewer epochs may lead to underfitting by stopping training too early.

EXAM FOCUS	*Balance complexity with regularization: Increase training data, use cross-validation, and regularize your model (L1/L2) to avoid overfitting and underfitting.*
CAUTION ALERT	*Don't increase model complexity blindly: Increasing model complexity without control can lead to overfitting. Use regularization to keep model complexity in check.*

QUESTION 37

Answer - A, B, D

A) Correct – L2 regularization (Ridge) penalizes large coefficients, helping to prevent overfitting.
B) Correct – Increasing the size of the training dataset allows the model to generalize better and reduces overfitting.
C) Incorrect – Adding irrelevant features can worsen model performance and increase overfitting risk.
D) Correct – Cross-validation is a technique to evaluate the model's ability to generalize by splitting the data into different subsets.
E) Incorrect – Adding more polynomial features can lead to overfitting, especially if not handled carefully.

EXAM FOCUS	*Prevent overfitting with regularization: Add L2 regularization, increase training data, and use cross-validation to avoid overfitting in your logistic regression model.*
CAUTION ALERT	*Irrelevant features increase overfitting: Avoid adding irrelevant features, as this may worsen overfitting and reduce the model's overall performance.*

QUESTION 38

Answer - A, D

A) Correct because it correctly creates a pivot table that counts returns grouped by product and reason.
B) Incorrect because it performs a sum() instead of a count of returns, which is not what the prompt asks for.
C) Incorrect as it mistakenly assigns product to values and returns to columns, which reverses the required roles of these variables.
D) Correct because it uses pivot_table to count the returns grouped by both product and reason, fulfilling the prompt's requirements.
E) Incorrect as it uses the pivot() method, which is not designed for counting or aggregation.

EXAM FOCUS	*Pivot tables for product returns: Use pivot_table() to calculate returns counts by grouping on product and return reasons. This ensures easy analysis of returns patterns.*
CAUTION ALERT	*Incorrect use of sum() for counting: Ensure you're using count() instead of sum() when the objective is to count occurrences, such as in the case of product returns.*

QUESTION 39

Answer - A, D

A) Correct because f1_score(y_true, y_pred) calculates the F1-score for binary classification.
B) Incorrect because precision_score calculates precision, not the F1-score.

C) Incorrect because recall_score calculates recall, not the F1-score.

D) Correct because f1_score(y_true, y_pred, average='macro') calculates the F1-score for multi-class classification using the macro average, though it can also work for binary classification.

E) Incorrect because accuracy_score measures overall accuracy, not the F1-score.

EXAM FOCUS	*F1-Score Computation: The F1-score is useful for imbalanced classification tasks as it balances precision and recall. Use f1_score() from sklearn.metrics to compute it.*
CAUTION ALERT	*Precision vs. F1-Score: Precision measures correct positive predictions, but F1-score considers both precision and recall. They should not be confused with each other.*

QUESTION 40

Answer - A, C

A) Correct because sns.lineplot() is the correct function to create a line plot, and the x and y values are assigned appropriately to visualize the trend of sales over time.

B) Incorrect because reversing x and y will not show the desired trend correctly.

C) Correct because plt.title() adds a title to the plot, improving clarity.

D) Incorrect because while plt.grid(True) adds gridlines, it alone does not fulfill the requirements of creating a line plot and adding a title.

E) Incorrect because plt.bar() generates a bar plot, not a line plot.

EXAM FOCUS	*Line Plot Tip: Seaborn's sns.lineplot() is perfect for visualizing trends over time, like sales trends. Don't forget to add a title and gridlines for better readability.*
CAUTION ALERT	*Incorrect Plot Type: Don't confuse line plots with bar plots. Use sns.lineplot() for continuous data over time, and plt.bar() for categorical comparisons.*

QUESTION 41

Answer - A, E

A) Correct because the loop places the plt.text() function to add the height label to each bar, using the x coordinate i and y coordinate as the sales value.

B) Incorrect because plt.annotate() is typically used for marking individual points rather than bars, and this might not function well for labeling multiple bars.

C) Incorrect because plt.bar_label() is not a valid function in Matplotlib.

D) Incorrect because plt.text() is missing the required x, y coordinates and is incomplete.

E) Correct because it uses plt.text() to label the bars with their sales value, adjusted with an offset to avoid overlap with the bars.

EXAM FOCUS	*Bar Labeling Tip: Use plt.text() to label each bar in a bar plot with its respective value. Position the labels carefully to avoid overlapping with the bars.*
CAUTION ALERT	*Common Mistake: Avoid using plt.bar_label()—it's not a valid function in Matplotlib. Instead, use loops and plt.text() for proper bar labeling.*

QUESTION 42

Answer - B

A) Suitable because a simple bar plot with one color keeps the visualization straightforward.

B) Least suitable because adding a legend without multiple categories can add unnecessary complexity for a non-technical audience.

C) Suitable because adding edge color can help clarify the visual without overwhelming the viewer.

D) Suitable because annotations can clarify key points for the audience.

E) Suitable because a basic bar plot with minimal styling is easy to understand for non-technical viewers.

EXAM FOCUS	*Minimalism Tip: Reduce unnecessary visual elements like legends in simple bar plots. Keep the plot minimal and clean for non-technical viewers.*
CAUTION ALERT	*Legend Complexity: Avoid using legends when unnecessary—especially for a single data series. Legends can add unnecessary complexity for a non-technical audience.*

QUESTION 43

Answer - D

A) Correct because presenting insights as concise bullet points next to the chart maintains clarity while highlighting essential data points.

B) Correct because using one visualization per slide with key takeaways ensures the audience focuses on each point without overwhelming them.

C) Suitable if the visuals are clear, though some text explanation is typically necessary.

D) Incorrect because removing visualizations entirely and relying only on text reduces engagement and makes it harder for the audience to understand data-driven insights.

EXAM FOCUS	*Balance Visuals and Text: Present concise bullet points beside the chart and ensure each slide focuses on one visualization to avoid overcrowding.*
CAUTION ALERT	*No Visuals: Avoid removing visualizations entirely. Presenting only text-based insights reduces engagement and makes data harder to interpret.*

QUESTION 44

Answer - B

A) Incorrect because the Greys color map lacks the contrasting colors necessary to effectively highlight high and low correlation values.

B) Correct because coolwarm is a diverging color palette, making it ideal for highlighting high and low correlation values with strong contrast in a heatmap.

C) Incorrect because the Blues palette is sequential and does not provide contrasting colors for showing high and low values effectively.

D) Incorrect because viridis is a perceptually uniform color map, which is more suited for gradients, not for contrasting extremes.

E) Incorrect because Purples is also sequential and not suited for showing contrasts effectively.

EXAM FOCUS	*Heatmap Palettes: Use cmap="coolwarm" for heatmaps to emphasize high and low correlation values with strong color contrasts, aiding clear interpretation.*
CAUTION ALERT	*Sequential Palettes: Avoid using sequential color maps like "Blues" or "Greys" for heatmaps, as they lack the necessary contrast to differentiate high and low values.*

QUESTION 45

Answer - A

A) Correct because scatter plots are ideal for visually representing the relationship between two continuous variables like marketing spend and sales. B) Incorrect because heatmaps are more useful for visualizing data relationships in a matrix, not for demonstrating a direct relationship between two variables. C) Incorrect because a bar plot is more suited for categorical comparisons, not for showing continuous relationships. D) Incorrect because pie charts don't show relationships between variables effectively. E) Incorrect because box plots are more suitable for showing distributions rather than relationships between two variables like marketing spend and sales.

EXAM FOCUS	*Scatter Plot for Relationships: Scatter plots are the go-to visualization for presenting relationships between two continuous variables, like marketing spend and overall sales.*
CAUTION ALERT	*Avoid Bar Plots for Continuous Variables: Bar plots are not ideal for showing relationships between continuous variables. Use scatter plots for this purpose.*

ABOUT THE AUTHOR

Step into the world of Anand, and you're in for a journey beyond just tech and algorithms. While his accolades in the tech realm are numerous, including penning various tech-centric and personal improvement ebooks, there's so much more to this multi-faceted author.

At the heart of Anand lies an AI enthusiast and investor, always on the hunt for the next big thing in artificial intelligence. But turn the page, and you might find him engrossed in a gripping cricket match or passionately cheering for his favorite football team. His weekends? They might be spent experimenting with a new recipe in the kitchen, penning down his latest musings, or crafting a unique design that blends creativity with functionality.

While his professional journey as a Solution Architect and AI Consultant, boasting over a decade of AI/ML expertise, is impressive, it's the fusion of this expertise with his diverse hobbies that makes Anand's writings truly distinctive.

So, as you navigate through his works, expect more than just information. Prepare for stories interwoven with passion, experiences peppered with life's many spices, and wisdom that transcends beyond the tech realm. Dive in and discover Anand, the author, the enthusiast, the chef, the sports lover, and above all, the storyteller.

Made in the USA
Coppell, TX
07 October 2024

38270719R00142